犬夜叉

INUYASHA

ANI-MANGA™

Vol. 18

CREATED BY
RUMIKO TAKAHASHI

Inuyasha Ani-Manga™
Vol. #18

Created by
Rumiko Takahashi

Translation based on the VIZ anime TV series
Translation Assistance/Katy Bridges
Lettering & Editorial Assistance/John Clark
Cover Design & Graphics/Hidemi Sahara
Editor/Ian Robertson

Editor in Chief, Books/Alvin Lu
Editor in Chief, Magazines/Marc Weidenbaum
Sr. Director of Acquisitions/Rika Inouye
Sr. VP of Marketing/Liza Coppola
Exec. VP of Sales & Marketing/John Easum
Publisher/Hyoe Narita

Published by VIZ Media, LLC
P.O. Box 77010
San Francisco, CA 94107

10 9 8 7 6 5 4 3 2
First printing, December 2006
Second printing, March 2007

www.viz.com
store.viz.com

Story thus far

Kagome's mundane teenage existence was
turned upside down when she was transported
into a mythical version of Japan's medieval past!
Kagome is the reincarnation of Lady Kikyo, a
great warrior and the defender of the Shikon
Jewel, or the Jewel of Four Souls. Kikyo was in

love with Inuyasha, a dog-like half-demon who wishes to possess the jewel in
order to transform himself into a full-fledged demon. But 50 years earlier,
the evil shape-shifting Naraku tricked Kikyo and Inuyasha into betraying one
another. The betrayal led to Kikyo's death and Inuyasha's imprisonment
under a binding spell...and Inuyasha remained trapped by the spell until
Kagome appeared in feudal Japan and unwittingly released him!

In a skirmish for possession of the Shikon Jewel, it
accidentally shatters and is strewn across the land.
Only Kagome has the power to find the jewel shards,
and only Inuyasha has the strength to defeat the
demons that now hold them, so the two unlikely
partners are bound together in the quest to reclaim
all the pieces of the sacred jewel. To prevent Inuyasha
from stealing the jewel, Kikyo's sister, Lady Kaede,
puts a magical necklace around Inuyasha's neck that
allows Kagome to make him "sit" on command.

Inuyasha's greatest tool in the fight to recover the sacred jewel shards is his
father's sword, the Tetsusaiga, but Inuyasha's half-brother Sesshomaru covets
the mighty blade and has tried to steal it more than once.

Kagome and Inuyasha are dealt a crushing blow when
Kikyo, resurrected through witchcraft, steals all the
shards of the sacred jewel that have been collected.
Although Kikyo has grown to hate Naraku, she gives
him all the jewel shards. Finding themselves under
attack by Naraku's new incarnations Juromaru and
Kageromaru, can Inuyasha and Koga the wolf-demon
put their differences aside long enough to join forces
against these formidable opponents?

INUYASHA
ANI-MANGA™ Vol. 18

Contents

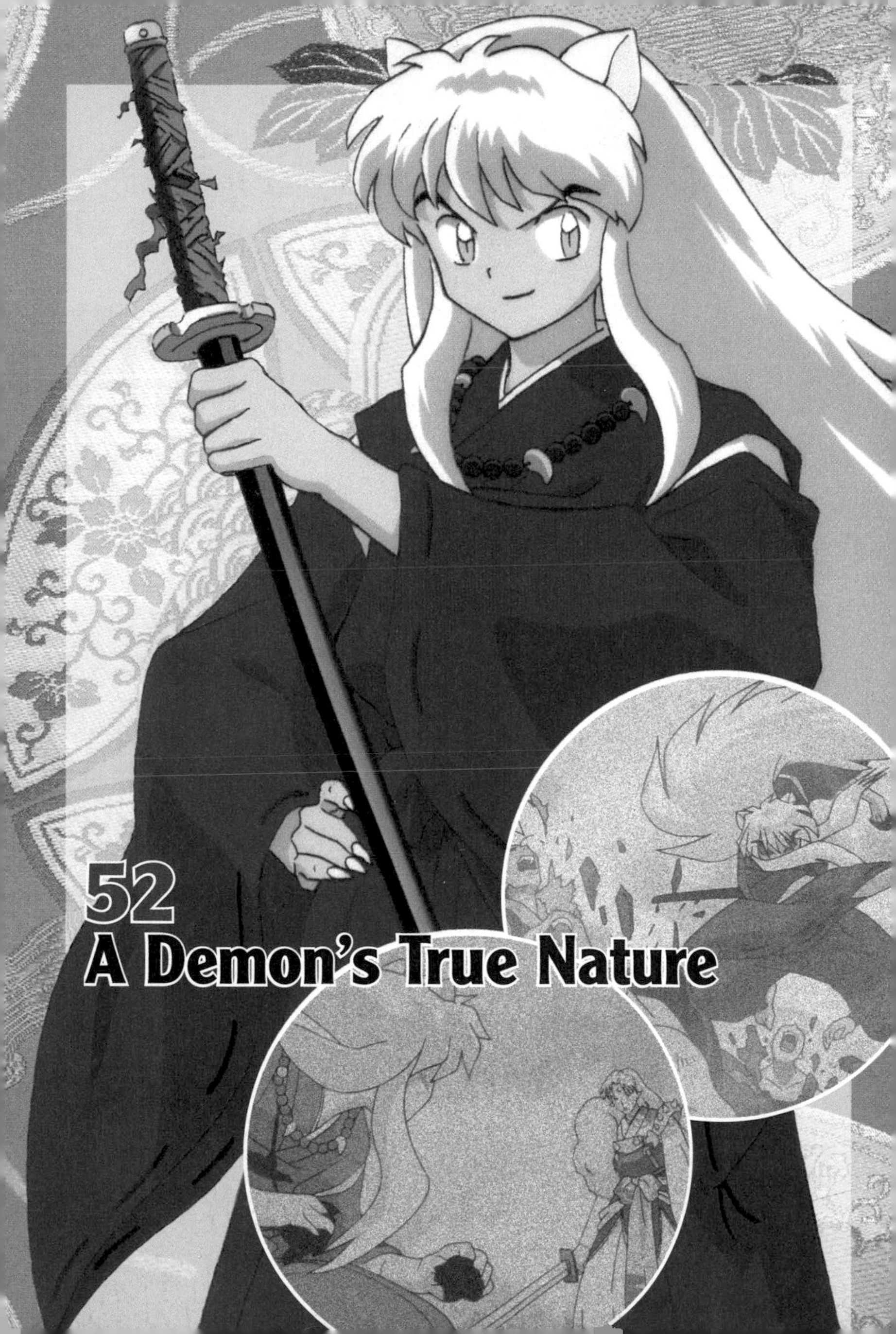

52
A Demon's True Nature

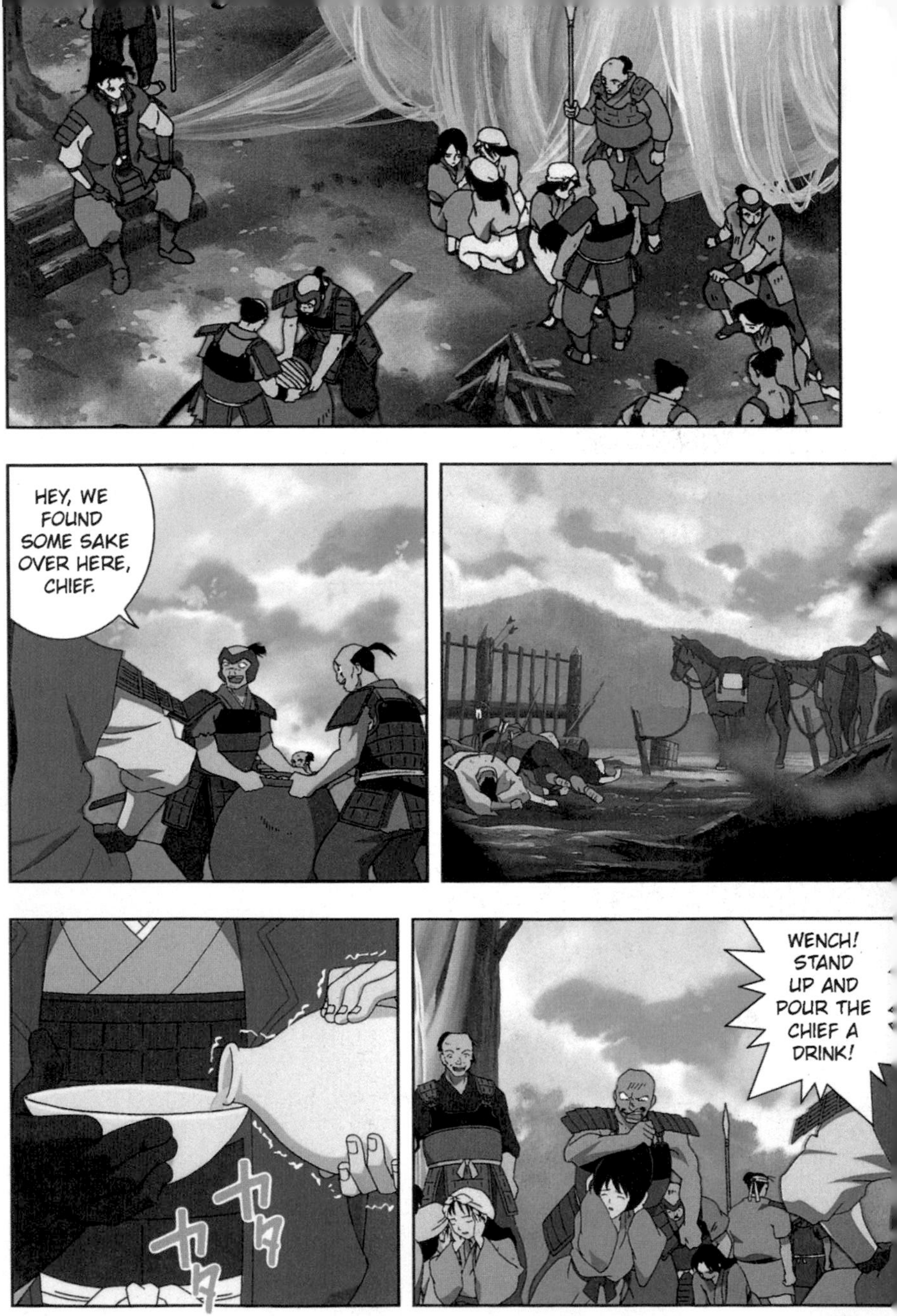
HEY, WE FOUND SOME SAKE OVER HERE, CHIEF.
WENCH! STAND UP AND POUR THE CHIEF A DRINK!

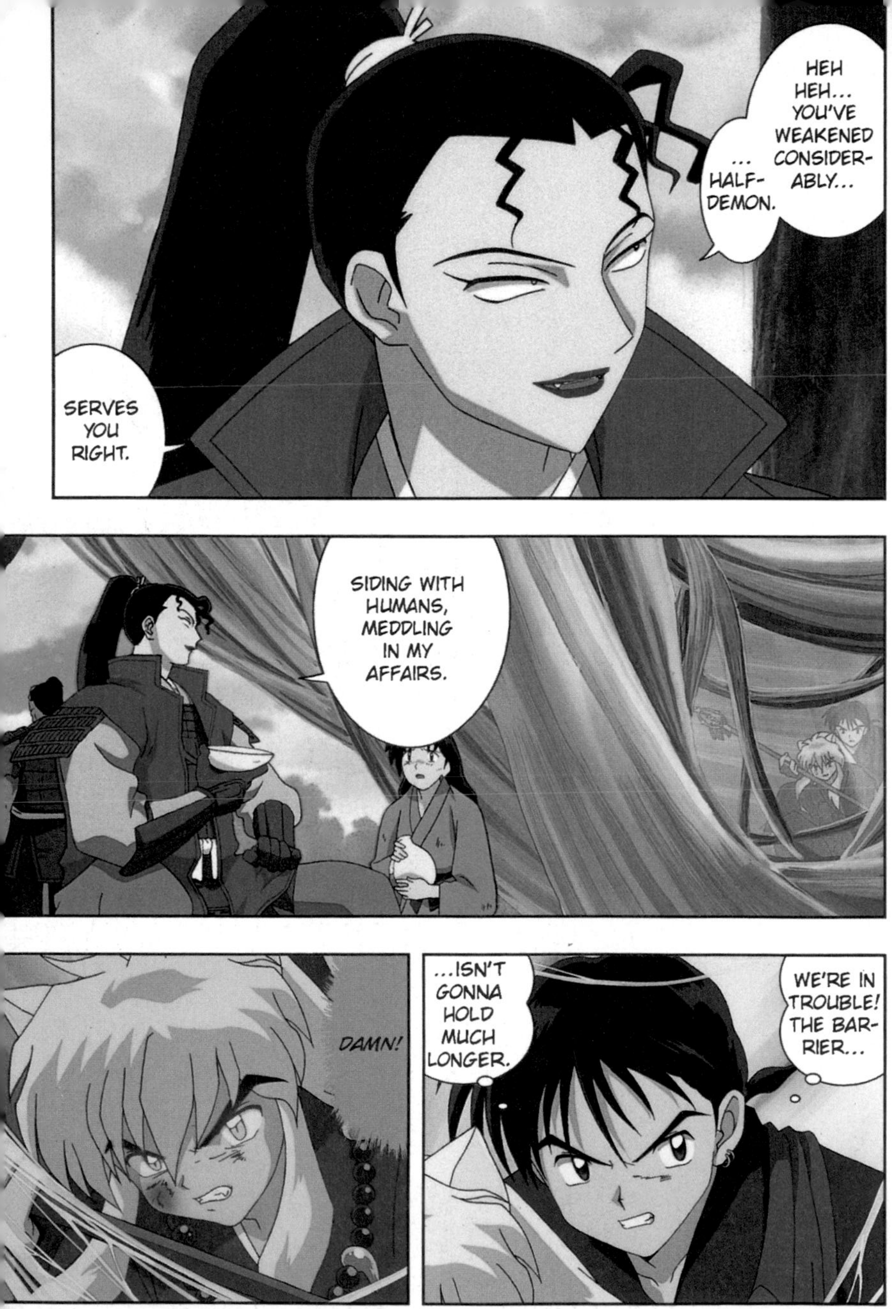
HEH HEH... YOU'VE WEAKENED CONSIDER-ABLY...
... HALF-DEMON.
SERVES YOU RIGHT.
SIDING WITH HUMANS, MEDDLING IN MY AFFAIRS.
WE'RE IN TROUBLE! THE BAR-RIER...
...ISN'T GONNA HOLD MUCH LONGER.
DAMN!

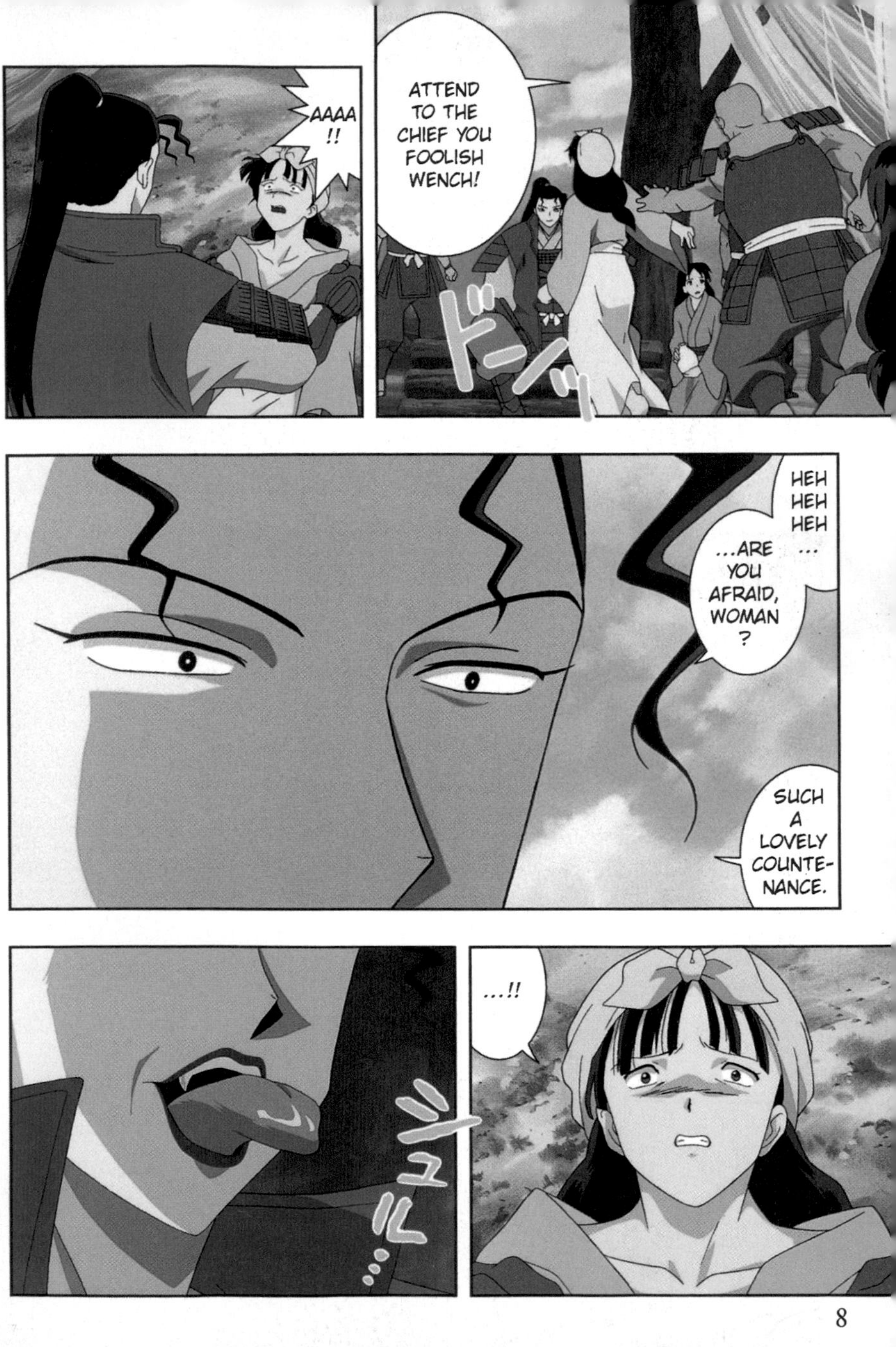
ATTEND TO THE CHIEF YOU FOOLISH WENCH!
ドーンッ
AAAA !!
HEH HEH HEH ...
...ARE YOU AFRAID, WOMAN ?
SUCH A LOVELY COUNTE-NANCE.
...!!
シュル...

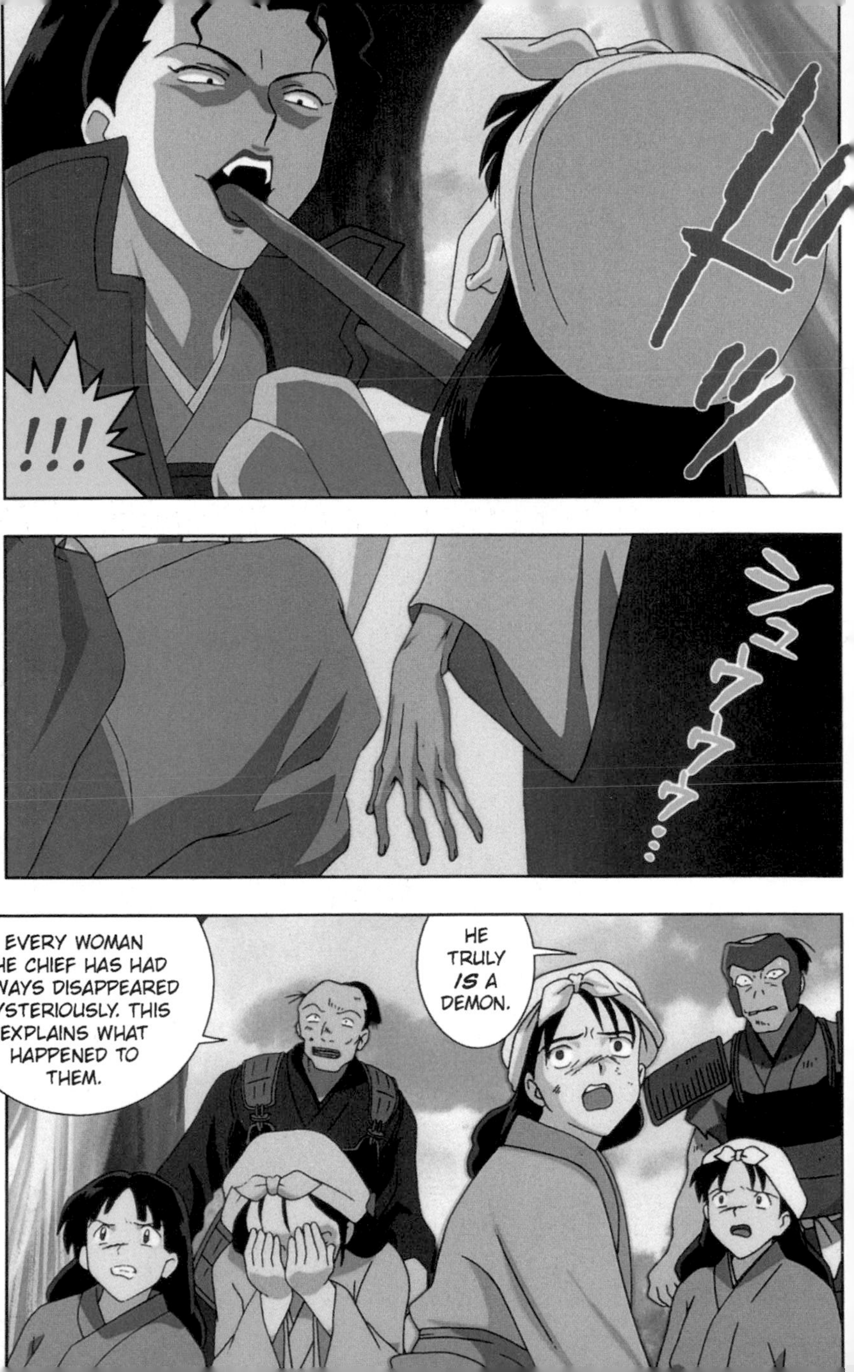
!!!
HE TRULY *IS* A DEMON.
EVERY WOMAN THE CHIEF HAS HAD ALWAYS DISAPPEARED MYSTERIOUSLY. THIS EXPLAINS WHAT HAPPENED TO THEM.

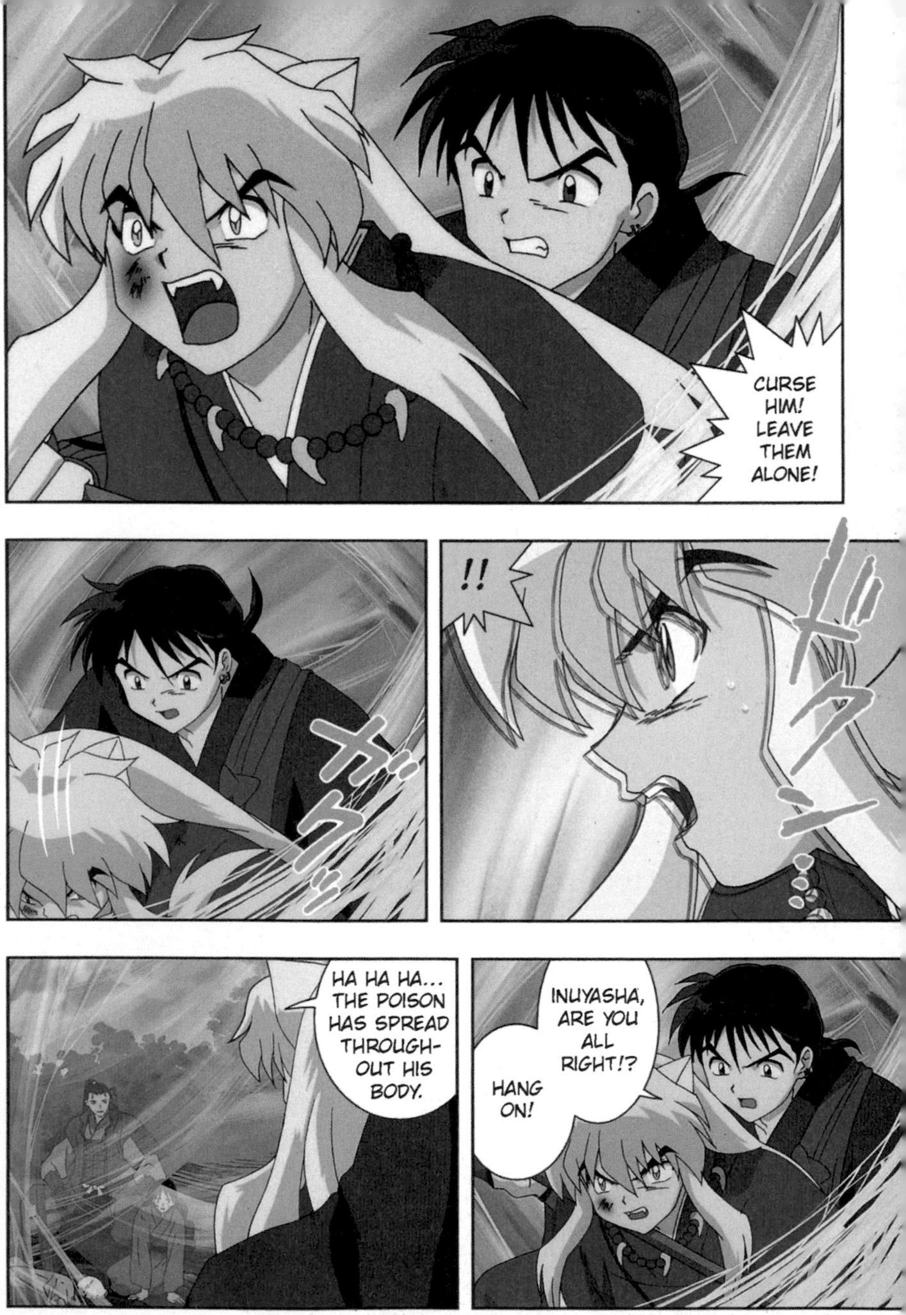
CURSE HIM! LEAVE THEM ALONE!
!!
ドクン
ガクッ
INUYASHA, ARE YOU ALL RIGHT!?
HANG ON!
HA HA HA... THE POISON HAS SPREAD THROUGH-OUT HIS BODY.

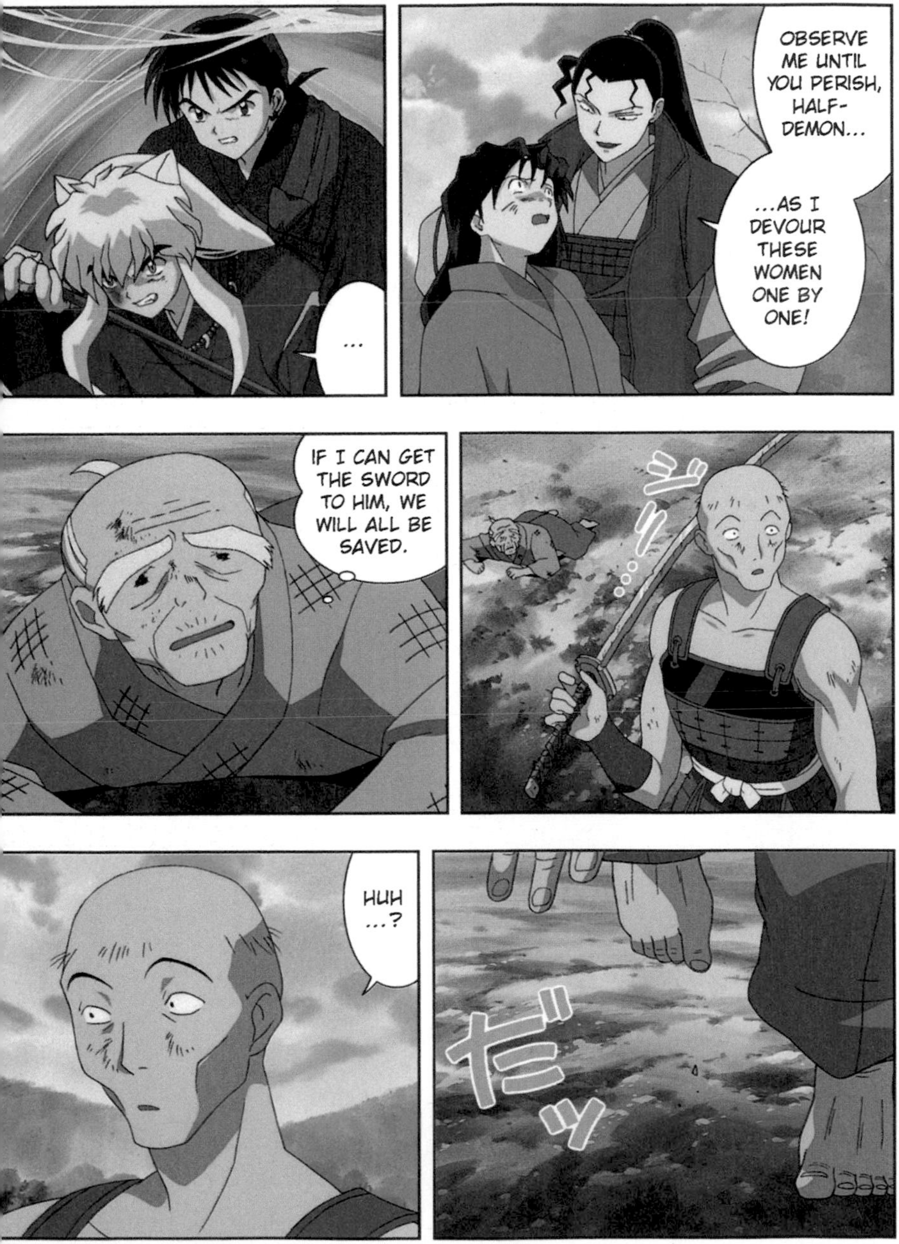
OBSERVE ME UNTIL YOU PERISH, HALF-DEMON...
...AS I DEVOUR THESE WOMEN ONE BY ONE!
...
ジリ...
IF I CAN GET THE SWORD TO HIM, WE WILL ALL BE SAVED.
だッ
HUH ...?

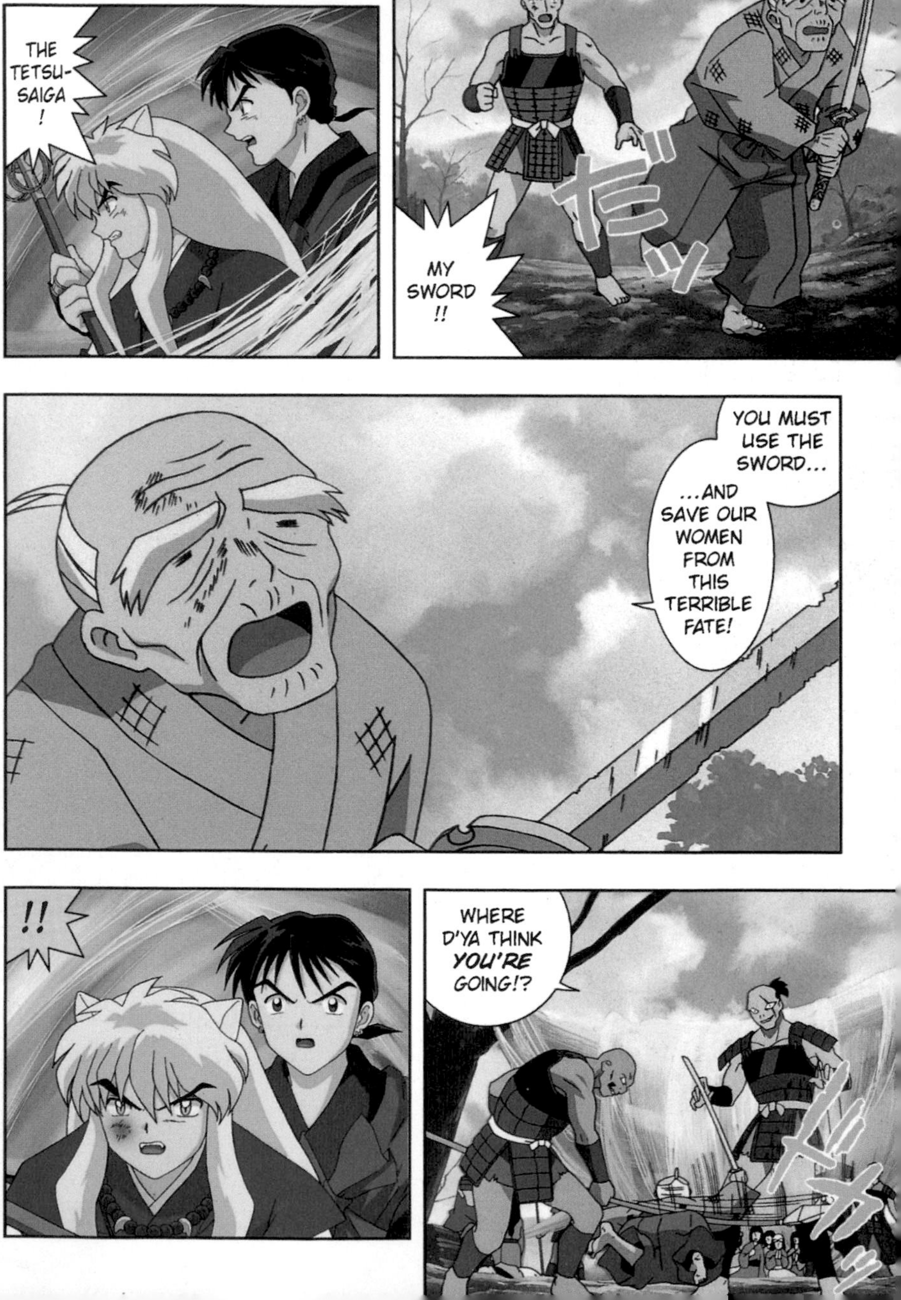
MY SWORD !!
ダッ
THE TETSU-SAIGA !
YOU MUST USE THE SWORD...
...AND SAVE OUR WOMEN FROM THIS TERRIBLE FATE!
WHERE D'YA THINK ***YOU'RE*** GOING!?
!!

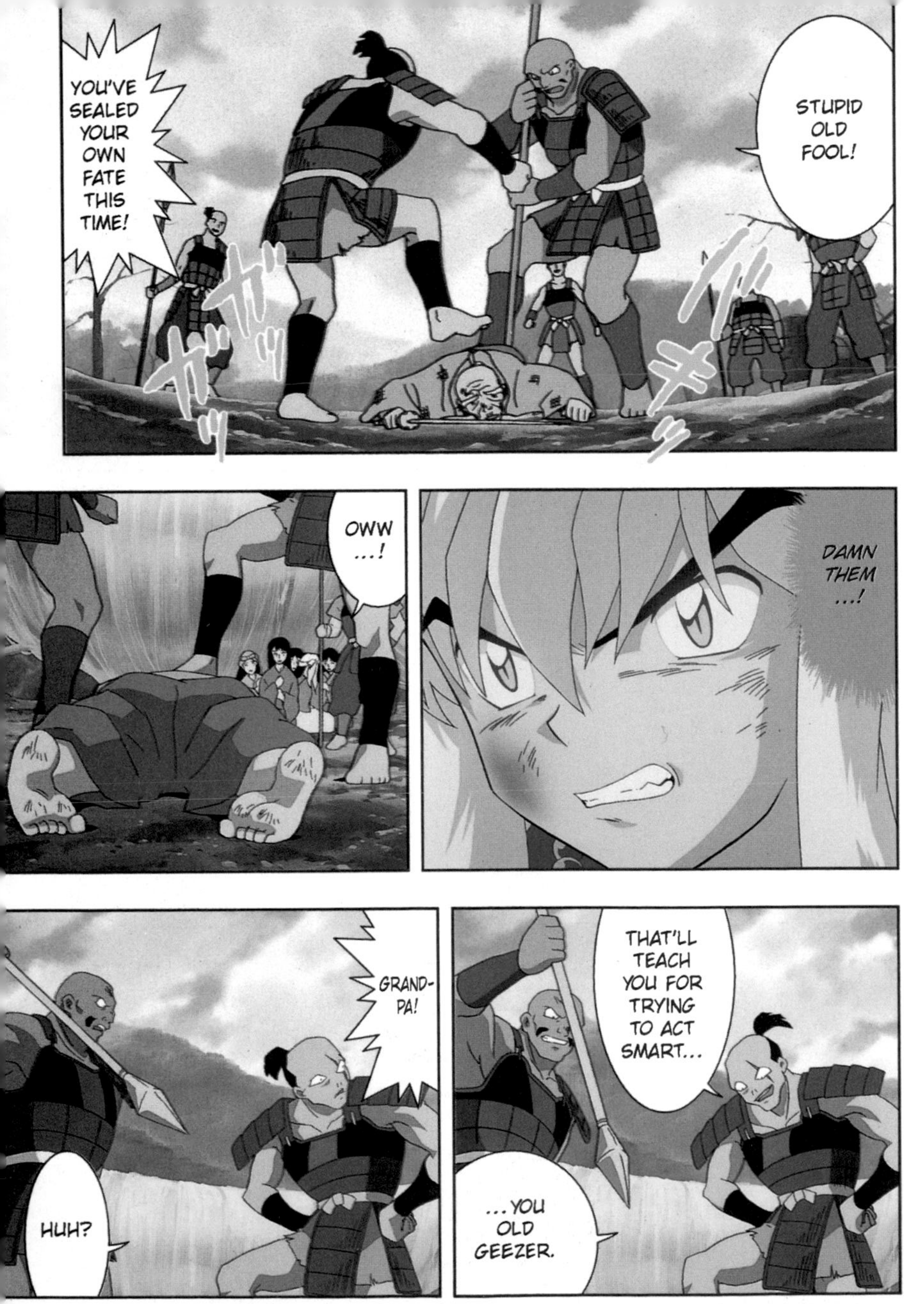
STUPID OLD FOOL!
YOU'VE SEALED YOUR OWN FATE THIS TIME!
DAMN THEM ...!
OWW ...!
THAT'LL TEACH YOU FOR TRYING TO ACT SMART...
...YOU OLD GEEZER.
GRAND-PA!
HUH?

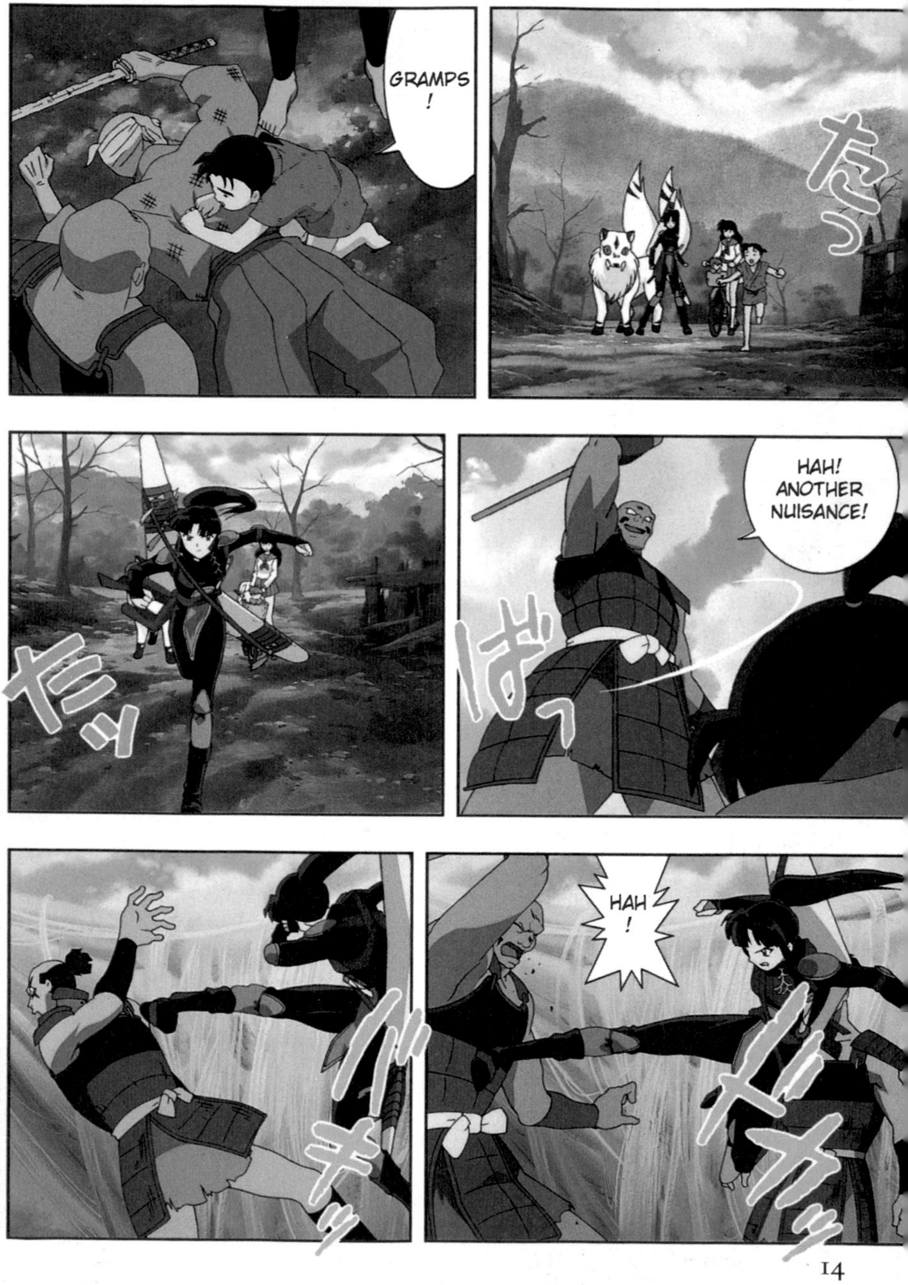
たっ
GRAMPS!
HAH! ANOTHER NUISANCE!
ばっ
ダッ
HAH!
ドカッ
ガキッ

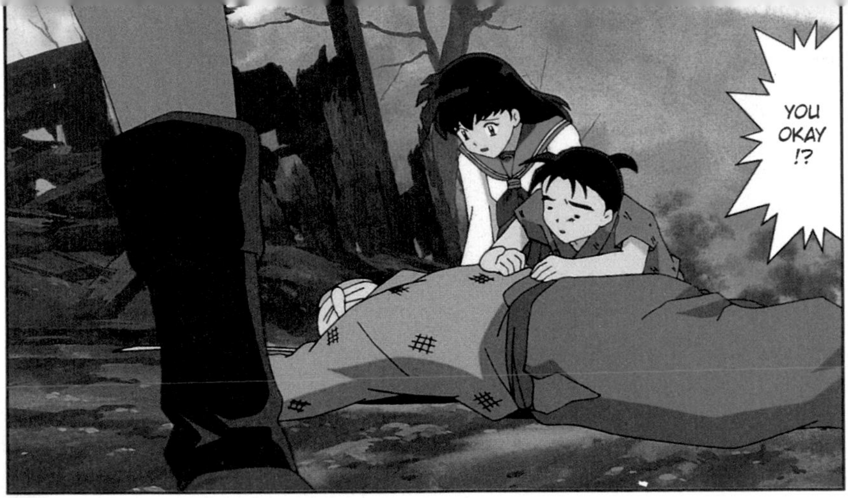
YOU OKAY !?

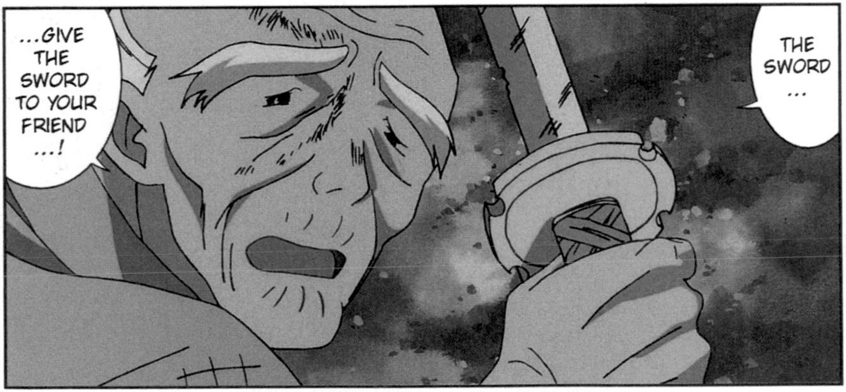
THE SWORD ...
...GIVE THE SWORD TO YOUR FRIEND ...!

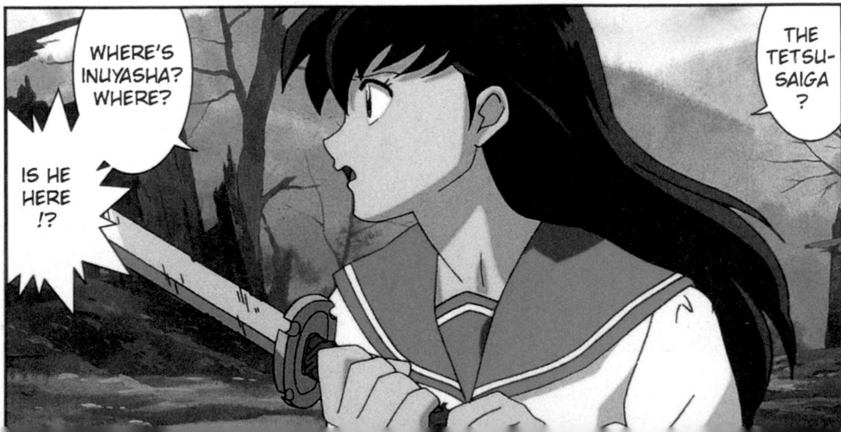
THE TETSU-SAIGA ?
WHERE'S INUYASHA? WHERE?
IS HE HERE !?

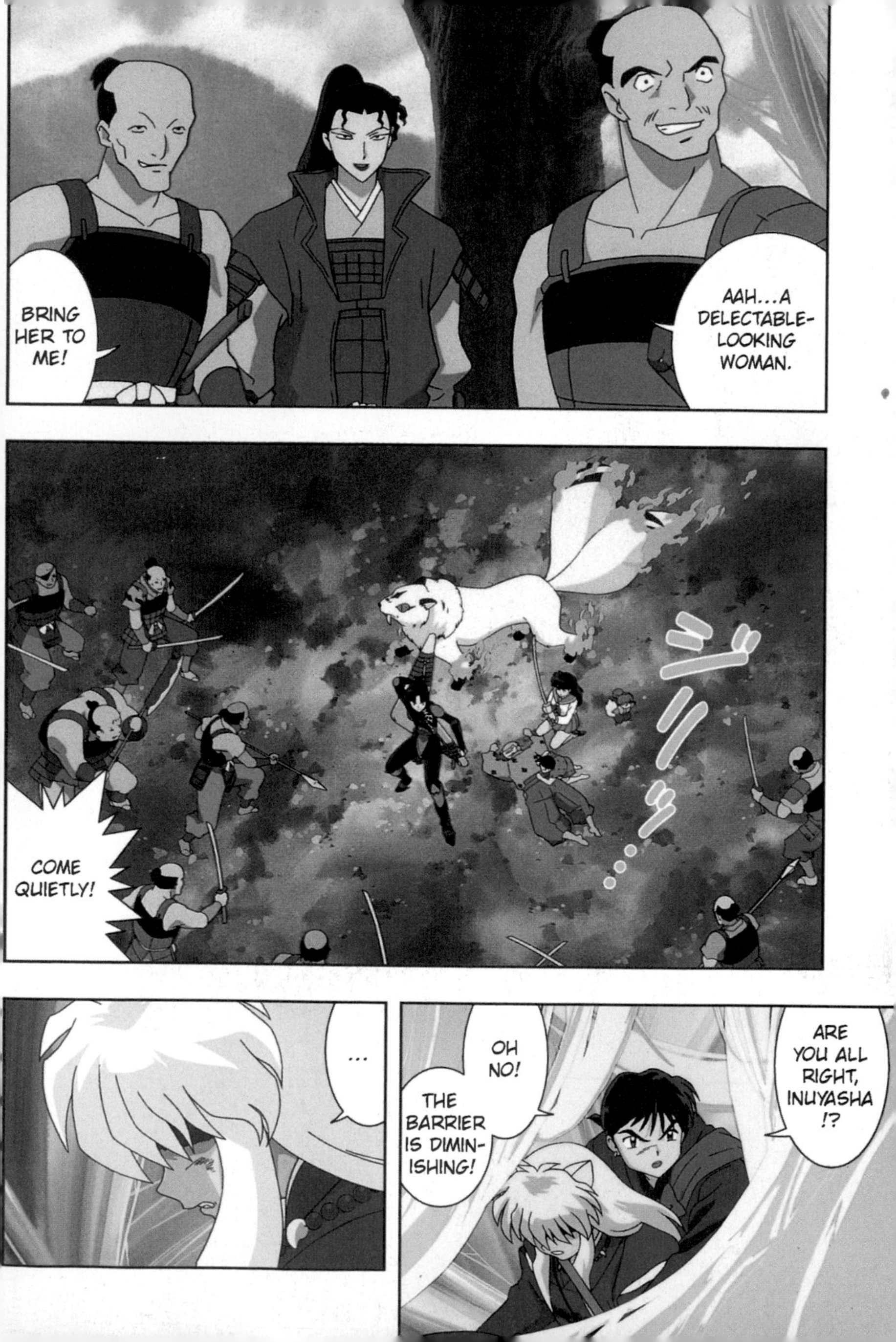
AAH...A DELECTABLE-LOOKING WOMAN.
BRING HER TO ME!
ジリリッ...
COME QUIETLY!
ARE YOU ALL RIGHT, INUYASHA!?
OH NO!
THE BARRIER IS DIMINISHING!
...

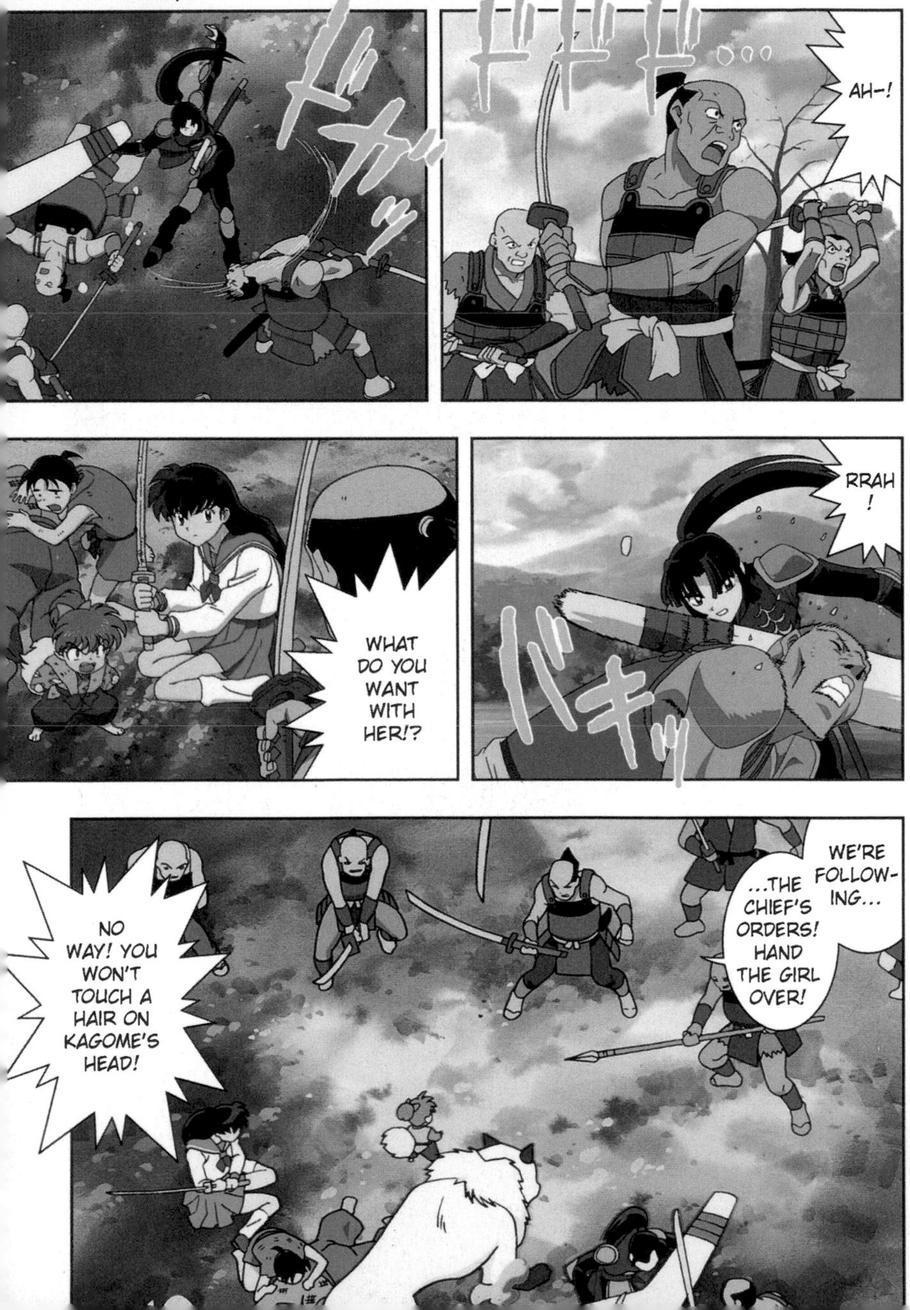
ドドド…
AH—!
ドガッ
RRAH!
バキッ
WHAT DO YOU WANT WITH HER!?
WE'RE FOLLOWING...
...THE CHIEF'S ORDERS! HAND THE GIRL OVER!
NO WAY! YOU WON'T TOUCH A HAIR ON KAGOME'S HEAD!

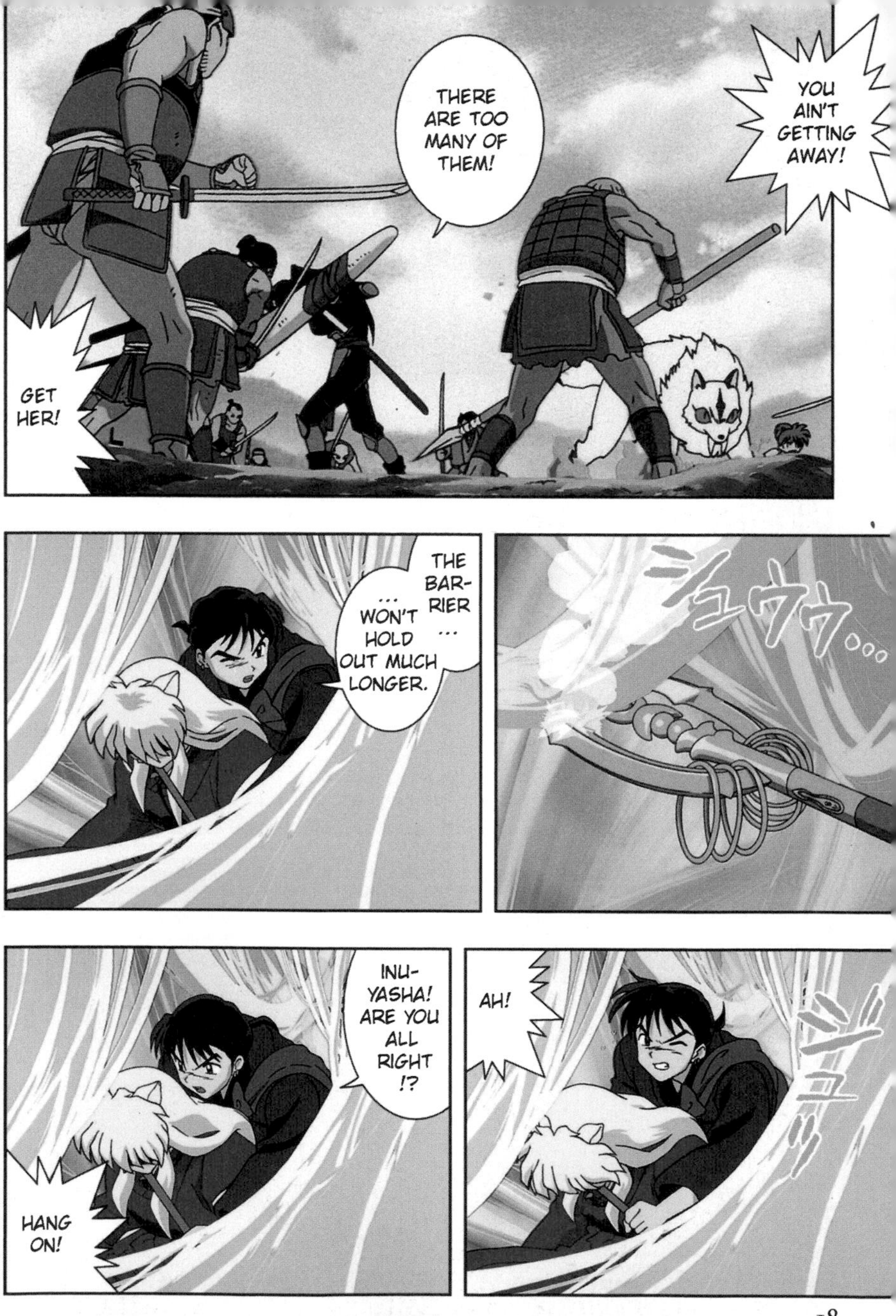
YOU AIN'T GETTING AWAY!
THERE ARE TOO MANY OF THEM!
GET HER!
シュウウ…
THE BAR-RIER ... WON'T HOLD OUT MUCH LONGER.
AH!
INU-YASHA! ARE YOU ALL RIGHT !?
HANG ON!

INU-YASHA!

WHAT'S HAPPEN-ING!?

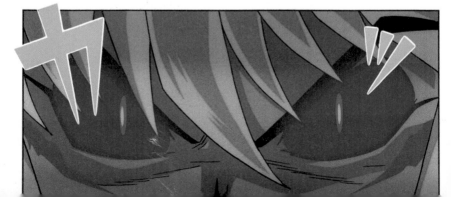

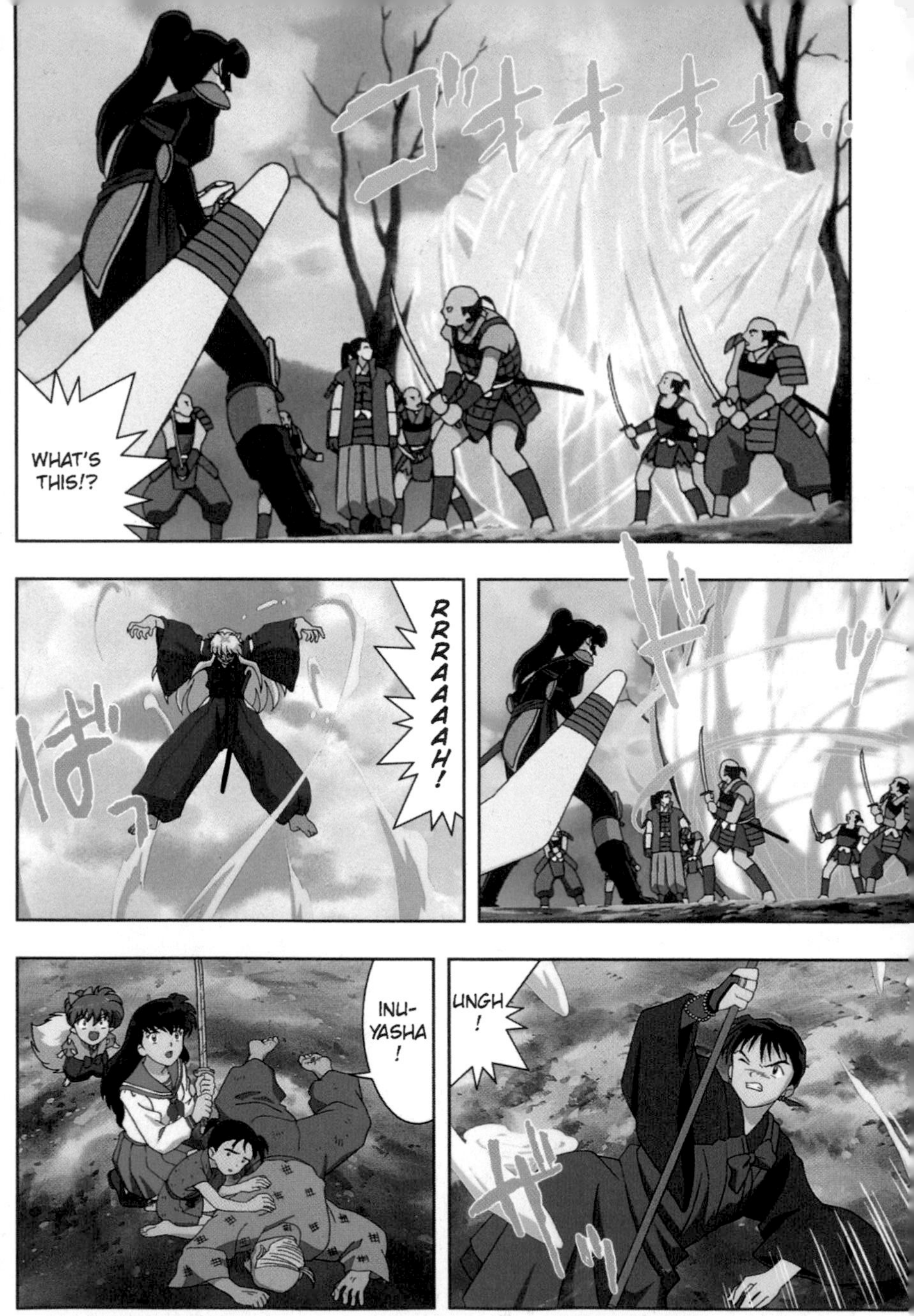

WHAT'S THIS!?
RRRAAAAAH!
UNGH!
INU-YASHA!

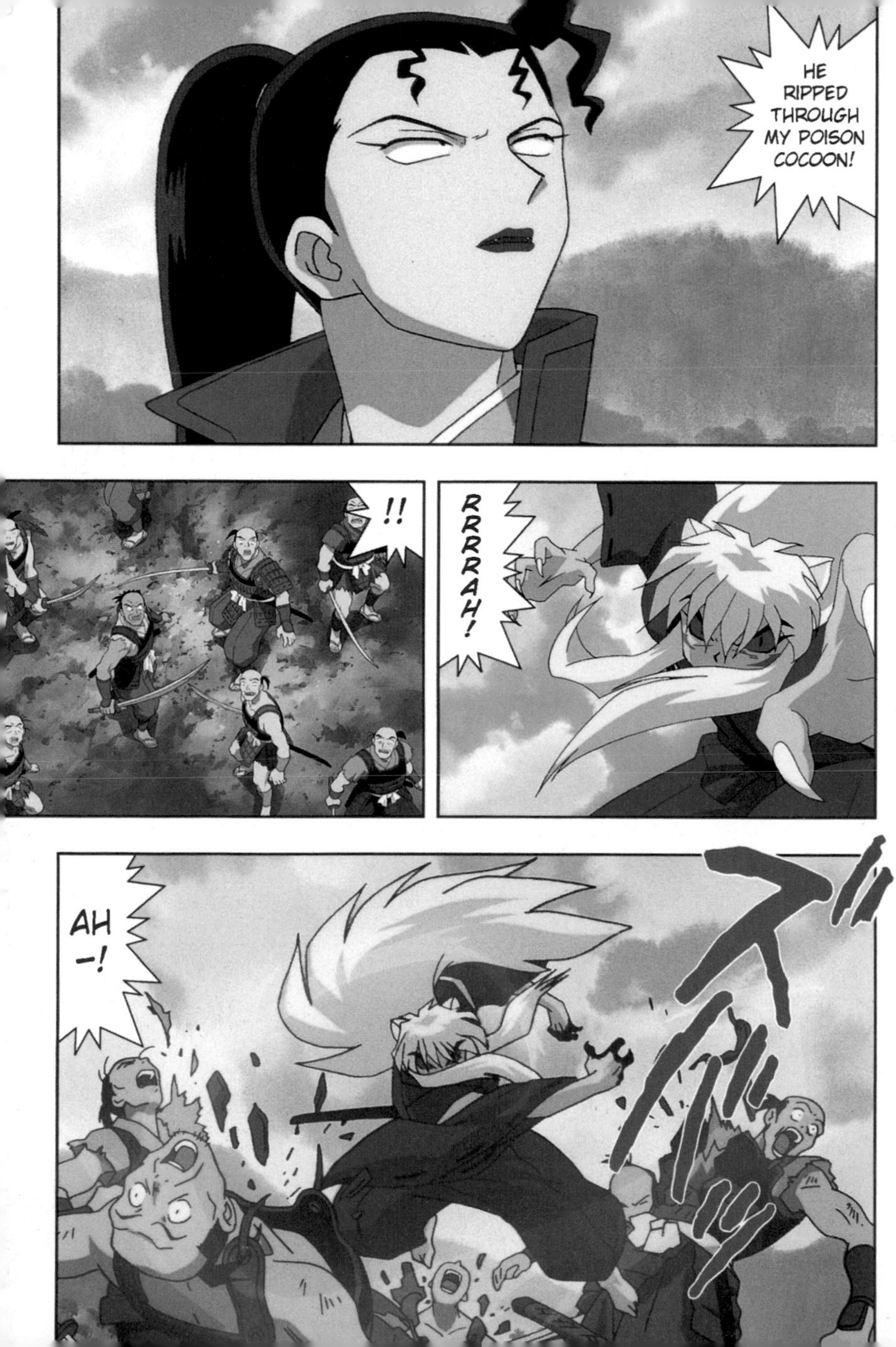
HE RIPPED THROUGH MY POISON COCOON!
RRRRAH!
!!
AH-!

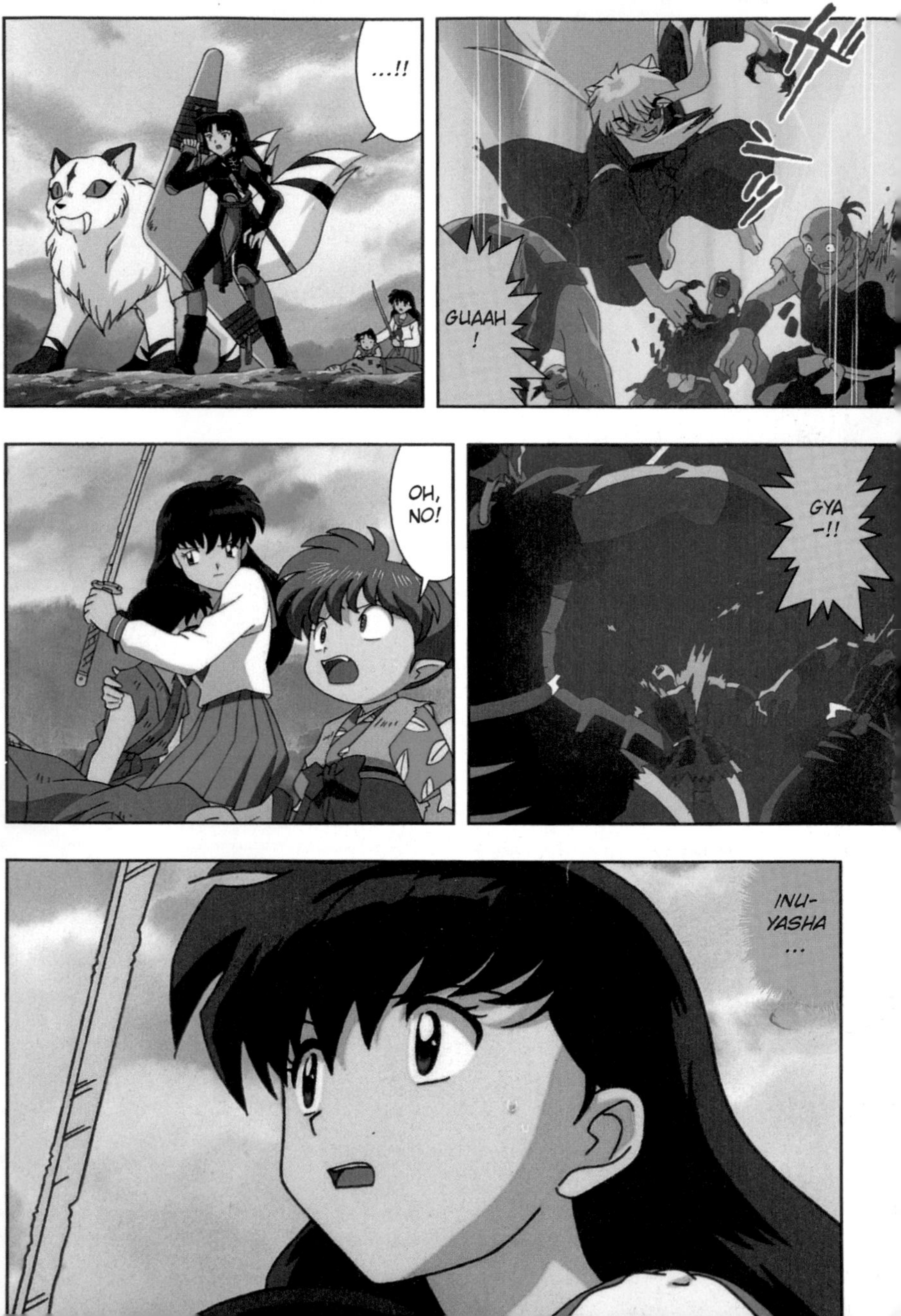
GUAAH!
...!!
GYA—!!
OH, NO!
INU-YASHA...

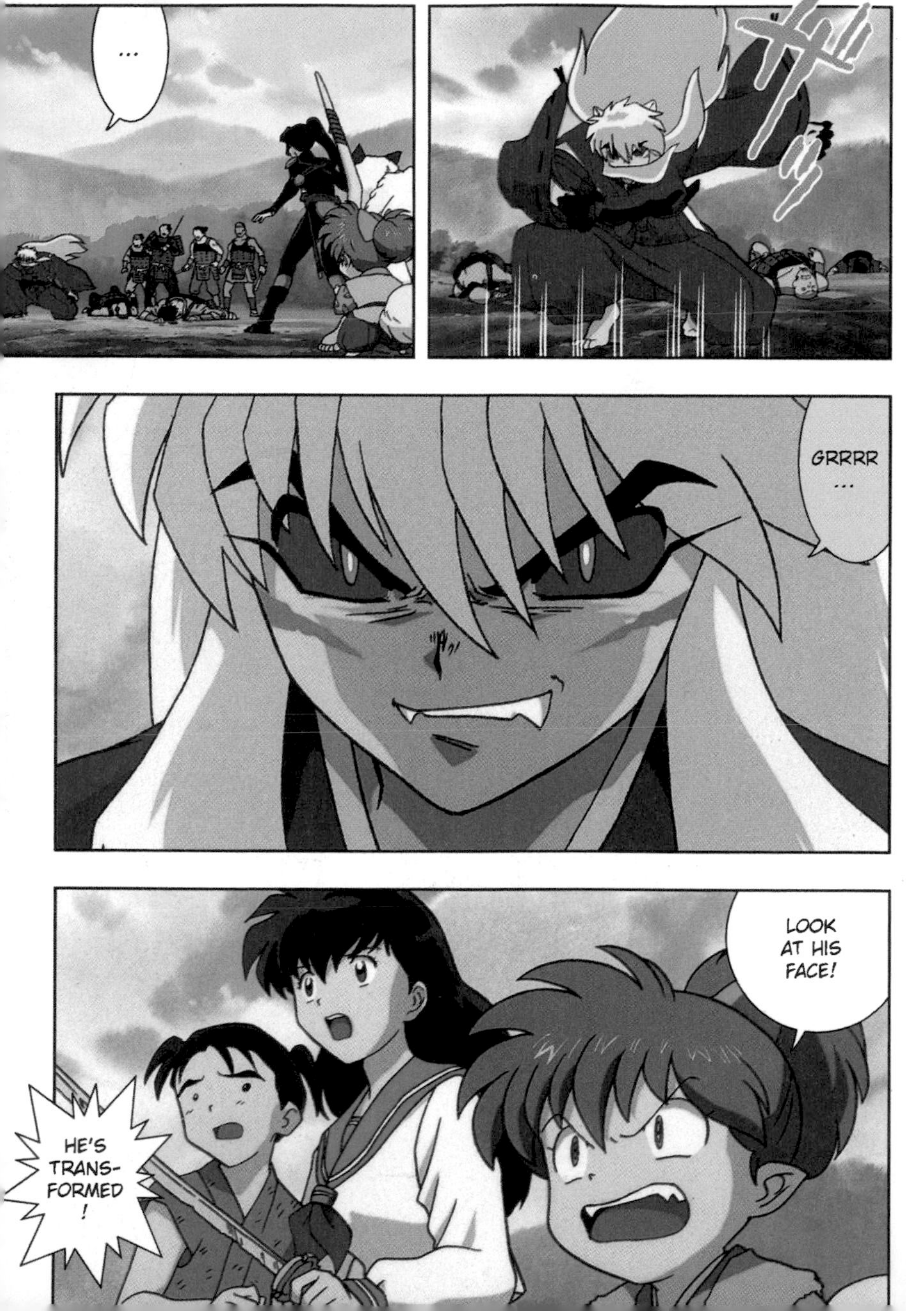
...
GRRRR ...
LOOK AT HIS FACE!
HE'S TRANS-FORMED!

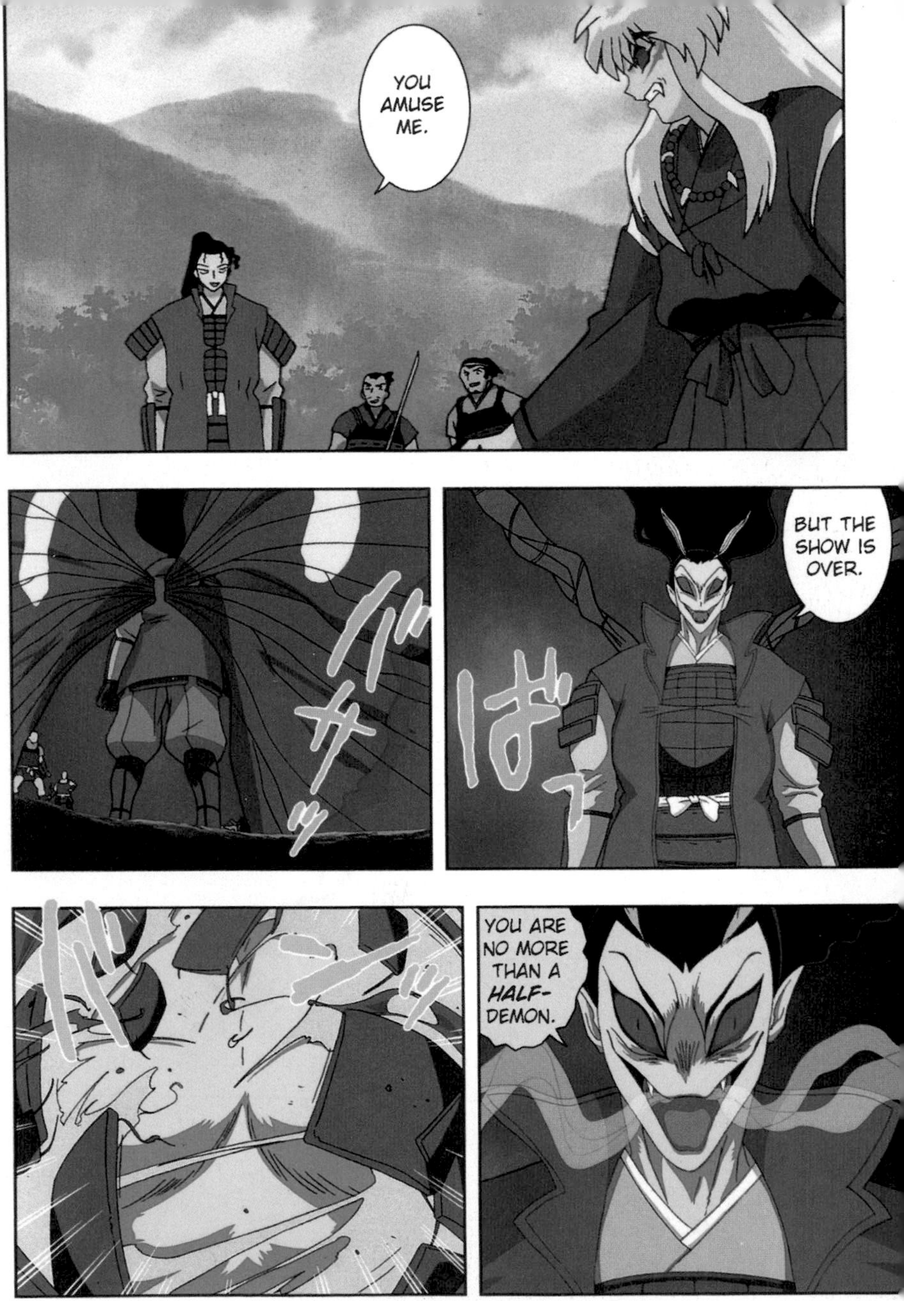
YOU AMUSE ME.
BUT THE SHOW IS OVER.
ばっ
YOU ARE NO MORE THAN A ***HALF***-DEMON.

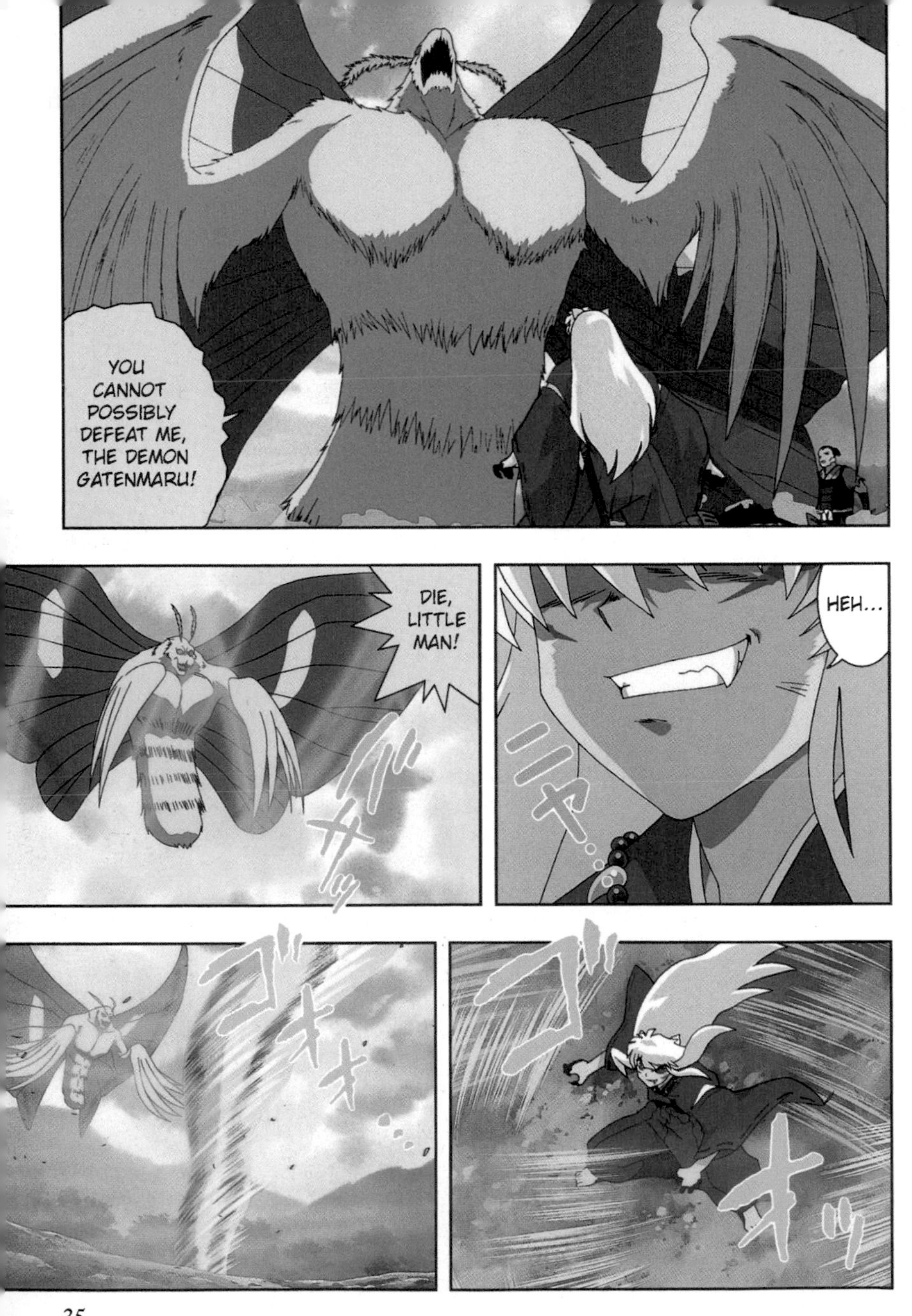
YOU CANNOT POSSIBLY DEFEAT ME, THE DEMON GATENMARU!
HEH...
ニヤ…
DIE, LITTLE MAN!
バサッ
ゴォッ
ゴォォ…

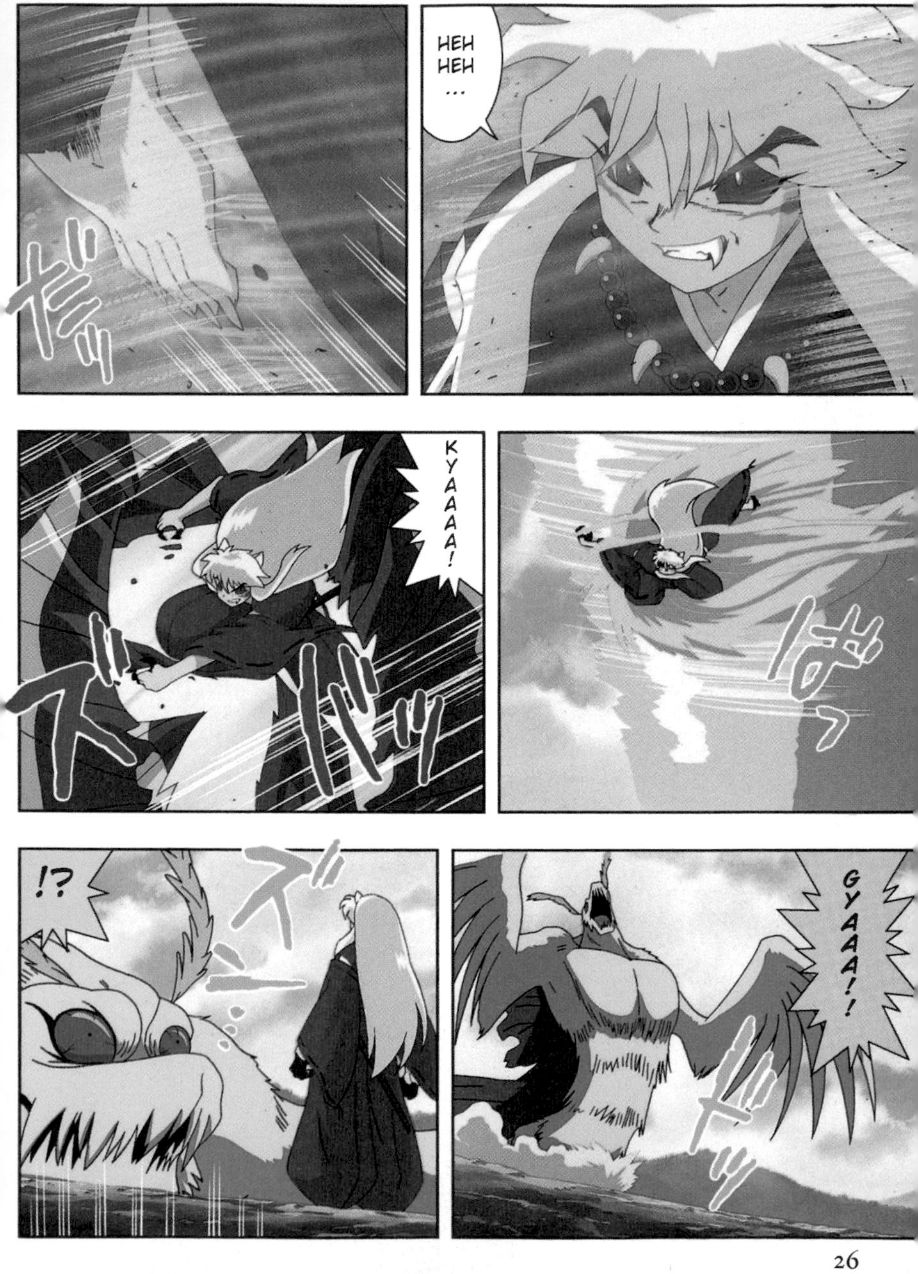
HEH HEH ...
ガッ
ばっ
KYAAAAA!
ズバッ
GYAAAA!!
ドッ
ズ
!?

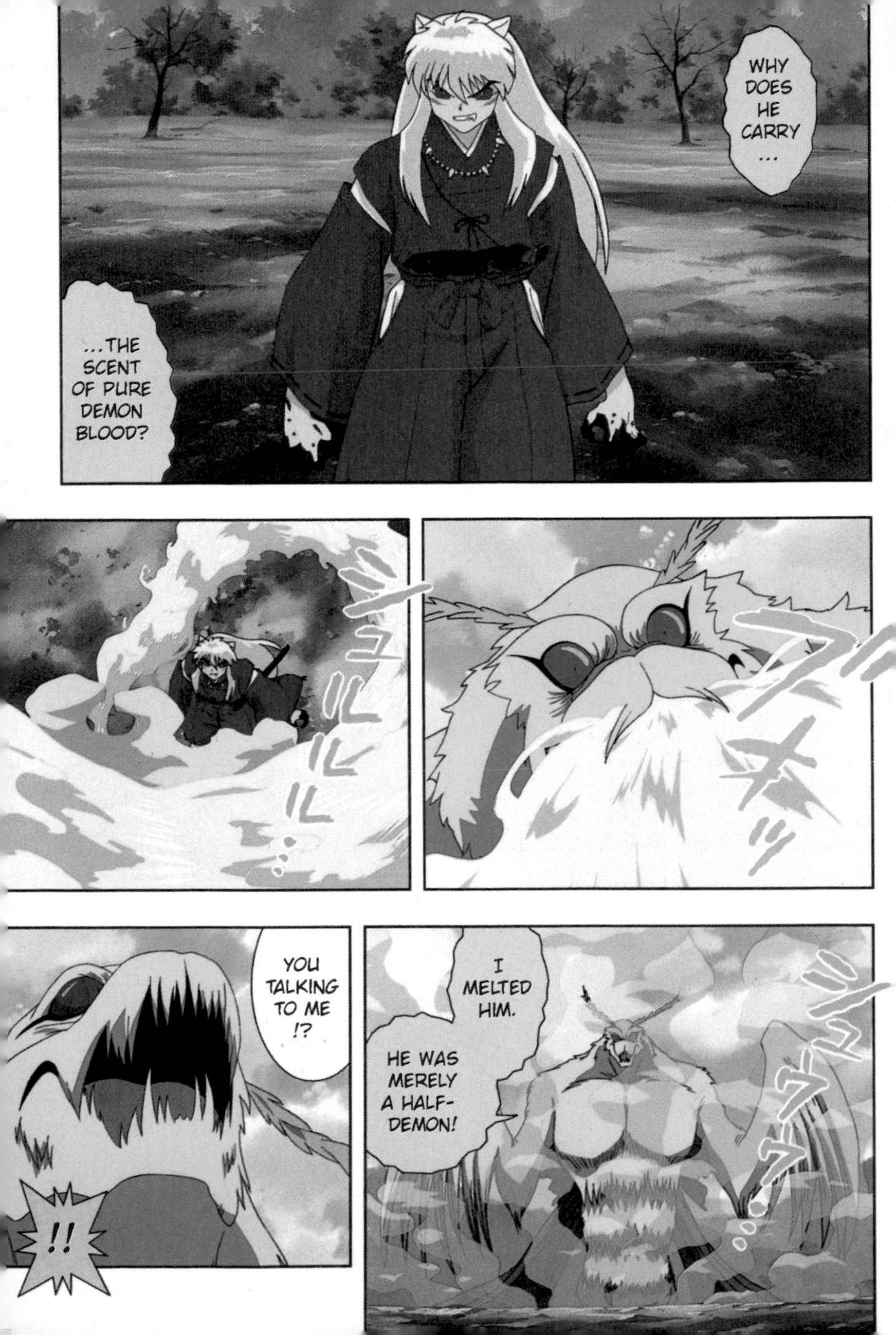
WHY DOES HE CARRY ...
...THE SCENT OF PURE DEMON BLOOD?
I MELTED HIM.
HE WAS MERELY A HALF-DEMON!
YOU TALKING TO ME !?
!!

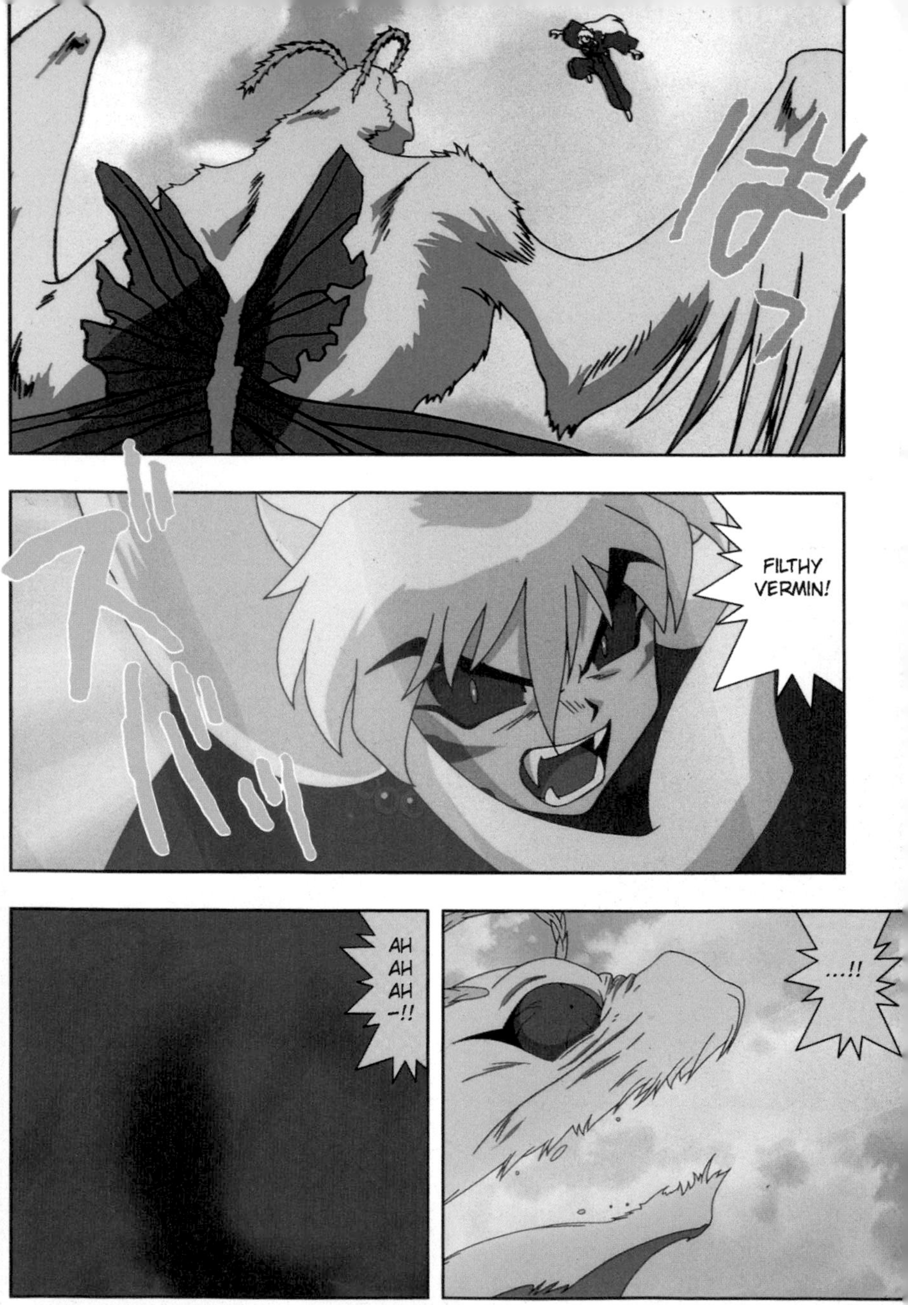
FILTHY VERMIN!
...!!
AH AH AH -!!

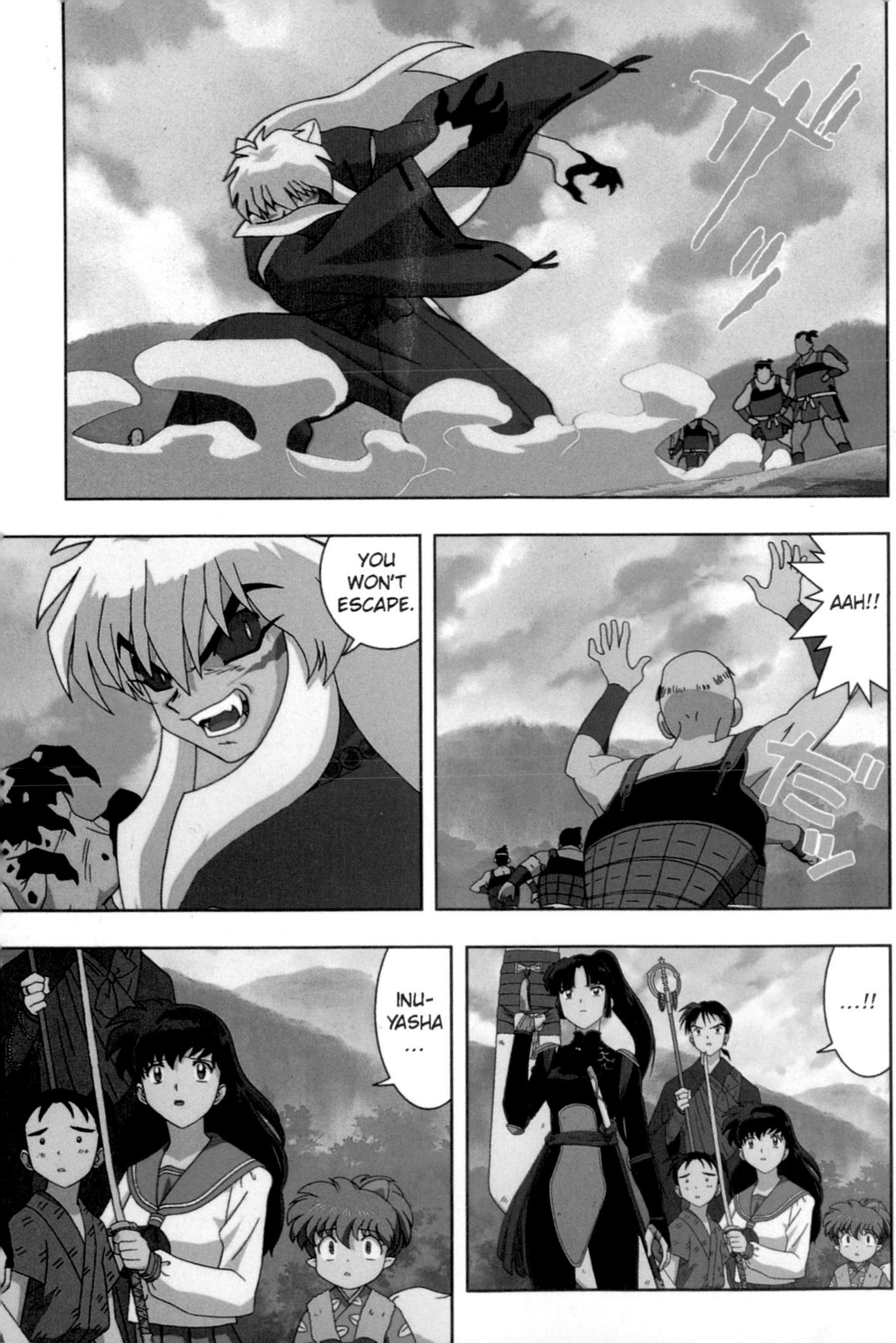
AAH!!
YOU WON'T ESCAPE.
...!!
INU-YASHA ...

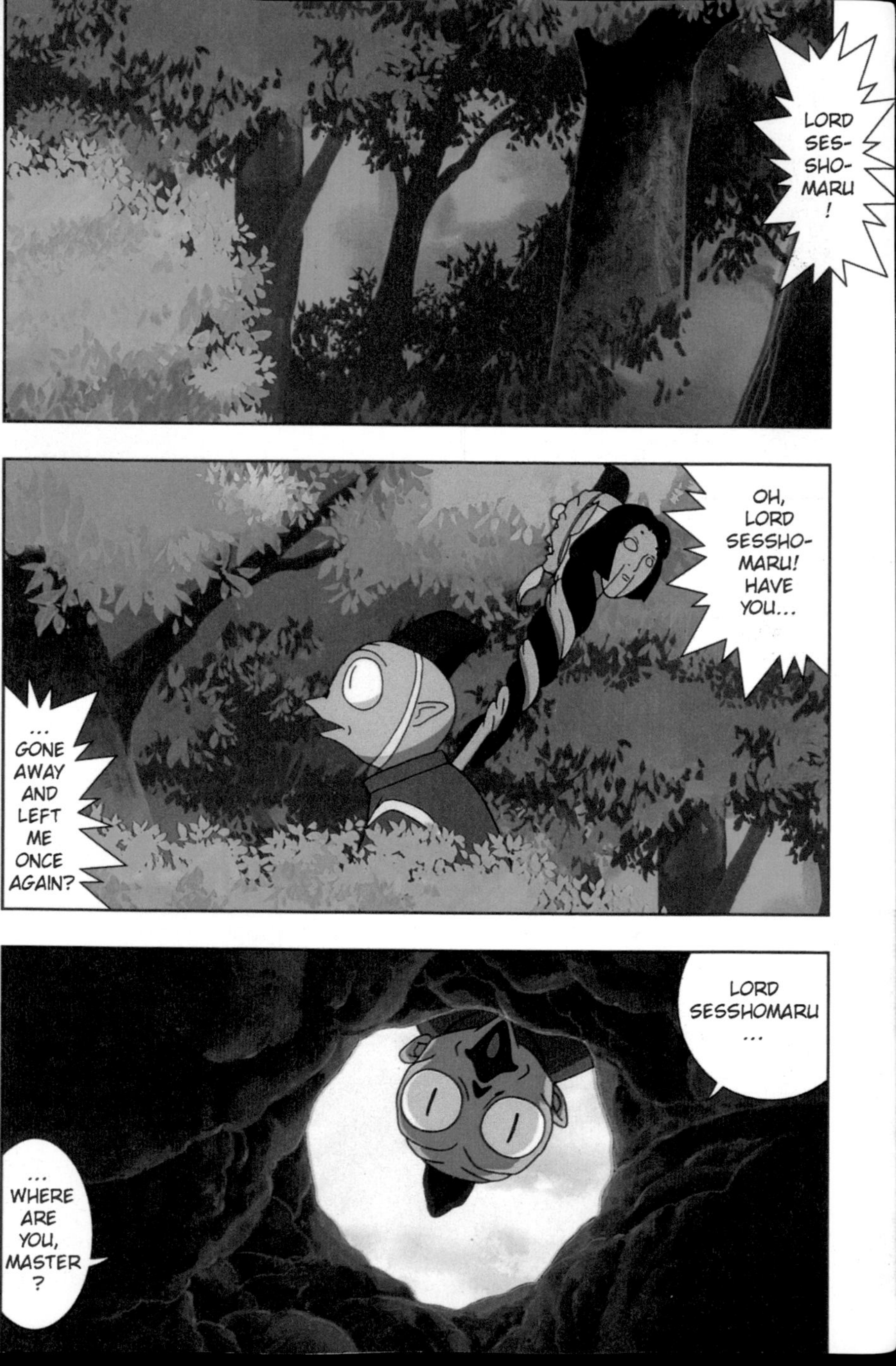
LORD SES-SHO-MARU!
OH, LORD SESSHO-MARU! HAVE YOU...
...GONE AWAY AND LEFT ME ONCE AGAIN?
LORD SESSHOMARU...
...WHERE ARE YOU, MASTER?

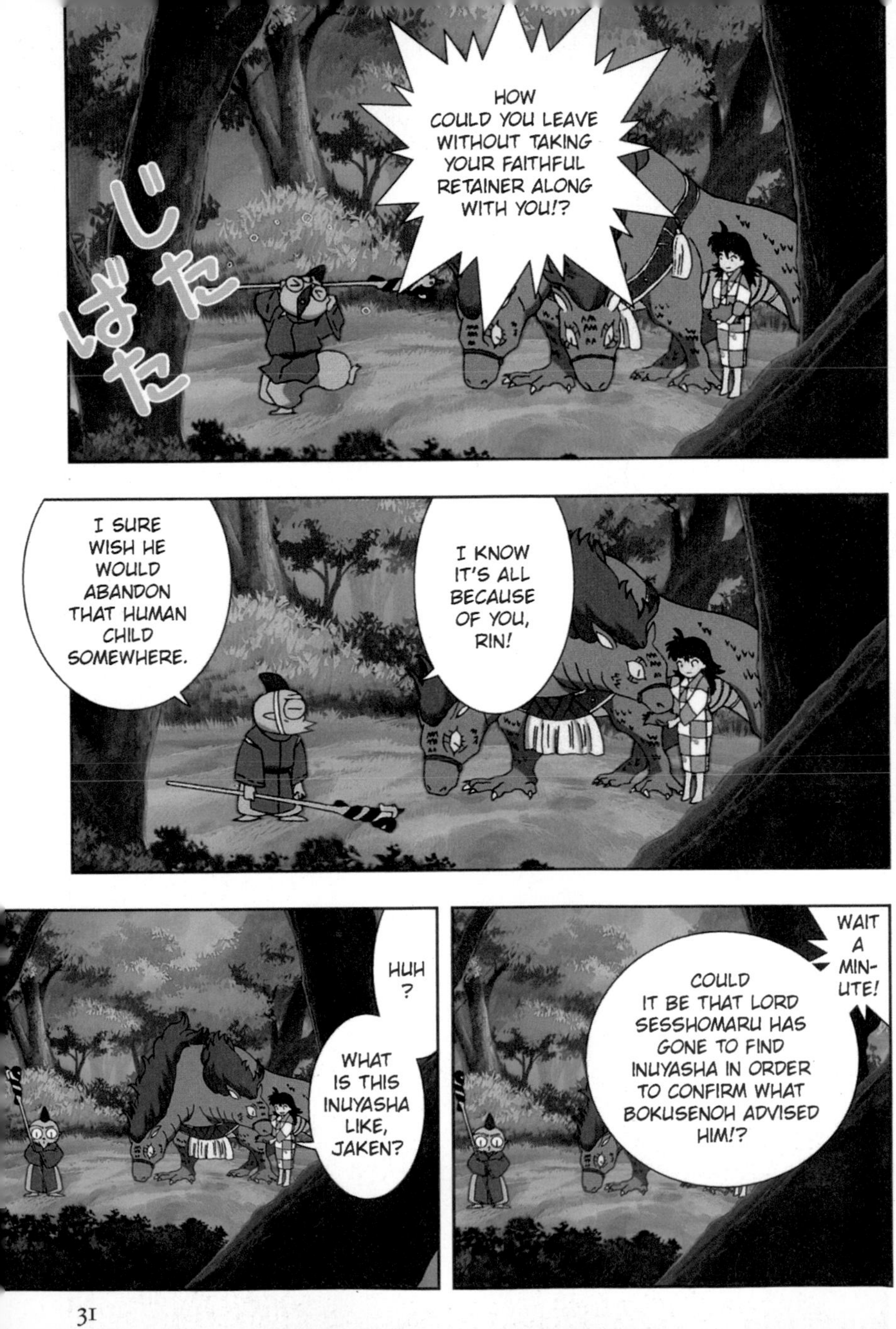
HOW COULD YOU LEAVE WITHOUT TAKING YOUR FAITHFUL RETAINER ALONG WITH YOU!?
じたばた
I KNOW IT'S ALL BECAUSE OF YOU, RIN!
I SURE WISH HE WOULD ABANDON THAT HUMAN CHILD SOMEWHERE.
WAIT A MIN-UTE!
COULD IT BE THAT LORD SESSHOMARU HAS GONE TO FIND INUYASHA IN ORDER TO CONFIRM WHAT BOKUSENOH ADVISED HIM!?
HUH ?
WHAT IS THIS INUYASHA LIKE, JAKEN?

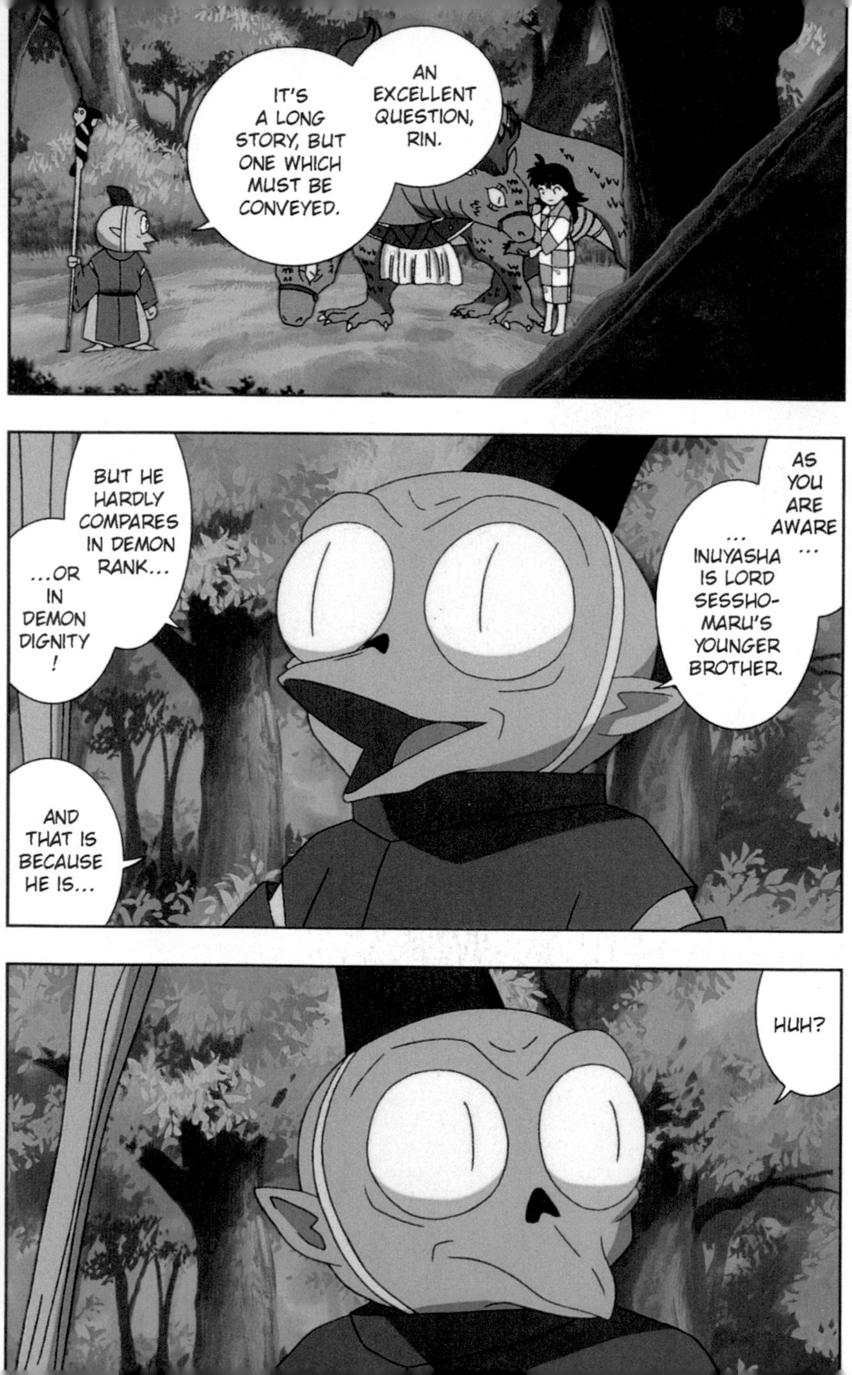
AN EXCELLENT QUESTION, RIN.
IT'S A LONG STORY, BUT ONE WHICH MUST BE CONVEYED.
AS YOU ARE AWARE...
...INUYASHA IS LORD SESSHO-MARU'S YOUNGER BROTHER.
BUT HE HARDLY COMPARES IN DEMON RANK...
...OR IN DEMON DIGNITY!
AND THAT IS BECAUSE HE IS...
HUH?

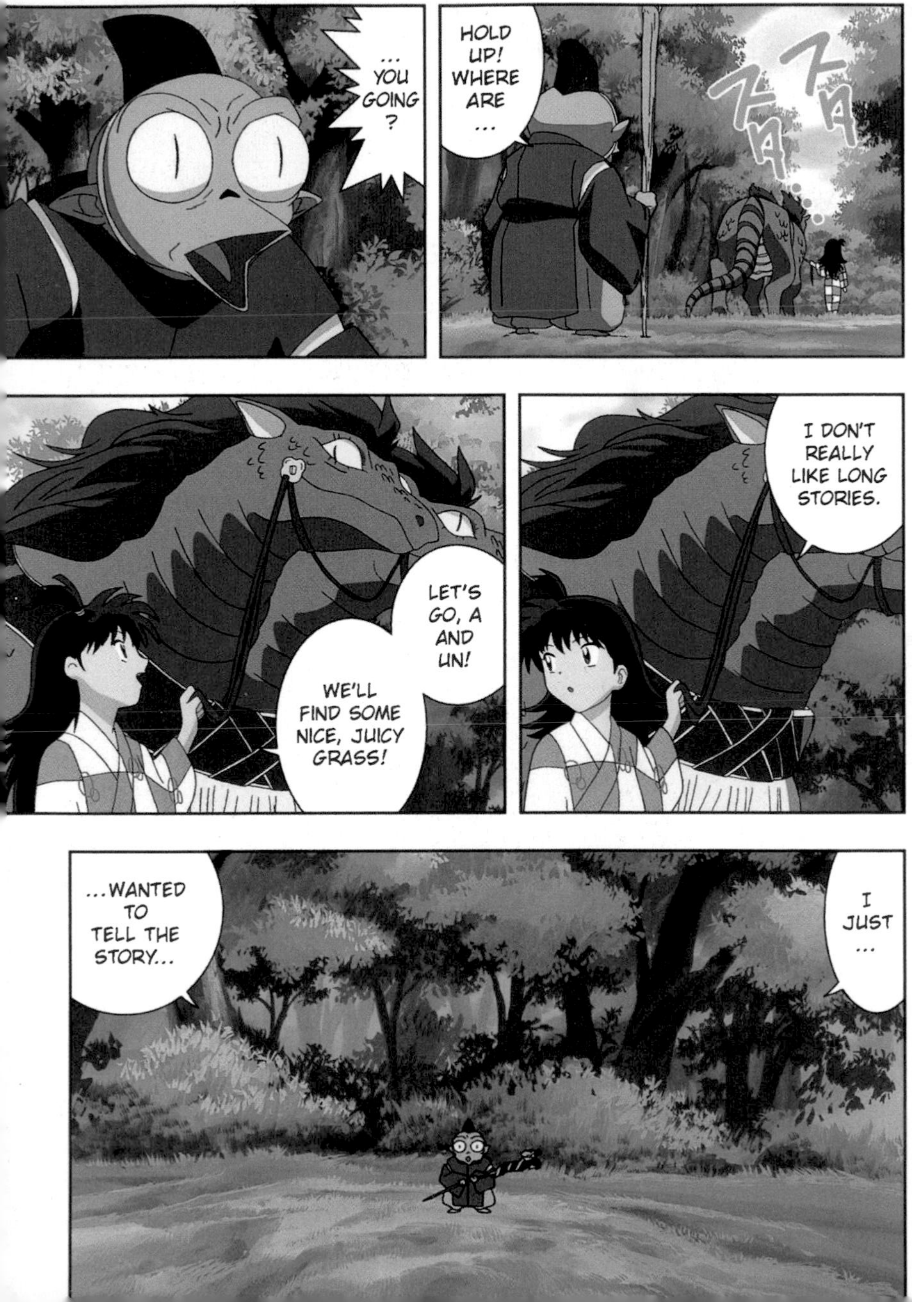
HOLD UP! WHERE ARE ...
... YOU GOING ?
I DON'T REALLY LIKE LONG STORIES.
LET'S GO, A AND UN!
WE'LL FIND SOME NICE, JUICY GRASS!
I JUST ...
...WANTED TO TELL THE STORY...

RUN FOR YOUR LIVES!

DEMON! WE'RE DOOMED!

YOU WON'T GET AWAY!

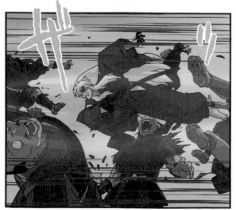

GYA-!!

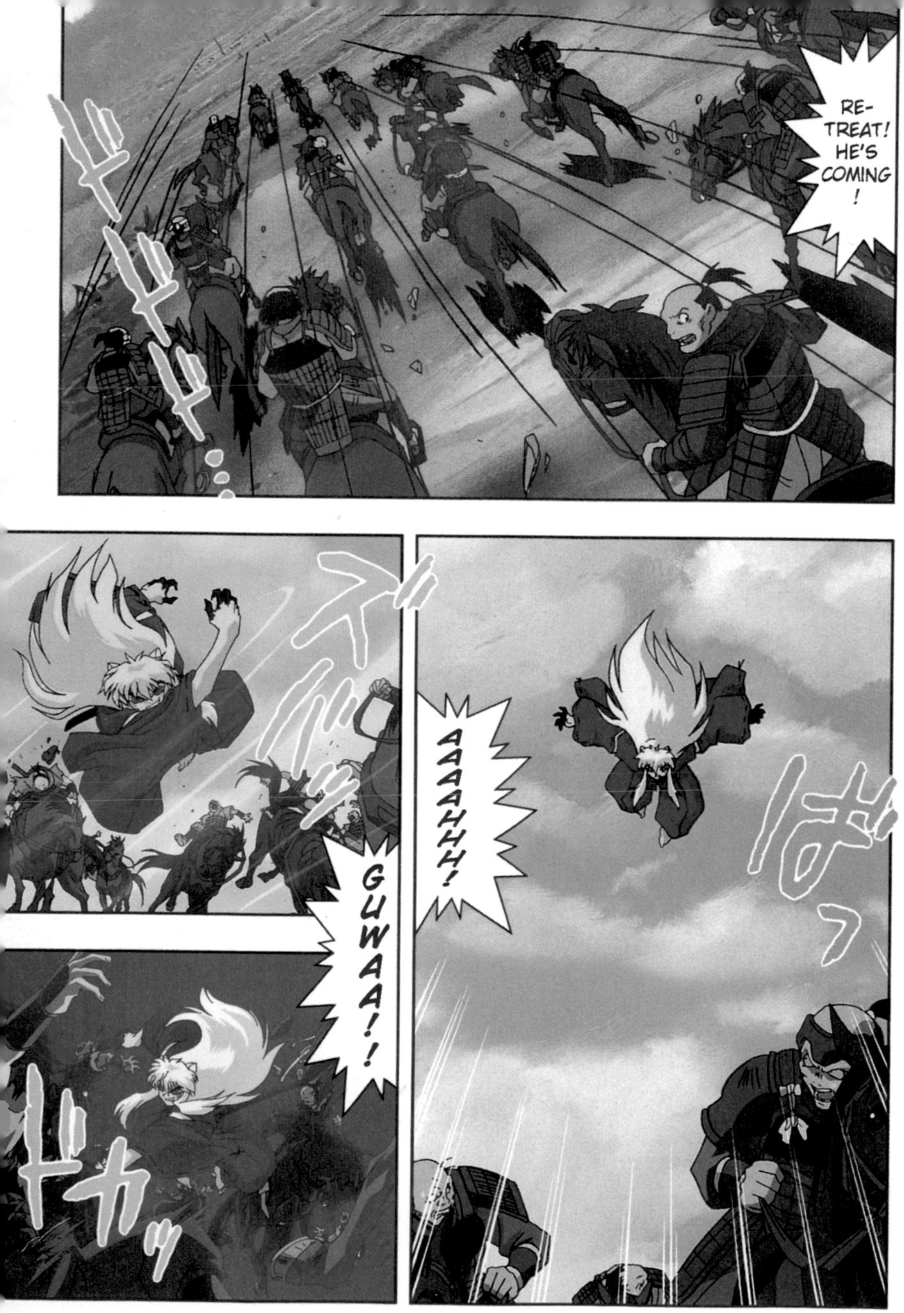
RE-TREAT! HE'S COMING!
ぱっ
AAAAAHHH!
GUWAAA!!
ドカッ

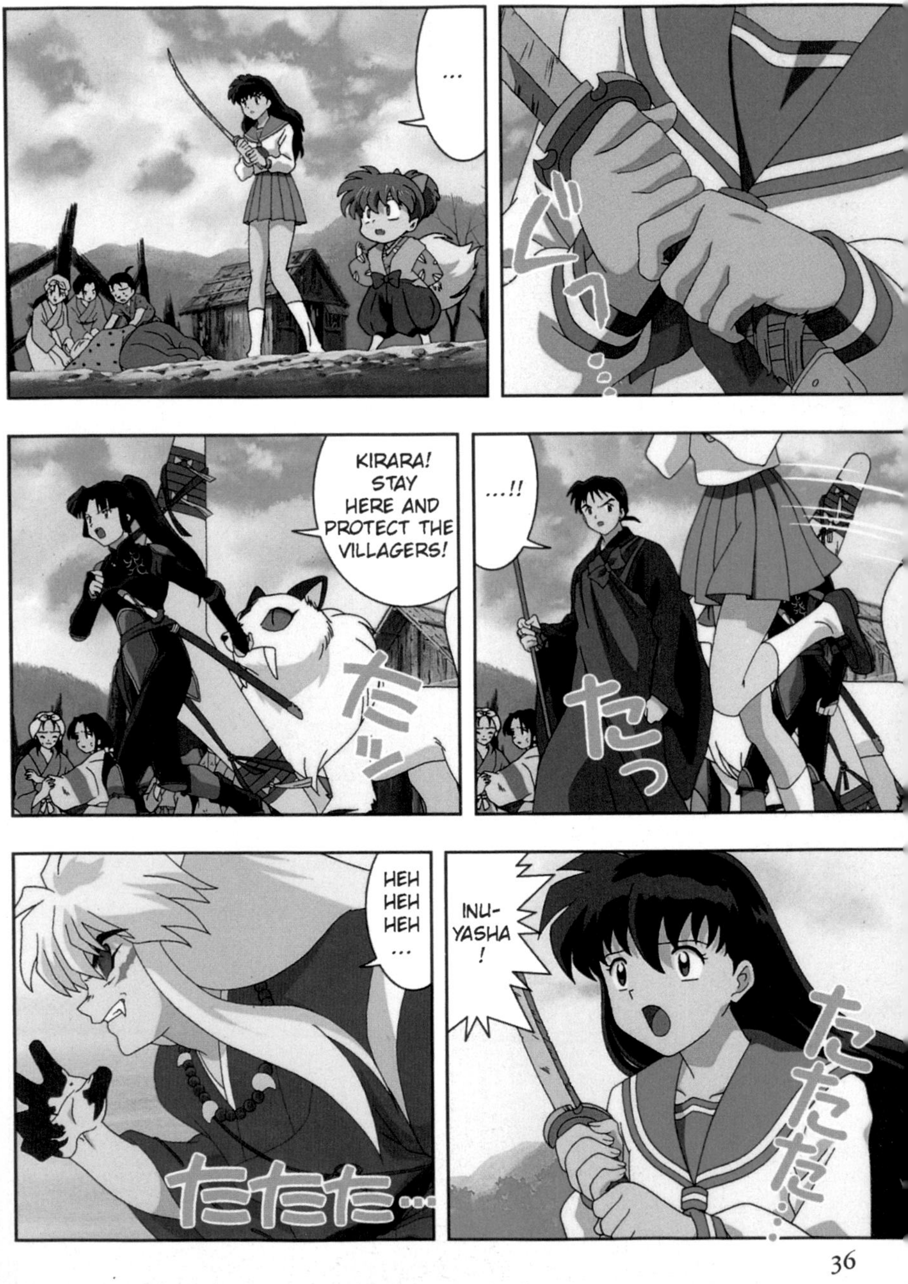
...
...!!
たっ
KIRARA! STAY HERE AND PROTECT THE VILLAGERS!
たッ
INU-YASHA!
たたた…
HEH HEH HEH ...
たたた…

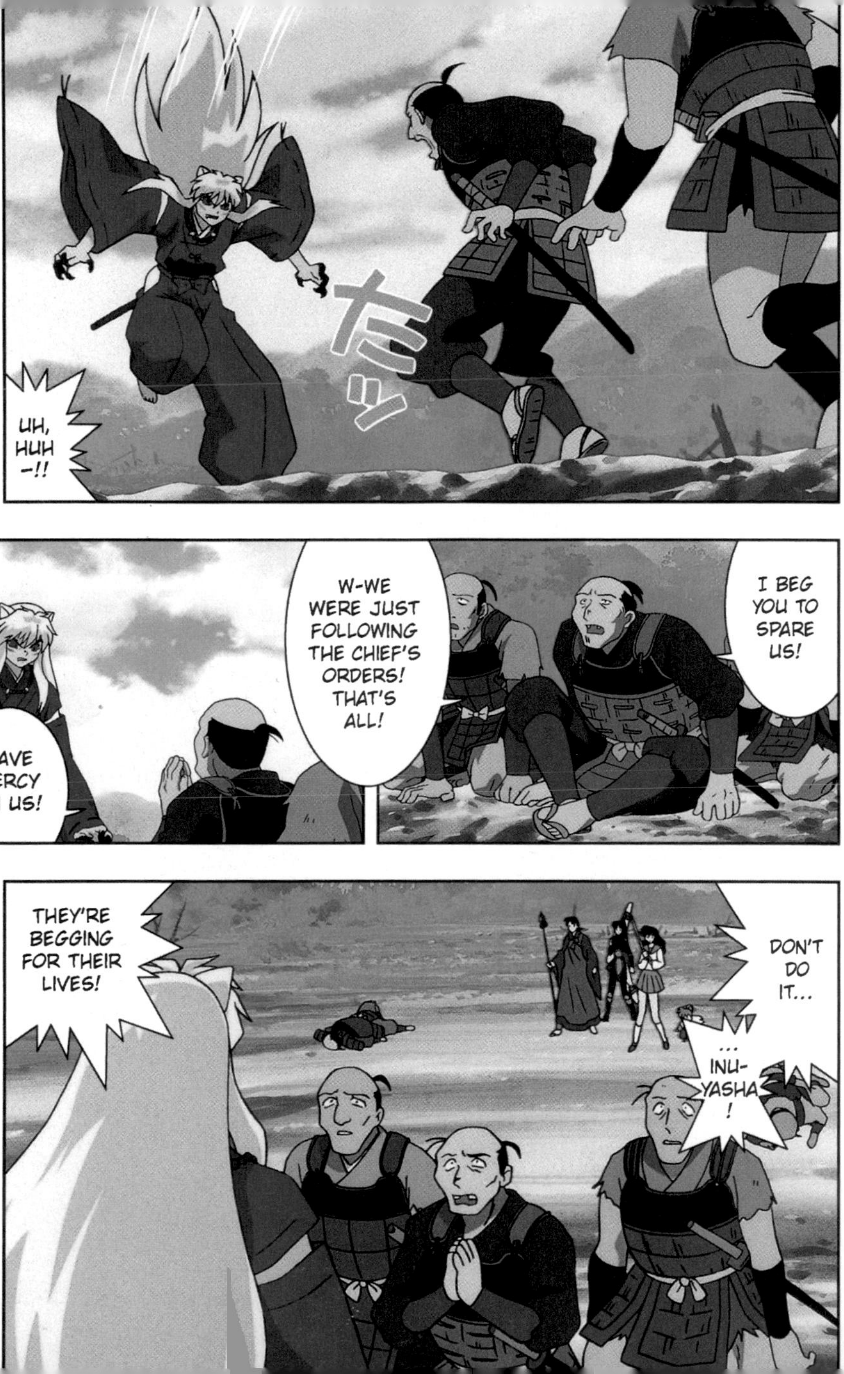
タッ
UH, HUH—!!
I BEG YOU TO SPARE US!
W-WE WERE JUST FOLLOWING THE CHIEF'S ORDERS! THAT'S ALL!
HAVE MERCY ON US!
DON'T DO IT...
...INU-YASHA!
THEY'RE BEGGING FOR THEIR LIVES!

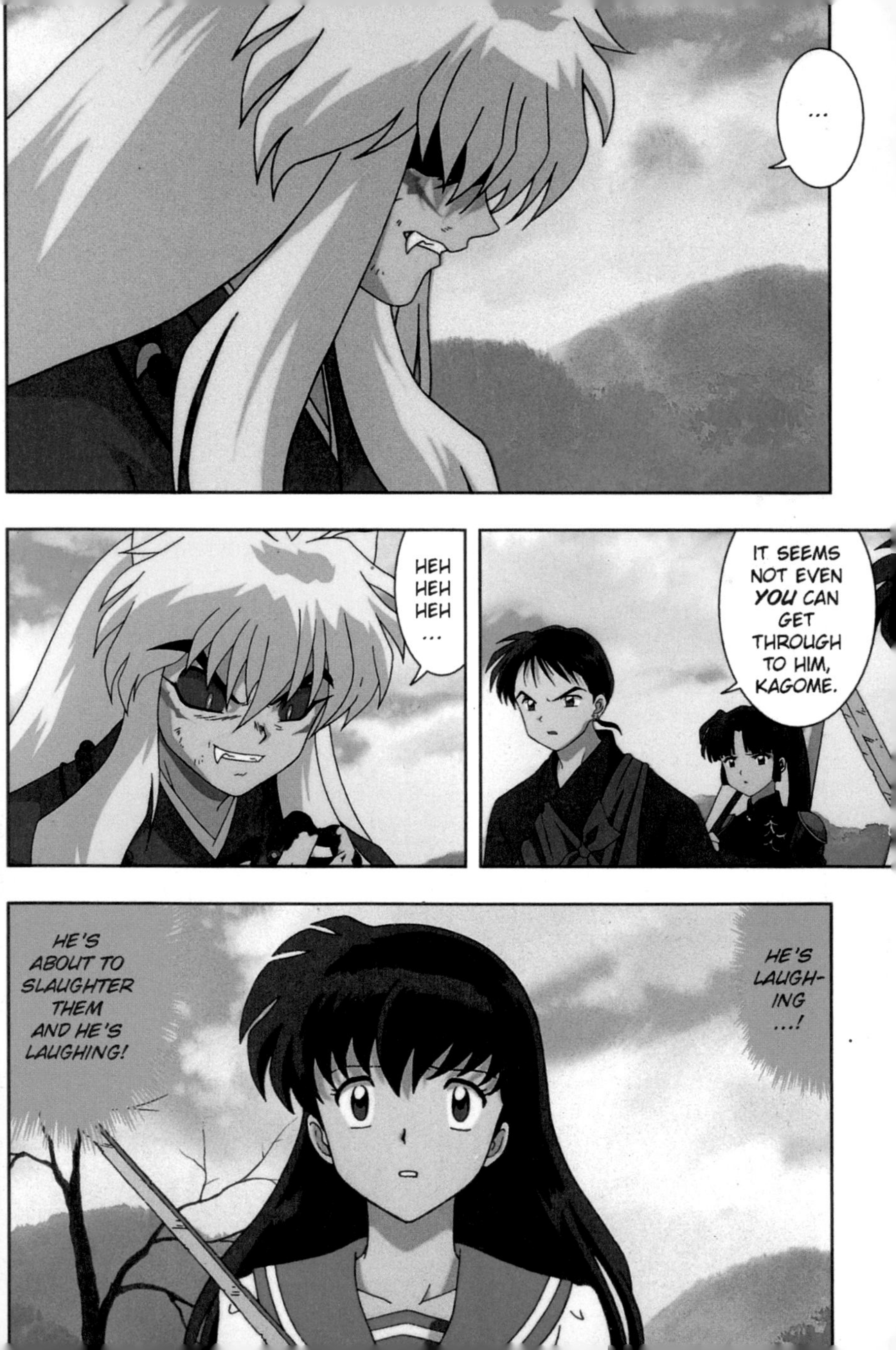
...
IT SEEMS NOT EVEN YOU CAN GET THROUGH TO HIM, KAGOME.
HEH HEH HEH ...
HE'S LAUGHING ...!
HE'S ABOUT TO SLAUGHTER THEM AND HE'S LAUGHING!

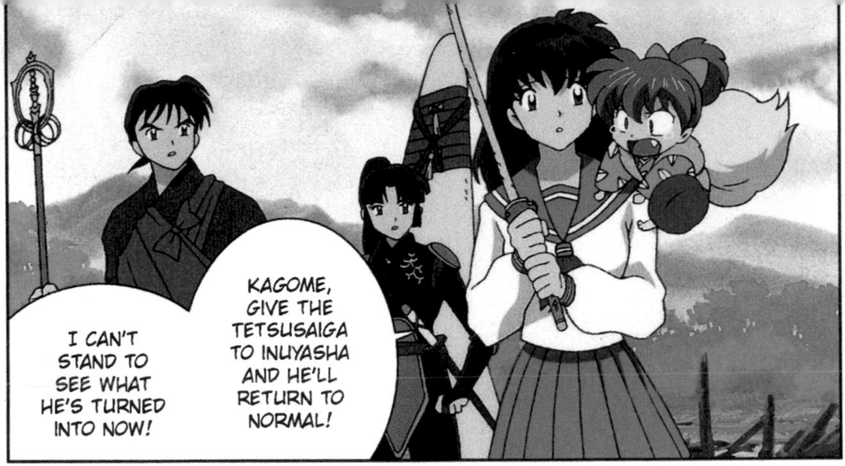
KAGOME, GIVE THE TETSUSAIGA TO INUYASHA AND HE'LL RETURN TO NORMAL!
I CAN'T STAND TO SEE WHAT HE'S TURNED INTO NOW!

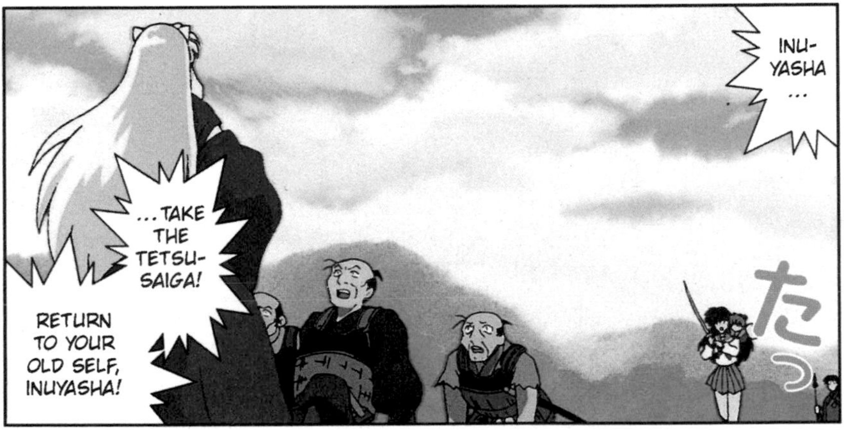
INU-YASHA ...
...TAKE THE TETSU-SAIGA!
RETURN TO YOUR OLD SELF, INUYASHA!
たっ

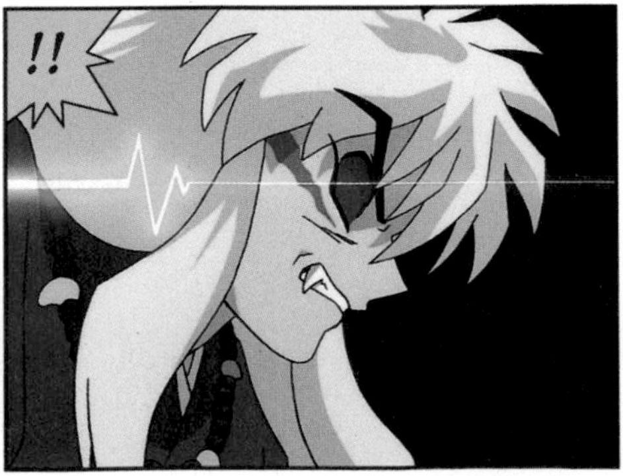
!!

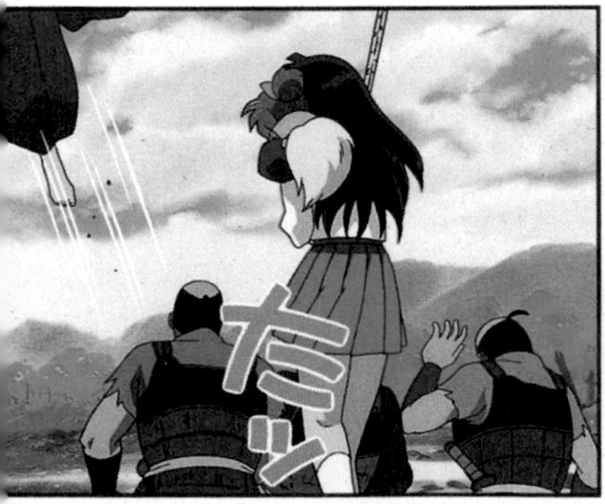

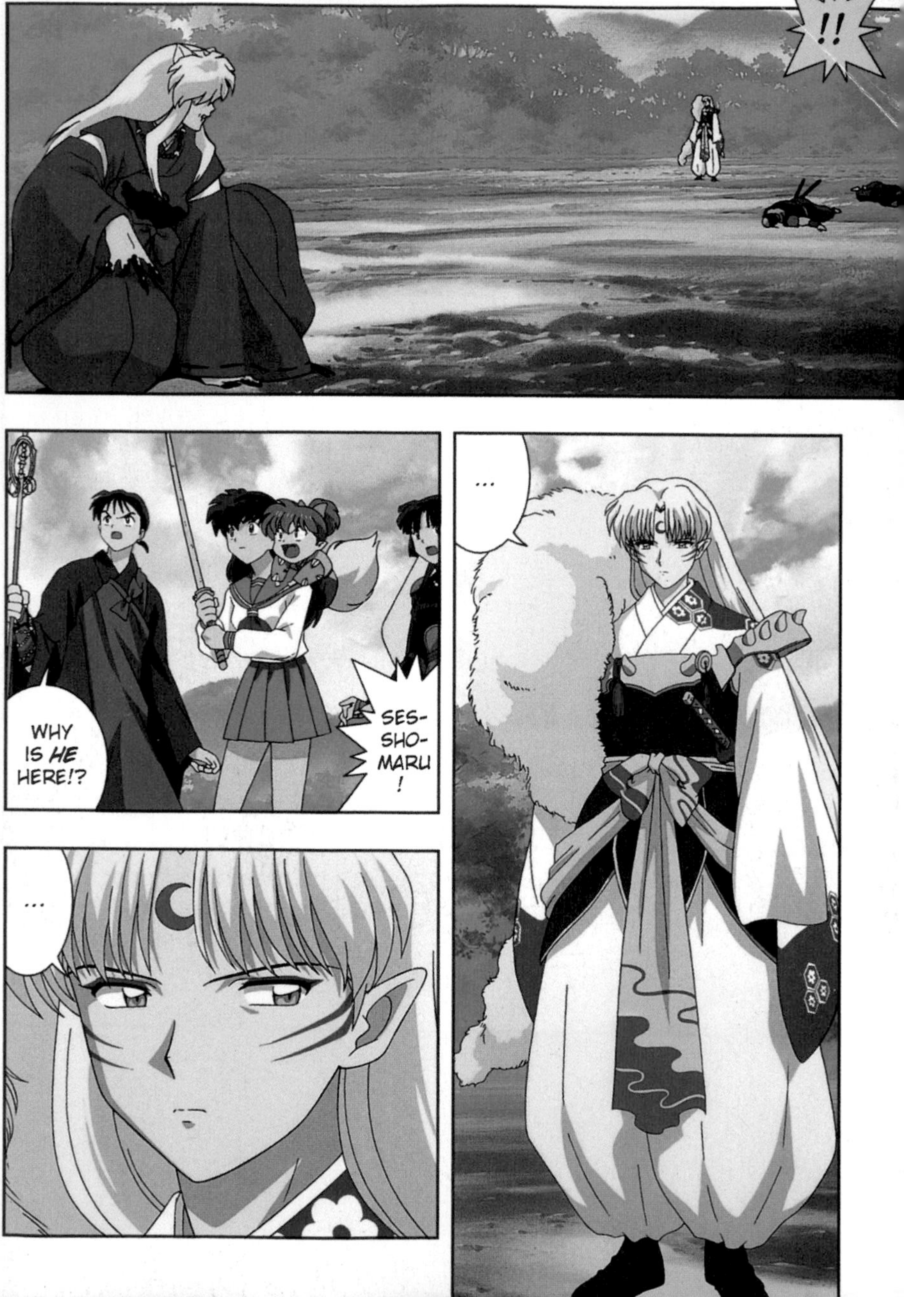
!!
...
SES-SHO-MARU!
WHY IS HE HERE!?
...

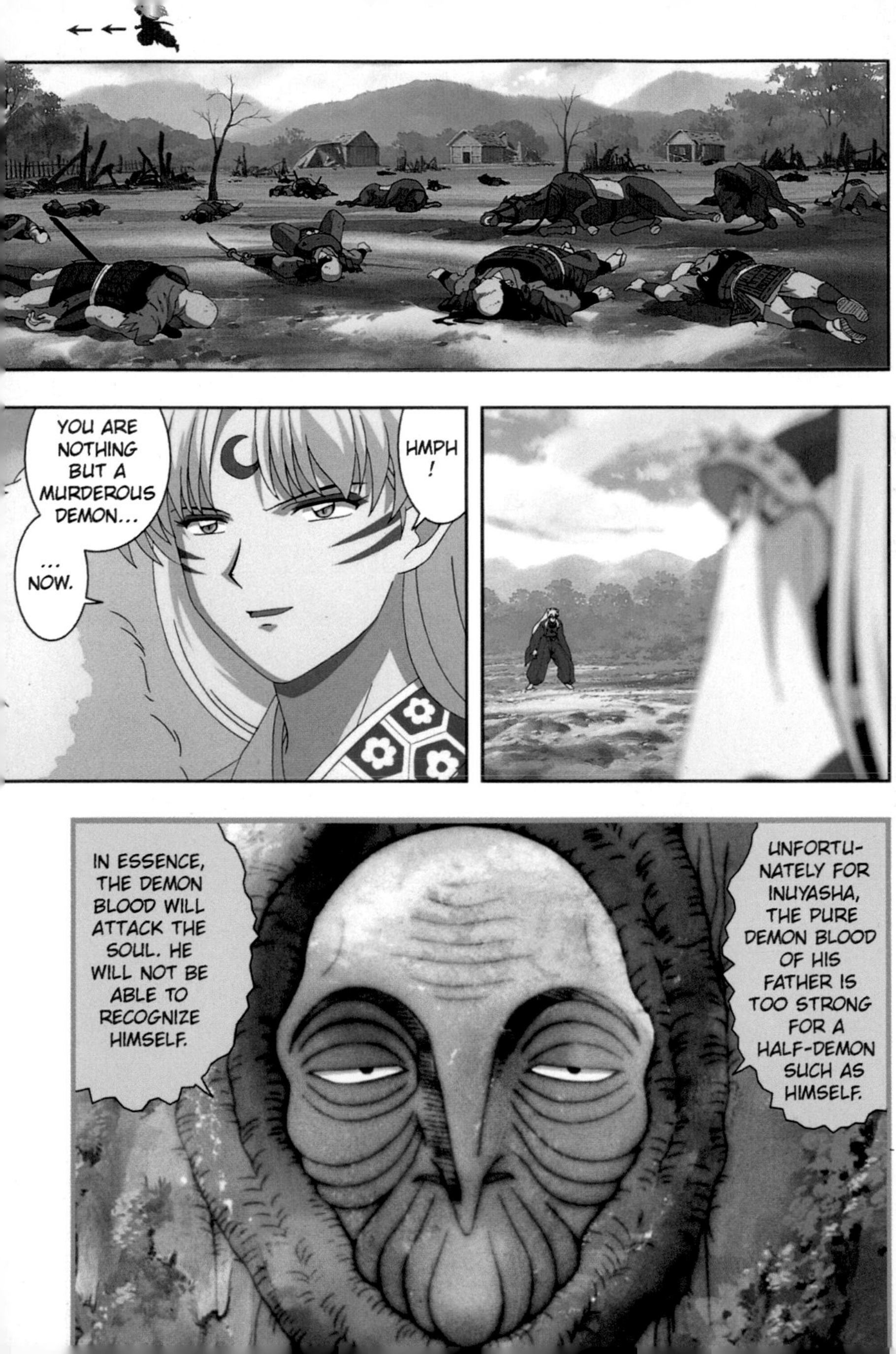
HMPH!
YOU ARE NOTHING BUT A MURDEROUS DEMON...
... NOW.
UNFORTUNATELY FOR INUYASHA, THE PURE DEMON BLOOD OF HIS FATHER IS TOO STRONG FOR A HALF-DEMON SUCH AS HIMSELF.
IN ESSENCE, THE DEMON BLOOD WILL ATTACK THE SOUL. HE WILL NOT BE ABLE TO RECOGNIZE HIMSELF.

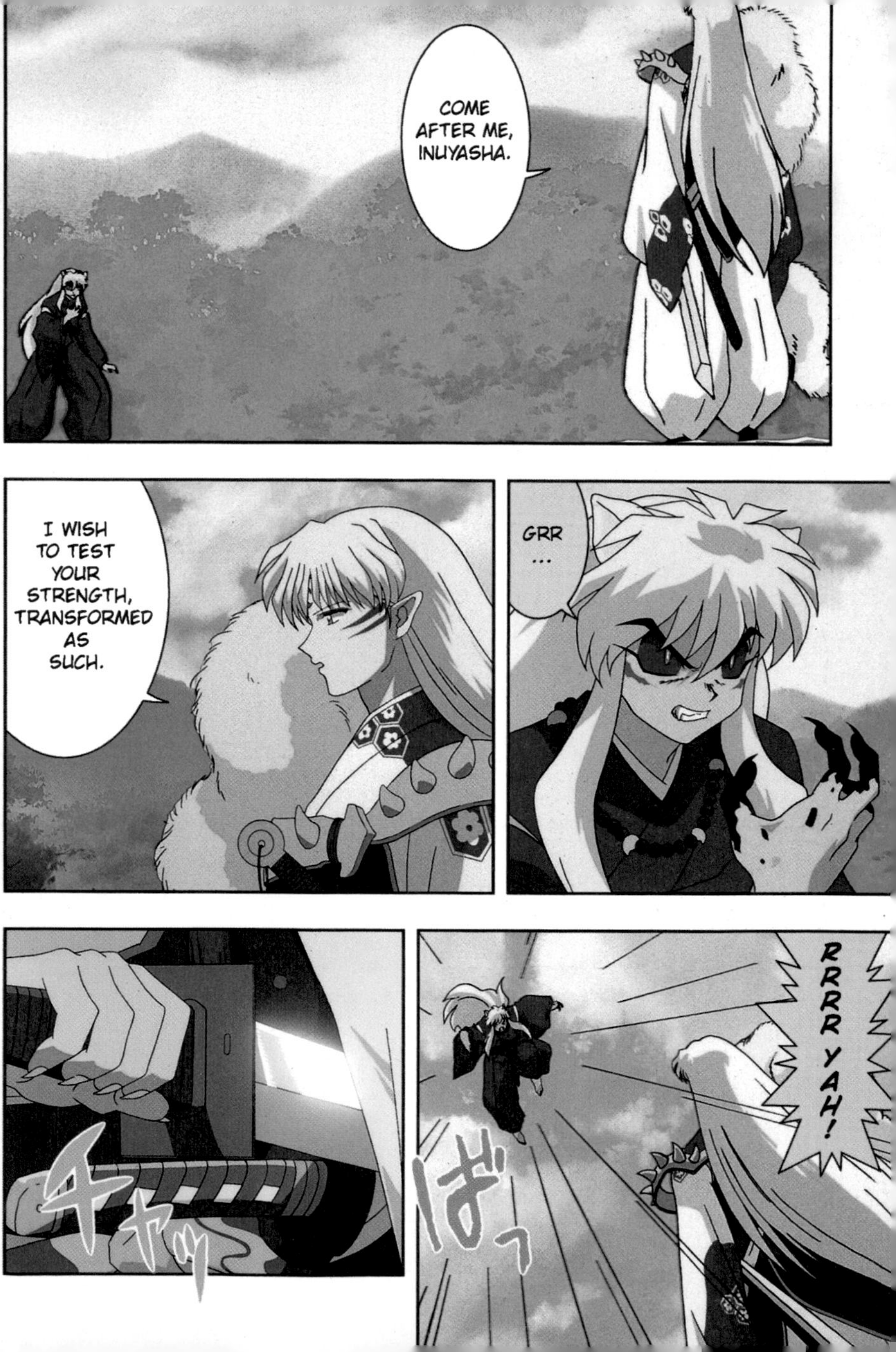
COME AFTER ME, INUYASHA.
GRR ...
I WISH TO TEST YOUR STRENGTH, TRANSFORMED AS SUCH.
RRRR YAH!
ばっ
チャッ

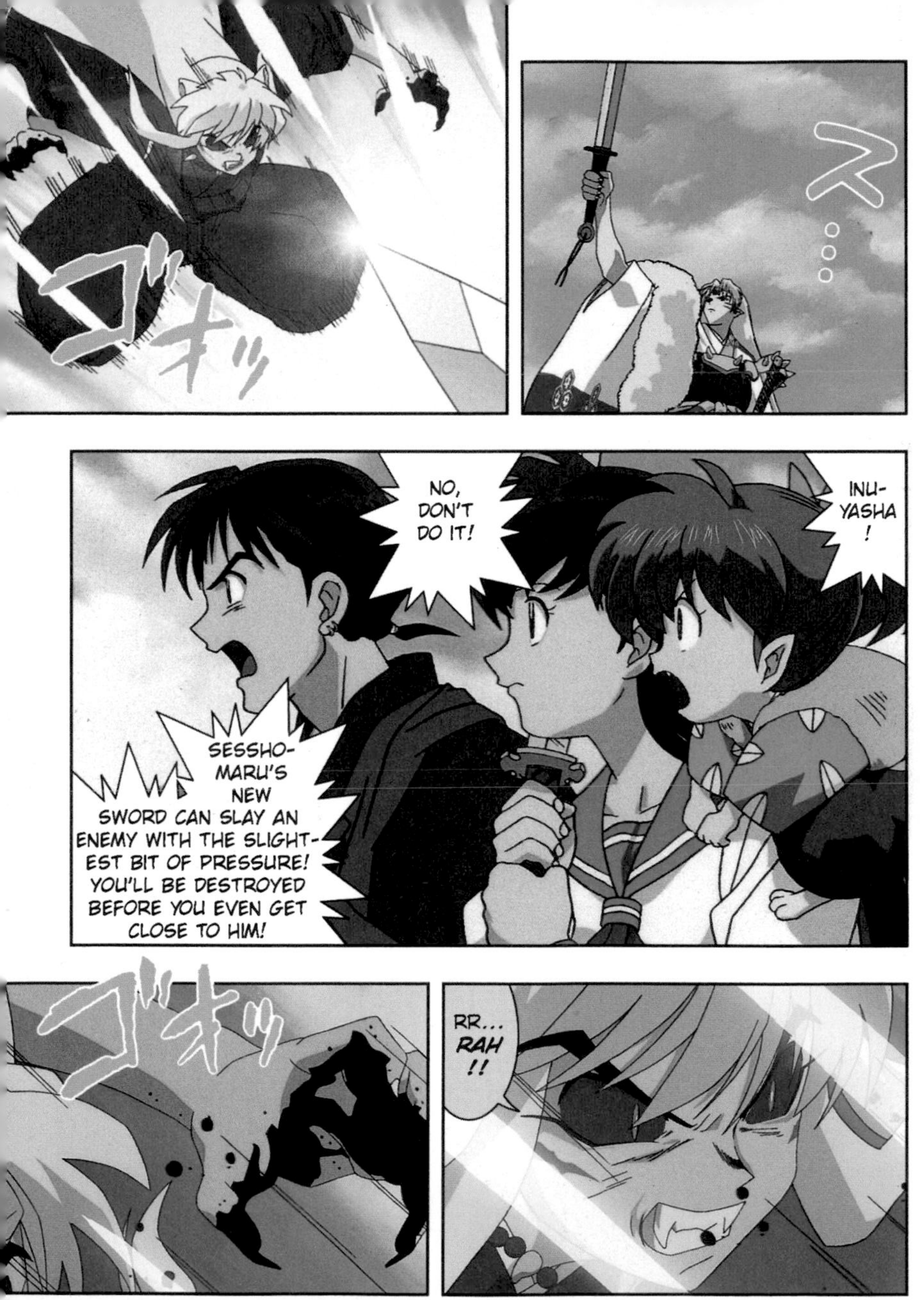
ス…
ゴオッ
INU-YASHA!
NO, DON'T DO IT!
SESSHO-MARU'S NEW SWORD CAN SLAY AN ENEMY WITH THE SLIGHT-EST BIT OF PRESSURE! YOU'LL BE DESTROYED BEFORE YOU EVEN GET CLOSE TO HIM!
RR... RAH!!
ゴオッ

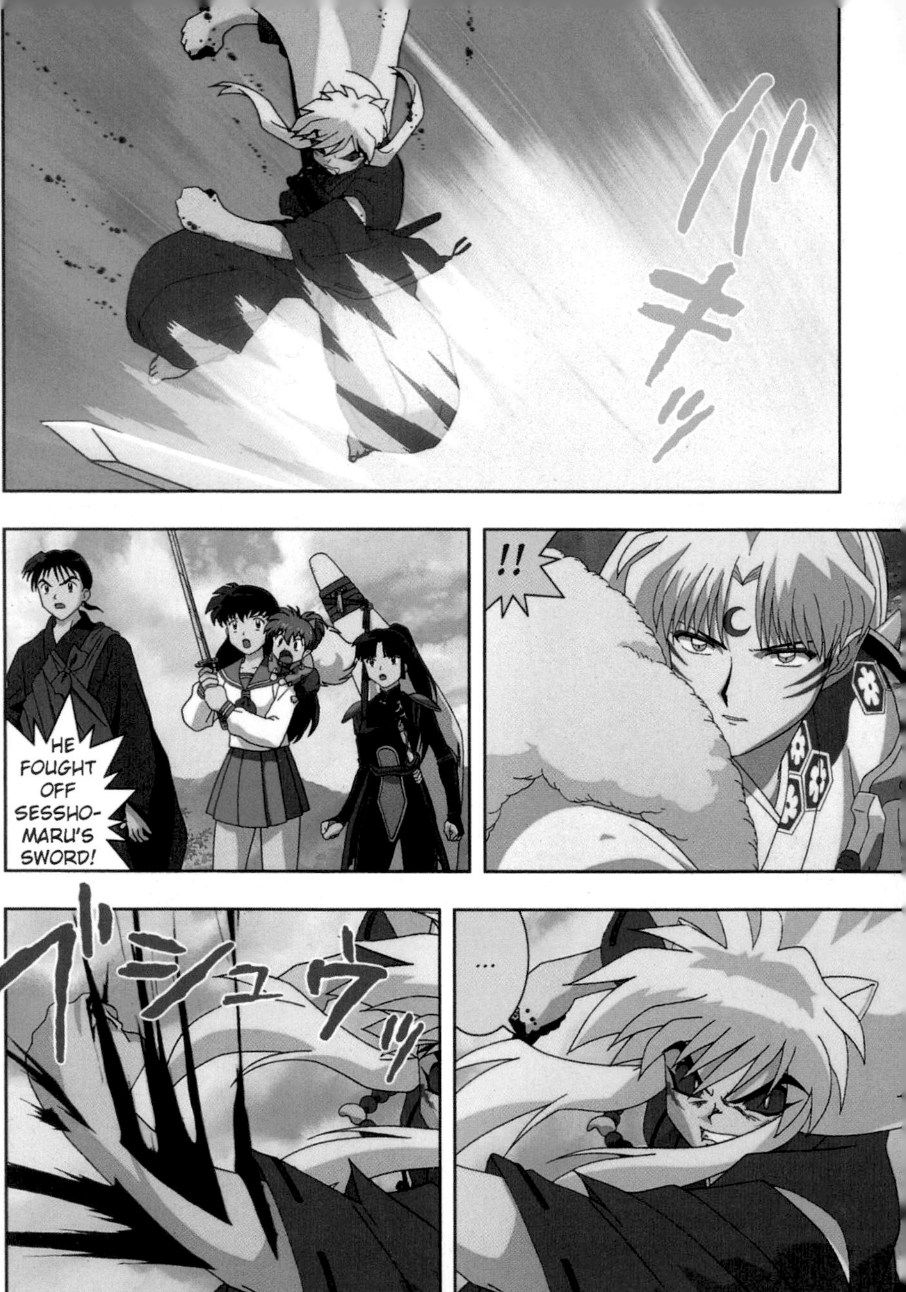
バキッ
!!
HE FOUGHT OFF SESSHO-MARU'S SWORD!
...
ブシュヴッ

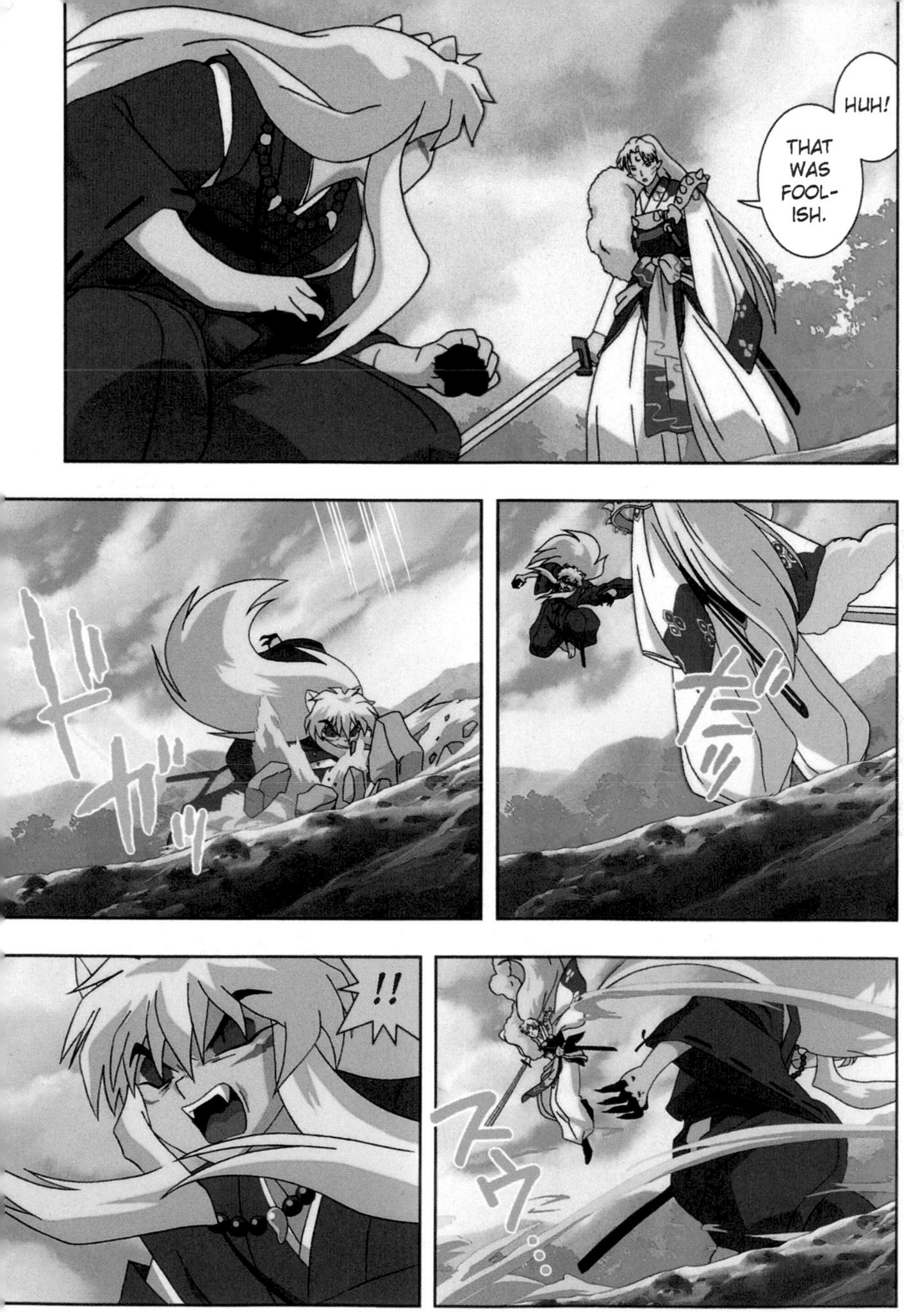
HUH!
THAT WAS FOOL-ISH.
ダッ
ドガッ
スゥ...
!!

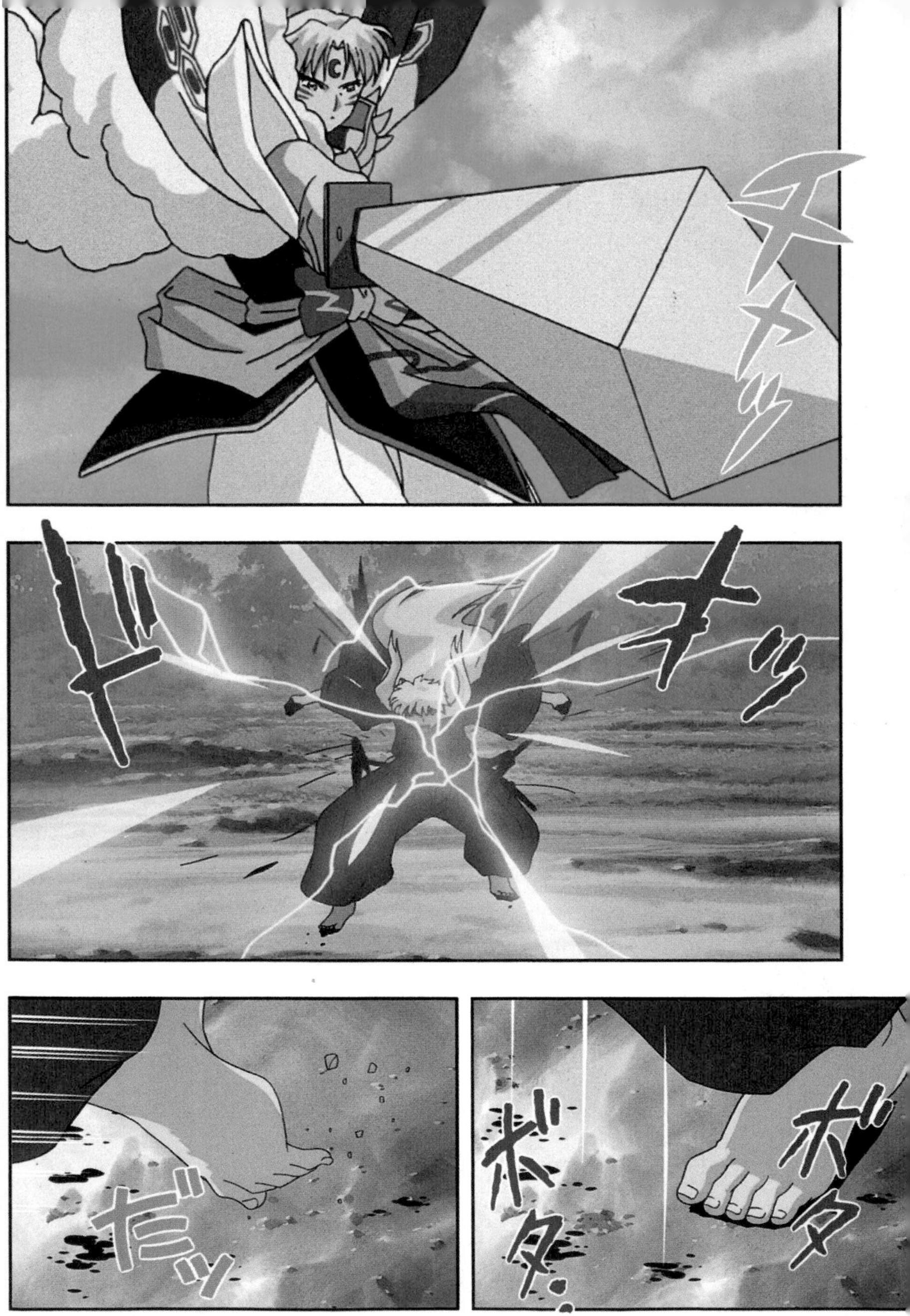
チャキッ
ドオッ
ボタ
ボタ…
ダッ

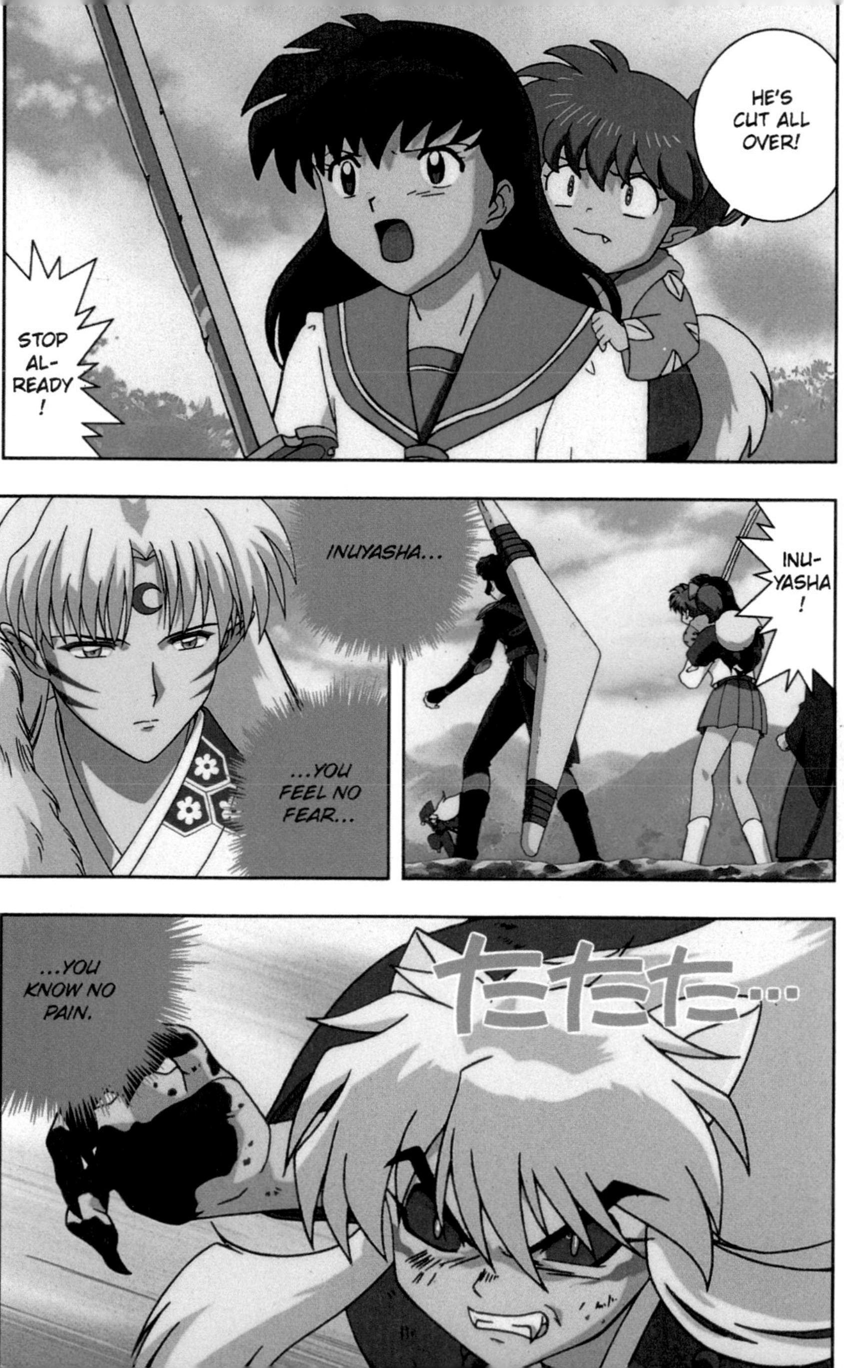
HE'S CUT ALL OVER!
STOP AL-READY!
INU-YASHA!
INUYASHA...
...YOU FEEL NO FEAR...
...YOU KNOW NO PAIN.
たたたた...

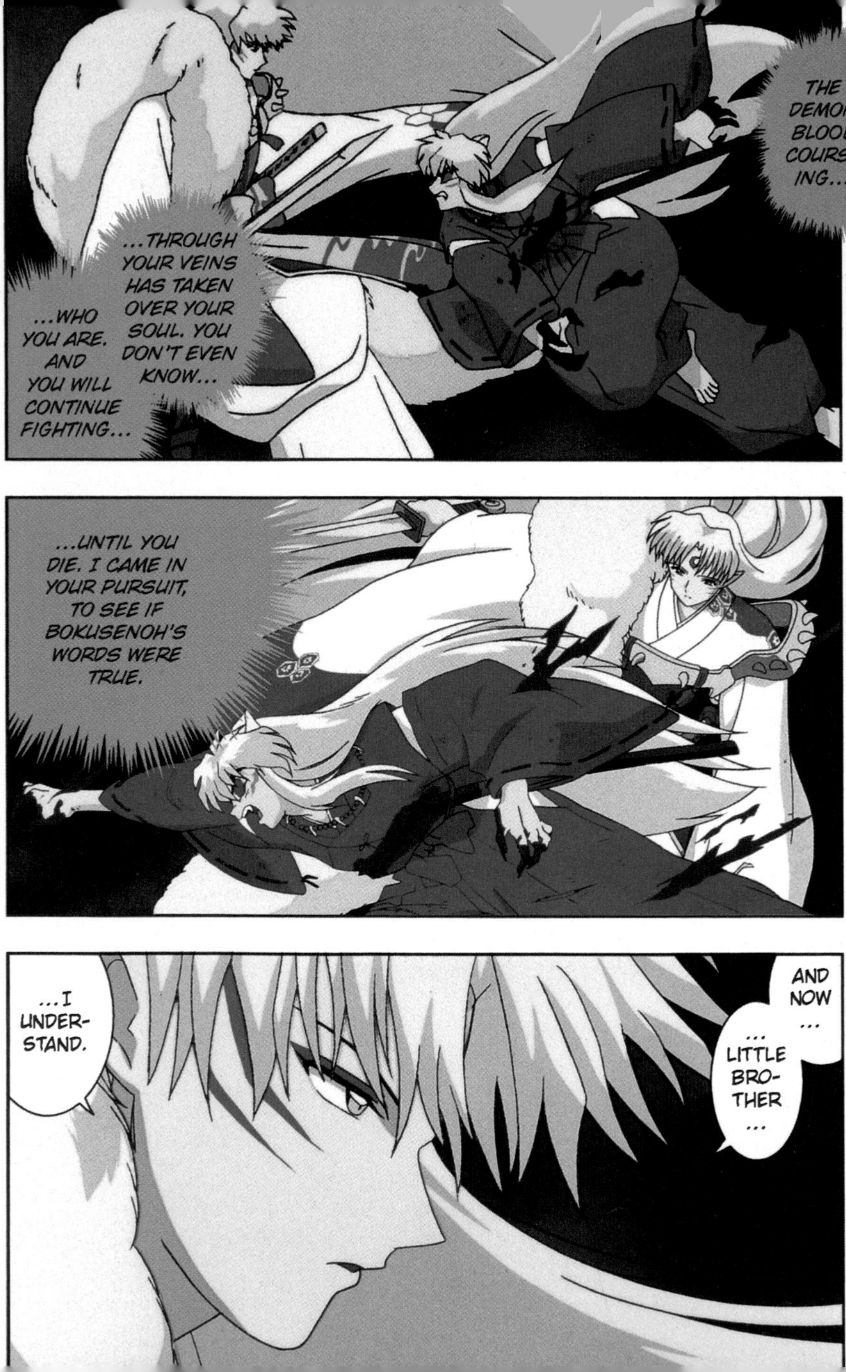
THE DEMON BLOOD COURSING...
...THROUGH YOUR VEINS HAS TAKEN OVER YOUR SOUL. YOU DON'T EVEN KNOW...
...WHO YOU ARE. AND YOU WILL CONTINUE FIGHTING...
...UNTIL YOU DIE. I CAME IN YOUR PURSUIT, TO SEE IF BOKUSENOH'S WORDS WERE TRUE.
AND NOW ... LITTLE BROTHER ...
...I UNDERSTAND.

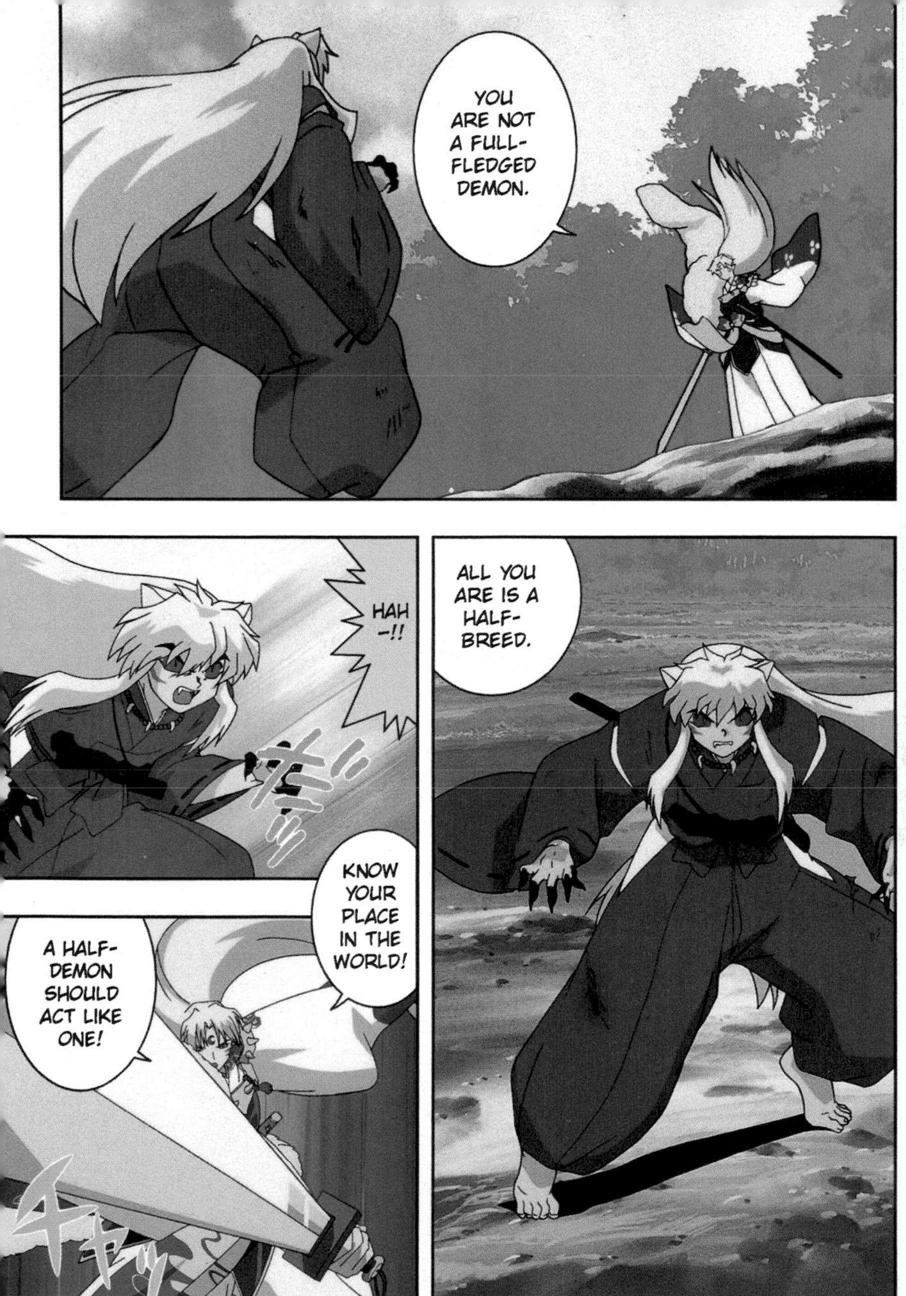
YOU ARE NOT A FULL-FLEDGED DEMON.
ALL YOU ARE IS A HALF-BREED.
HAH-!!
KNOW YOUR PLACE IN THE WORLD!
A HALF-DEMON SHOULD ACT LIKE ONE!

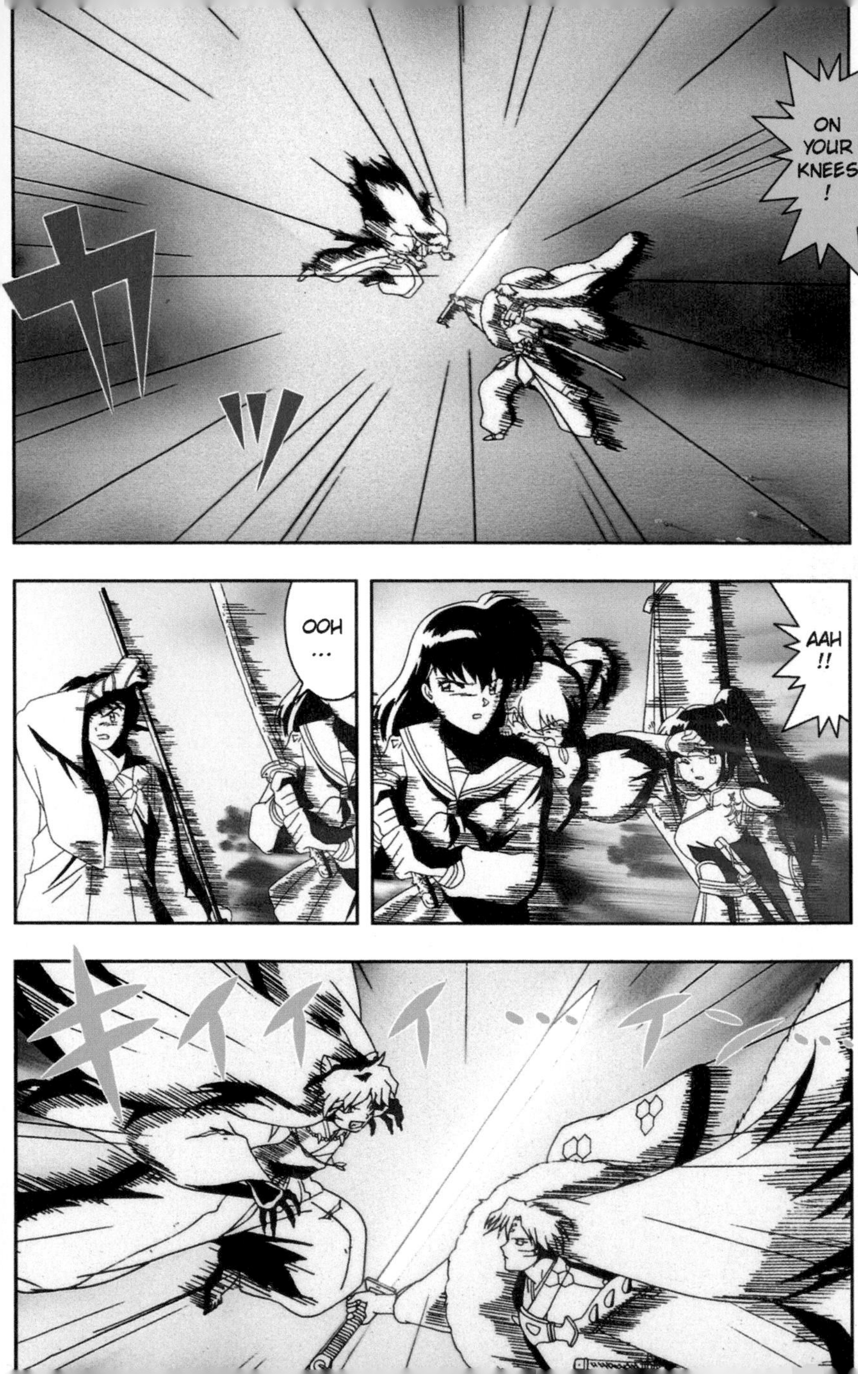
ON YOUR KNEES!
ガッ
AAH!!
OOH...
キイイ…イーン…

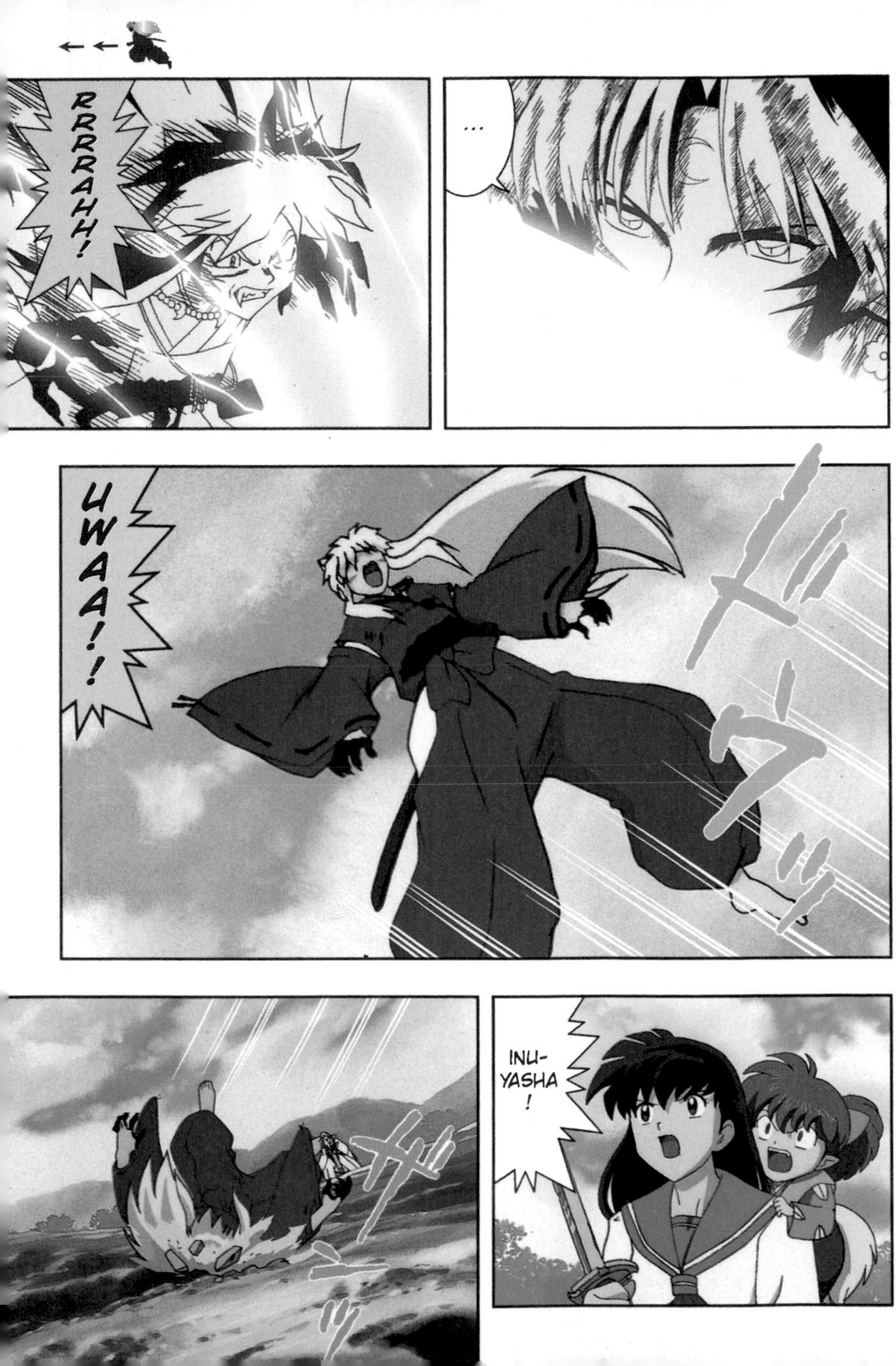
...
RRRRAHH!
UWAAA!!
INU-YASHA!

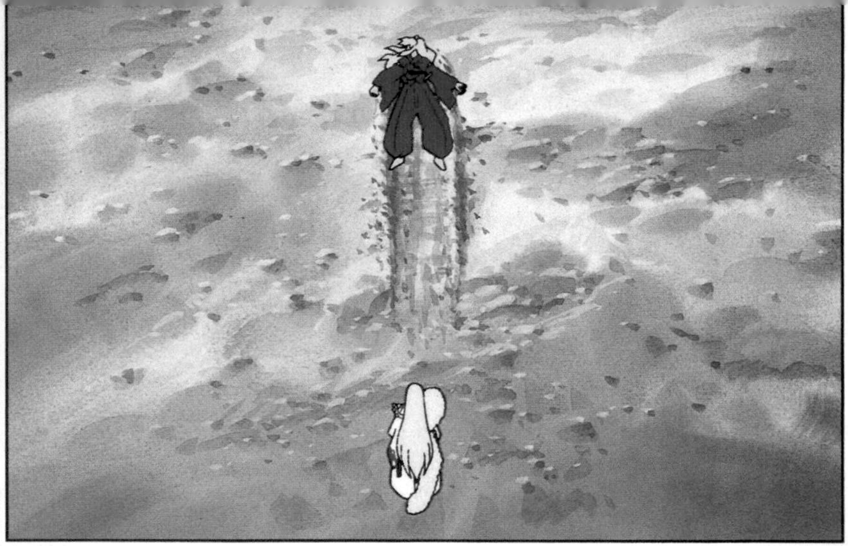

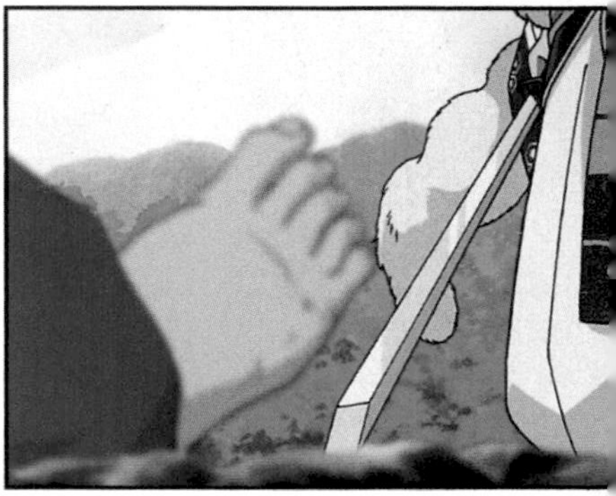

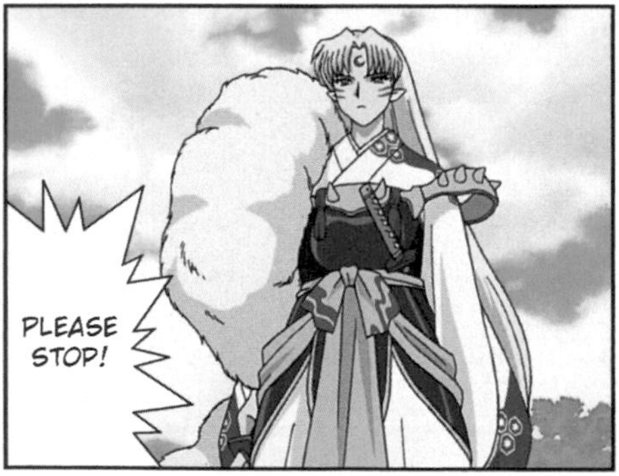
PLEASE STOP!

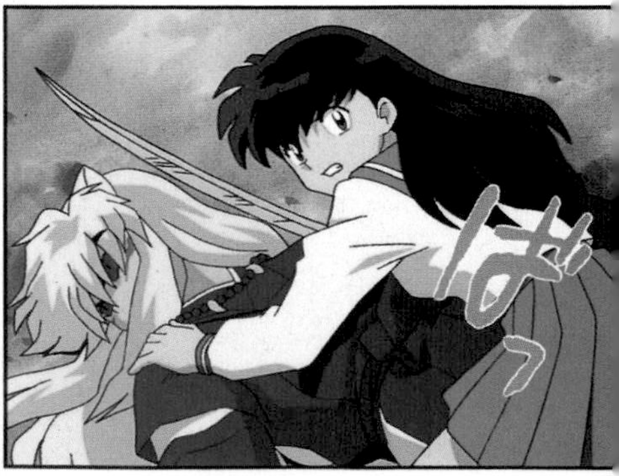

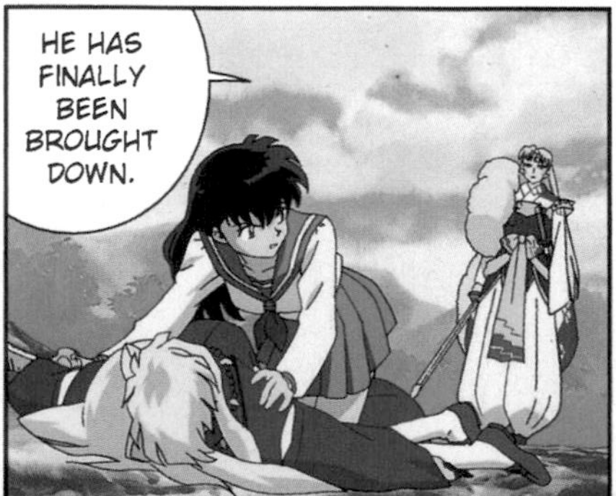
HE HAS FINALLY BEEN BROUGHT DOWN.

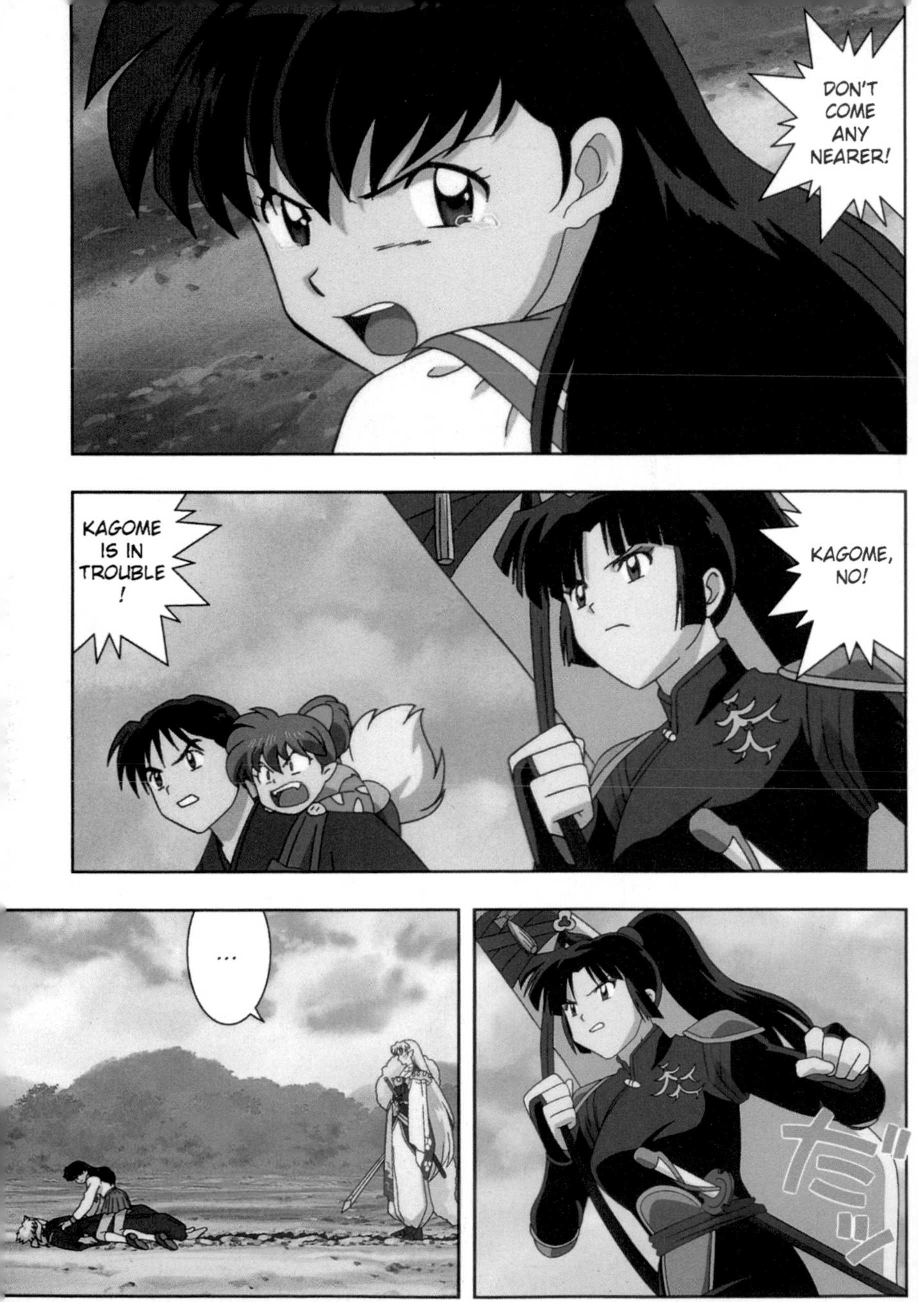
DON'T COME ANY NEARER!
KAGOME, NO!
KAGOME IS IN TROUBLE!
ダッ
...

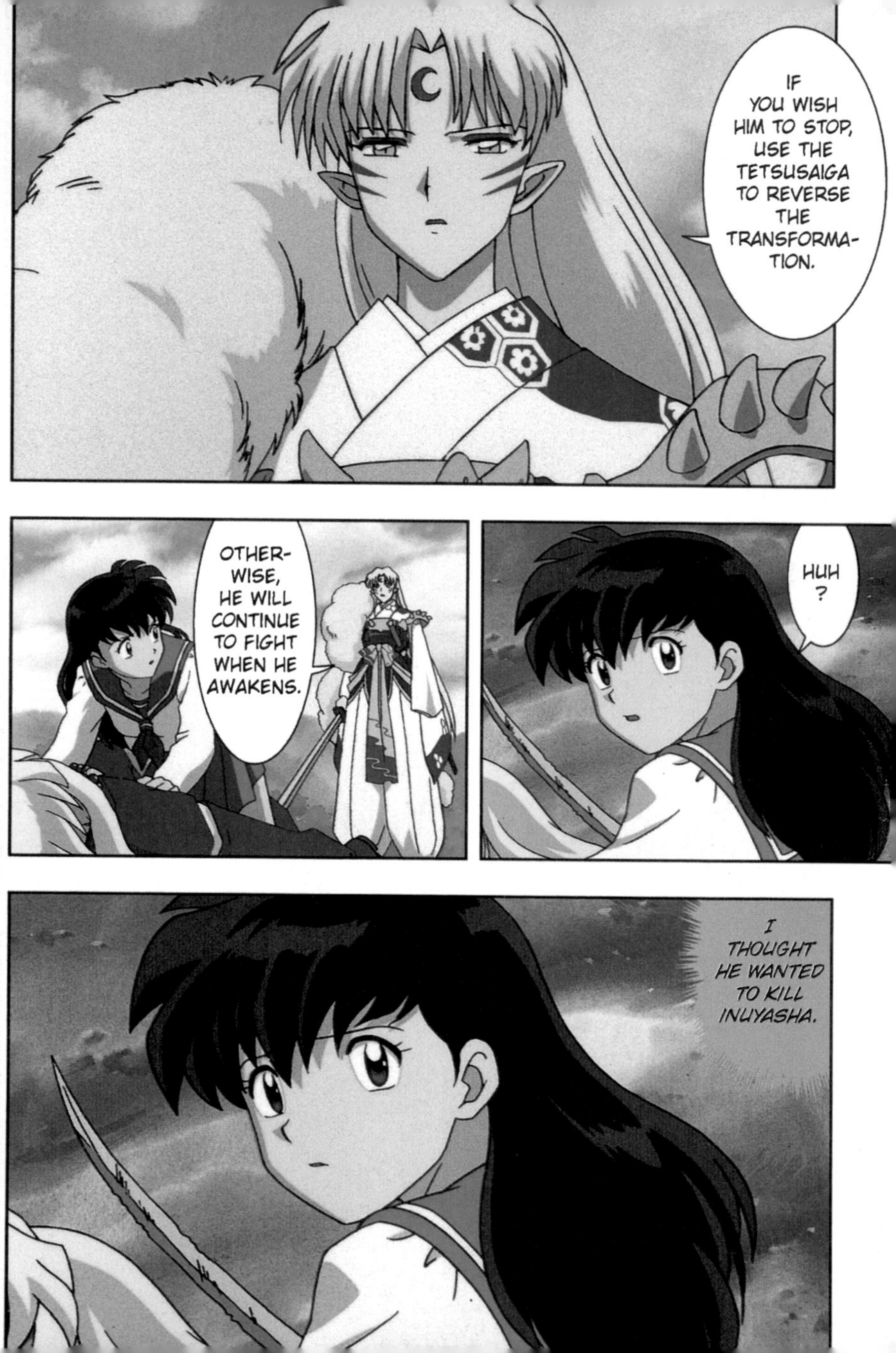
IF YOU WISH HIM TO STOP, USE THE TETSUSAIGA TO REVERSE THE TRANSFORMATION.
HUH?
OTHERWISE, HE WILL CONTINUE TO FIGHT WHEN HE AWAKENS.
I THOUGHT HE WANTED TO KILL INUYASHA.

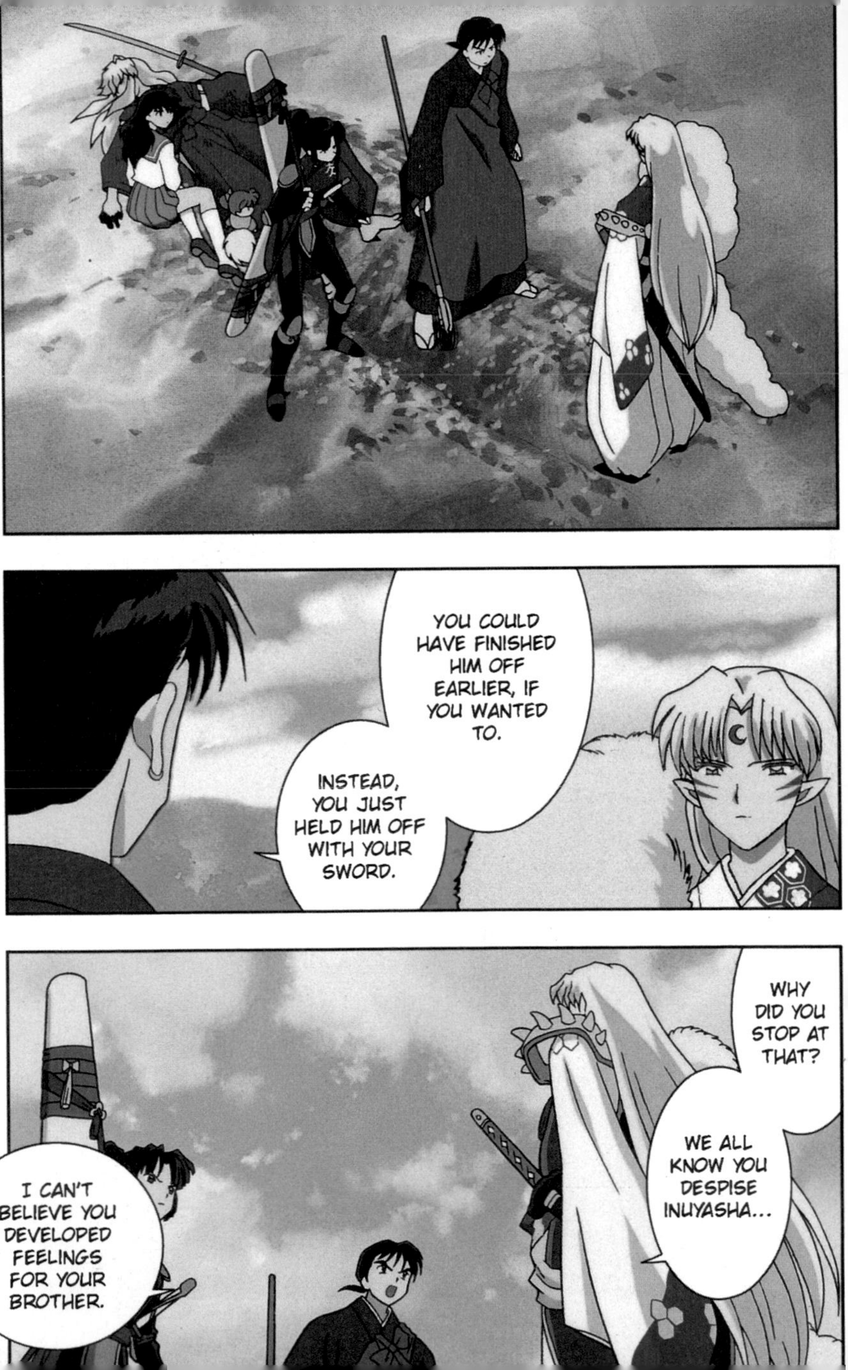
YOU COULD HAVE FINISHED HIM OFF EARLIER, IF YOU WANTED TO.
INSTEAD, YOU JUST HELD HIM OFF WITH YOUR SWORD.
WHY DID YOU STOP AT THAT?
WE ALL KNOW YOU DESPISE INUYASHA...
I CAN'T BELIEVE YOU DEVELOPED FEELINGS FOR YOUR BROTHER.

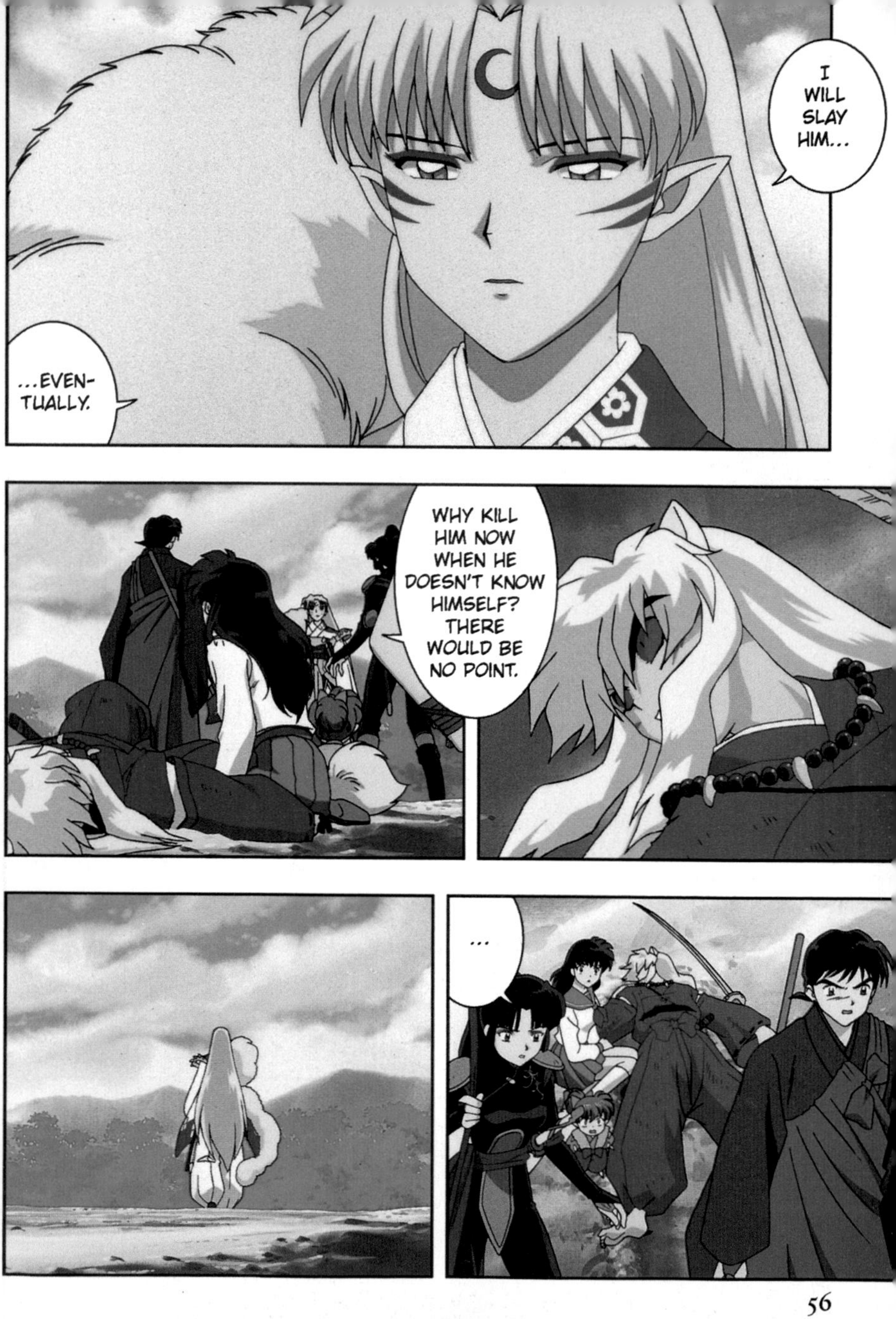
I WILL SLAY HIM...
...EVEN-TUALLY.
WHY KILL HIM NOW WHEN HE DOESN'T KNOW HIMSELF? THERE WOULD BE NO POINT.
...

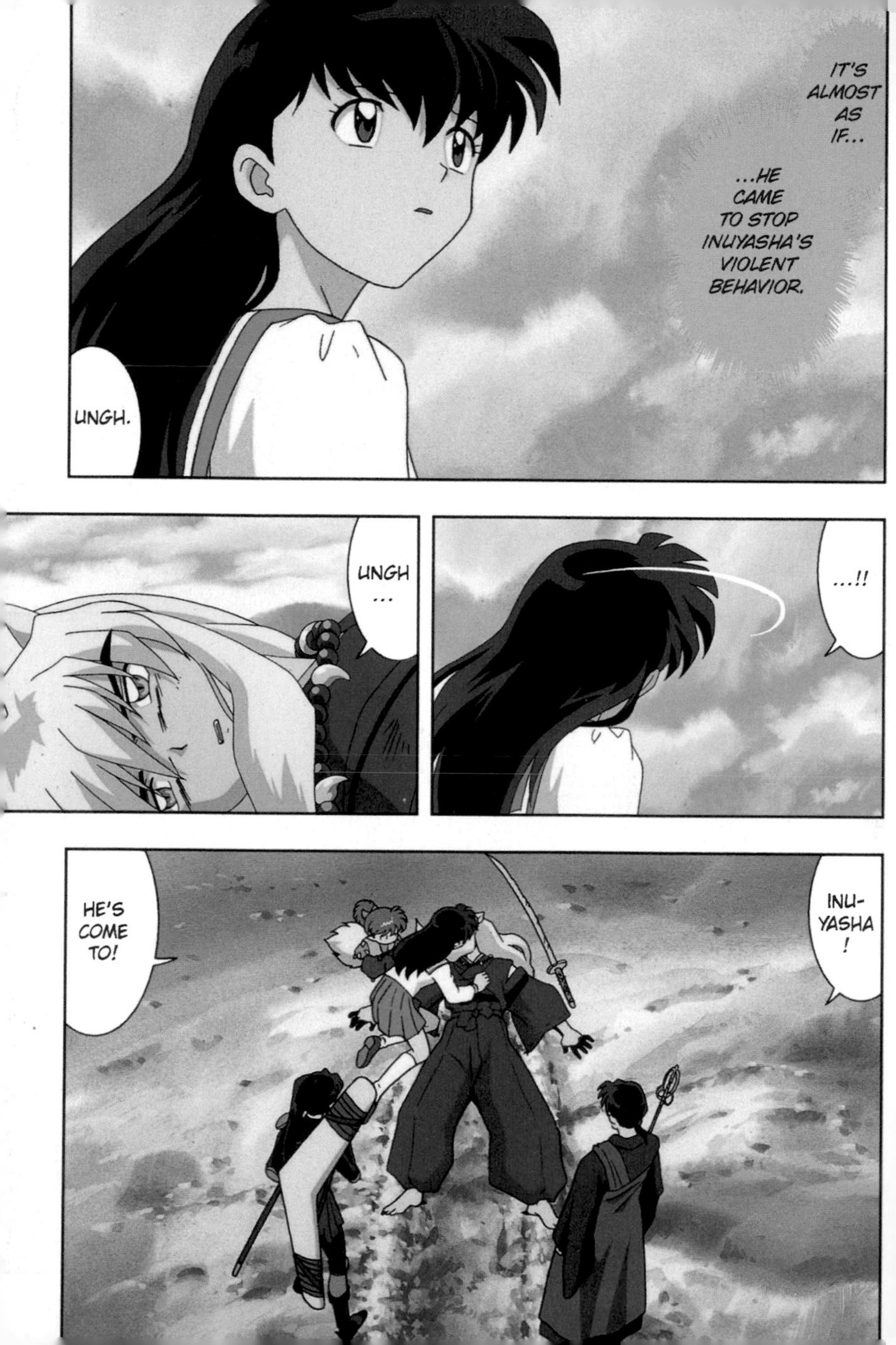
IT'S ALMOST AS IF...
...HE CAME TO STOP INUYASHA'S VIOLENT BEHAVIOR.
UNGH.
...!!
UNGH ...
INU-YASHA!
HE'S COME TO!

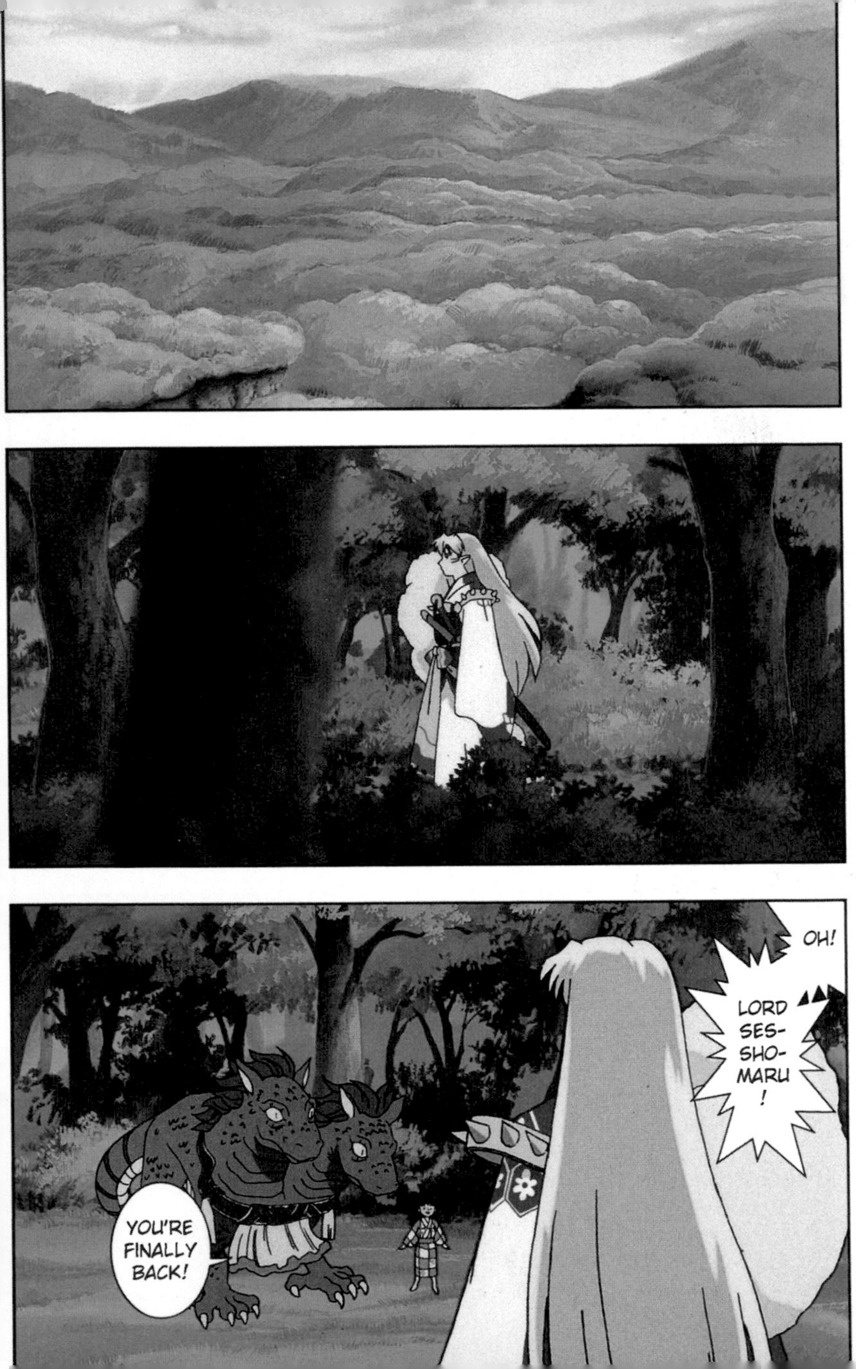
OH!
LORD SES-SHO-MARU!
YOU'RE FINALLY BACK!

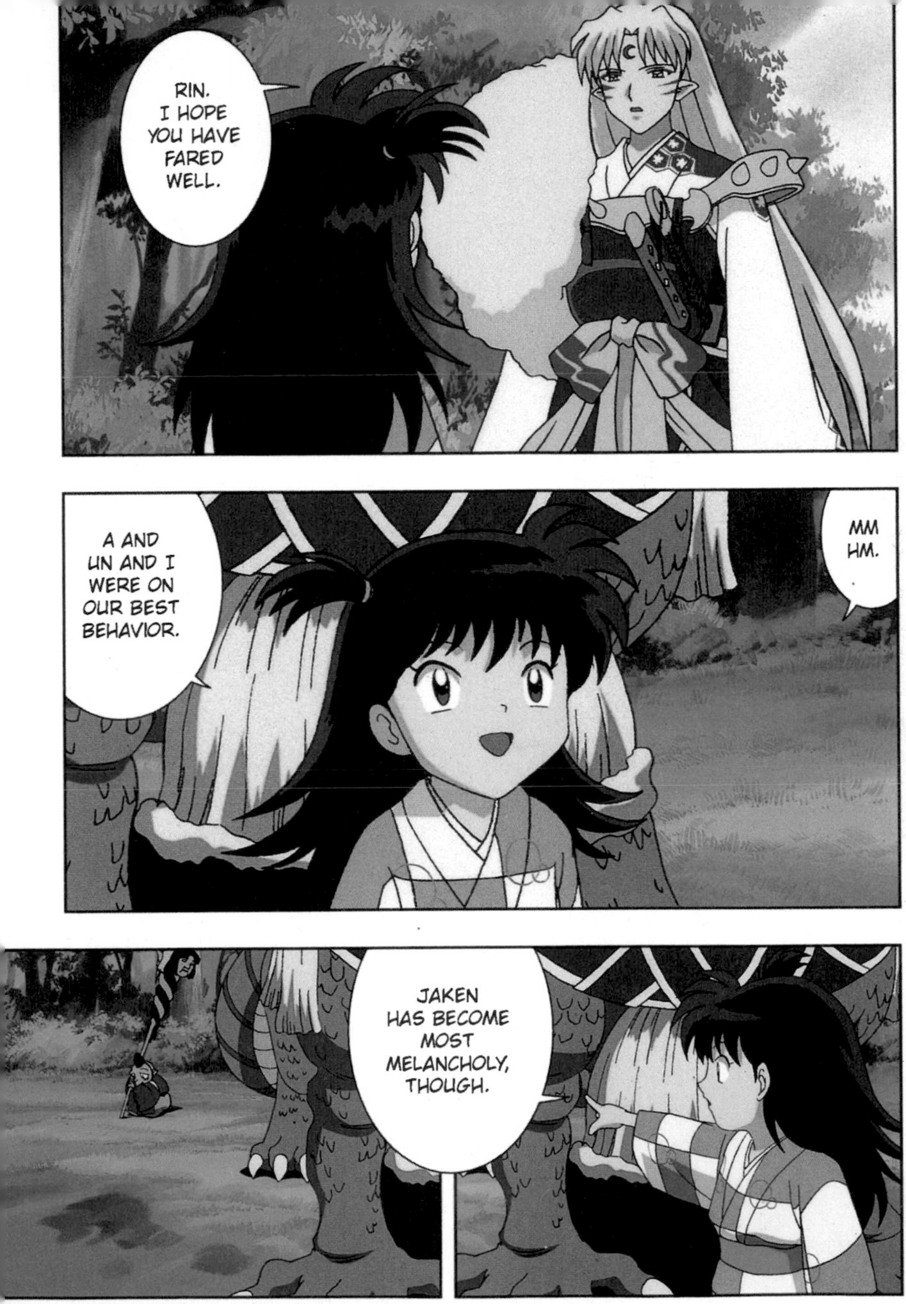
RIN. I HOPE YOU HAVE FARED WELL.
MM HM.
A AND UN AND I WERE ON OUR BEST BEHAVIOR.
JAKEN HAS BECOME MOST MELANCHOLY, THOUGH.

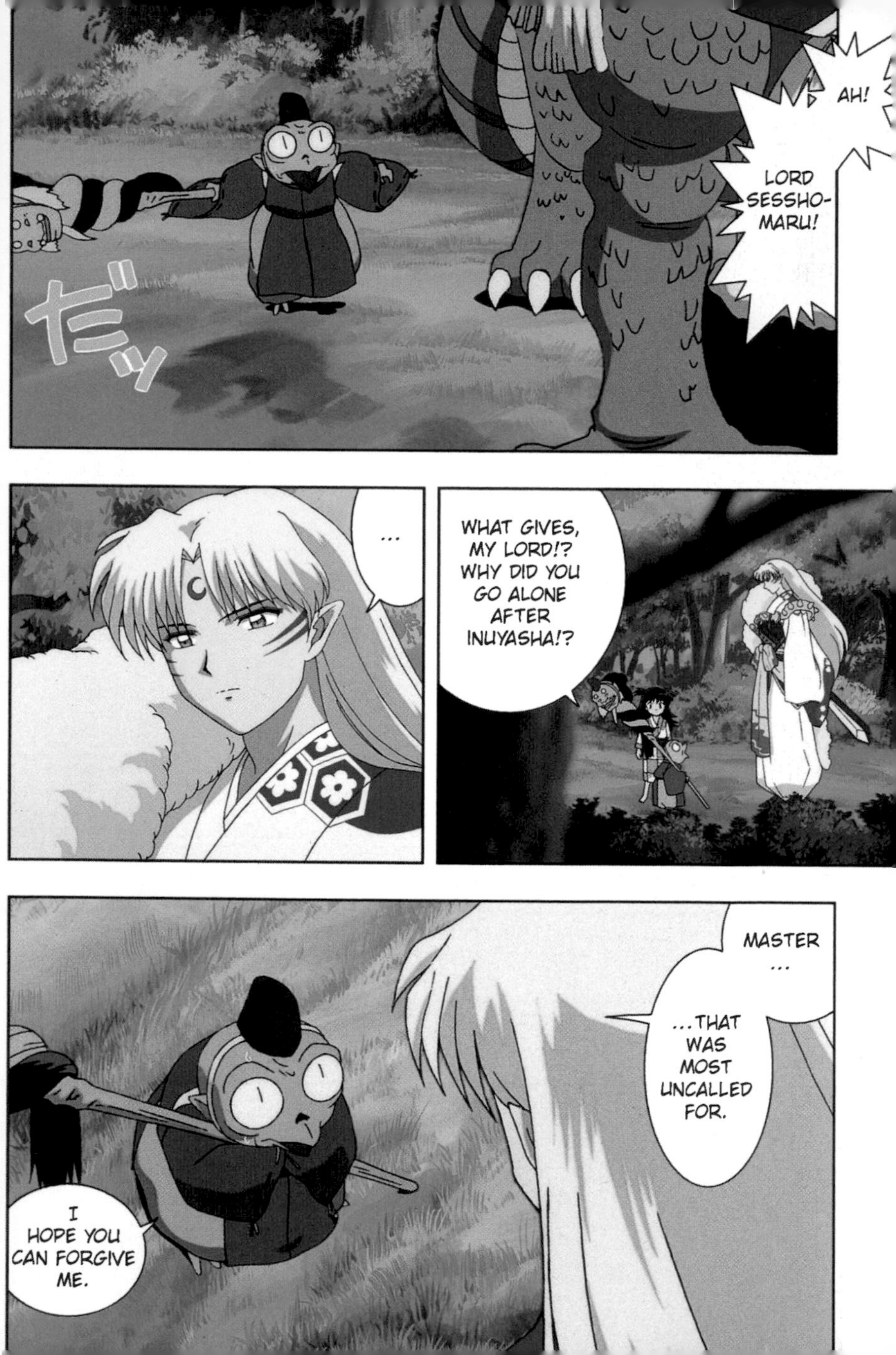
AH!
LORD SESSHO-MARU!
ダッ
WHAT GIVES, MY LORD!? WHY DID YOU GO ALONE AFTER INUYASHA!?
...
MASTER ...
...THAT WAS MOST UNCALLED FOR.
I HOPE YOU CAN FORGIVE ME.

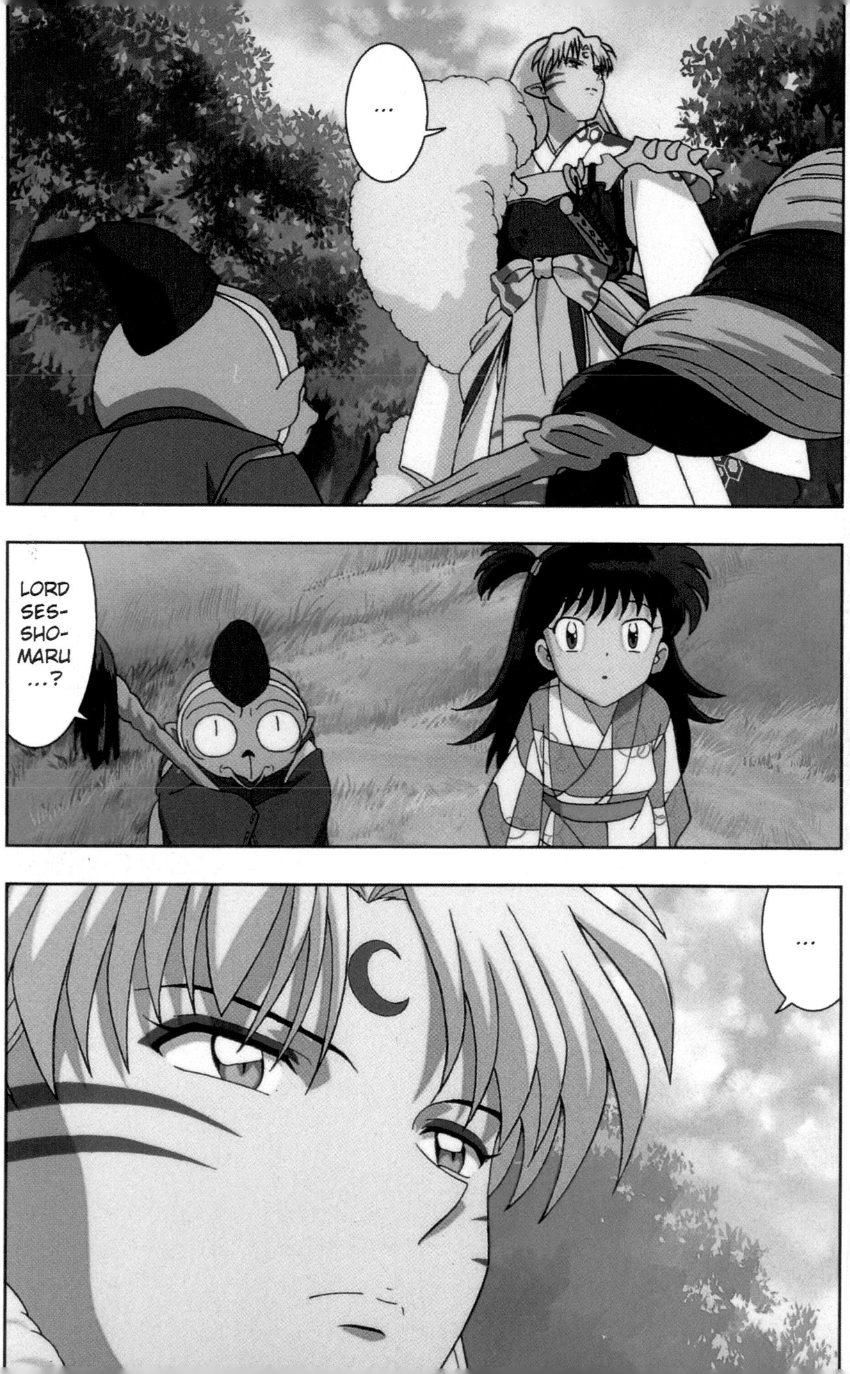
...
LORD SES-SHO-MARU ...?
...

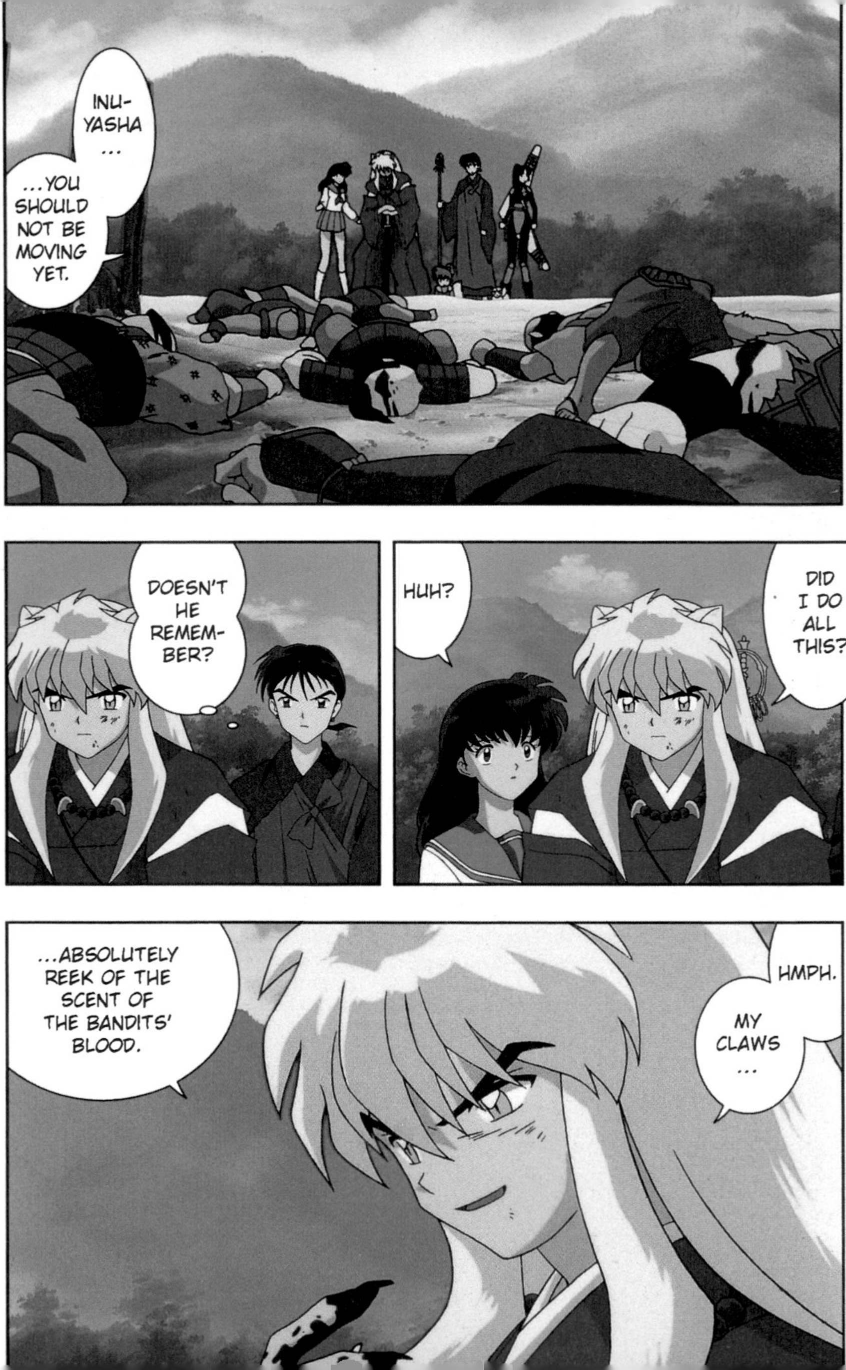
INU-YASHA ...
...YOU SHOULD NOT BE MOVING YET.
DID I DO ALL THIS?
HUH?
DOESN'T HE REMEMBER?
HMPH.
MY CLAWS ...
...ABSOLUTELY REEK OF THE SCENT OF THE BANDITS' BLOOD.

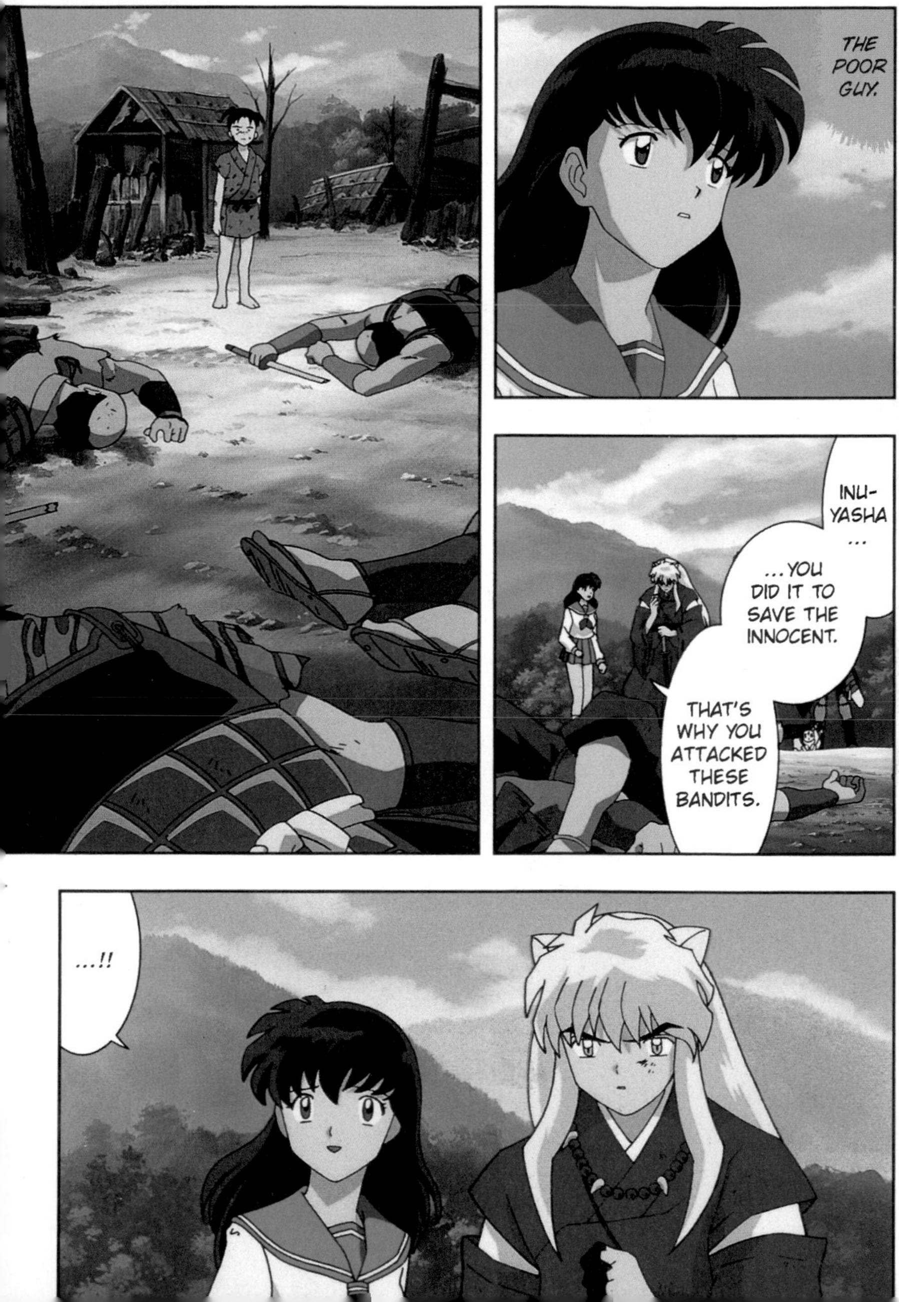
THE POOR GUY.
INU-YASHA ...
...YOU DID IT TO SAVE THE INNOCENT.
THAT'S WHY YOU ATTACKED THESE BANDITS.
...!!

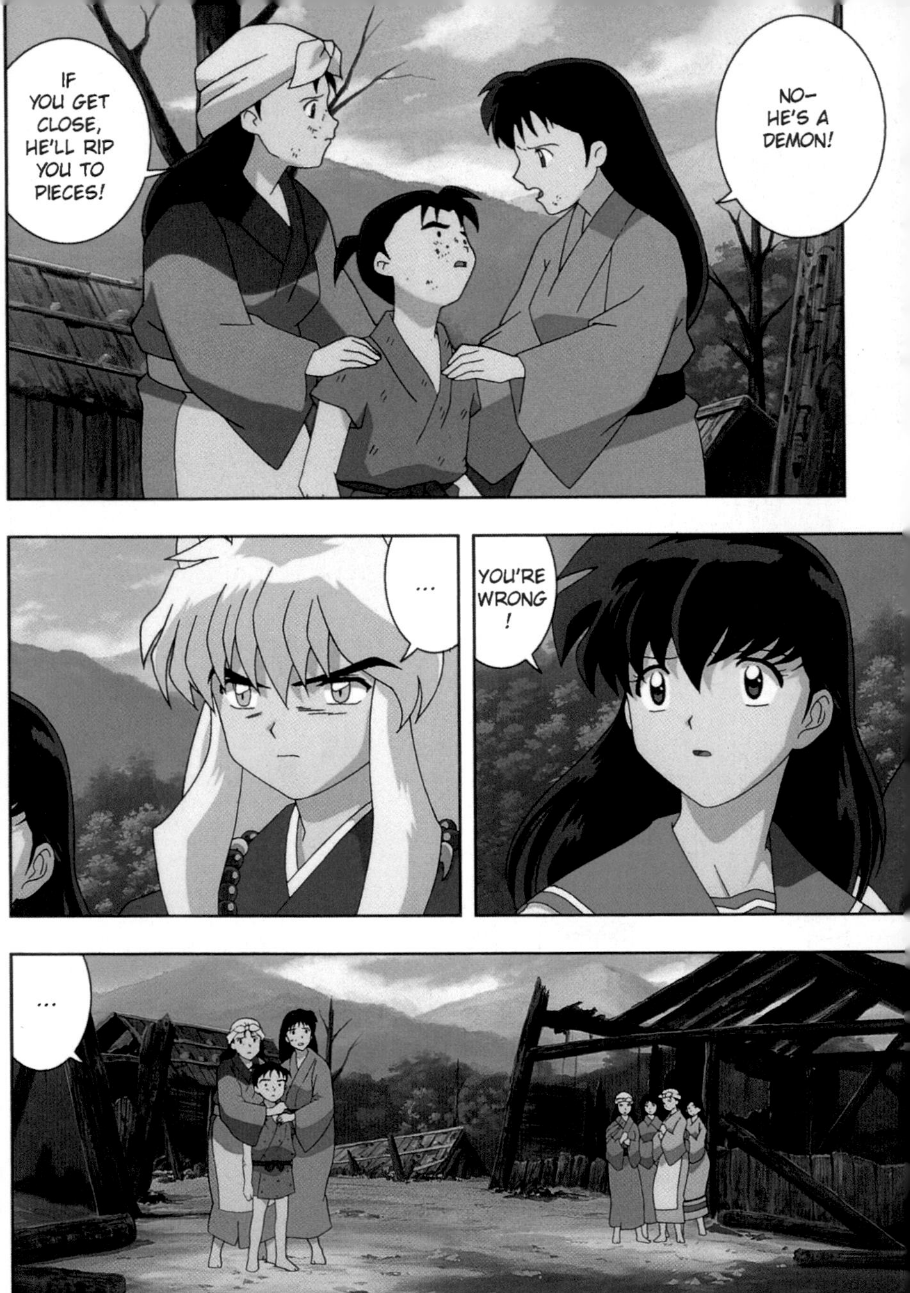
NO— HE'S A DEMON!
IF YOU GET CLOSE, HE'LL RIP YOU TO PIECES!
YOU'RE WRONG!
...
...

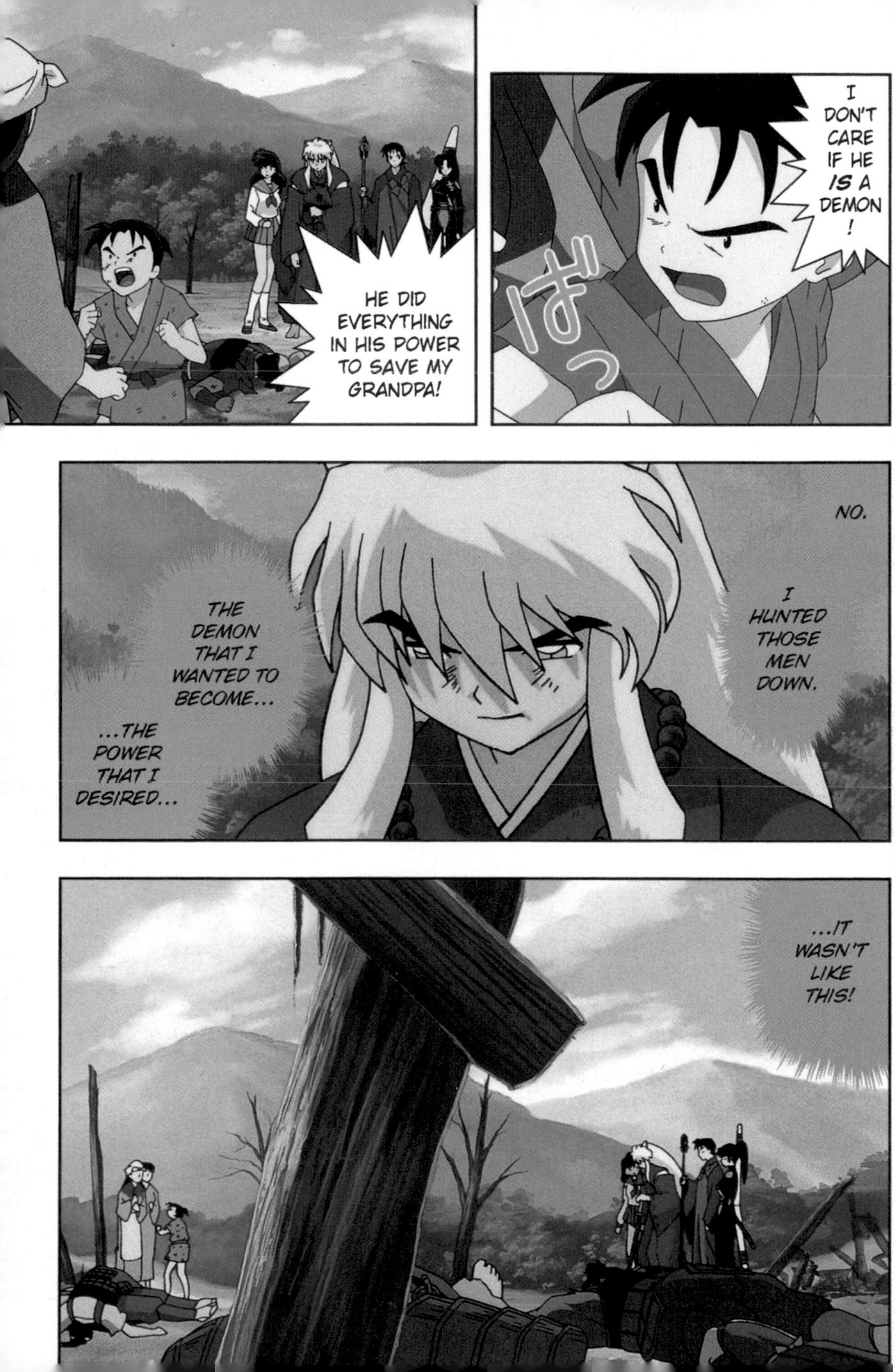
I DON'T CARE IF HE *IS* A DEMON!
ばっ
HE DID EVERYTHING IN HIS POWER TO SAVE MY GRANDPA!
NO.
I HUNTED THOSE MEN DOWN.
THE DEMON THAT I WANTED TO BECOME...
...THE POWER THAT I DESIRED...
...IT WASN'T LIKE THIS!

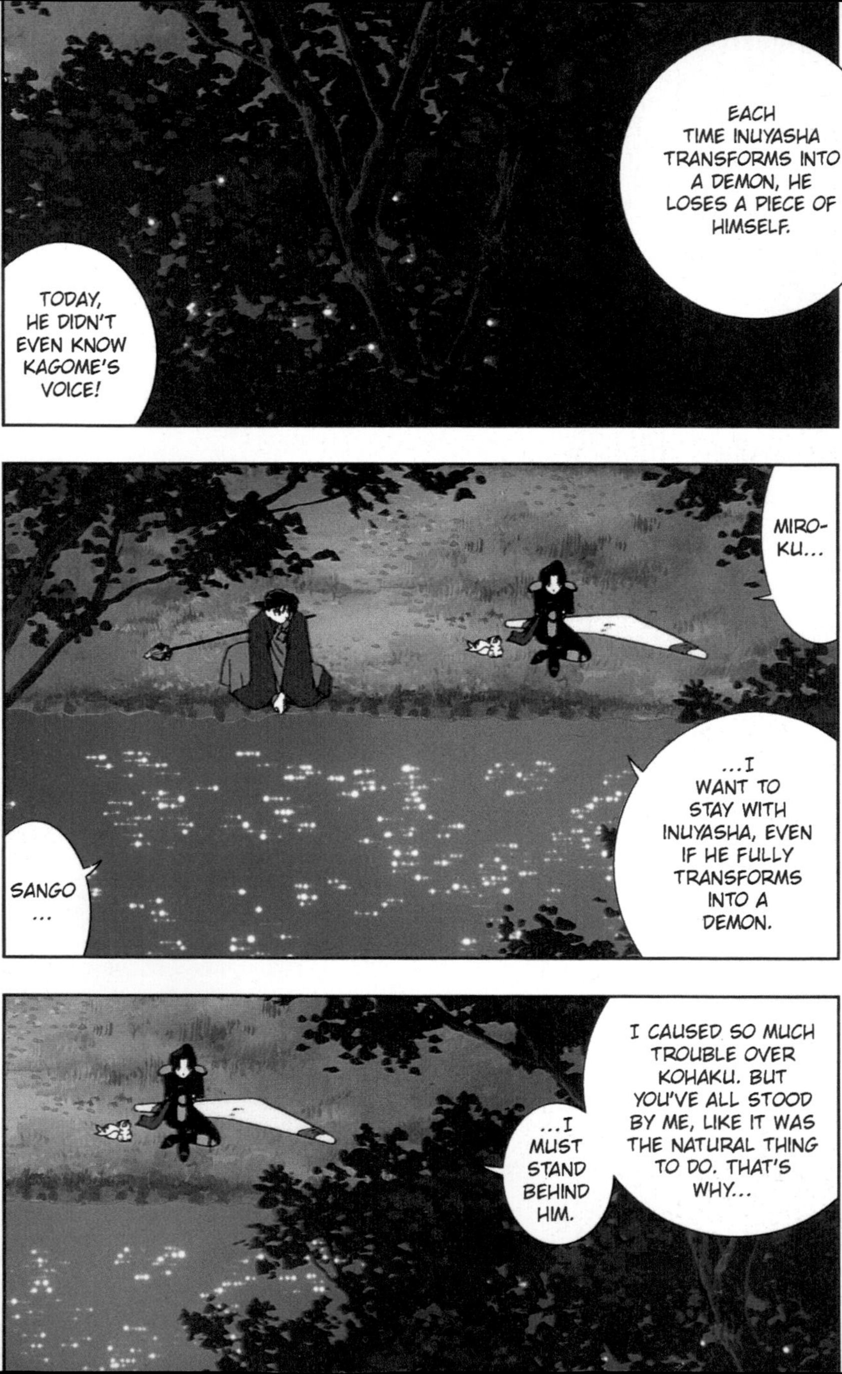
EACH TIME INUYASHA TRANSFORMS INTO A DEMON, HE LOSES A PIECE OF HIMSELF.
TODAY, HE DIDN'T EVEN KNOW KAGOME'S VOICE!
MIRO-KU...
...I WANT TO STAY WITH INUYASHA, EVEN IF HE FULLY TRANSFORMS INTO A DEMON.
SANGO ...
I CAUSED SO MUCH TROUBLE OVER KOHAKU. BUT YOU'VE ALL STOOD BY ME, LIKE IT WAS THE NATURAL THING TO DO. THAT'S WHY...
...I MUST STAND BEHIND HIM.

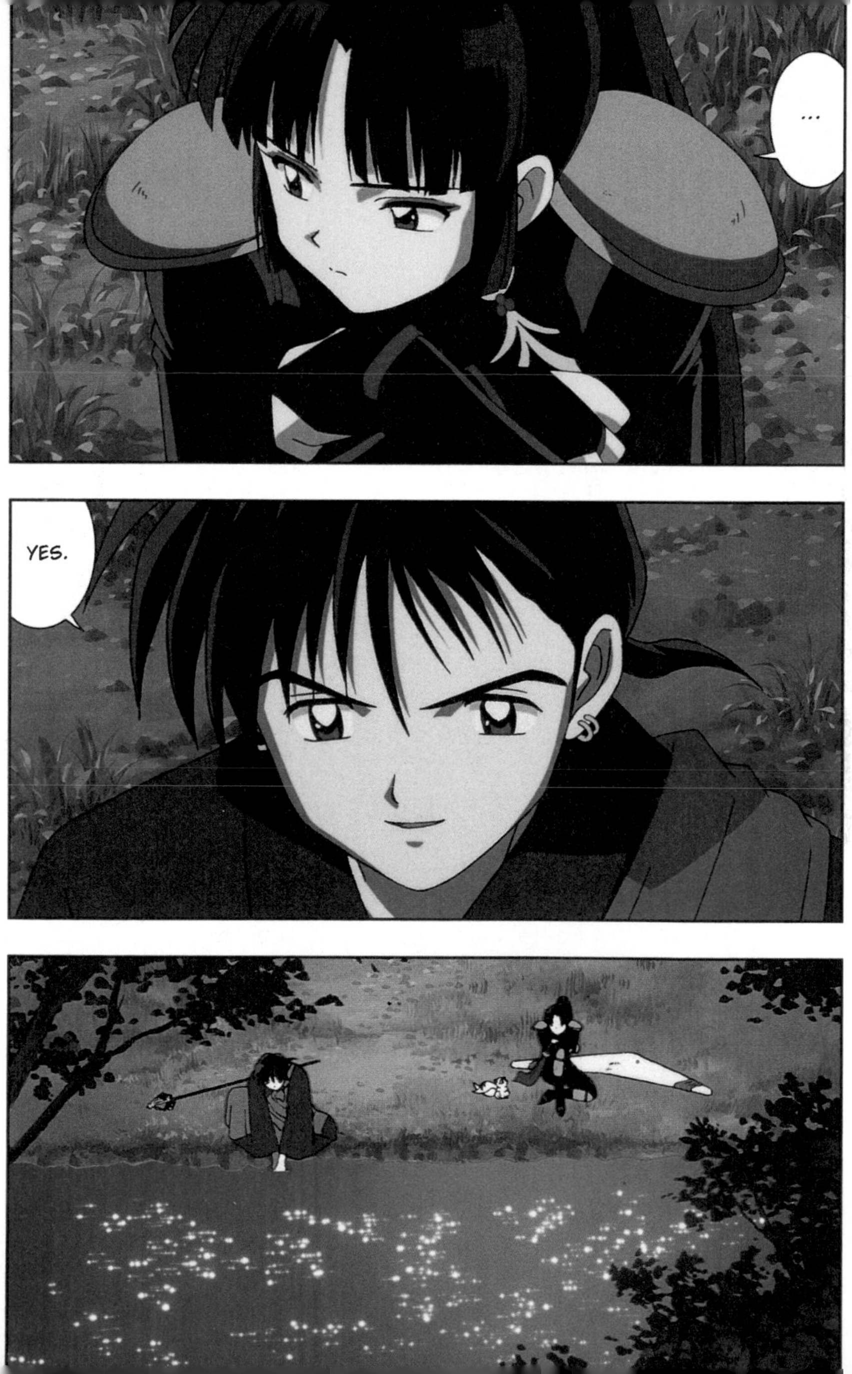
...
YES.

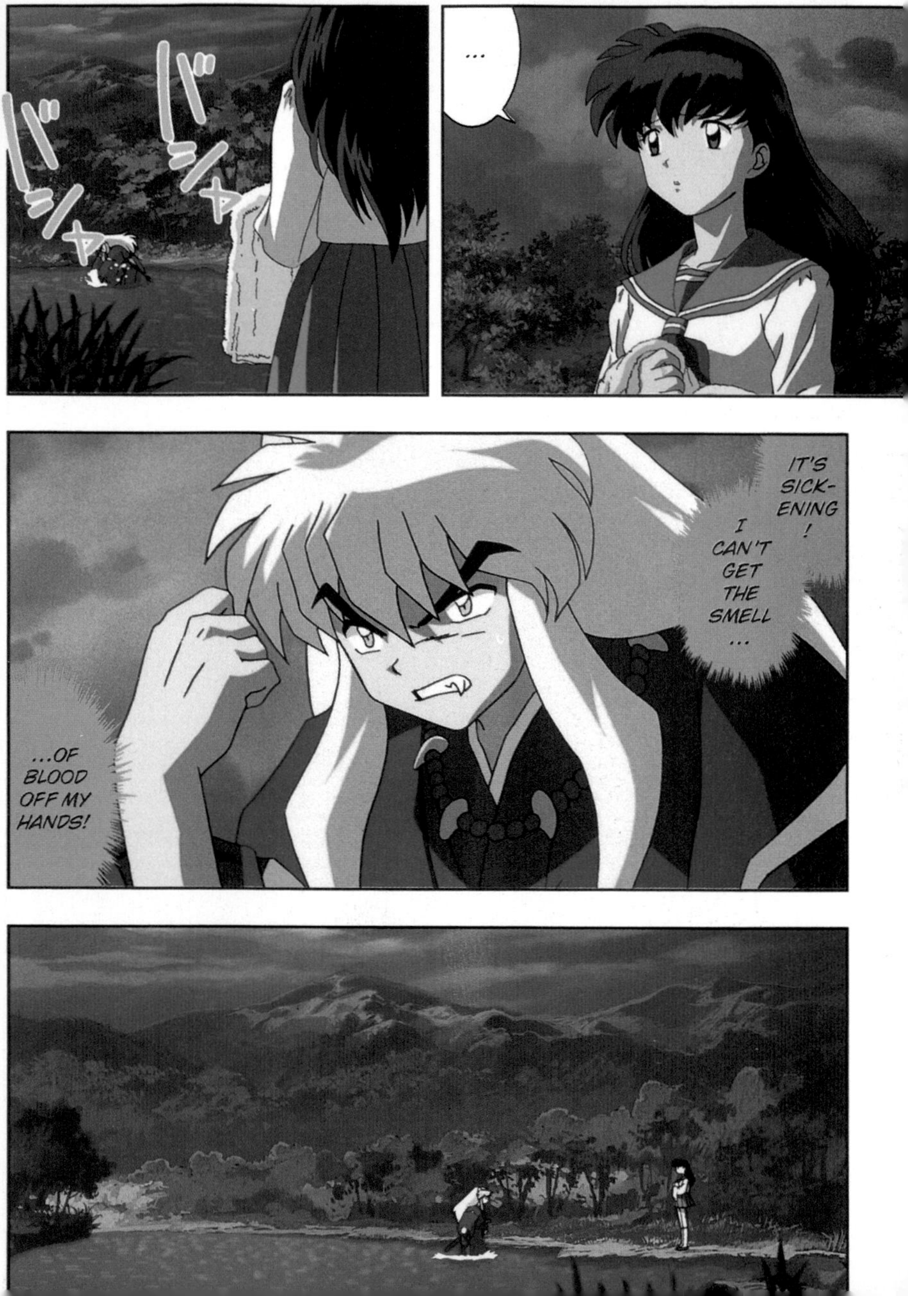
...
バシャ
バシャ
IT'S SICKENING!
I CAN'T GET THE SMELL...
...OF BLOOD OFF MY HANDS!

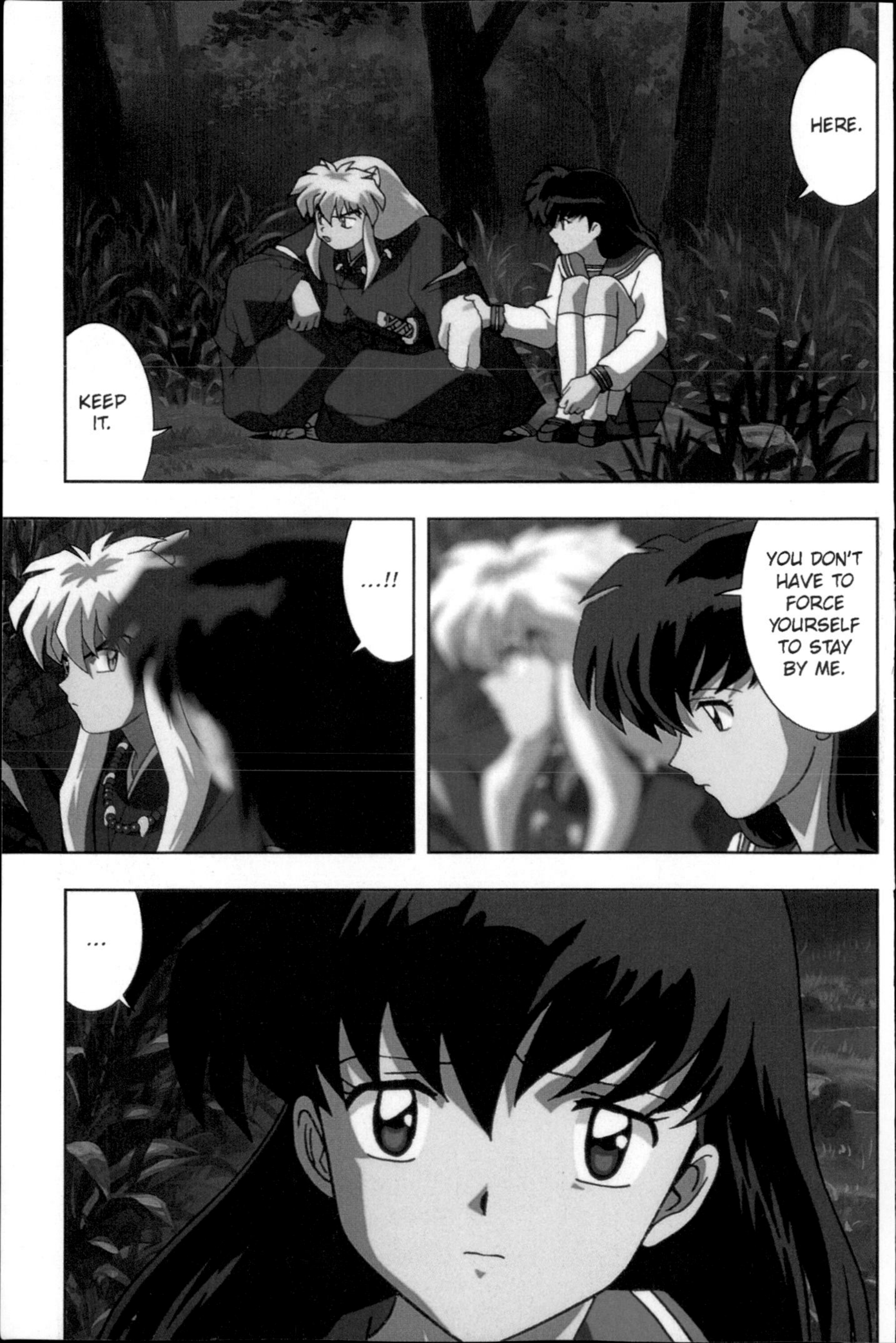
HERE.
KEEP IT.
YOU DON'T HAVE TO FORCE YOURSELF TO STAY BY ME.
...!!
...

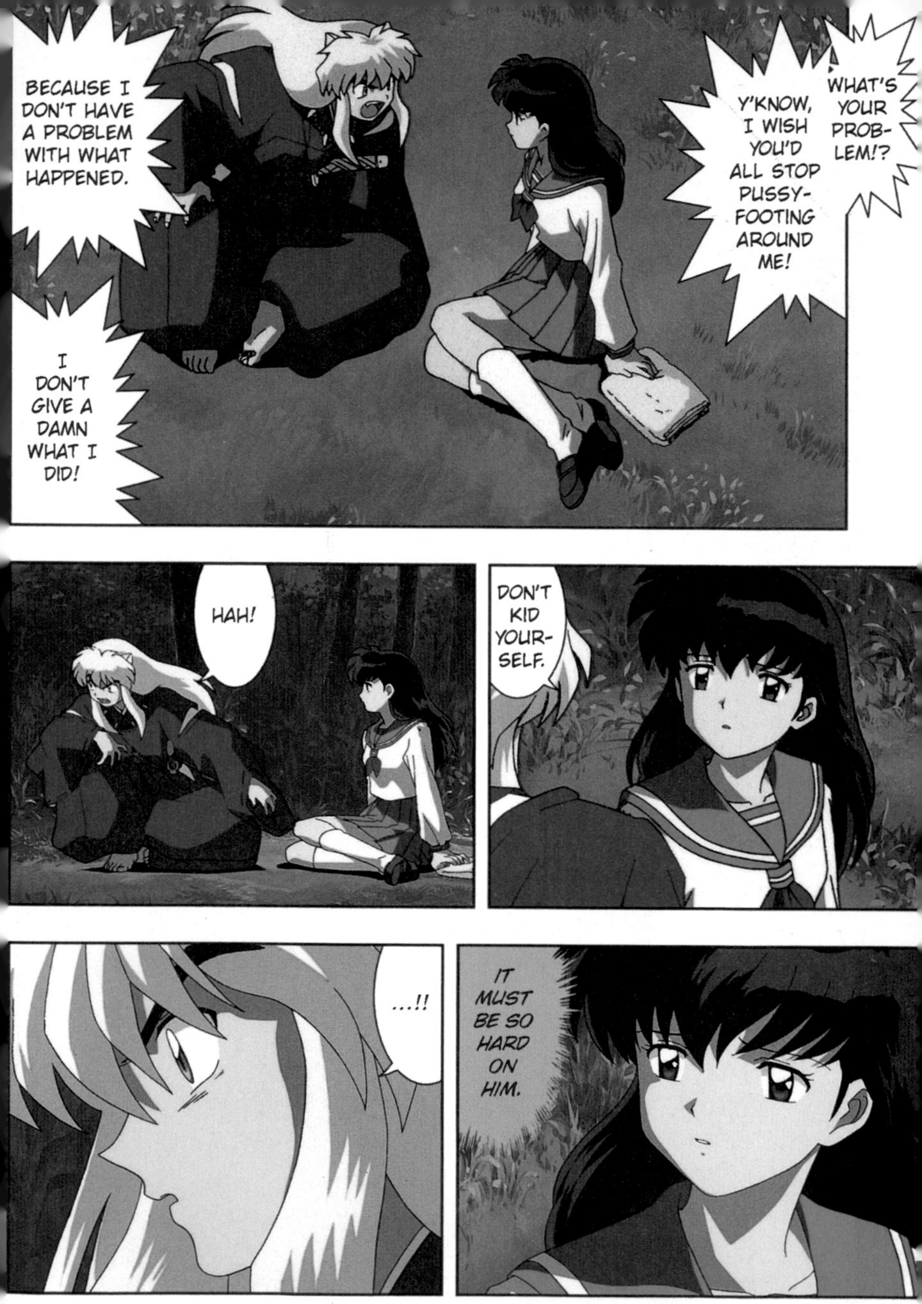
WHAT'S YOUR PROB-LEM!?
Y'KNOW, I WISH YOU'D ALL STOP PUSSY-FOOTING AROUND ME!
BECAUSE I DON'T HAVE A PROBLEM WITH WHAT HAPPENED.
I DON'T GIVE A DAMN WHAT I DID!
DON'T KID YOUR-SELF.
HAH!
IT MUST BE SO HARD ON HIM.
...!!

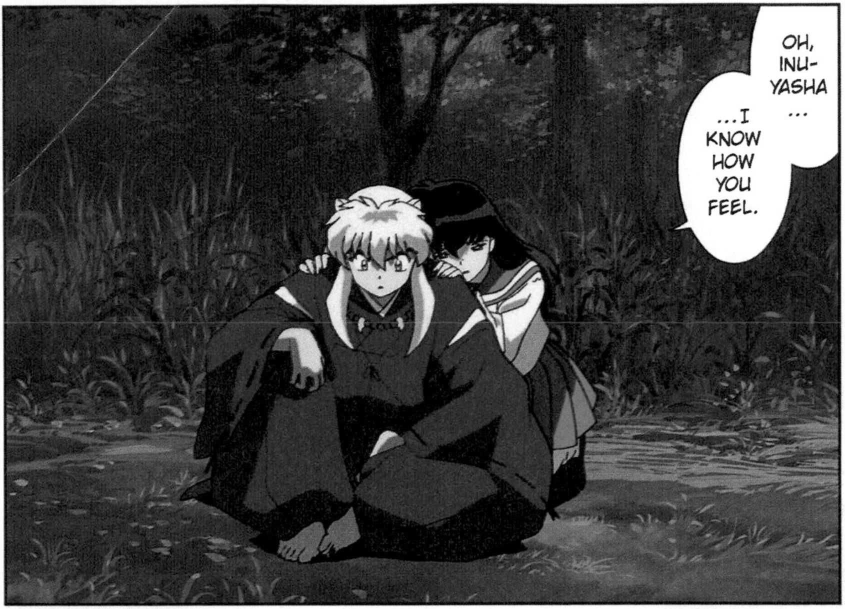
OH, INU-YASHA ...
...I KNOW HOW YOU FEEL.

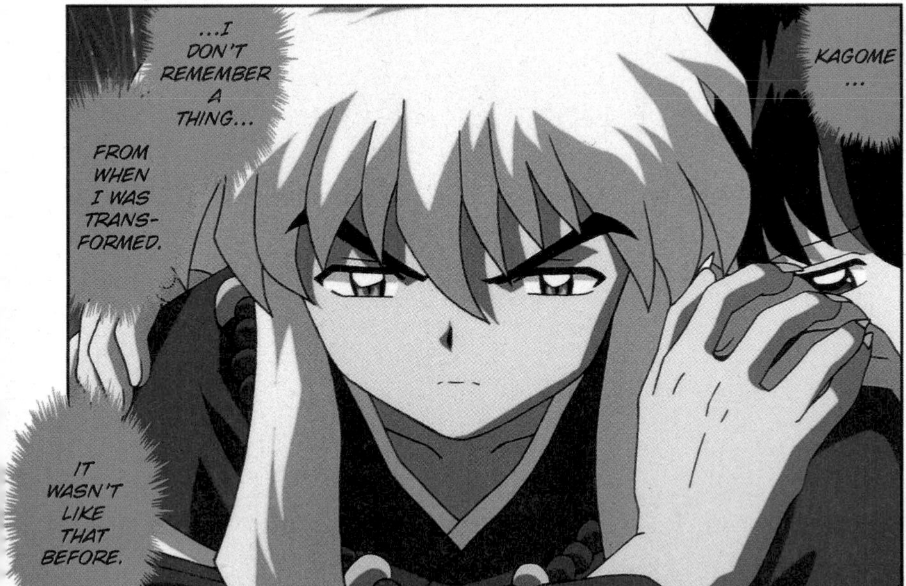
KAGOME ...
...I DON'T REMEMBER A THING...
FROM WHEN I WAS TRANS-FORMED.
IT WASN'T LIKE THAT BEFORE.

THE NEXT TIME...

...I TRANS- FORM...

...COME AFTER YOU WITH THESE CLAWS, KAGOME.

...I MAY EVEN ...

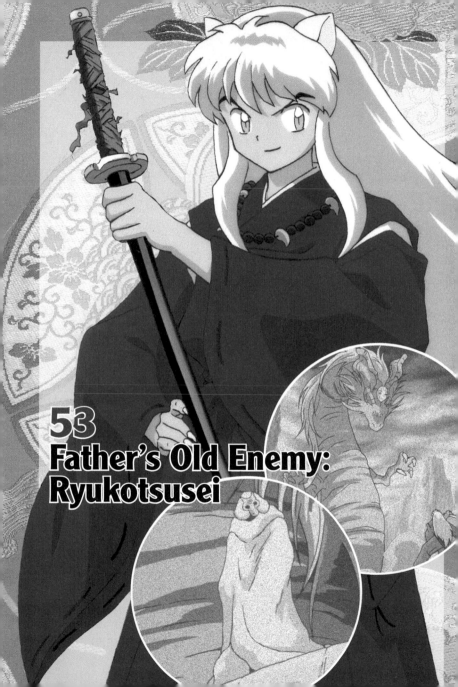

53
Father's Old Enemy:
Ryukotsusei

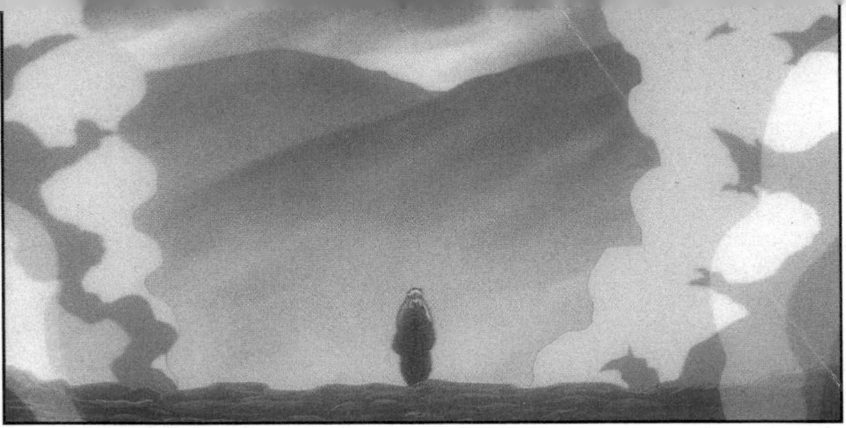

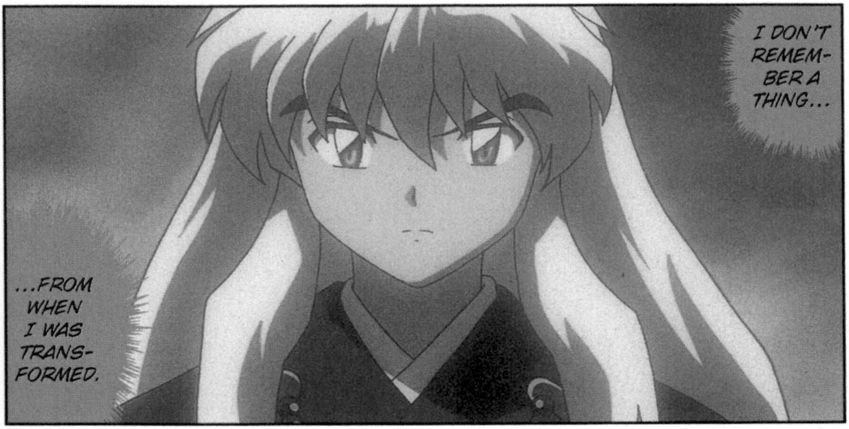
I DON'T REMEMBER A THING...
...FROM WHEN I WAS TRANSFORMED.

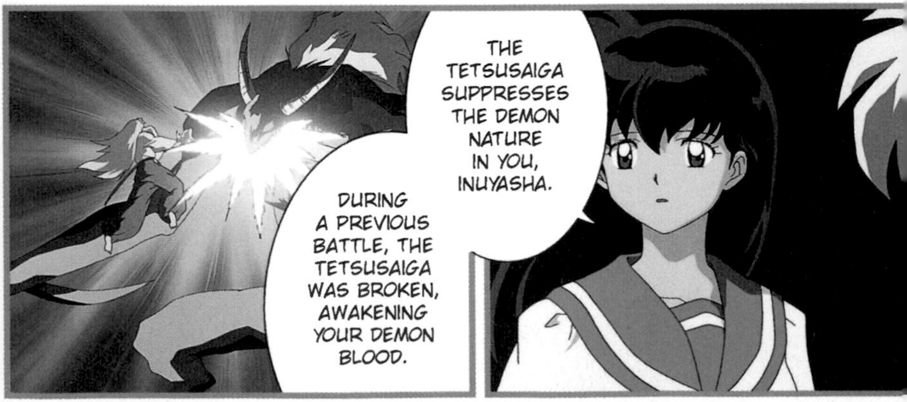
THE TETSUSAIGA SUPPRESSES THE DEMON NATURE IN YOU, INUYASHA.
DURING A PREVIOUS BATTLE, THE TETSUSAIGA WAS BROKEN, AWAKENING YOUR DEMON BLOOD.

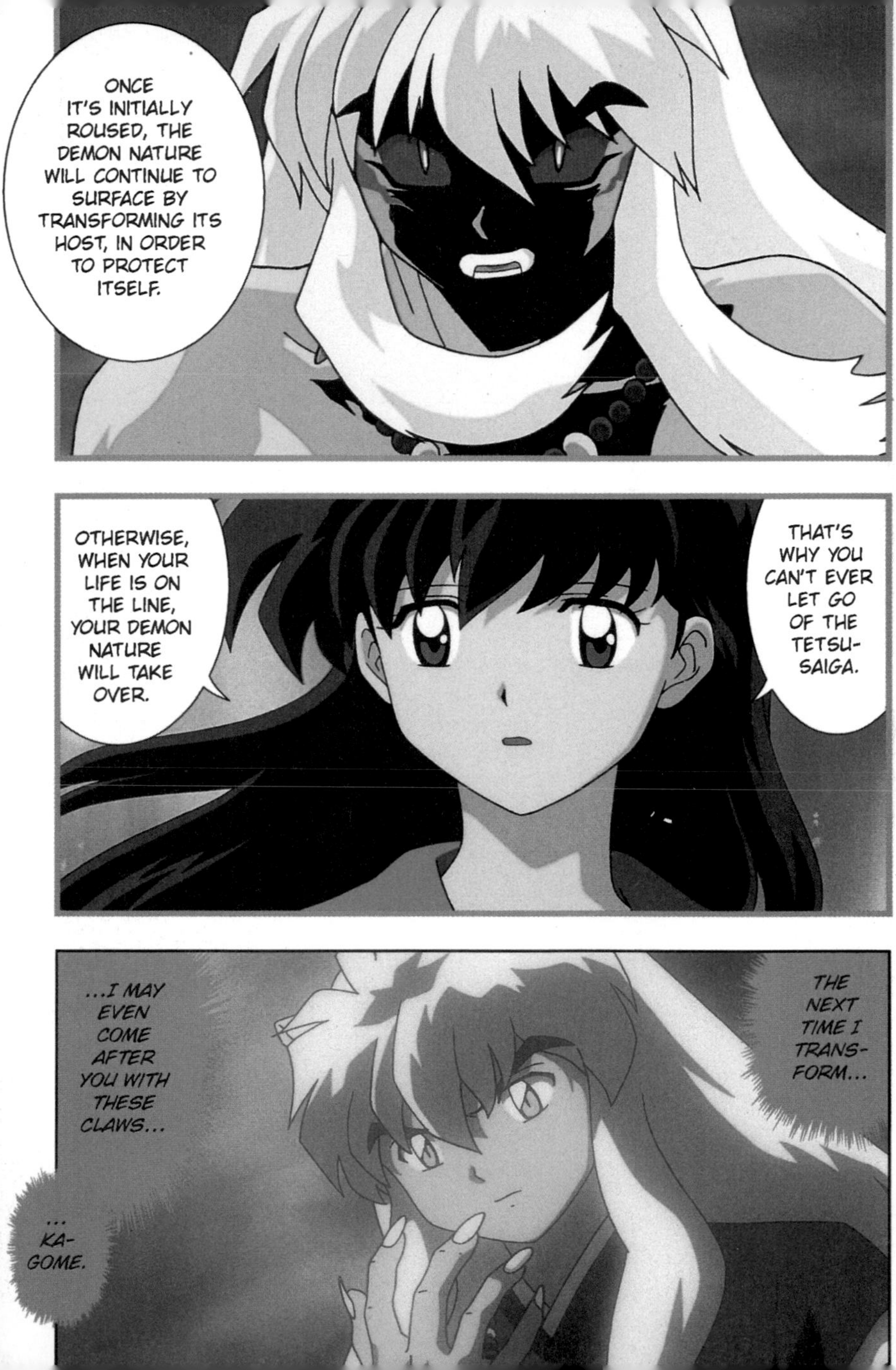
ONCE IT'S INITIALLY ROUSED, THE DEMON NATURE WILL CONTINUE TO SURFACE BY TRANSFORMING ITS HOST, IN ORDER TO PROTECT ITSELF.
THAT'S WHY YOU CAN'T EVER LET GO OF THE TETSU-SAIGA.
OTHERWISE, WHEN YOUR LIFE IS ON THE LINE, YOUR DEMON NATURE WILL TAKE OVER.
THE NEXT TIME I TRANS-FORM...
...I MAY EVEN COME AFTER YOU WITH THESE CLAWS...
...KA-GOME.

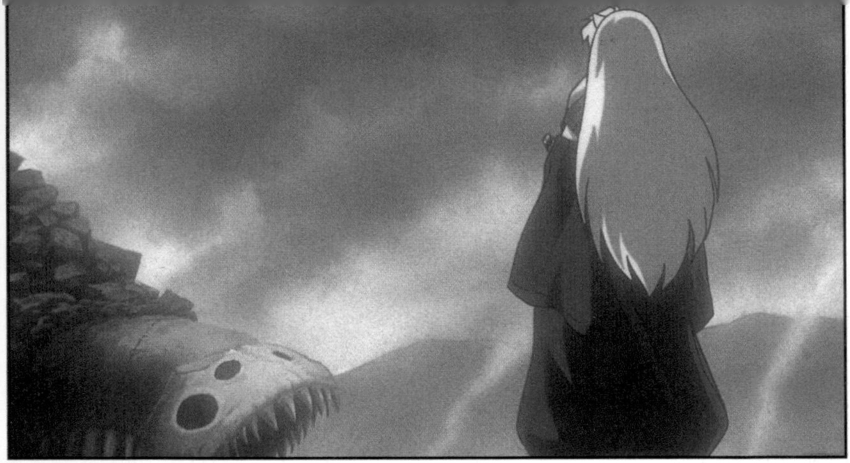

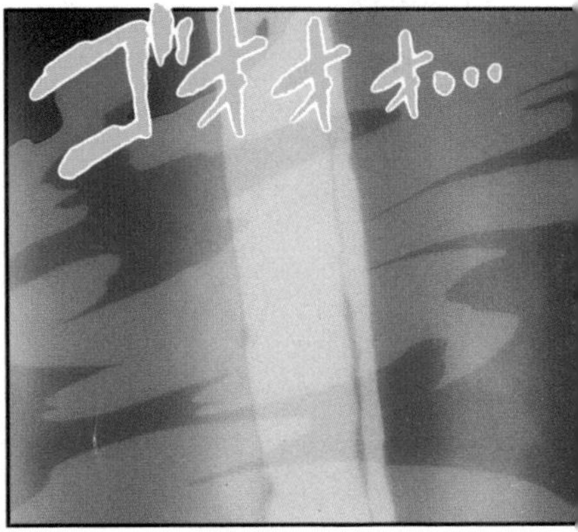
ゴオオオ…

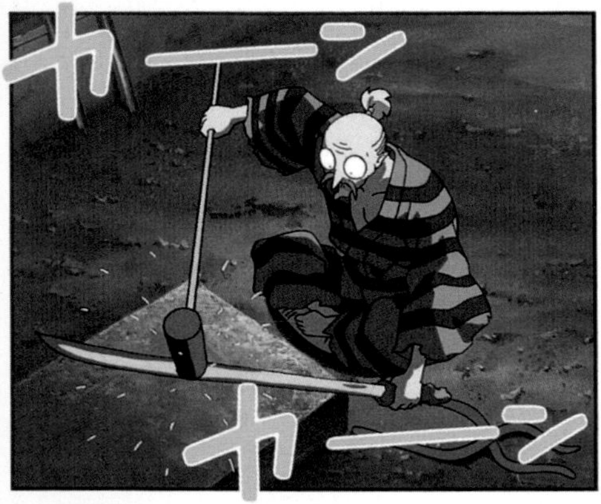
カーン
カーン

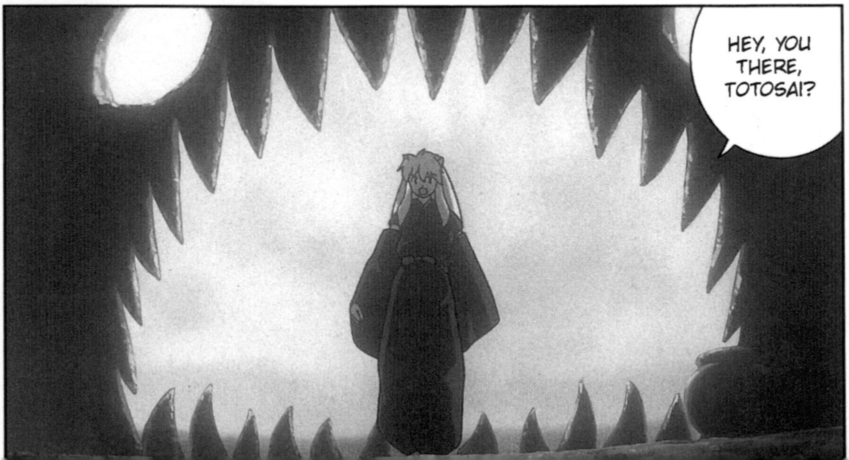
HEY, YOU THERE, TOTOSAI?

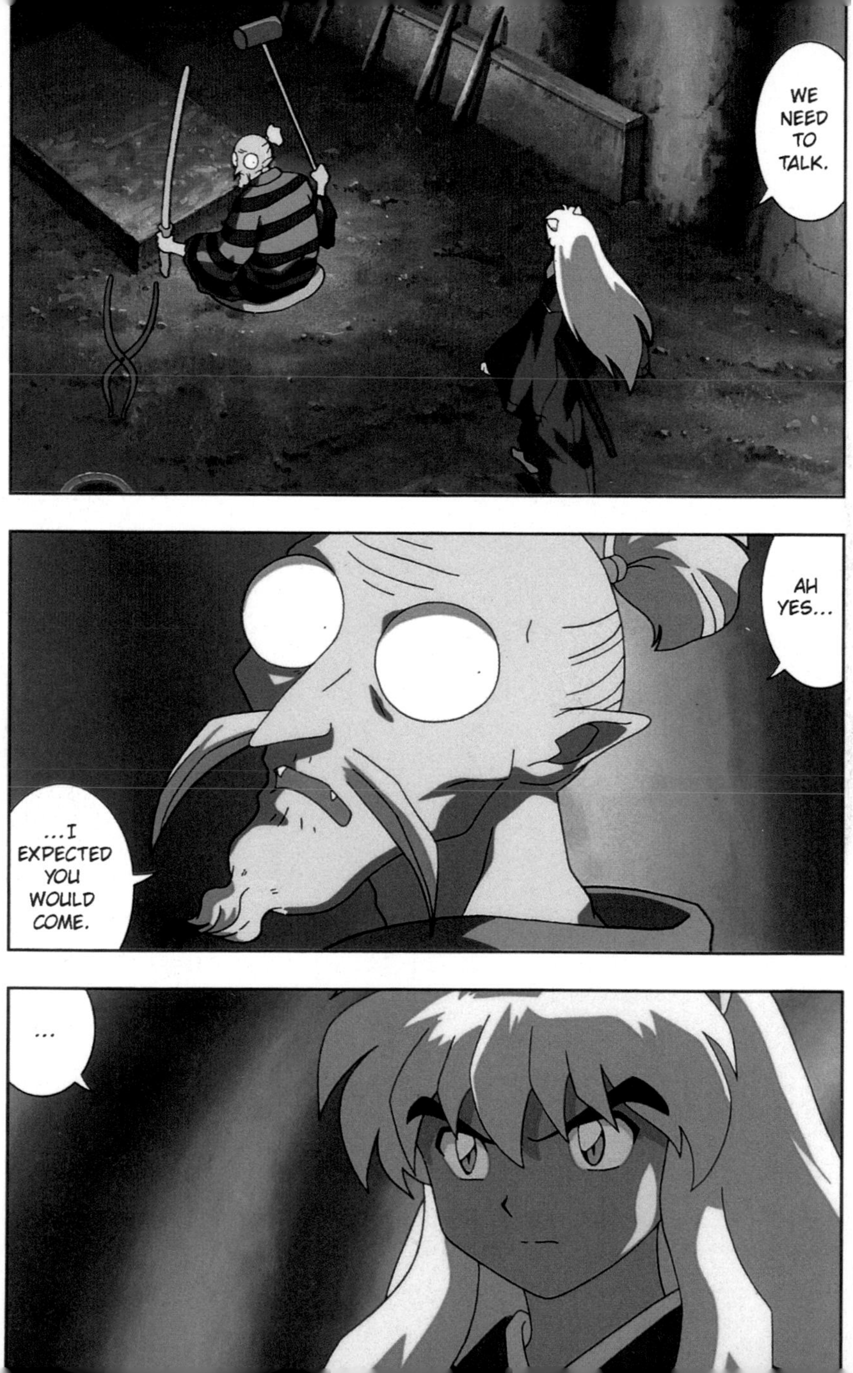
WE NEED TO TALK.
AH YES...
...I EXPECTED YOU WOULD COME.
...

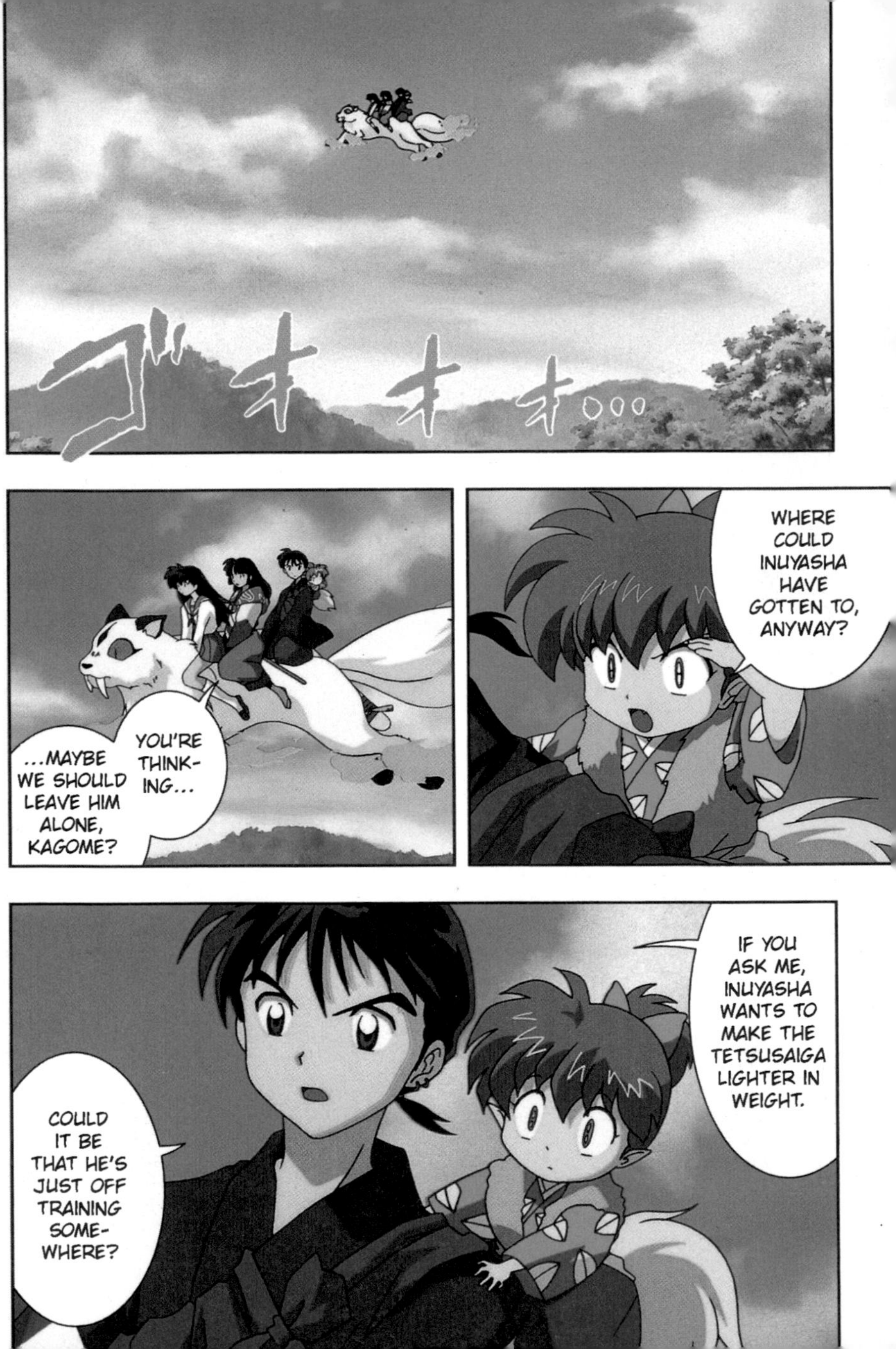
ゴオオオ…
WHERE COULD INUYASHA HAVE GOTTEN TO, ANYWAY?
YOU'RE THINK-ING...
...MAYBE WE SHOULD LEAVE HIM ALONE, KAGOME?
IF YOU ASK ME, INUYASHA WANTS TO MAKE THE TETSUSAIGA LIGHTER IN WEIGHT.
COULD IT BE THAT HE'S JUST OFF TRAINING SOME-WHERE?

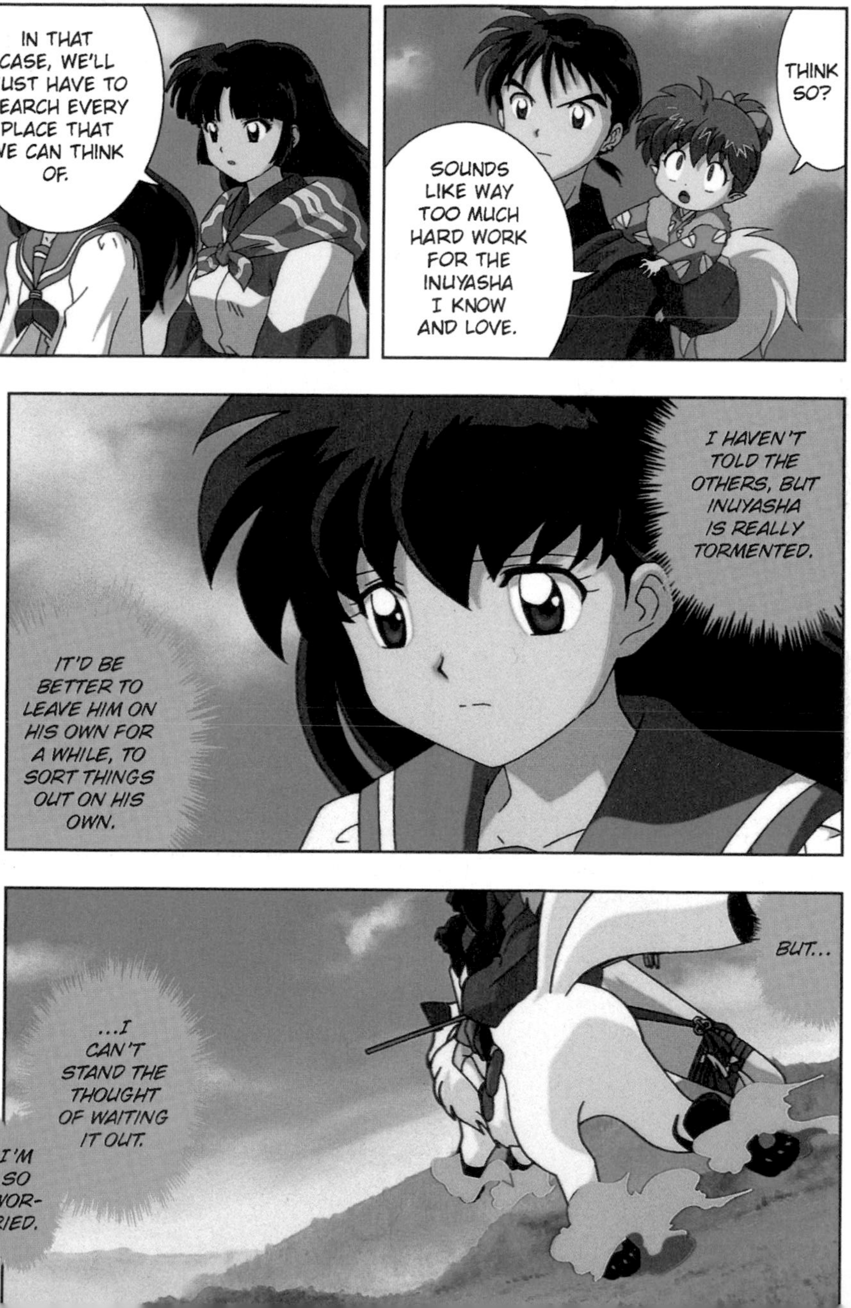
THINK SO?
SOUNDS LIKE WAY TOO MUCH HARD WORK FOR THE INUYASHA I KNOW AND LOVE.
IN THAT CASE, WE'LL JUST HAVE TO SEARCH EVERY PLACE THAT WE CAN THINK OF.
I HAVEN'T TOLD THE OTHERS, BUT INUYASHA IS REALLY TORMENTED.
IT'D BE BETTER TO LEAVE HIM ON HIS OWN FOR A WHILE, TO SORT THINGS OUT ON HIS OWN.
BUT...
...I CAN'T STAND THE THOUGHT OF WAITING IT OUT.
I'M SO WOR-RIED.

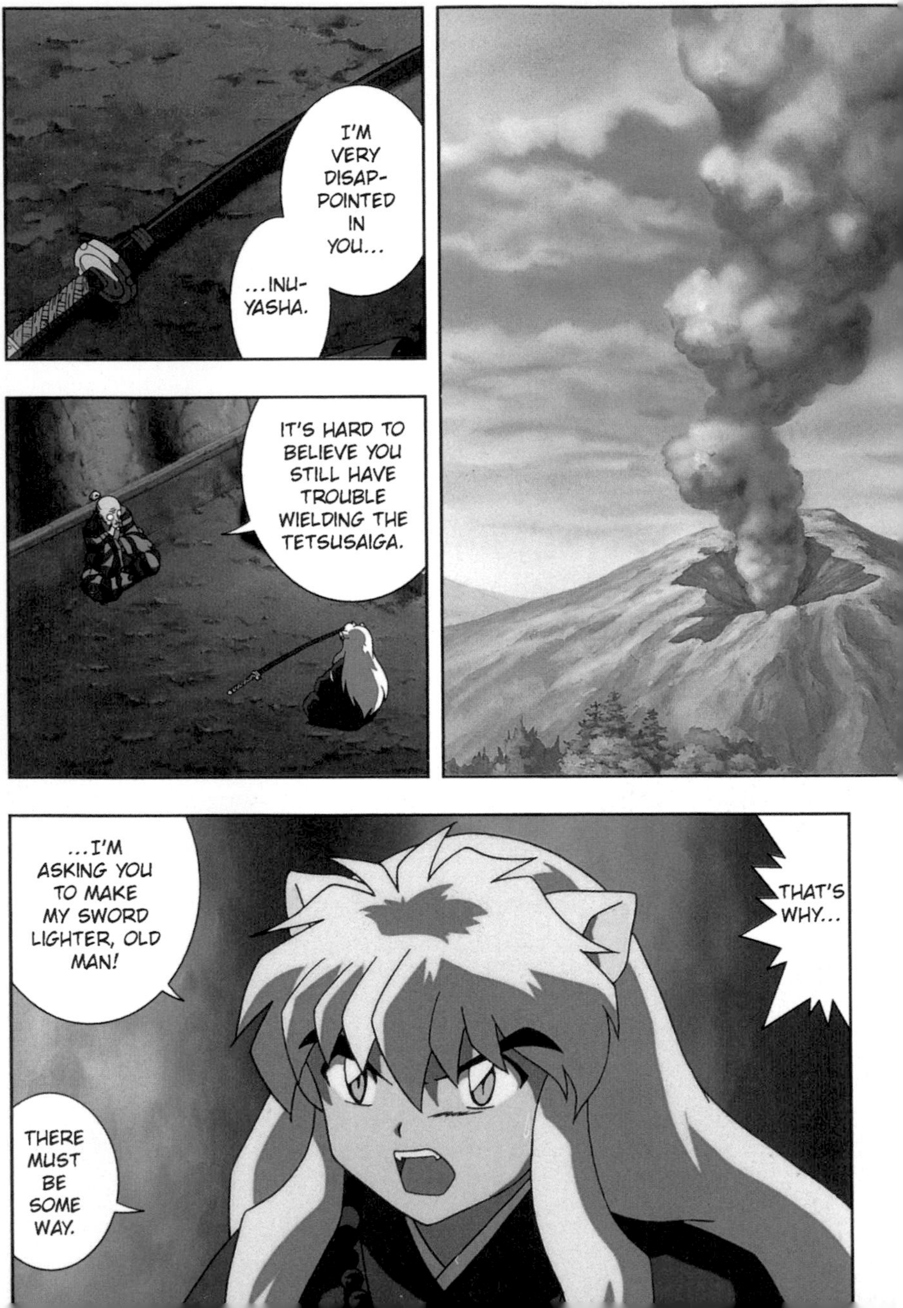
I'M VERY DISAP-POINTED IN YOU...
...INU-YASHA.
IT'S HARD TO BELIEVE YOU STILL HAVE TROUBLE WIELDING THE TETSUSAIGA.
THAT'S WHY...
...I'M ASKING YOU TO MAKE MY SWORD LIGHTER, OLD MAN!
THERE MUST BE SOME WAY.

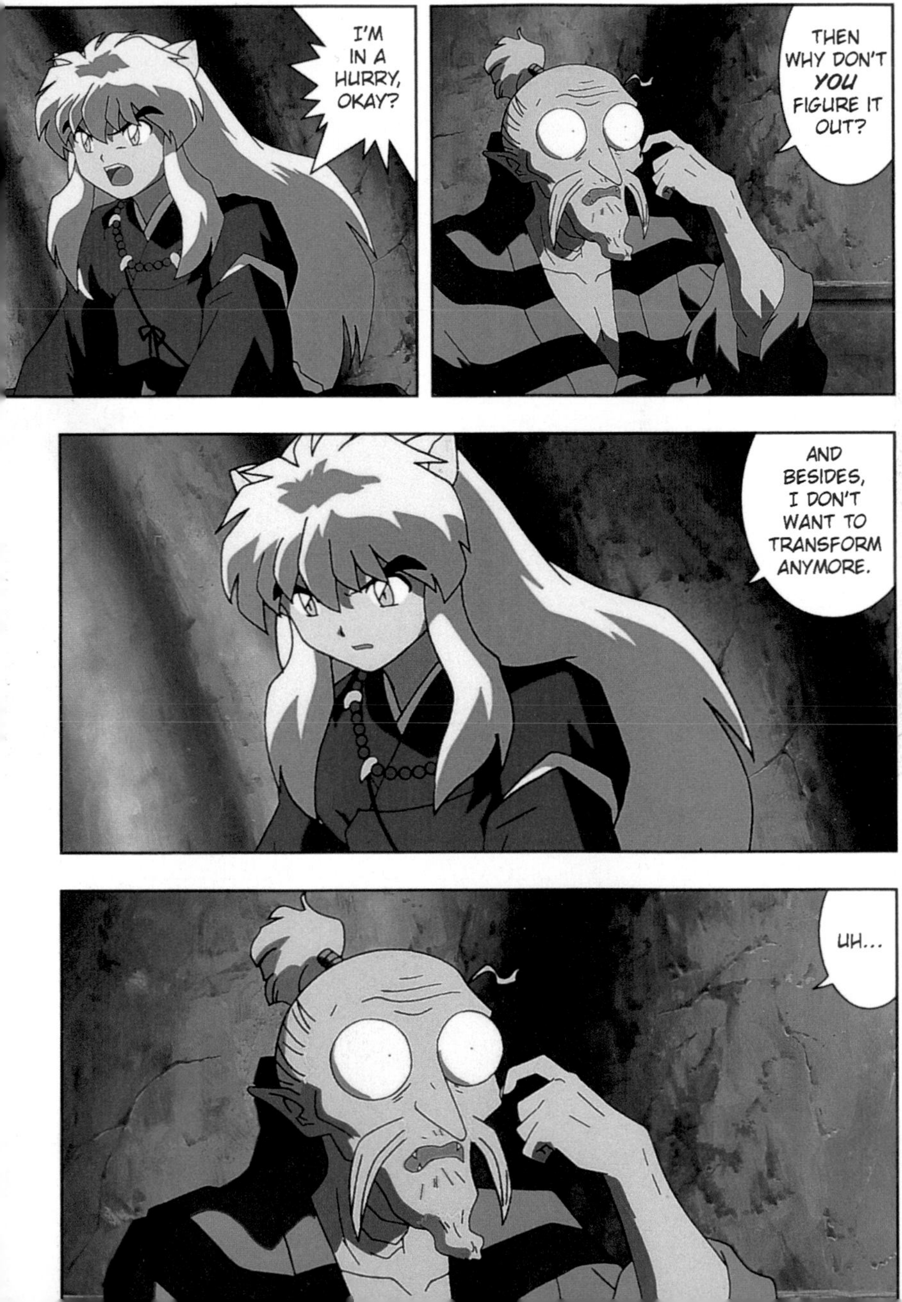
THEN WHY DON'T ***YOU*** FIGURE IT OUT?
I'M IN A HURRY, OKAY?
AND BESIDES, I DON'T WANT TO TRANSFORM ANYMORE.
UH...

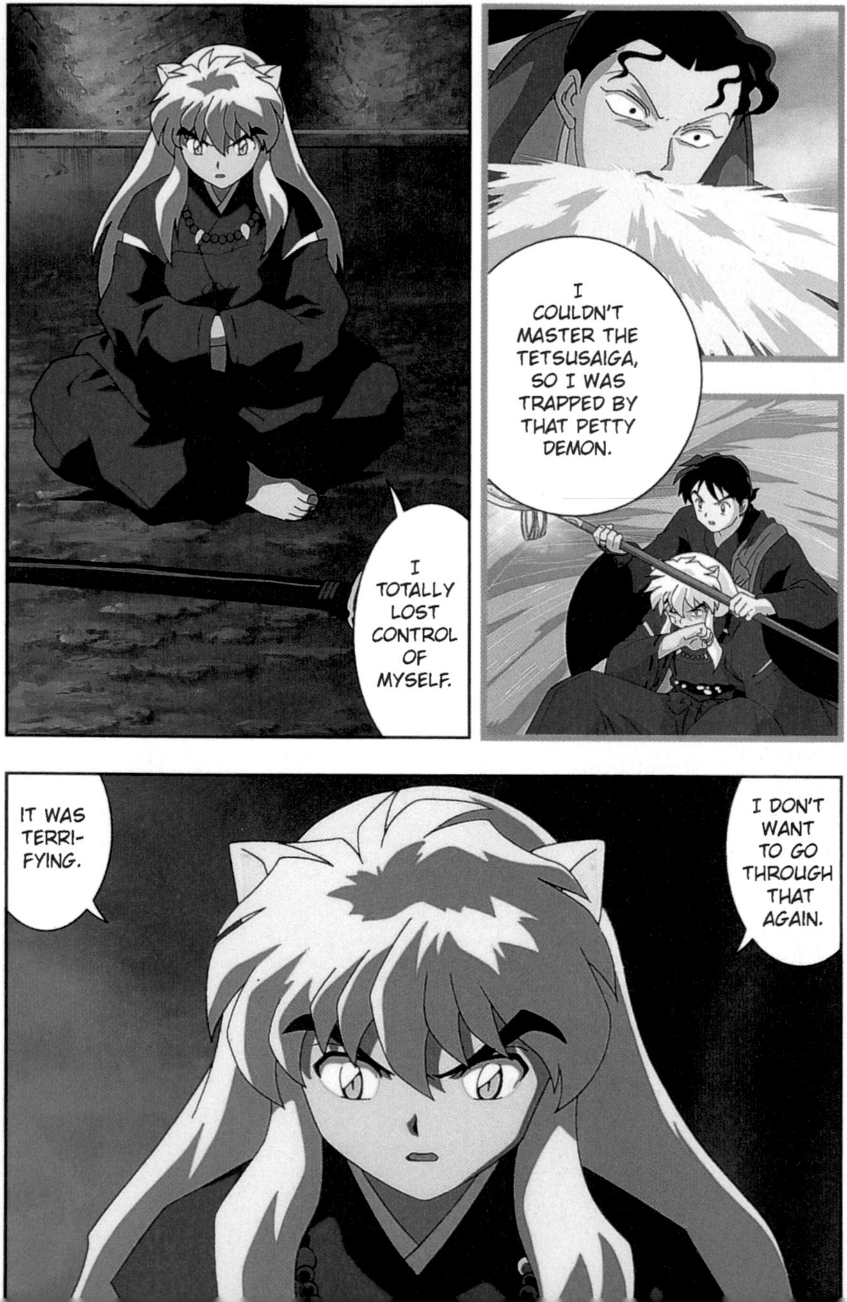
I COULDN'T MASTER THE TETSUSAIGA, SO I WAS TRAPPED BY THAT PETTY DEMON.
I TOTALLY LOST CONTROL OF MYSELF.
I DON'T WANT TO GO THROUGH THAT AGAIN.
IT WAS TERRI-FYING.

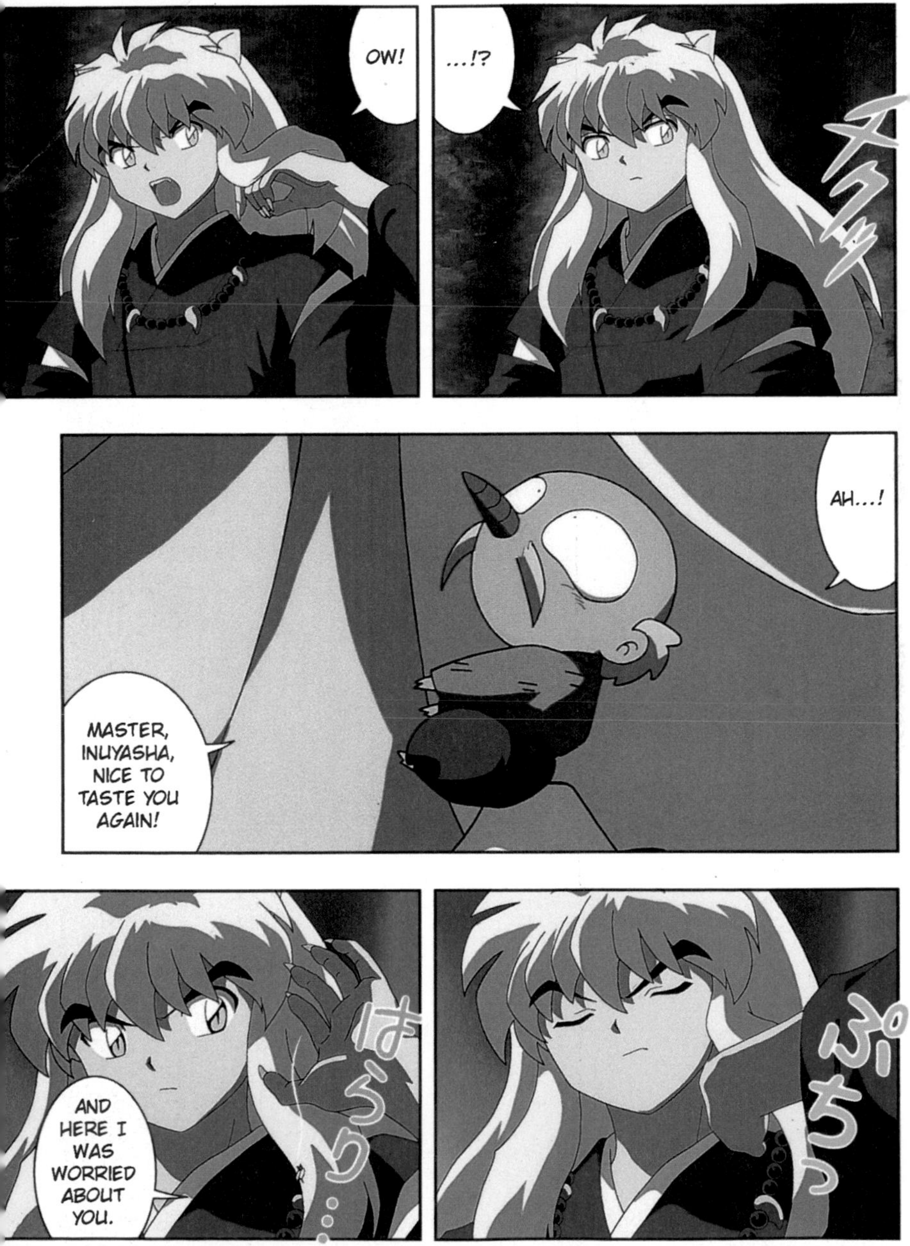
...!?
OW!
AH...!
MASTER, INUYASHA, NICE TO TASTE YOU AGAIN!
ぷちっ
AND HERE I WAS WORRIED ABOUT YOU.
はらり…

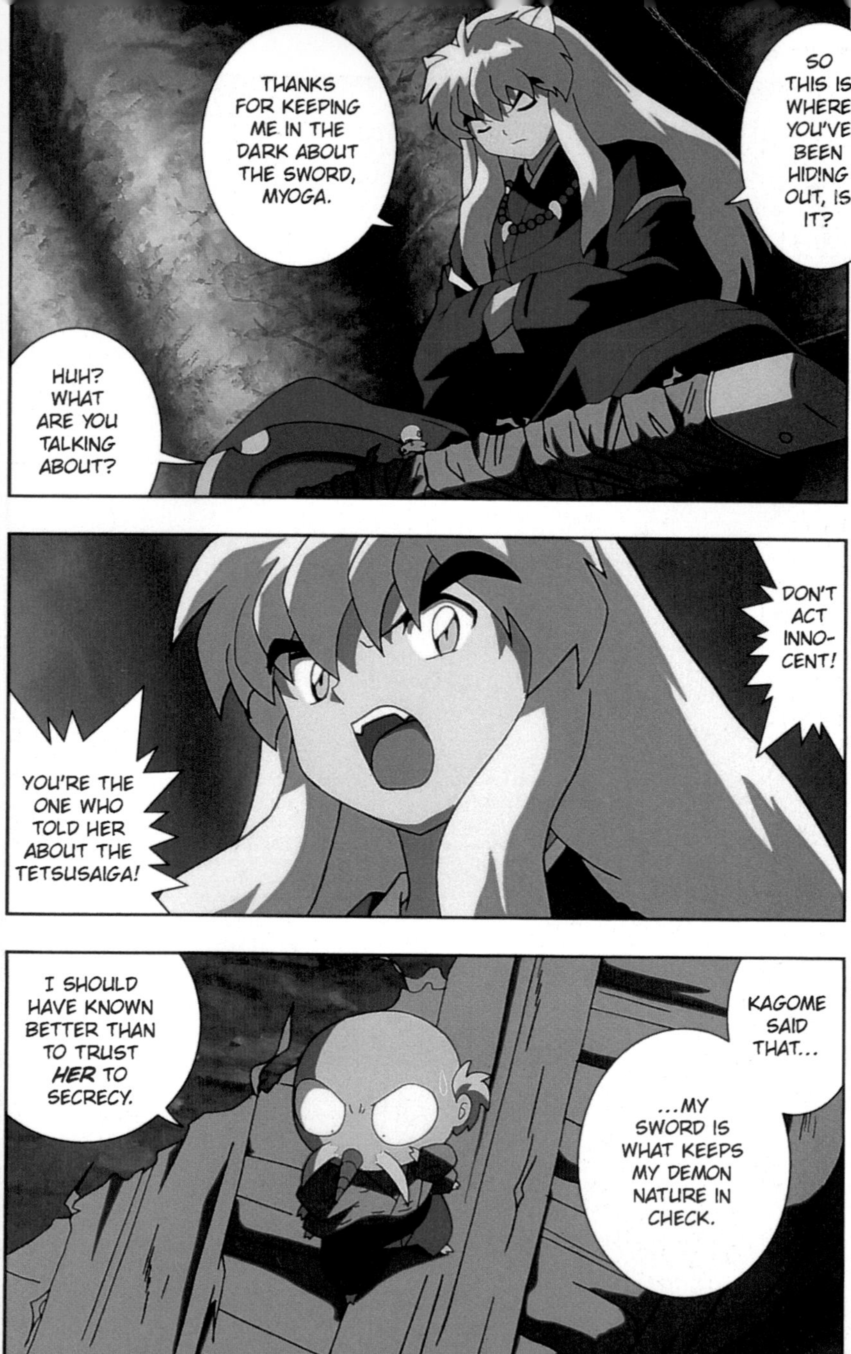
SO THIS IS WHERE YOU'VE BEEN HIDING OUT, IS IT?
THANKS FOR KEEPING ME IN THE DARK ABOUT THE SWORD, MYOGA.
HUH? WHAT ARE YOU TALKING ABOUT?
DON'T ACT INNO-CENT!
YOU'RE THE ONE WHO TOLD HER ABOUT THE TETSUSAIGA!
KAGOME SAID THAT...
...MY SWORD IS WHAT KEEPS MY DEMON NATURE IN CHECK.
I SHOULD HAVE KNOWN BETTER THAN TO TRUST *HER* TO SECRECY.

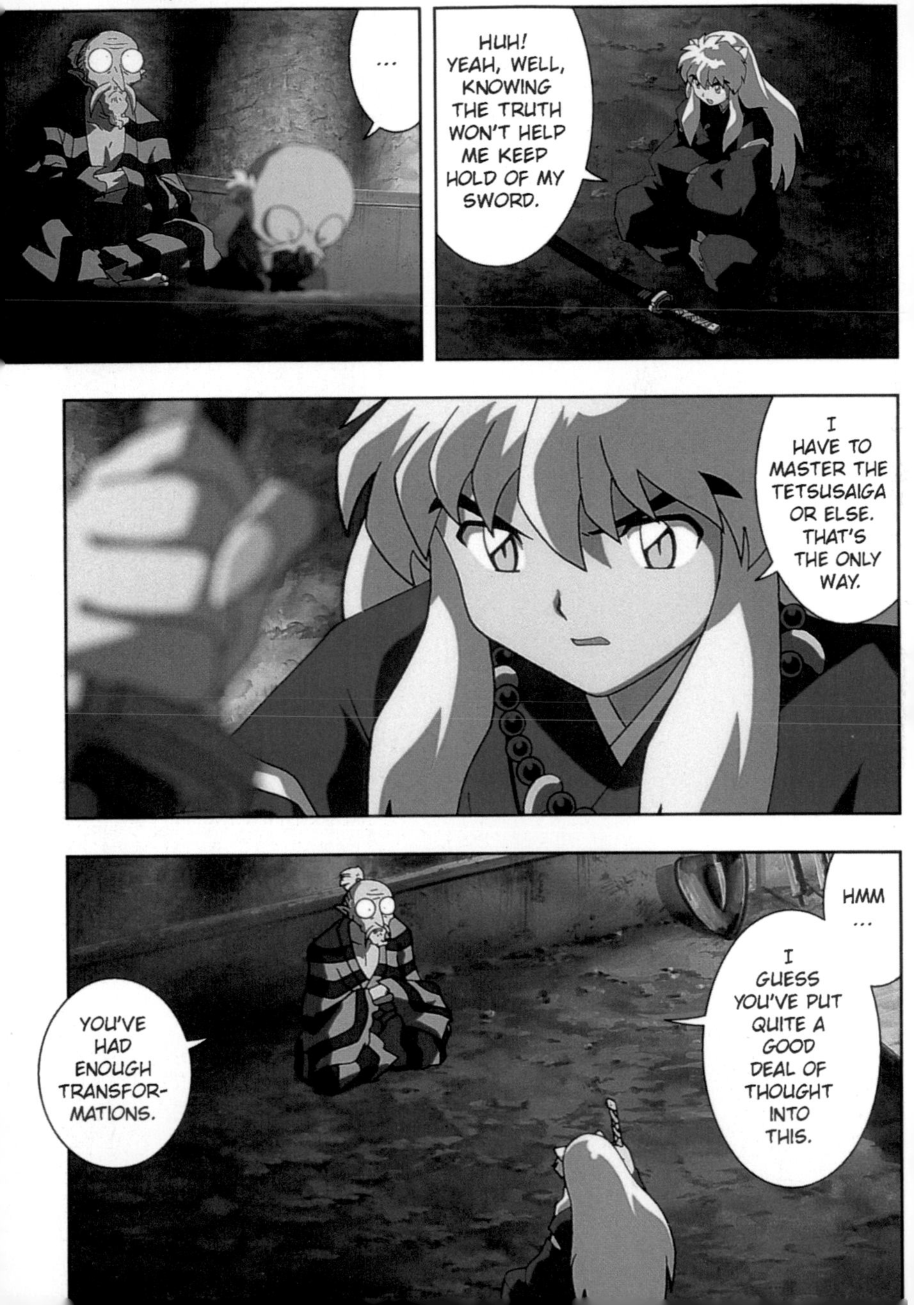
HUH! YEAH, WELL, KNOWING THE TRUTH WON'T HELP ME KEEP HOLD OF MY SWORD.
...
I HAVE TO MASTER THE TETSUSAIGA OR ELSE. THAT'S THE ONLY WAY.
HMM ...
I GUESS YOU'VE PUT QUITE A GOOD DEAL OF THOUGHT INTO THIS.
YOU'VE HAD ENOUGH TRANSFOR-MATIONS.

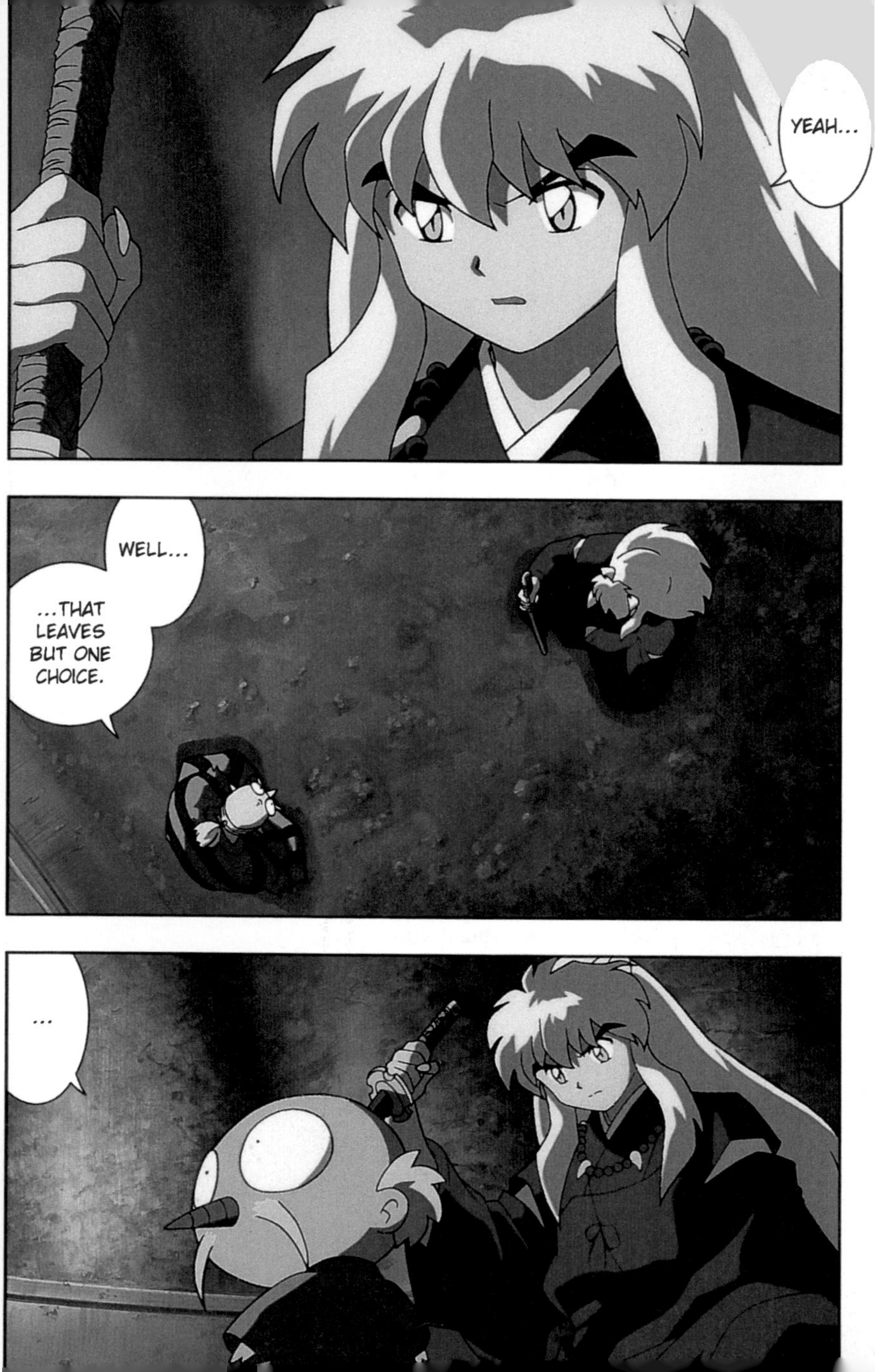
YEAH...
WELL...
...THAT LEAVES BUT ONE CHOICE.
...

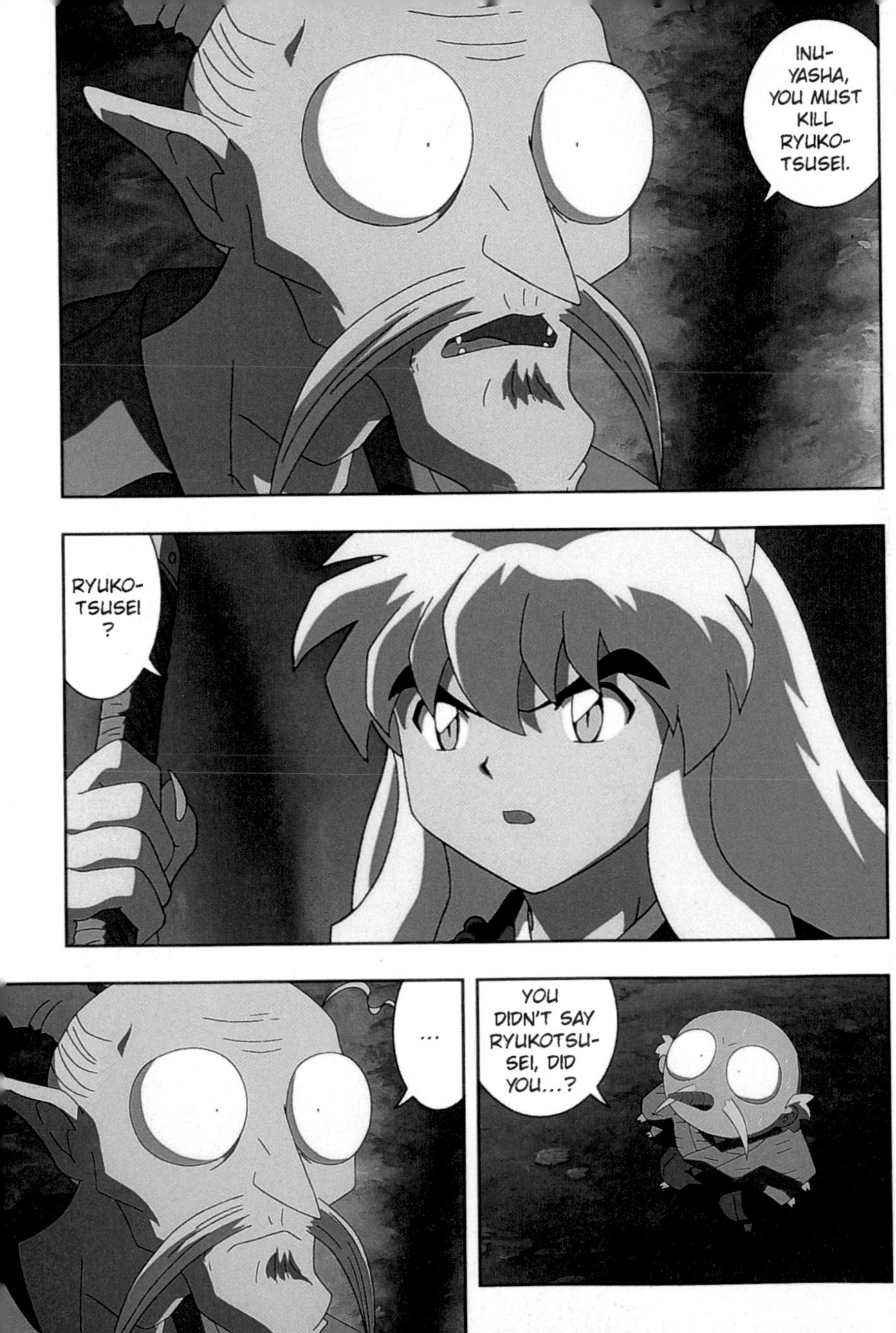
INU-YASHA, YOU MUST KILL RYUKO-TSUSEI.
RYUKO-TSUSEI ?
YOU DIDN'T SAY RYUKOTSU-SEI, DID YOU...?
...

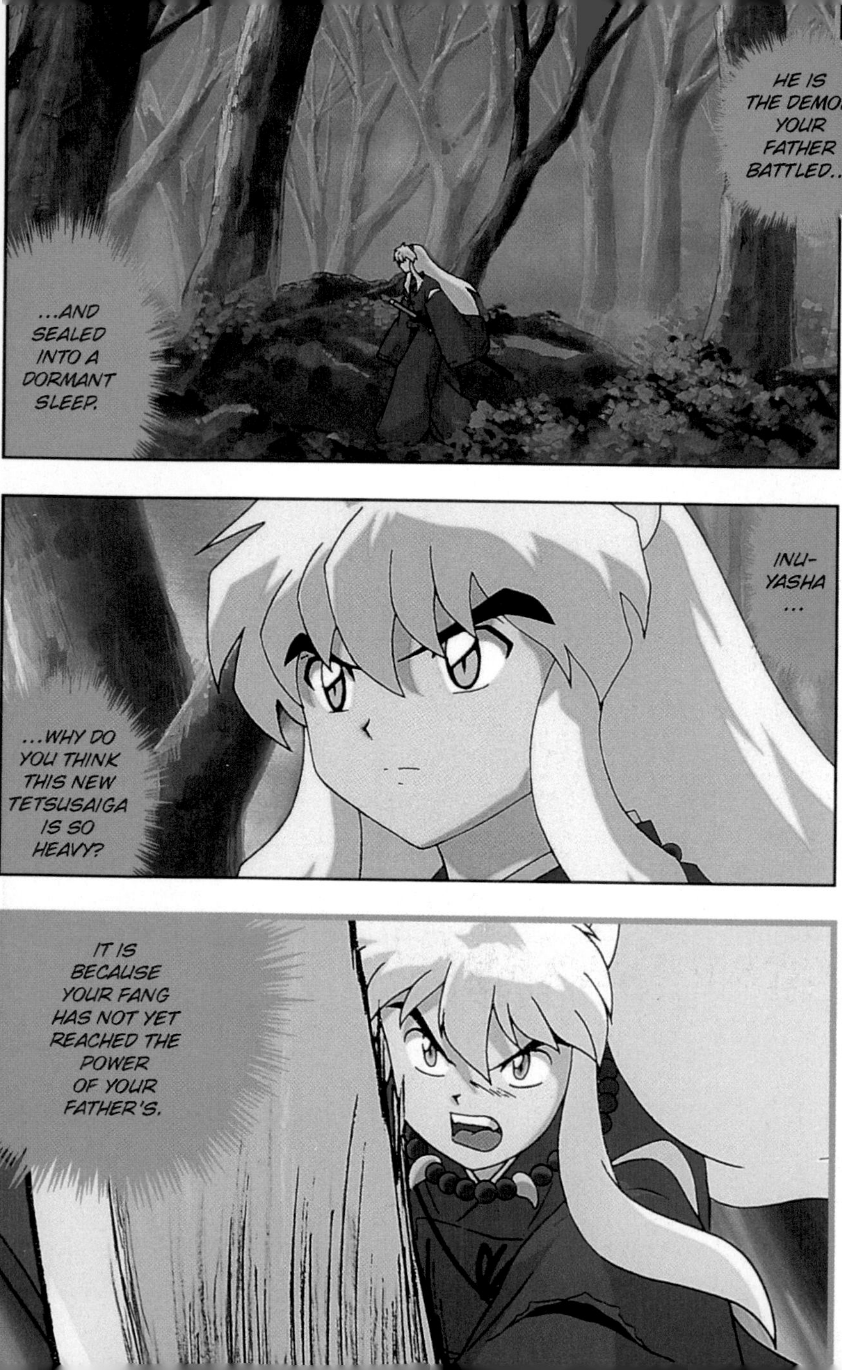
HE IS THE DEMON YOUR FATHER BATTLED...
...AND SEALED INTO A DORMANT SLEEP.
INU-YASHA...
...WHY DO YOU THINK THIS NEW TETSUSAIGA IS SO HEAVY?
IT IS BECAUSE YOUR FANG HAS NOT YET REACHED THE POWER OF YOUR FATHER'S.

IN OTHER WORDS, IF I DESTROY THE DEMON MY FATHER FOUGHT, THEN I'LL SURPASS THE OLD MAN IN STRENGTH?

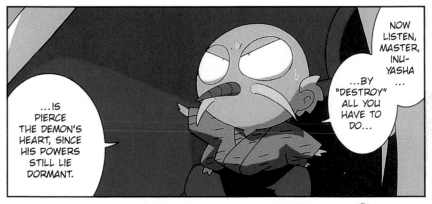

NOW LISTEN, MASTER, INU-YASHA...

...BY "DESTROY" ALL YOU HAVE TO DO...

...IS PIERCE THE DEMON'S HEART, SINCE HIS POWERS STILL LIE DORMANT.

WHAT?

I DON'T HAVE TO FIGHT HIM?

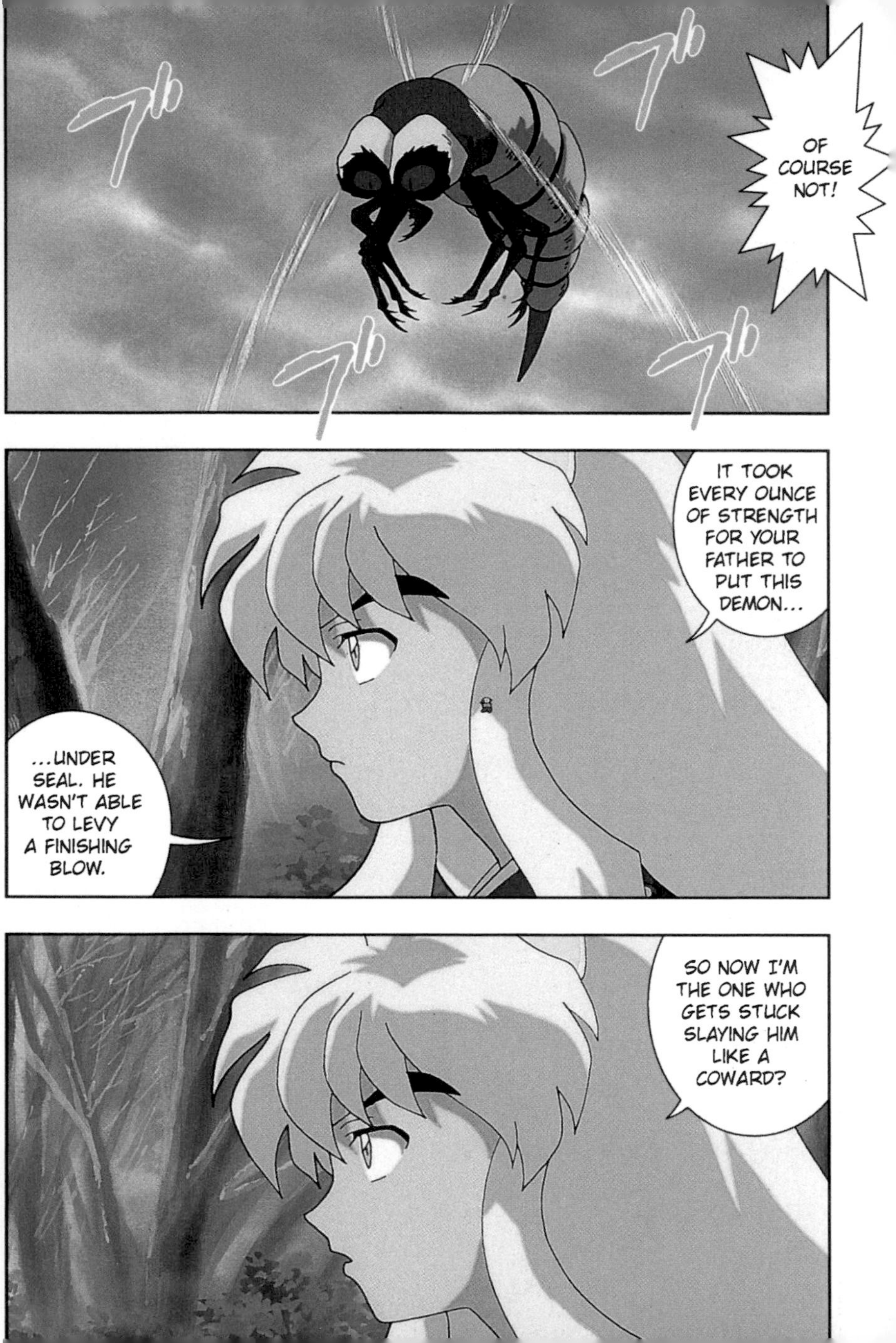
OF COURSE NOT!
IT TOOK EVERY OUNCE OF STRENGTH FOR YOUR FATHER TO PUT THIS DEMON...
...UNDER SEAL. HE WASN'T ABLE TO LEVY A FINISHING BLOW.
SO NOW I'M THE ONE WHO GETS STUCK SLAYING HIM LIKE A COWARD?

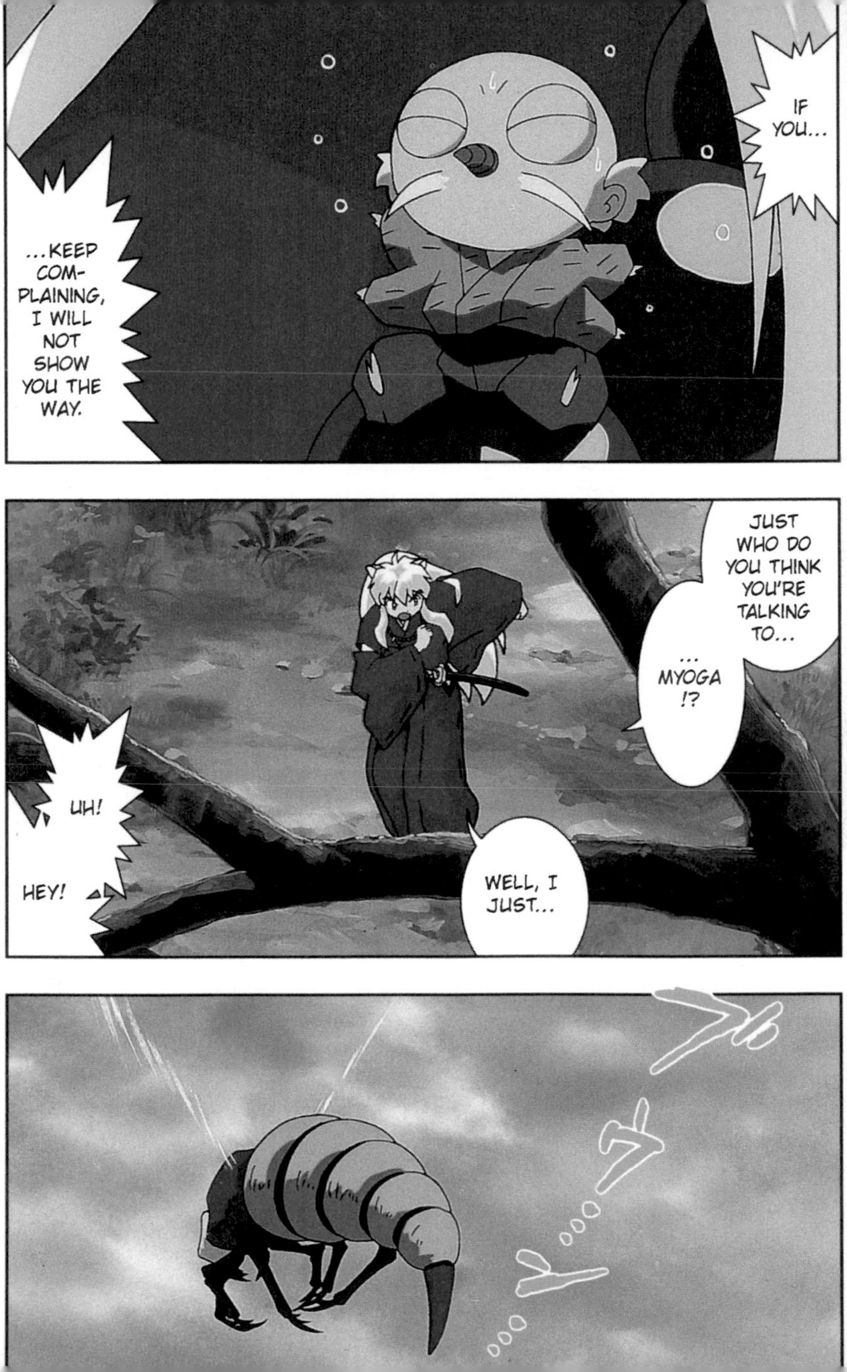
IF YOU...
...KEEP COMPLAINING, I WILL NOT SHOW YOU THE WAY.
JUST WHO DO YOU THINK YOU'RE TALKING TO...
...MYOGA!?
WELL, I JUST...
UH!
HEY!

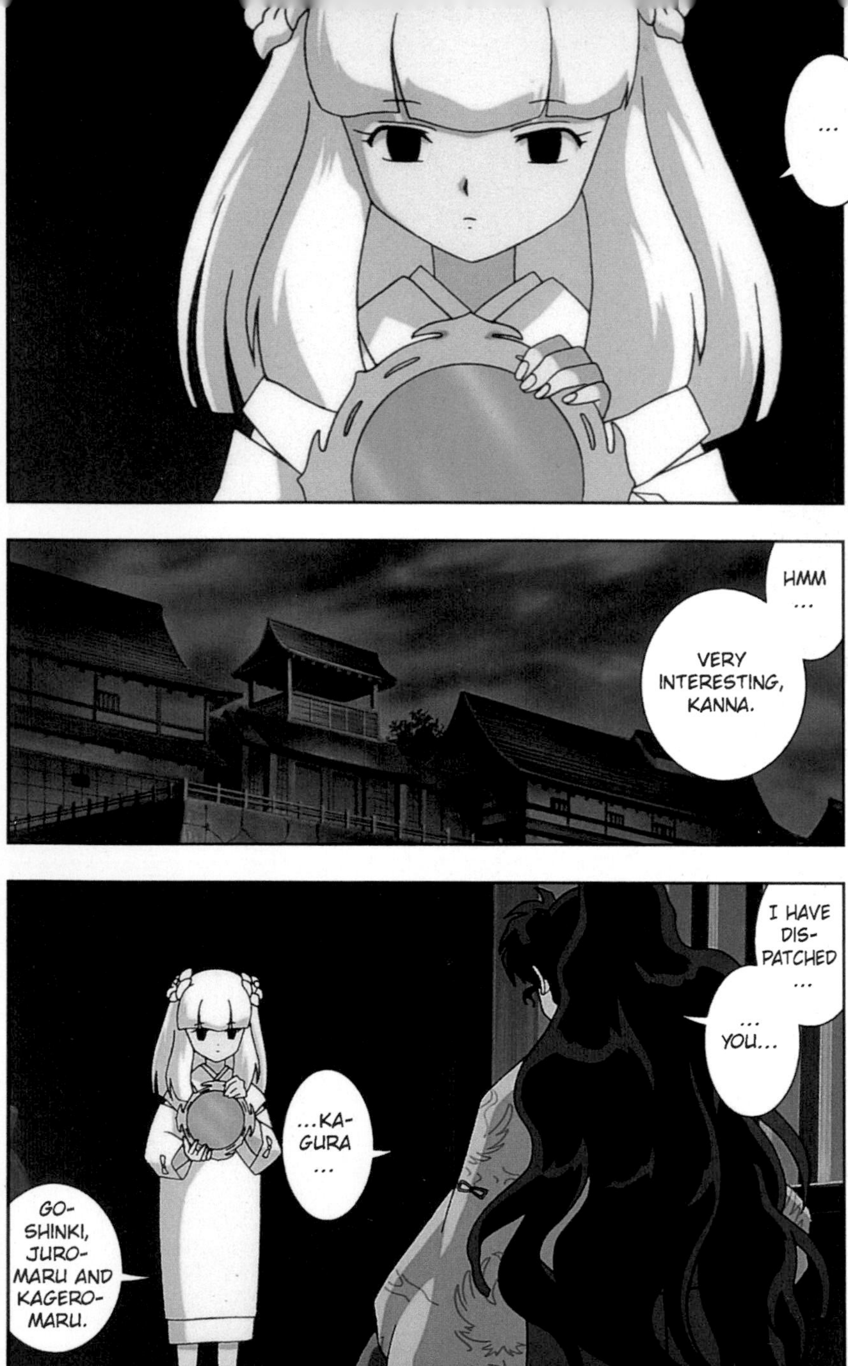
...
HMM ...
VERY INTERESTING, KANNA.
I HAVE DIS-PATCHED ...
... YOU...
...KA-GURA ...
GO-SHINKI, JURO-MARU AND KAGERO-MARU.

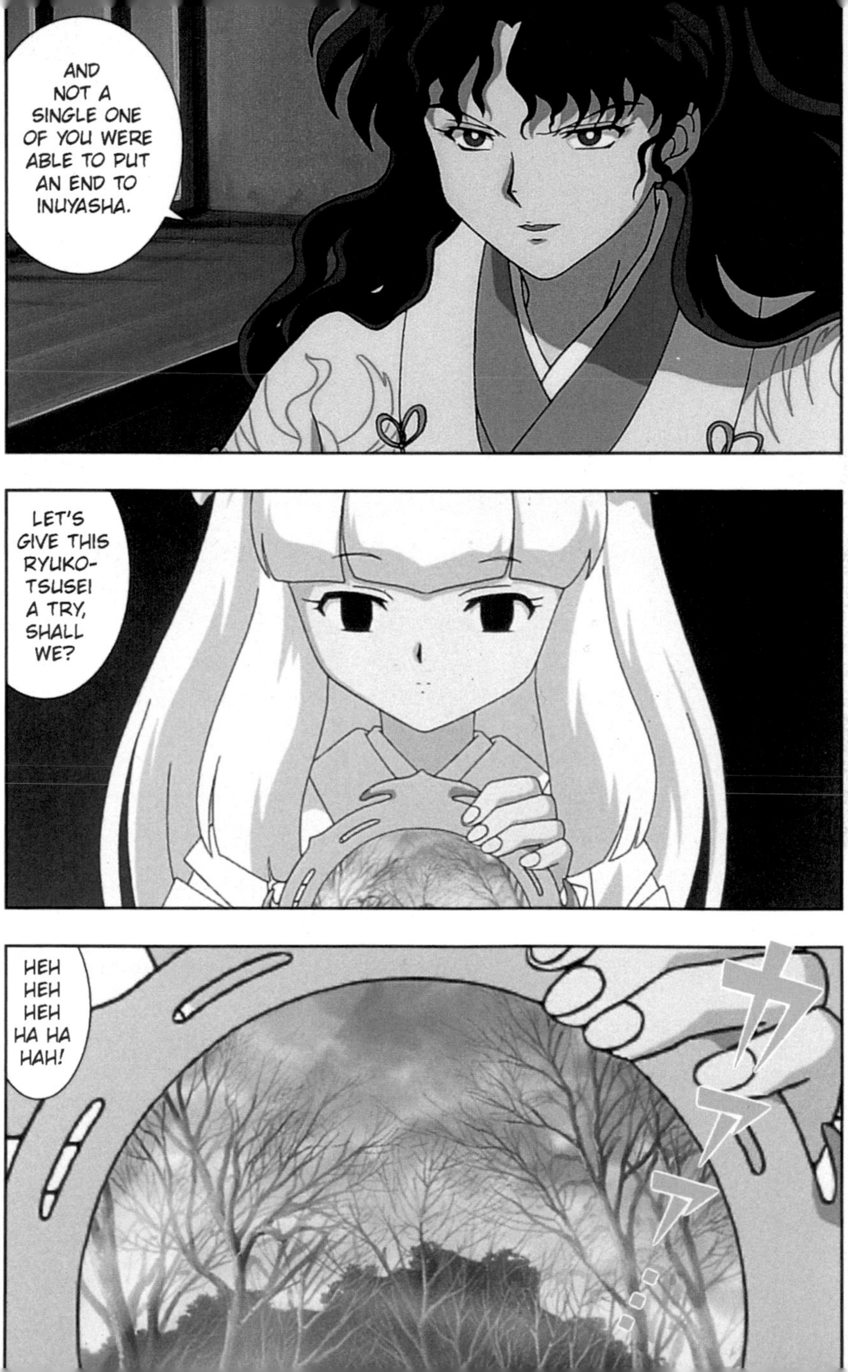
AND NOT A SINGLE ONE OF YOU WERE ABLE TO PUT AN END TO INUYASHA.
LET'S GIVE THIS RYUKO-TSUSEI A TRY, SHALL WE?
カァァ…
HEH HEH HEH HA HA HAH!

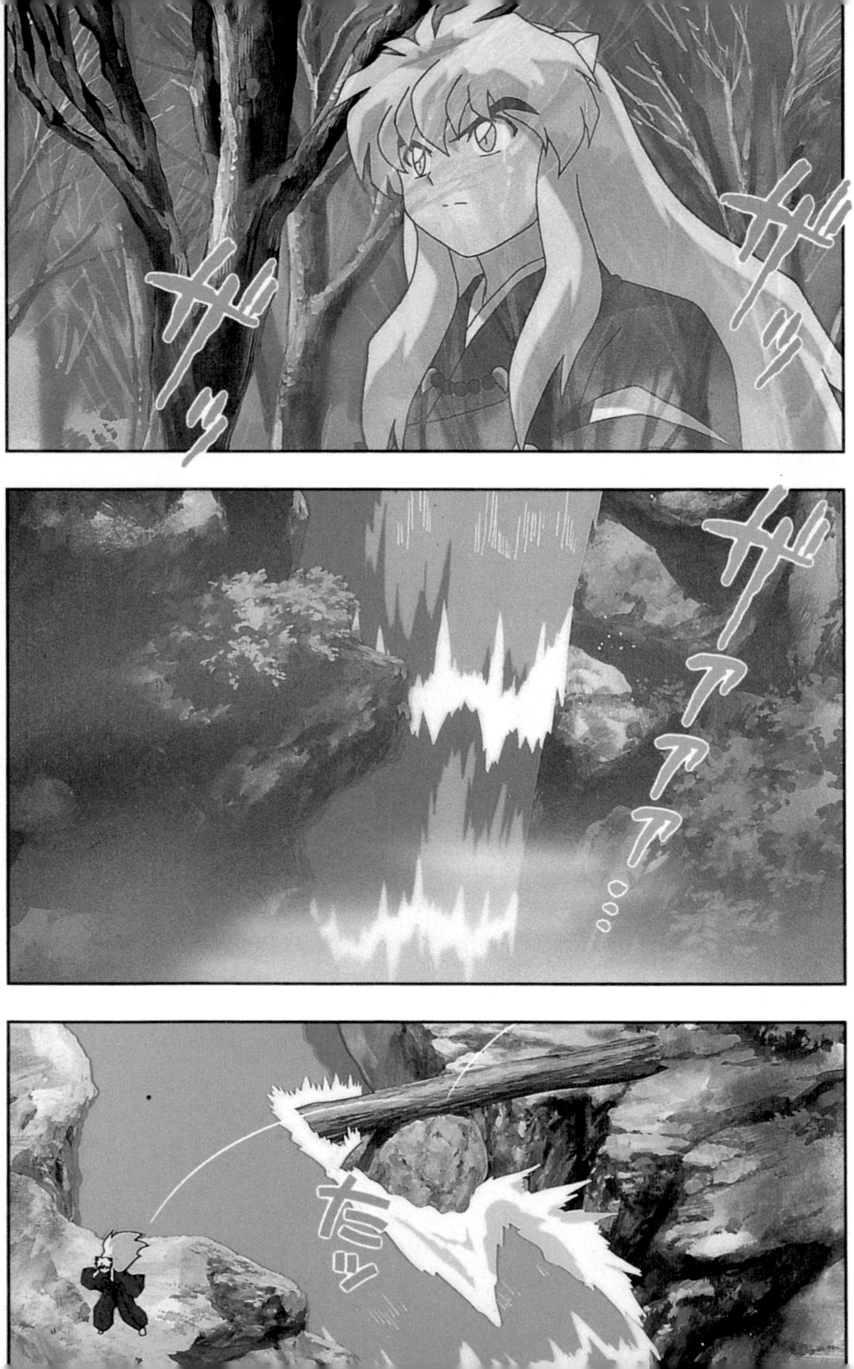
ザッ
ザッ
ザアアア…
たッ

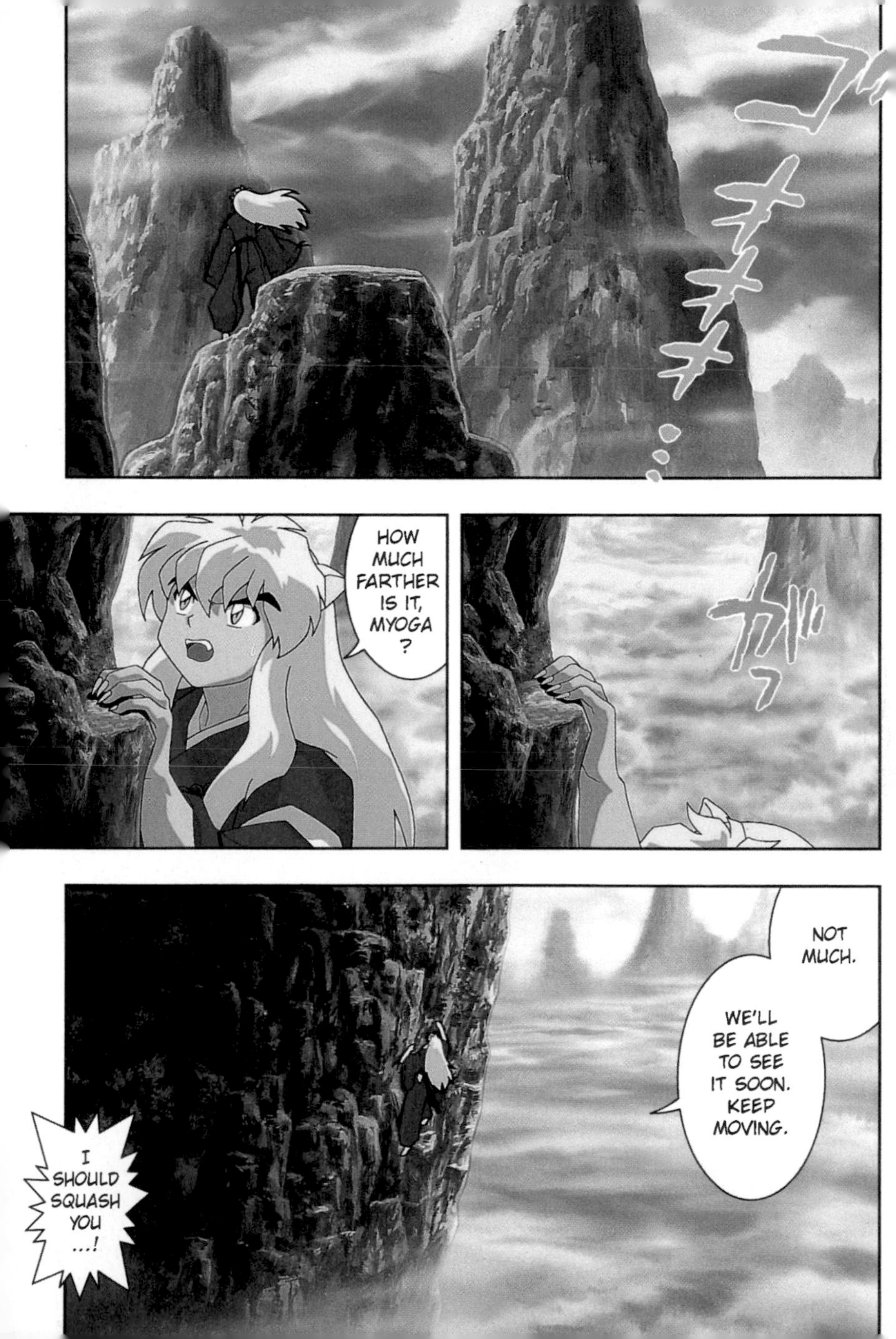
HOW MUCH FARTHER IS IT, MYOGA?
NOT MUCH.
WE'LL BE ABLE TO SEE IT SOON. KEEP MOVING.
I SHOULD SQUASH YOU ...!

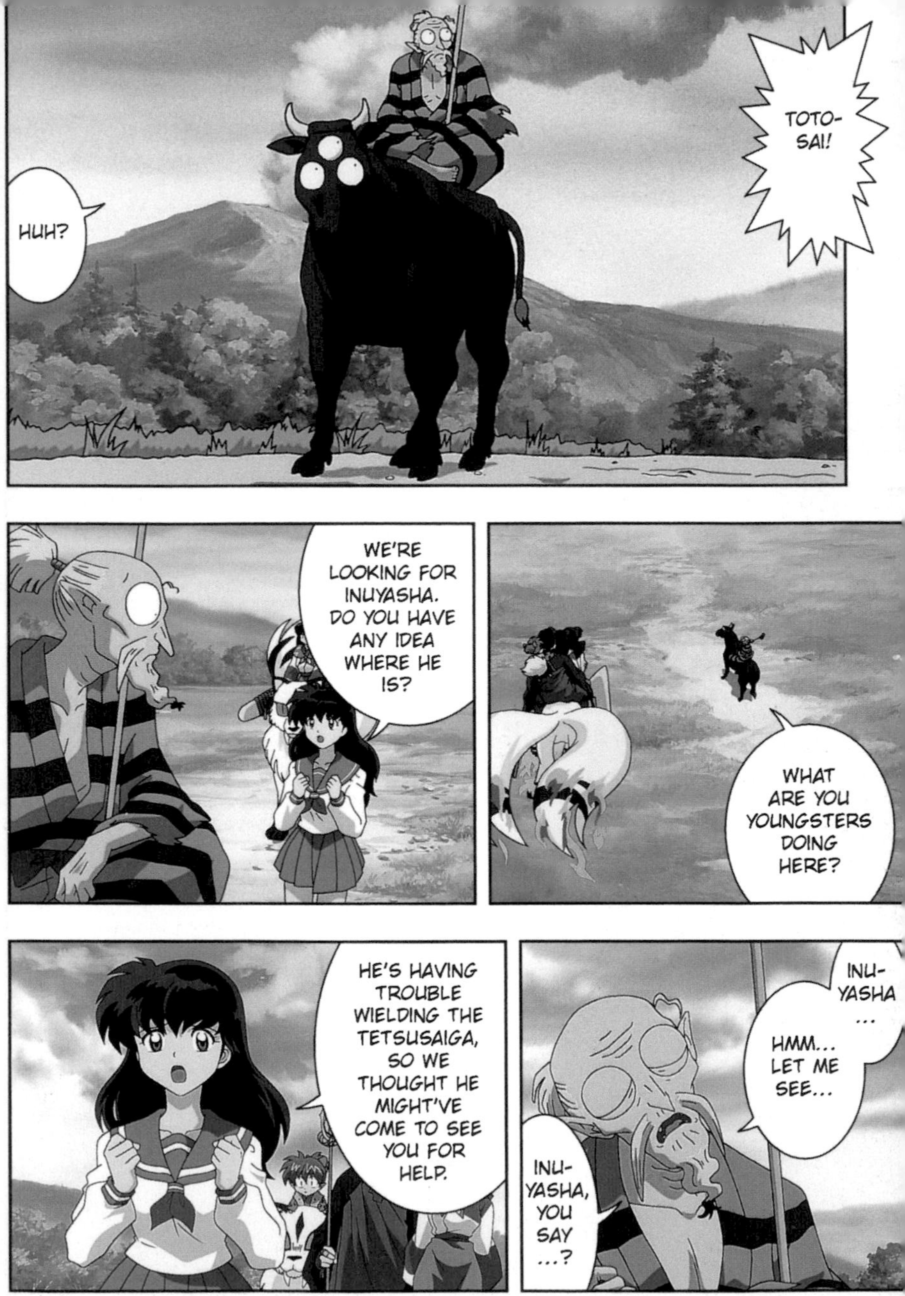
TOTO-SAI!
HUH?
WHAT ARE YOU YOUNGSTERS DOING HERE?
WE'RE LOOKING FOR INUYASHA. DO YOU HAVE ANY IDEA WHERE HE IS?
INU-YASHA...
HMM... LET ME SEE...
INU-YASHA, YOU SAY...?
HE'S HAVING TROUBLE WIELDING THE TETSUSAIGA, SO WE THOUGHT HE MIGHT'VE COME TO SEE YOU FOR HELP.

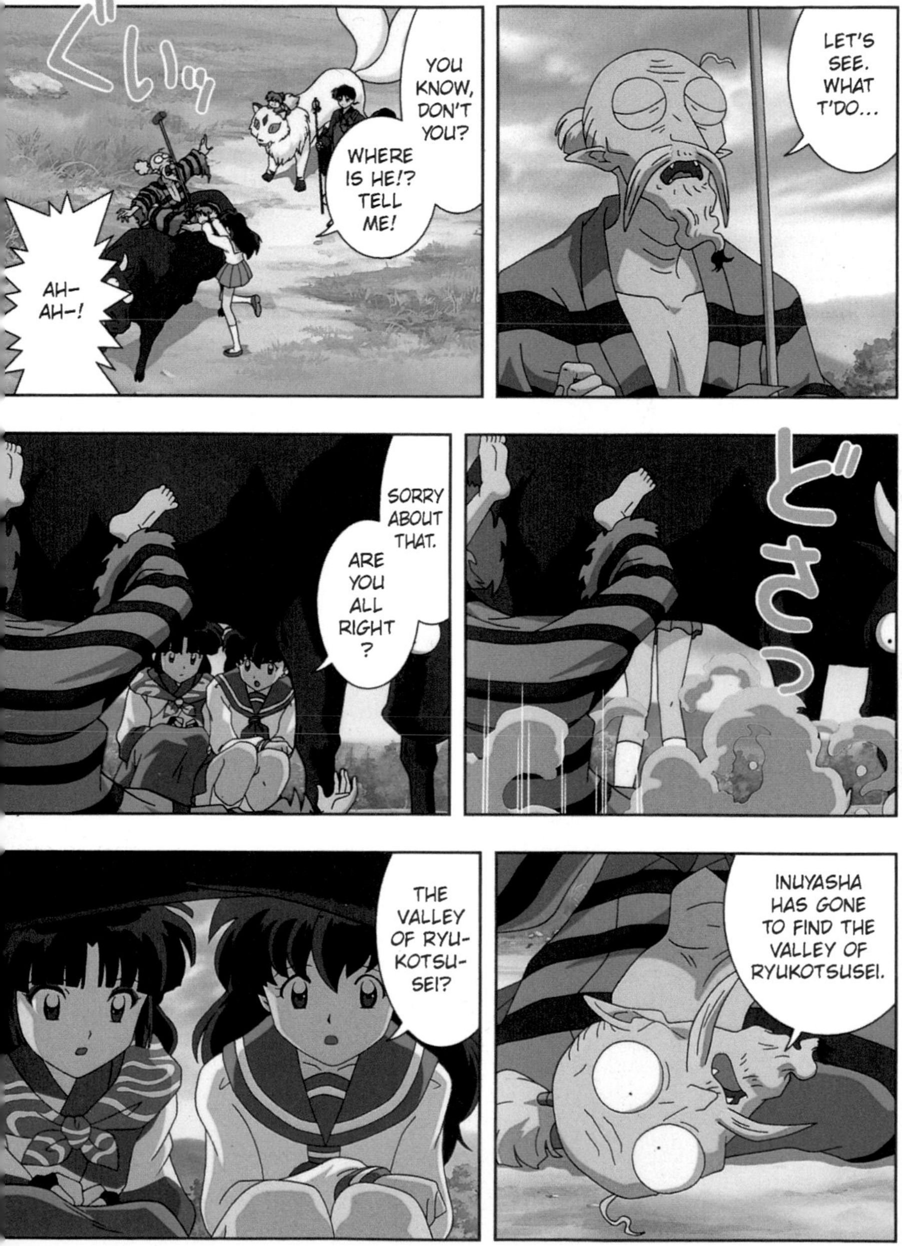
LET'S SEE. WHAT T'DO...
ぐいっ
YOU KNOW, DON'T YOU?
WHERE IS HE!? TELL ME!
AH- AH-!
どさっ
SORRY ABOUT THAT.
ARE YOU ALL RIGHT?
INUYASHA HAS GONE TO FIND THE VALLEY OF RYUKOTSUSEI.
THE VALLEY OF RYU-KOTSU-SEI?

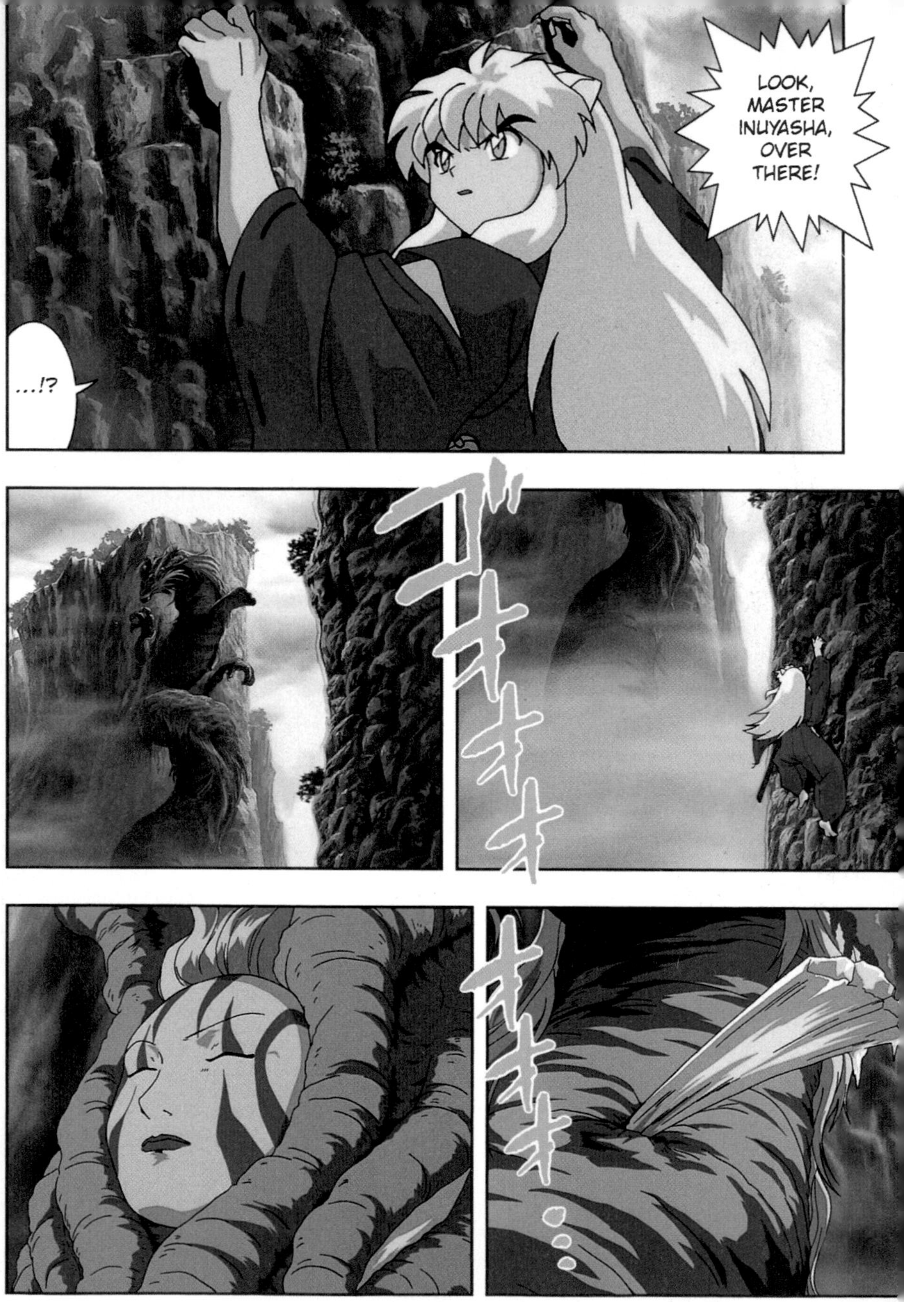
LOOK, MASTER INUYASHA, OVER THERE!
...!?
ゴオオオオオオオ…

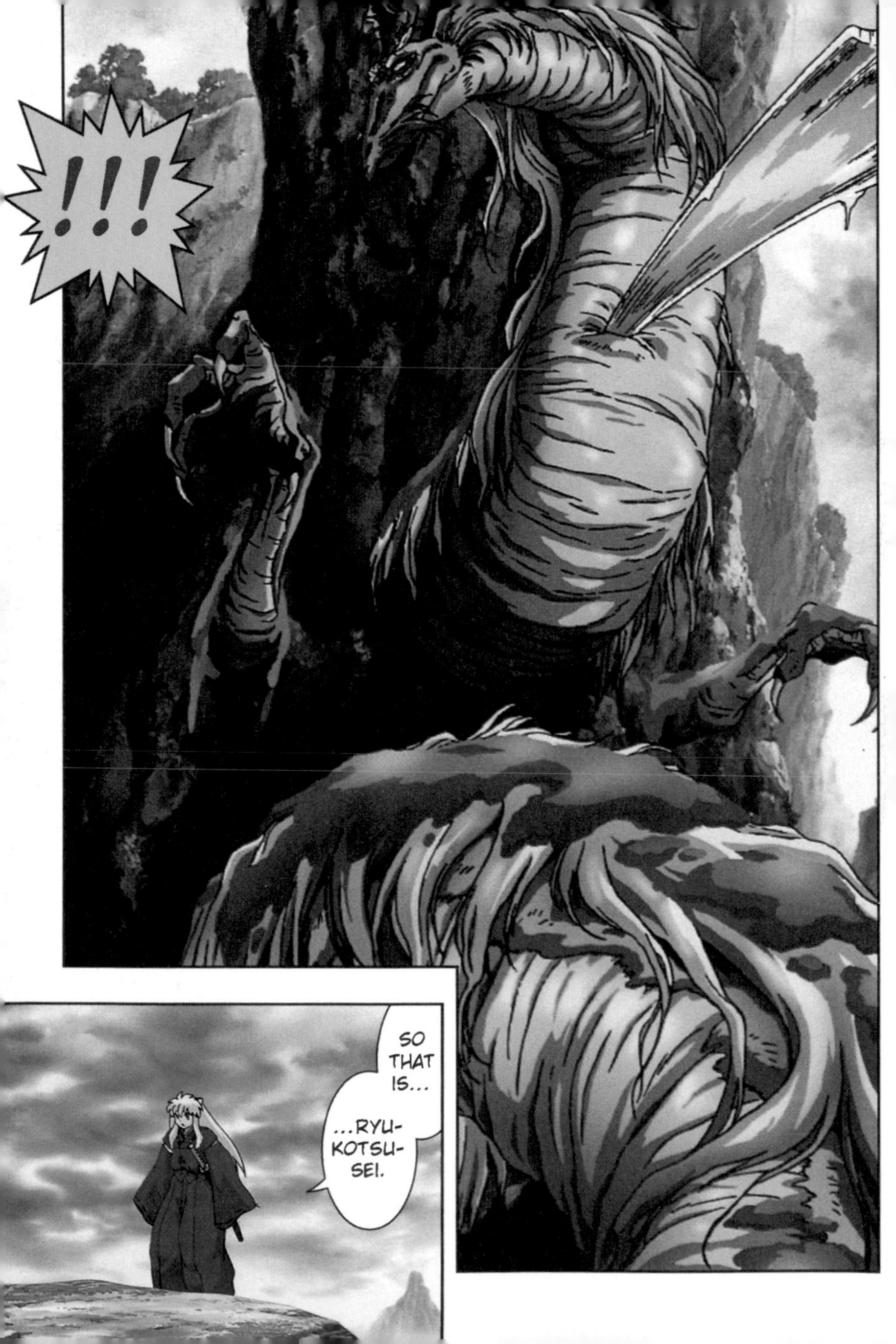
!!!
SO THAT IS...
...RYU-KOTSU-SEI.

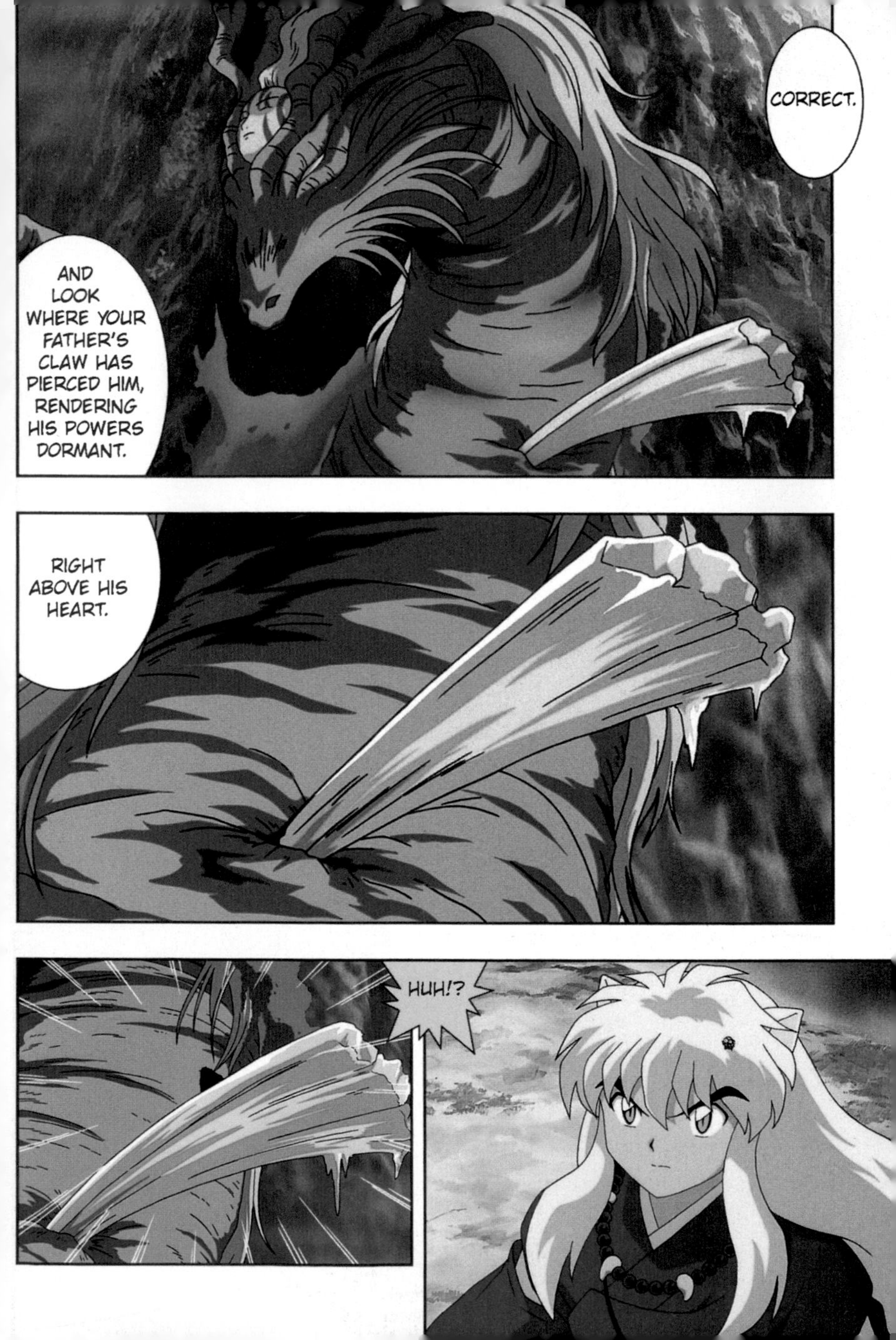
CORRECT.
AND LOOK WHERE YOUR FATHER'S CLAW HAS PIERCED HIM, RENDERING HIS POWERS DORMANT.
RIGHT ABOVE HIS HEART.
HUH!?

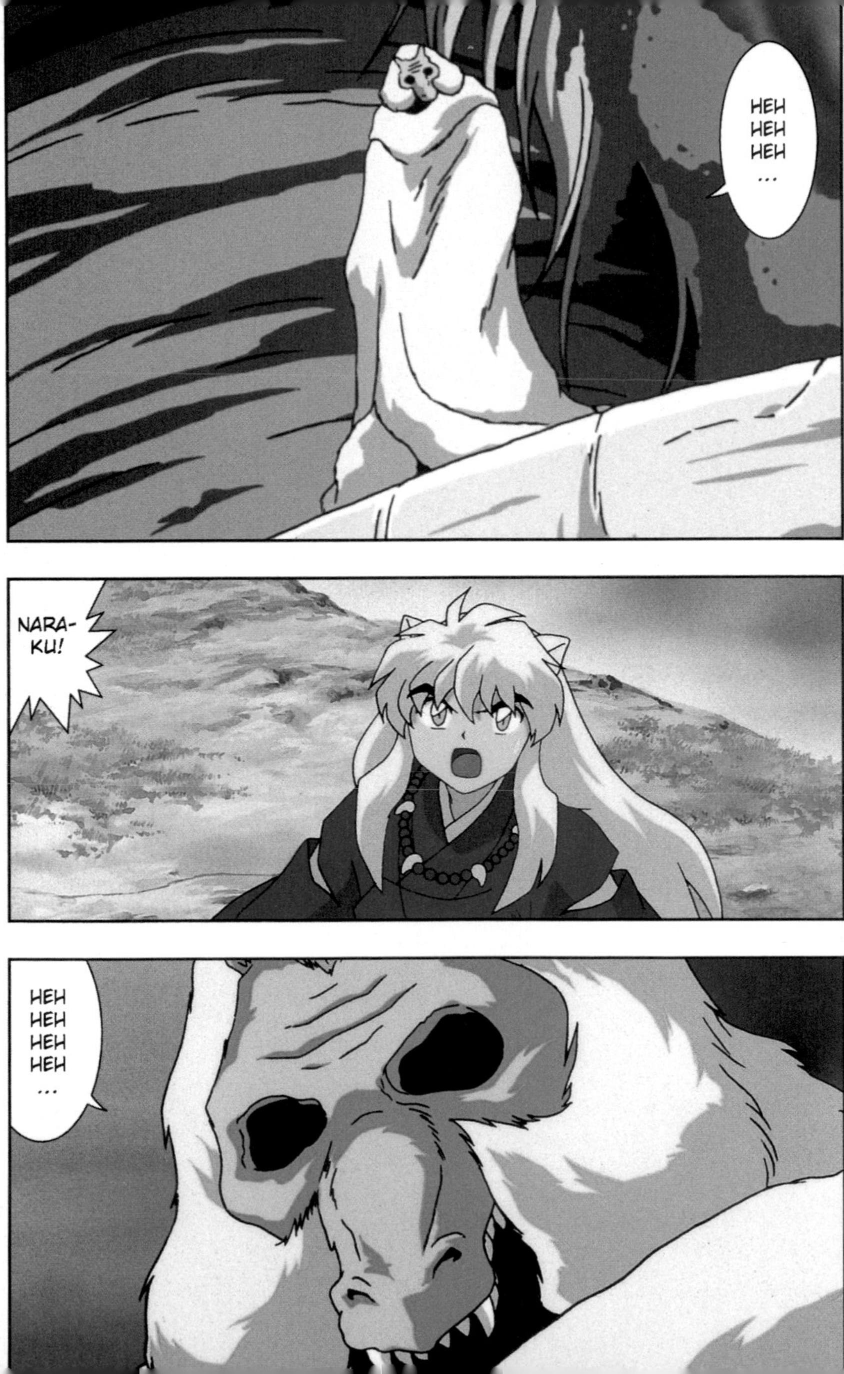
HEH HEH HEH ...
NARA-KU!
HEH HEH HEH HEH ...

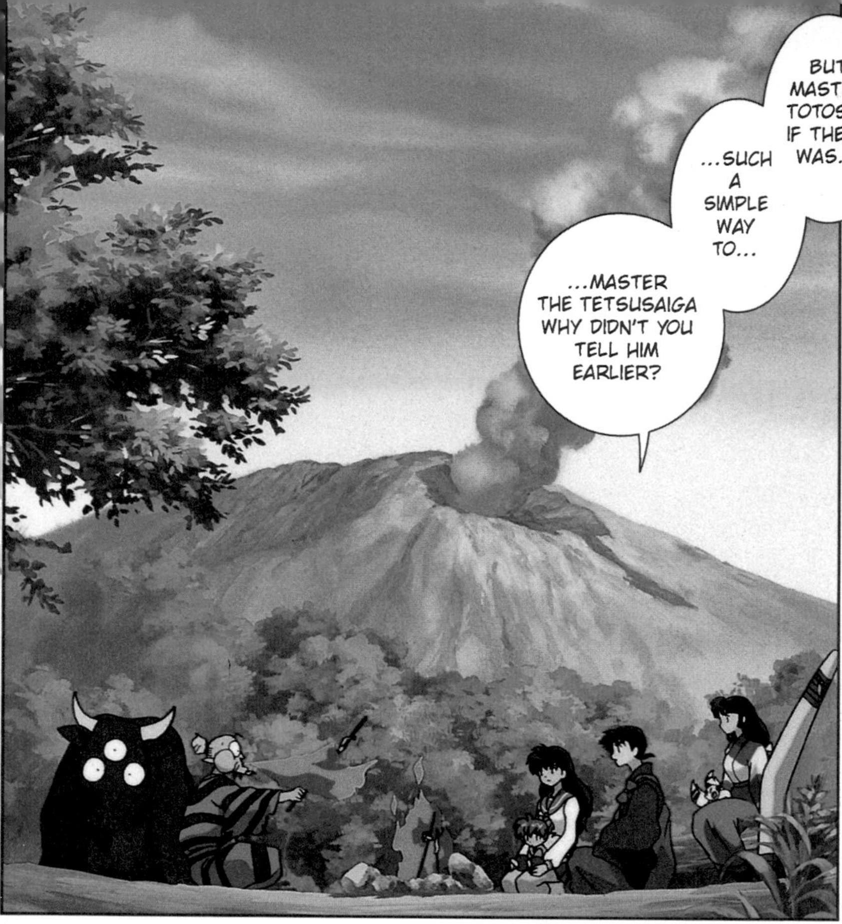
BUT MASTER TOTOSAI, IF THERE WAS...
...SUCH A SIMPLE WAY TO...
...MASTER THE TETSUSAIGA WHY DIDN'T YOU TELL HIM EARLIER?

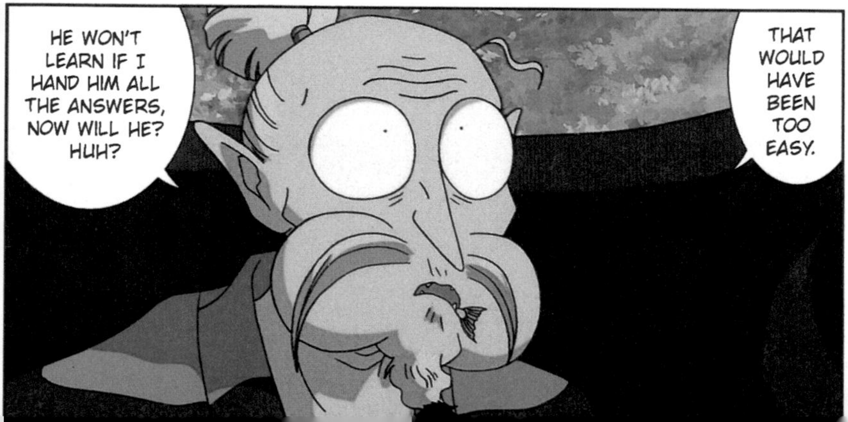
THAT WOULD HAVE BEEN TOO EASY.
HE WON'T LEARN IF I HAND HIM ALL THE ANSWERS, NOW WILL HE? HUH?

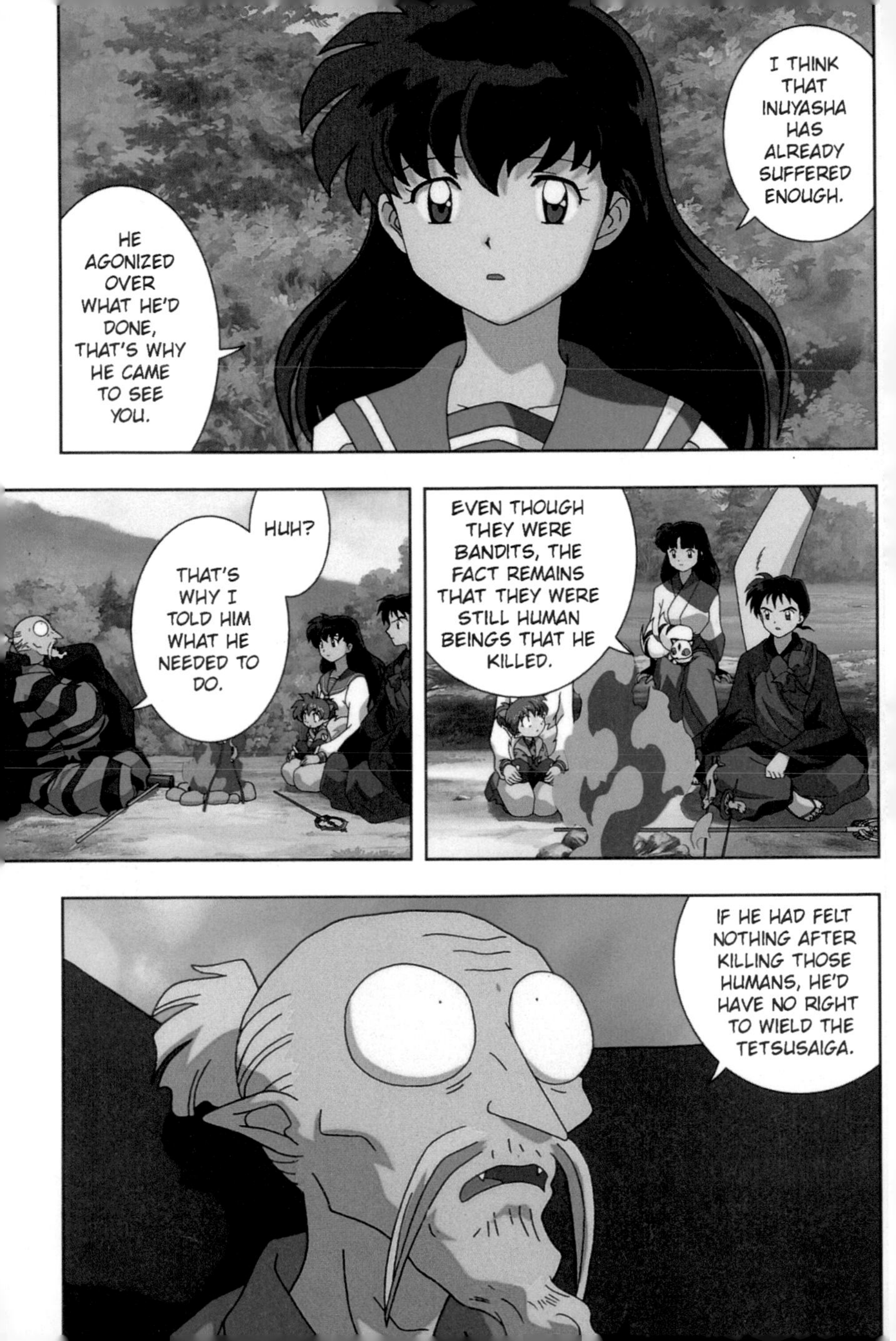
I THINK THAT INUYASHA HAS ALREADY SUFFERED ENOUGH.
HE AGONIZED OVER WHAT HE'D DONE, THAT'S WHY HE CAME TO SEE YOU.
HUH?
THAT'S WHY I TOLD HIM WHAT HE NEEDED TO DO.
EVEN THOUGH THEY WERE BANDITS, THE FACT REMAINS THAT THEY WERE STILL HUMAN BEINGS THAT HE KILLED.
IF HE HAD FELT NOTHING AFTER KILLING THOSE HUMANS, HE'D HAVE NO RIGHT TO WIELD THE TETSUSAIGA.

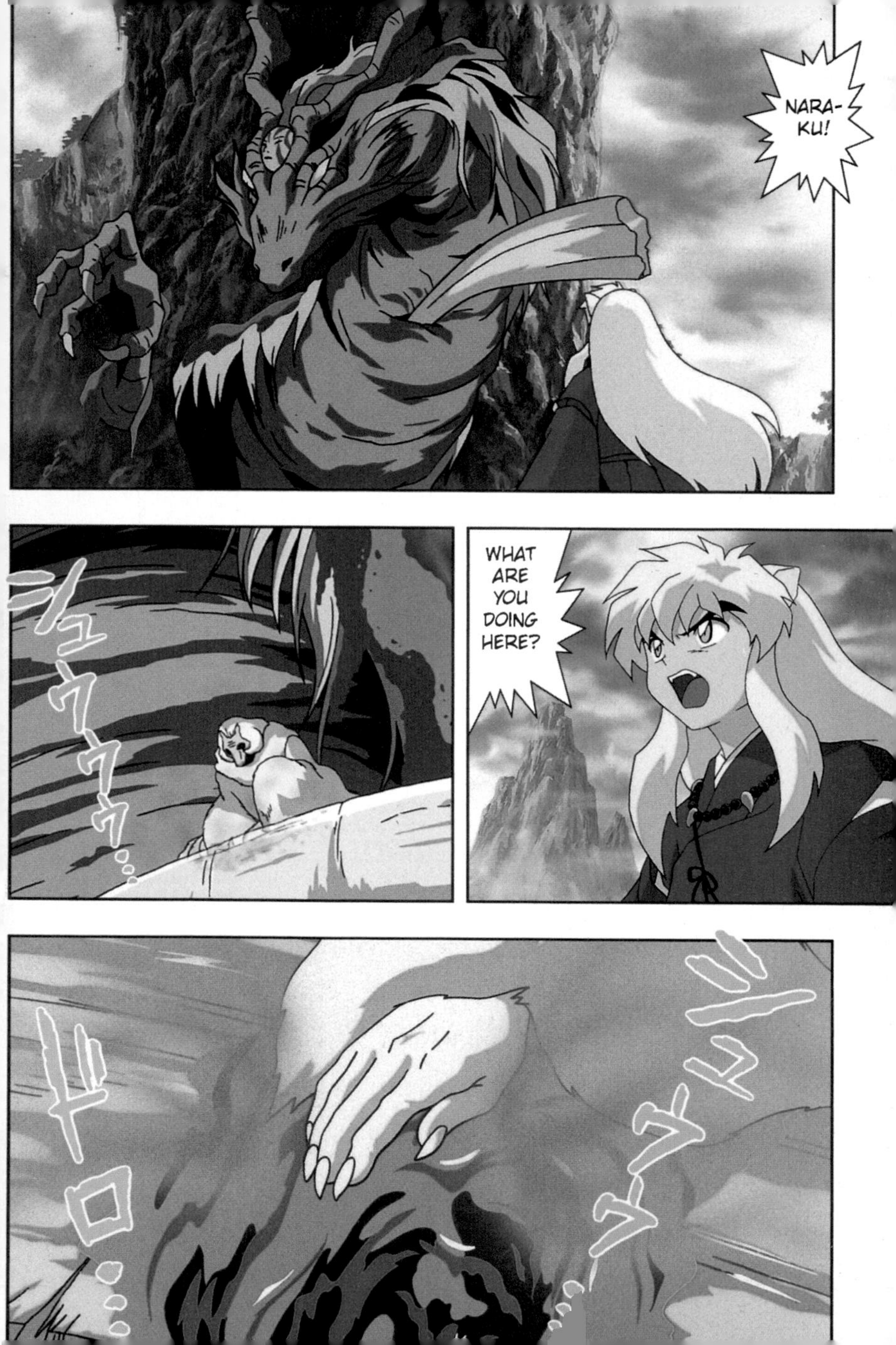
NARAKU!
WHAT ARE YOU DOING HERE?
シュウウウ…
ジュワァ…
ドロ…

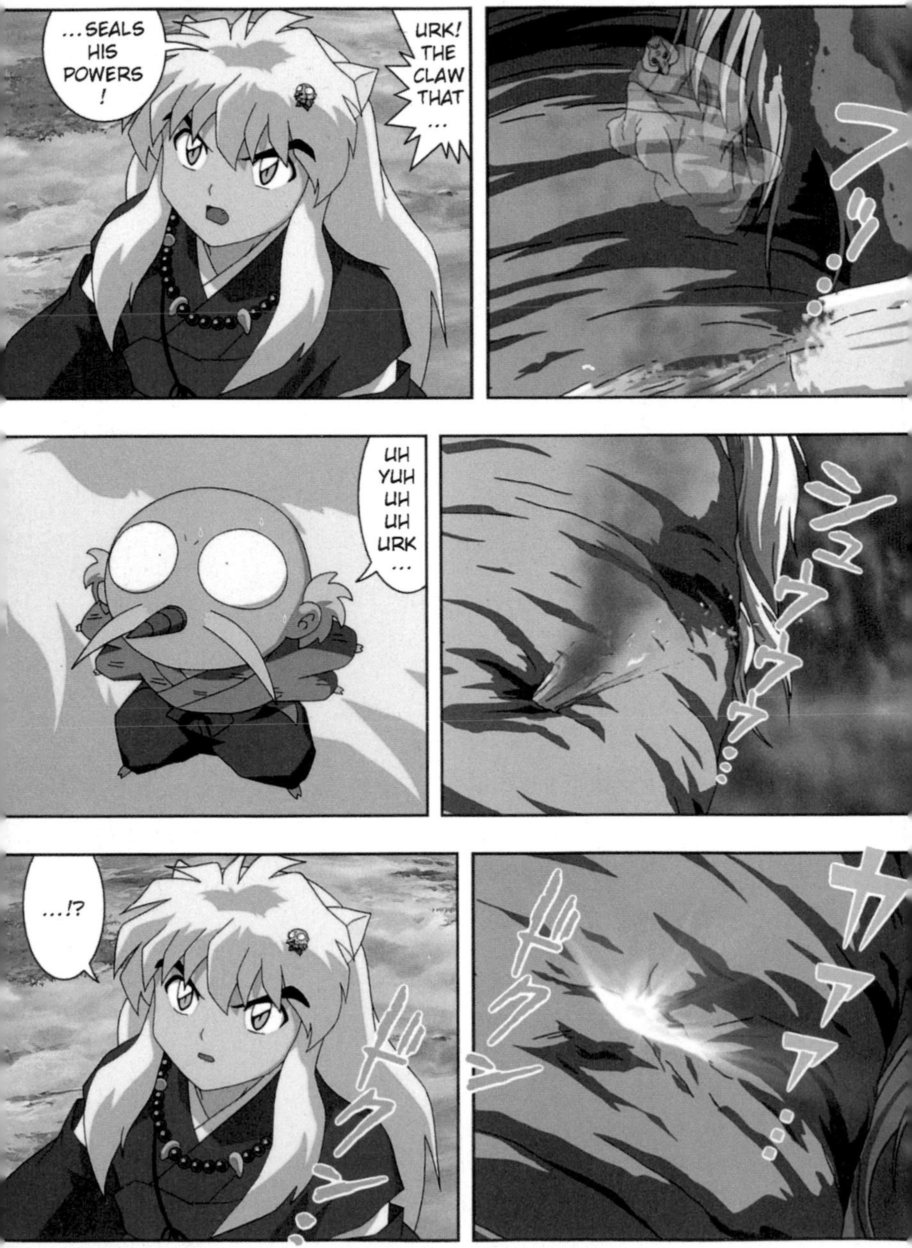
フッ…
URK! THE CLAW THAT ...
...SEALS HIS POWERS!
シュウウウウ…
UH YUH UH UH URK ...
ザァァァ…
ドクン
ドクン…
...!?

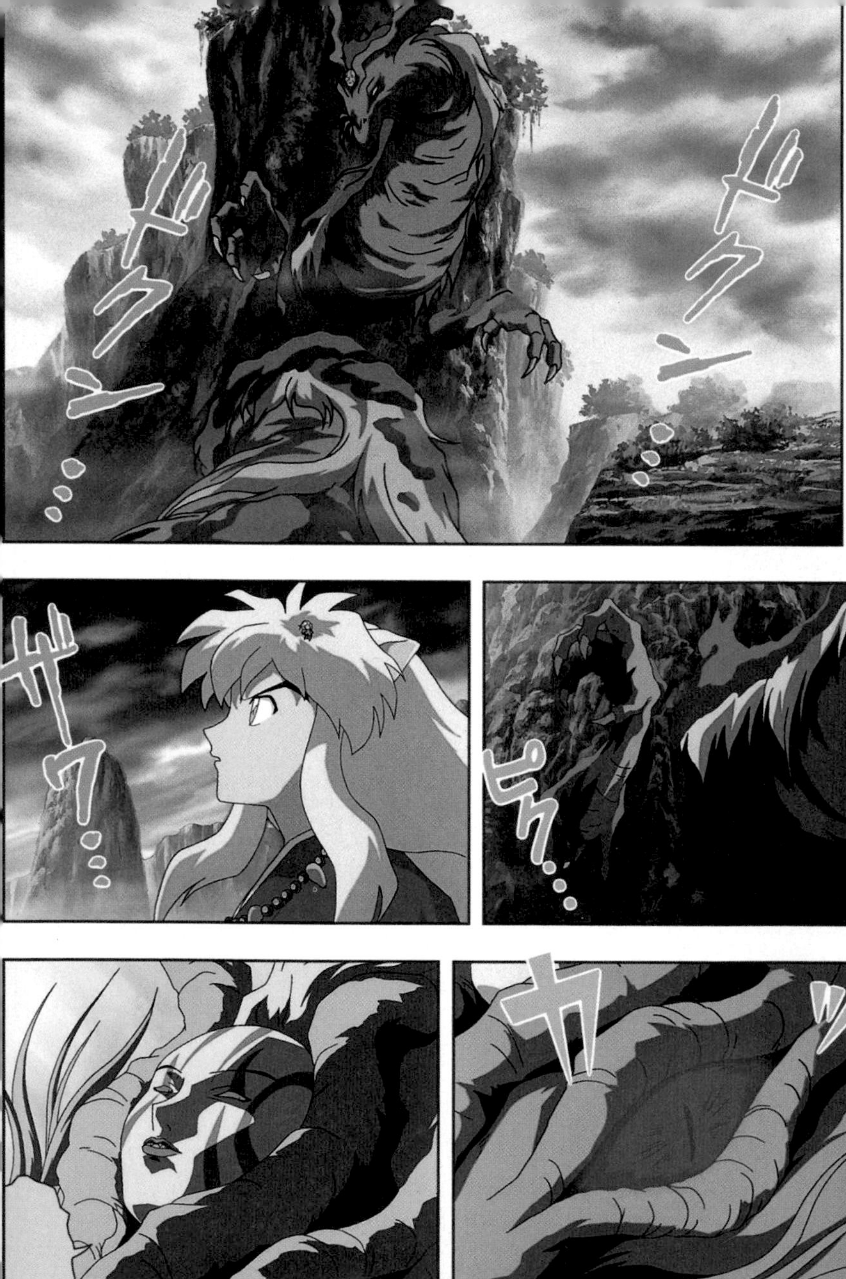
ドクン…
ドクン…
ピク…
ザワ…
カッ

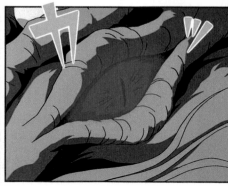

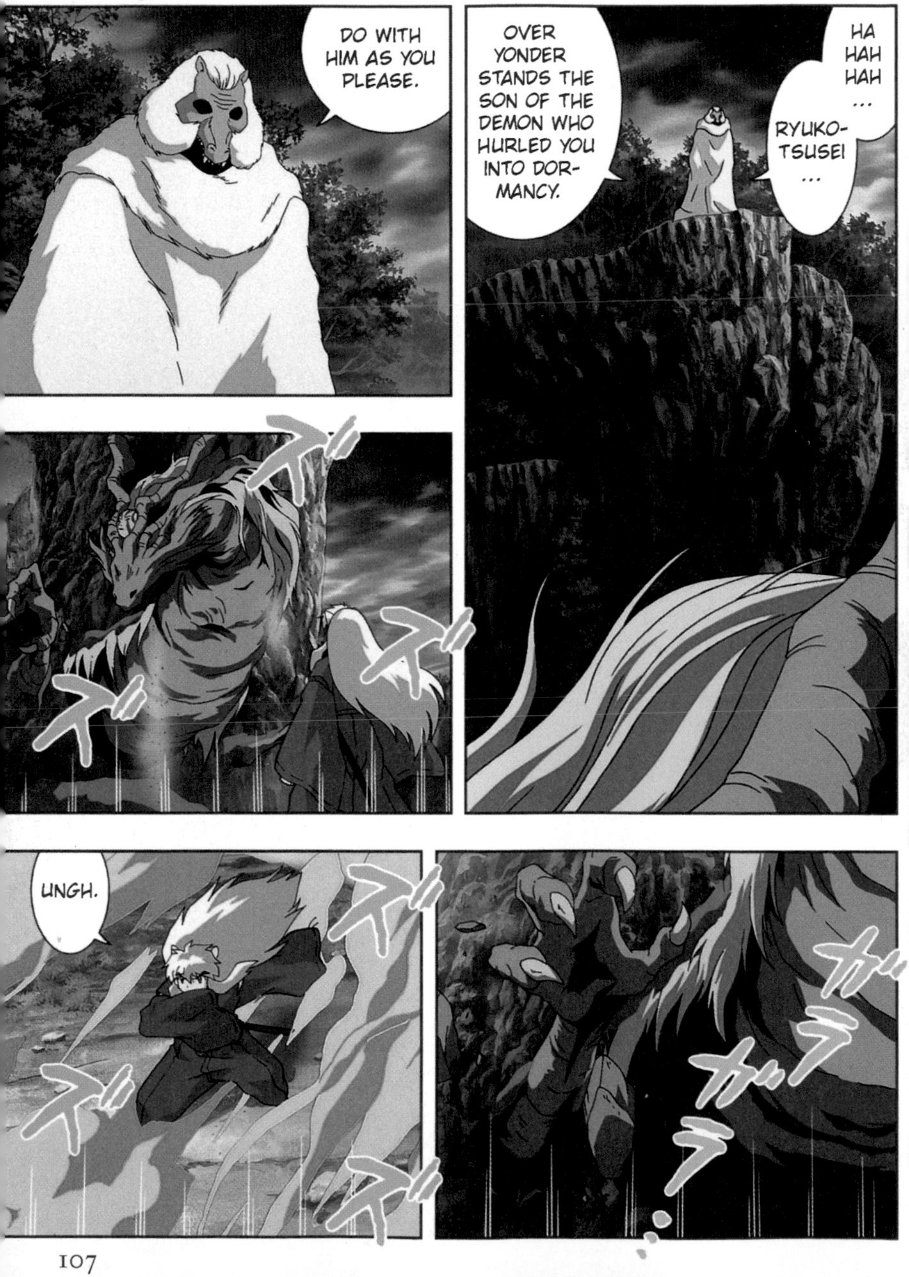
HA HAH HAH ...
RYUKO-TSUSEI ...
OVER YONDER STANDS THE SON OF THE DEMON WHO HURLED YOU INTO DORMANCY.
DO WITH HIM AS YOU PLEASE.
ズ
ズ
ズ
ガラ
ガラ
UNGH.
ズ
ズ
ズ

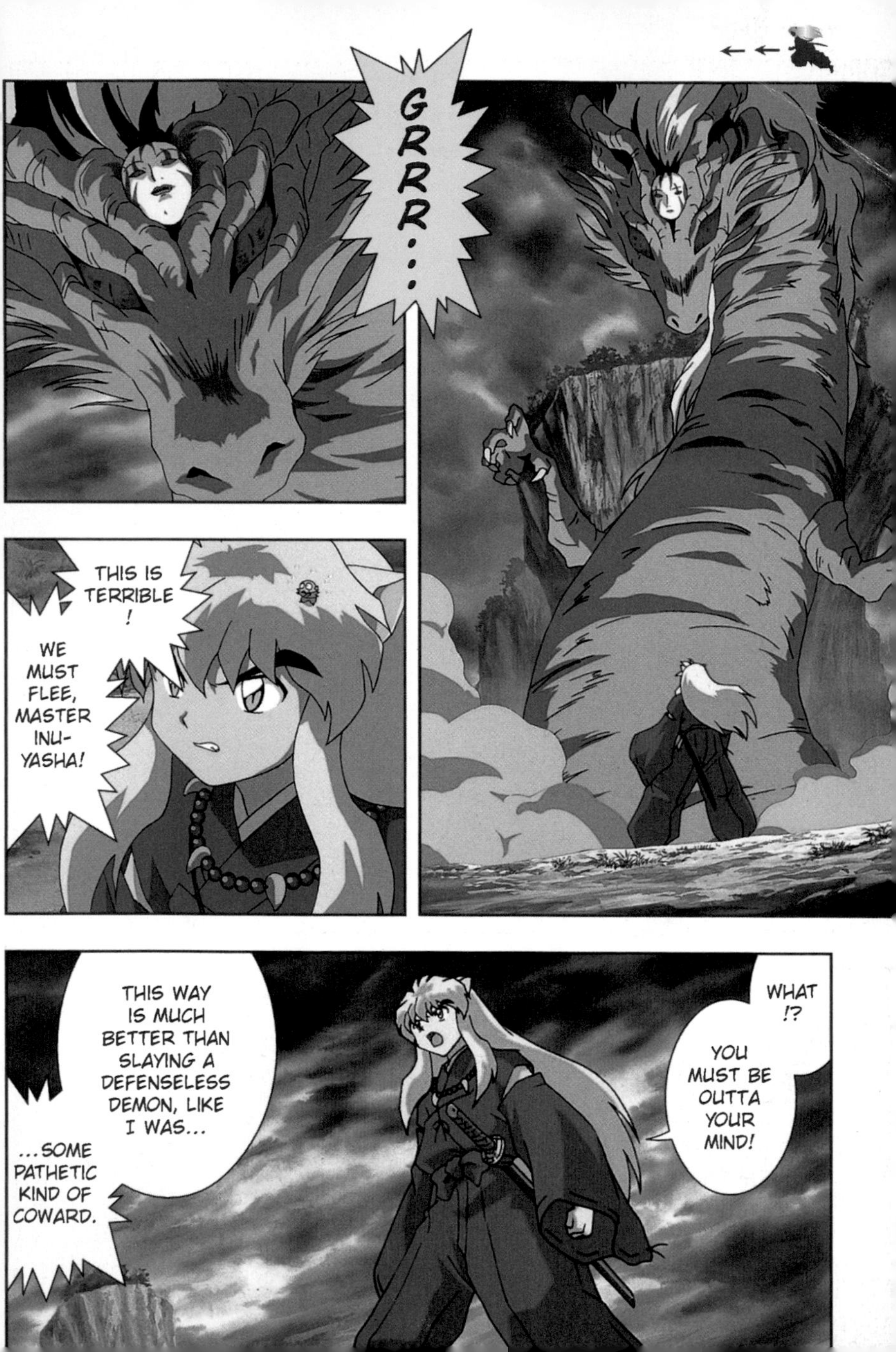
GRRR...
THIS IS TERRIBLE!
WE MUST FLEE, MASTER INU-YASHA!
WHAT!?
YOU MUST BE OUTTA YOUR MIND!
THIS WAY IS MUCH BETTER THAN SLAYING A DEFENSELESS DEMON, LIKE I WAS...
...SOME PATHETIC KIND OF COWARD.

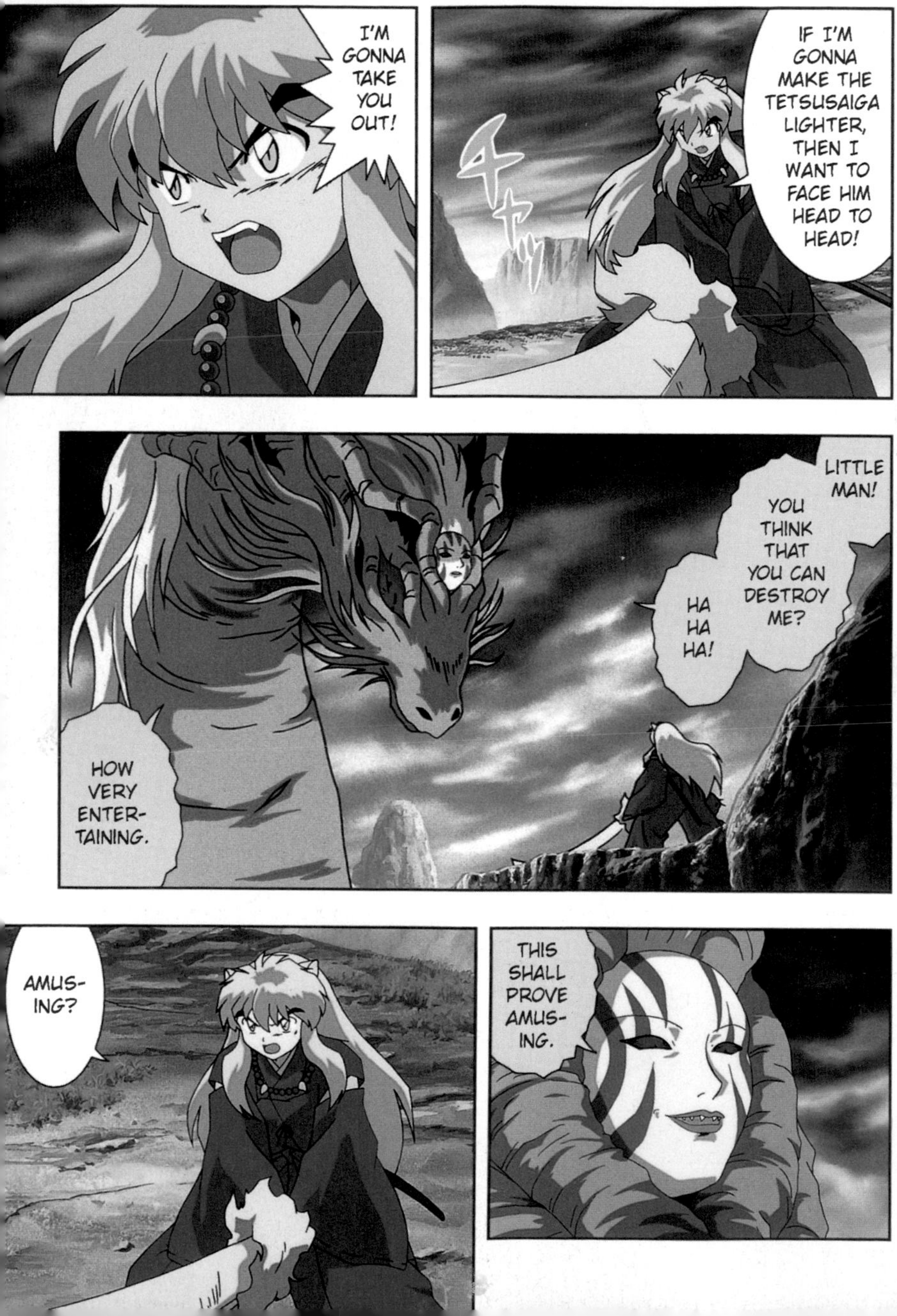
IF I'M GONNA MAKE THE TETSUSAIGA LIGHTER, THEN I WANT TO FACE HIM HEAD TO HEAD!
I'M GONNA TAKE YOU OUT!
LITTLE MAN!
YOU THINK THAT YOU CAN DESTROY ME?
HA HA HA!
HOW VERY ENTER-TAINING.
THIS SHALL PROVE AMUS-ING.
AMUS-ING?

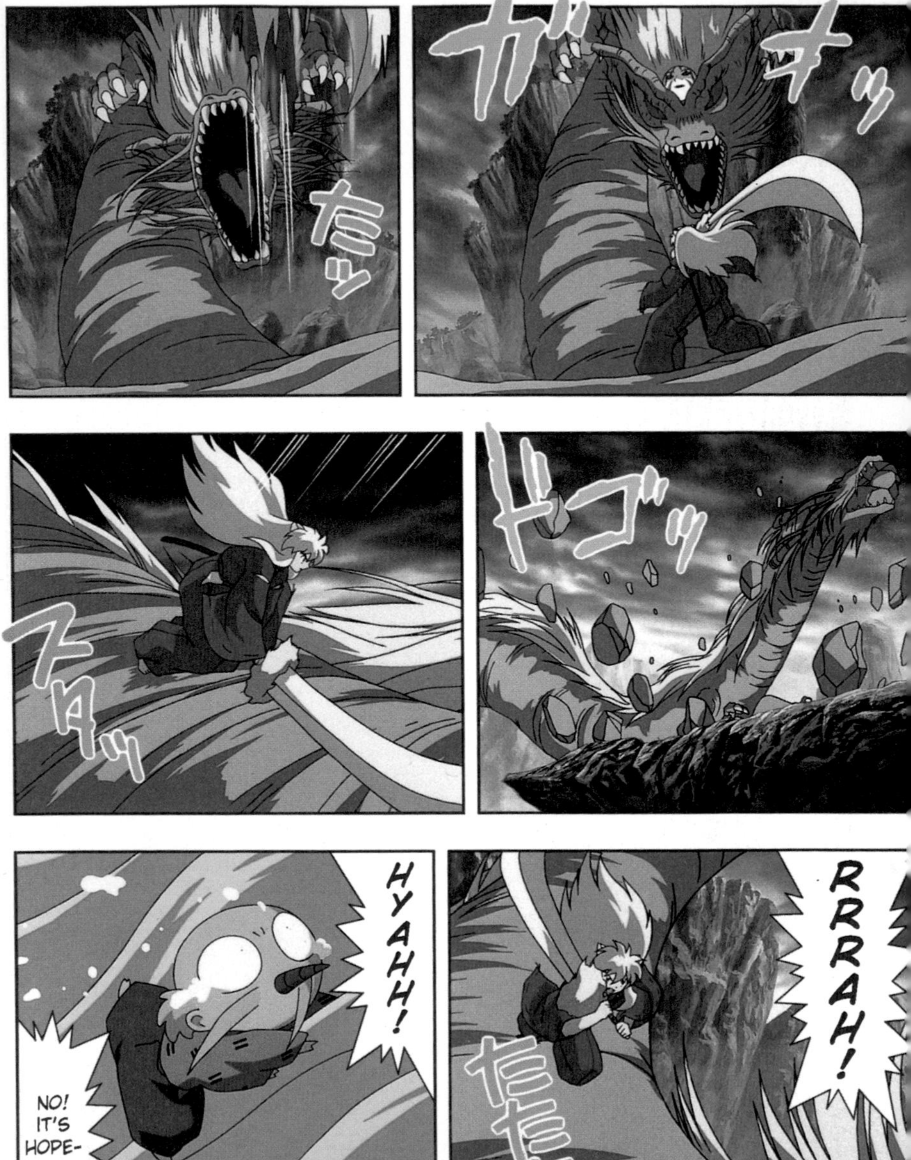

ガオッ
たッ
ドゴッ
スタッ
RRRAH!
たたた…
HYAHH!
NO! IT'S HOPE-LESS!

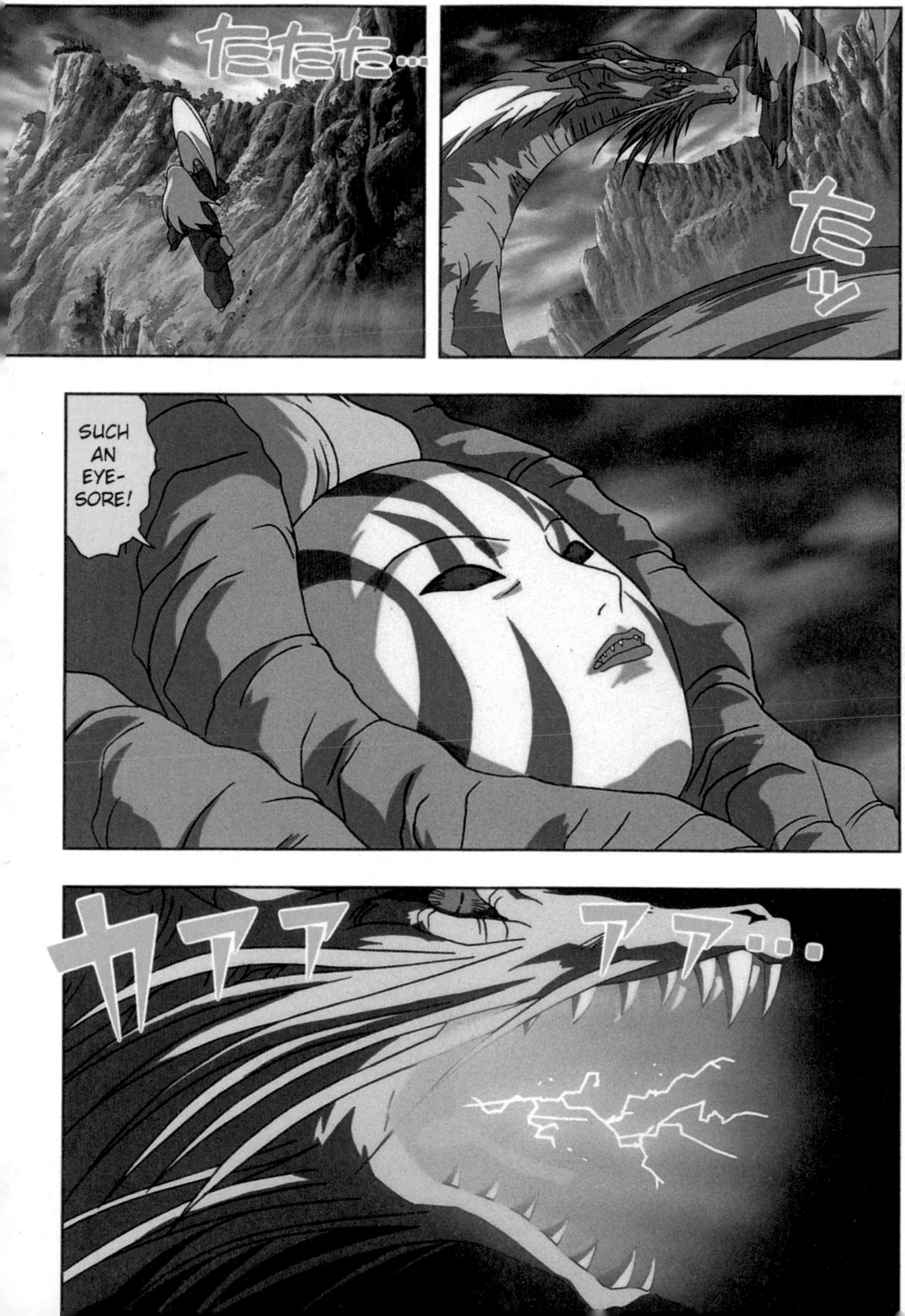
タッ
たたた…
SUCH AN EYE-SORE!
カァァァァ…

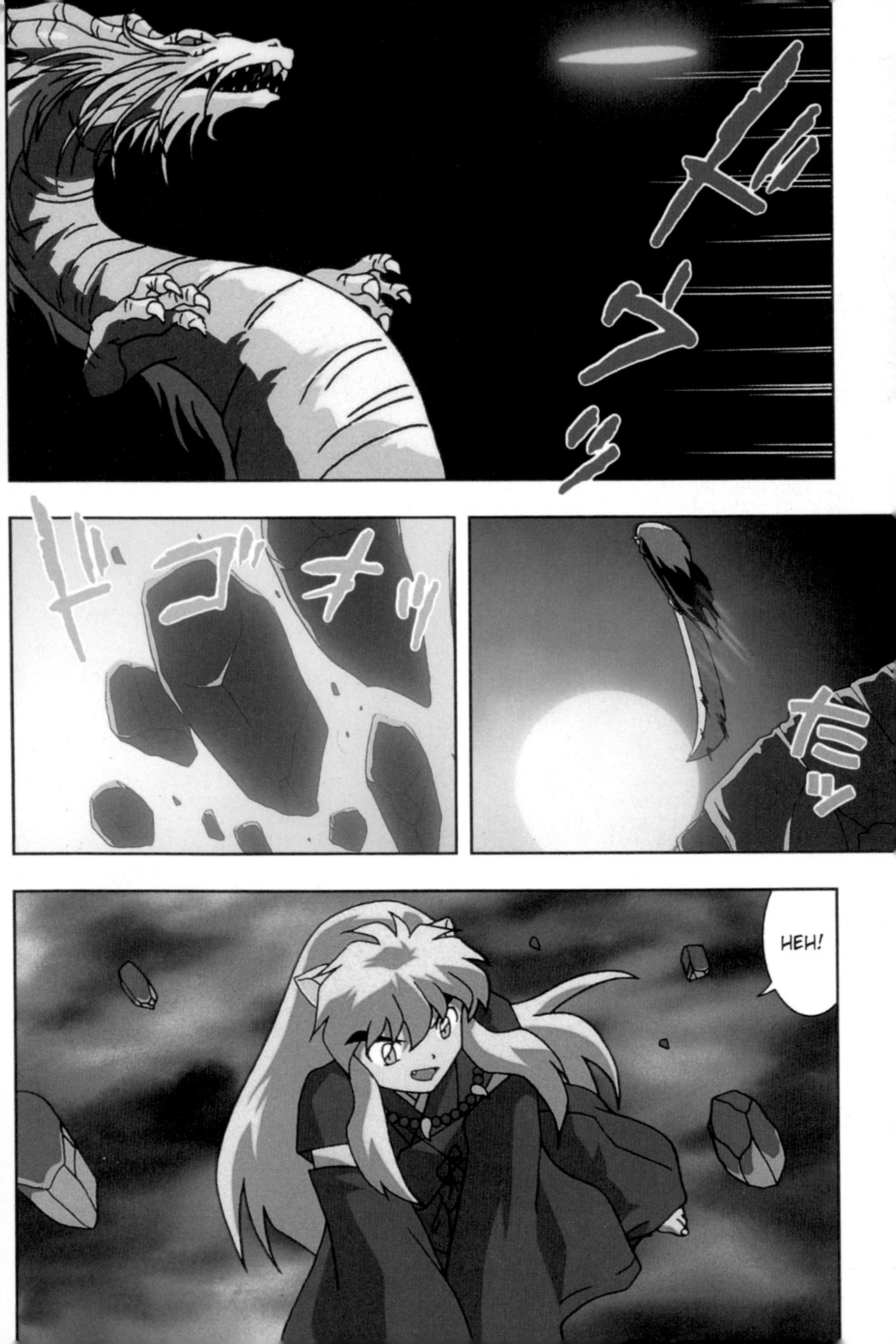
ドゴォッ
HEH!

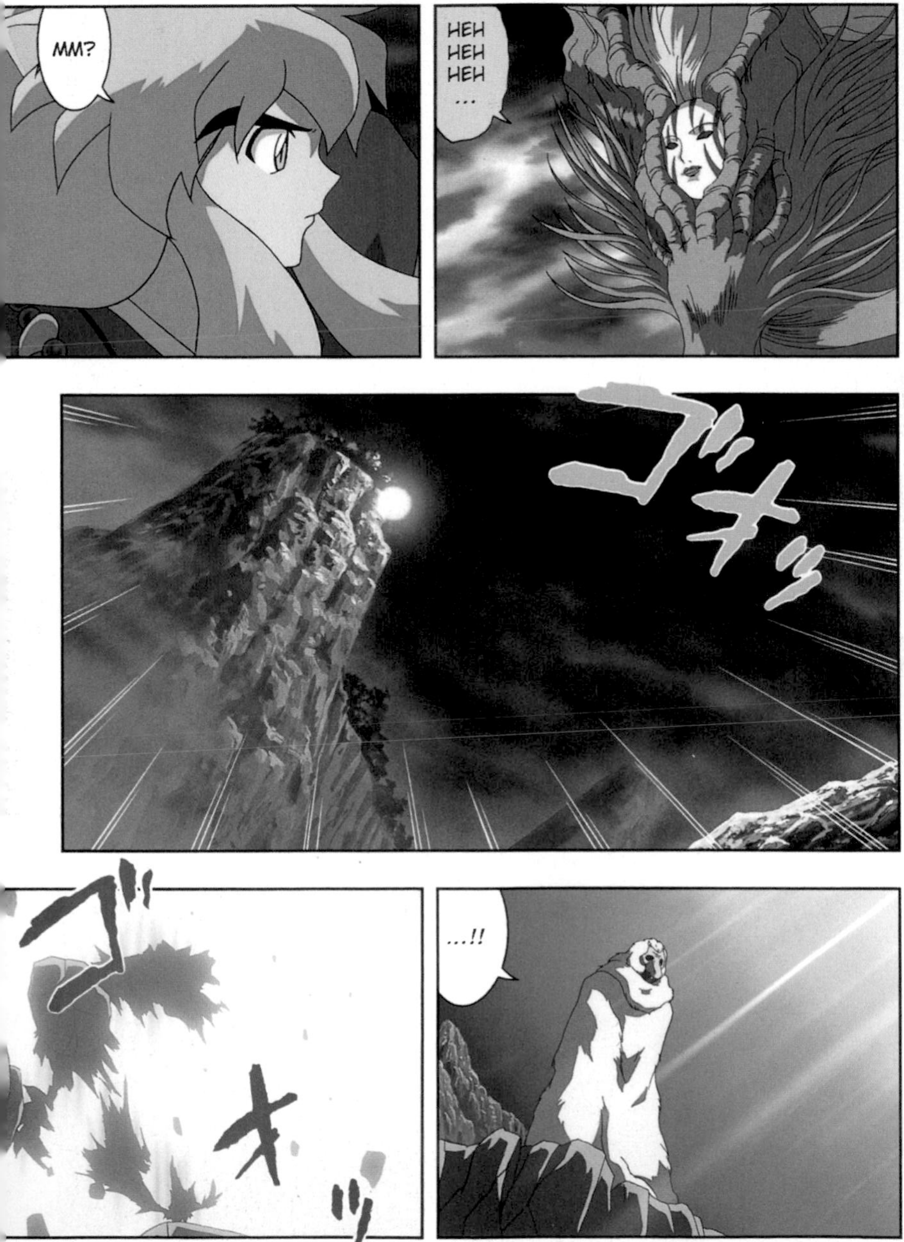
HEH HEH HEH ...
MM?
ゴキッ
...!!
ゴキッ

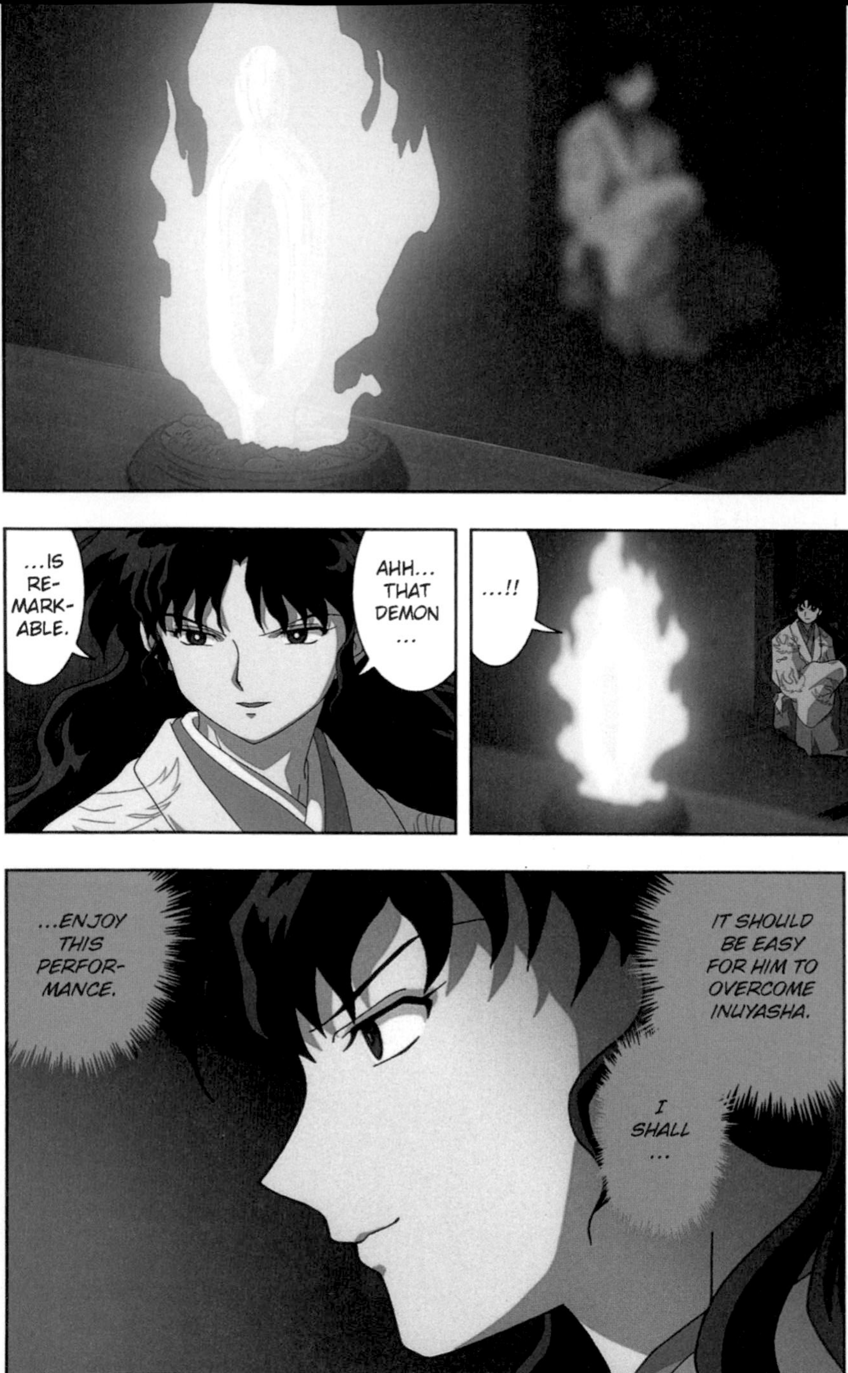
...!!
AHH... THAT DEMON...
...IS RE-MARK-ABLE.
IT SHOULD BE EASY FOR HIM TO OVERCOME INUYASHA.
I SHALL...
...ENJOY THIS PERFOR-MANCE.

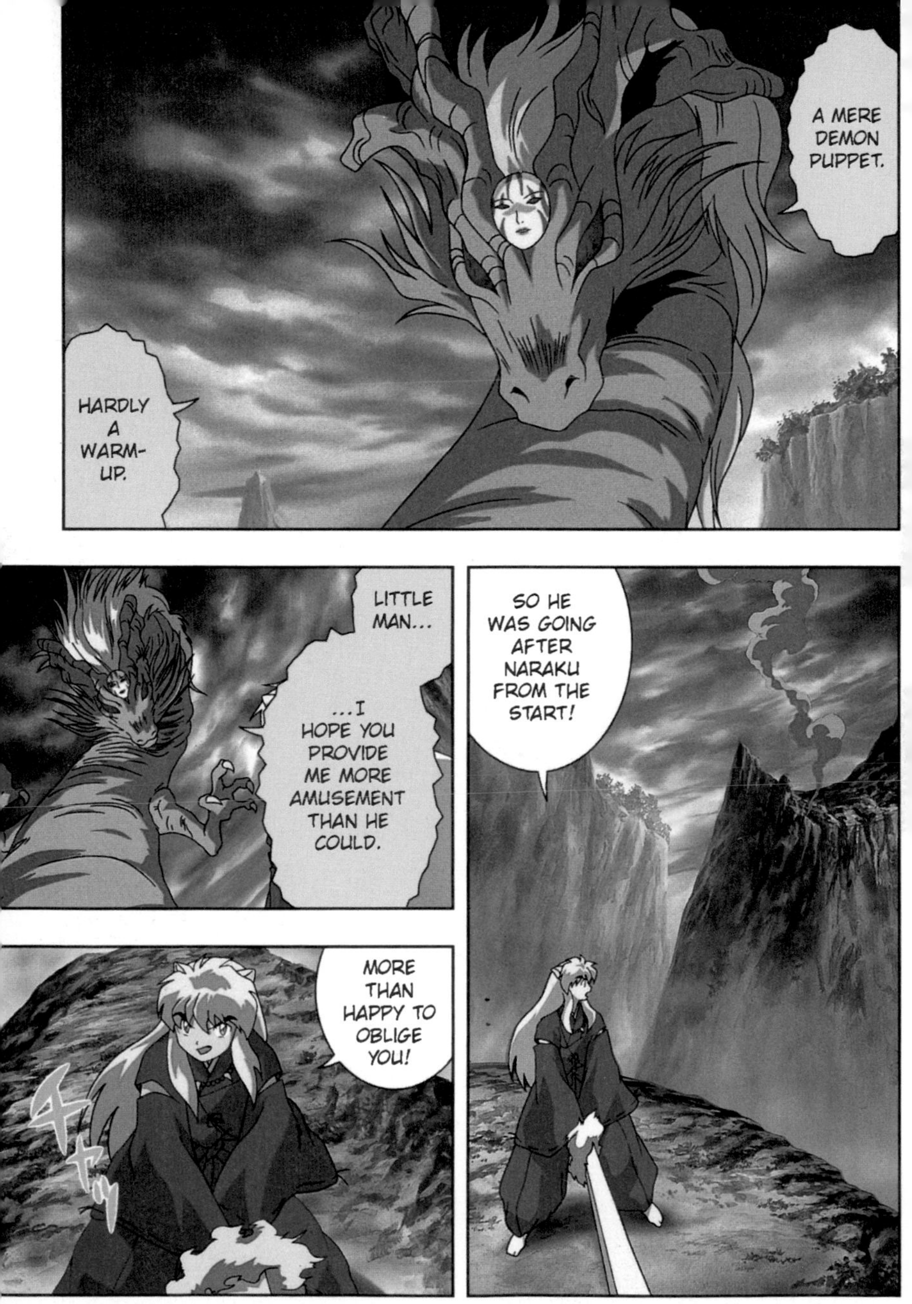
A MERE DEMON PUPPET.
HARDLY A WARM-UP.
SO HE WAS GOING AFTER NARAKU FROM THE START!
LITTLE MAN...
...I HOPE YOU PROVIDE ME MORE AMUSEMENT THAN HE COULD.
MORE THAN HAPPY TO OBLIGE YOU!

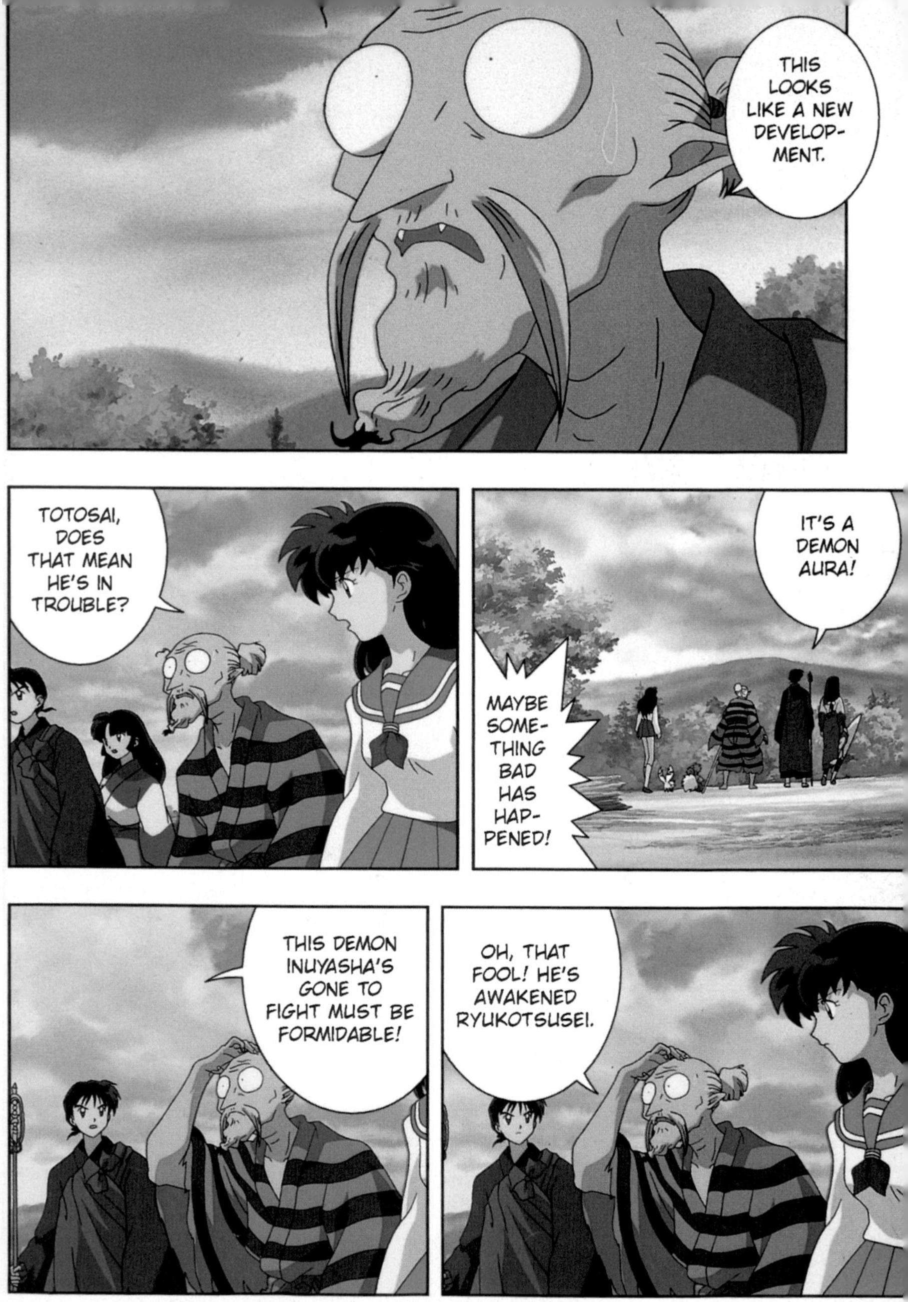
THIS LOOKS LIKE A NEW DEVELOP-MENT.
TOTOSAI, DOES THAT MEAN HE'S IN TROUBLE?
IT'S A DEMON AURA!
MAYBE SOME-THING BAD HAS HAP-PENED!
THIS DEMON INUYASHA'S GONE TO FIGHT MUST BE FORMIDABLE!
OH, THAT FOOL! HE'S AWAKENED RYUKOTSUSEI.

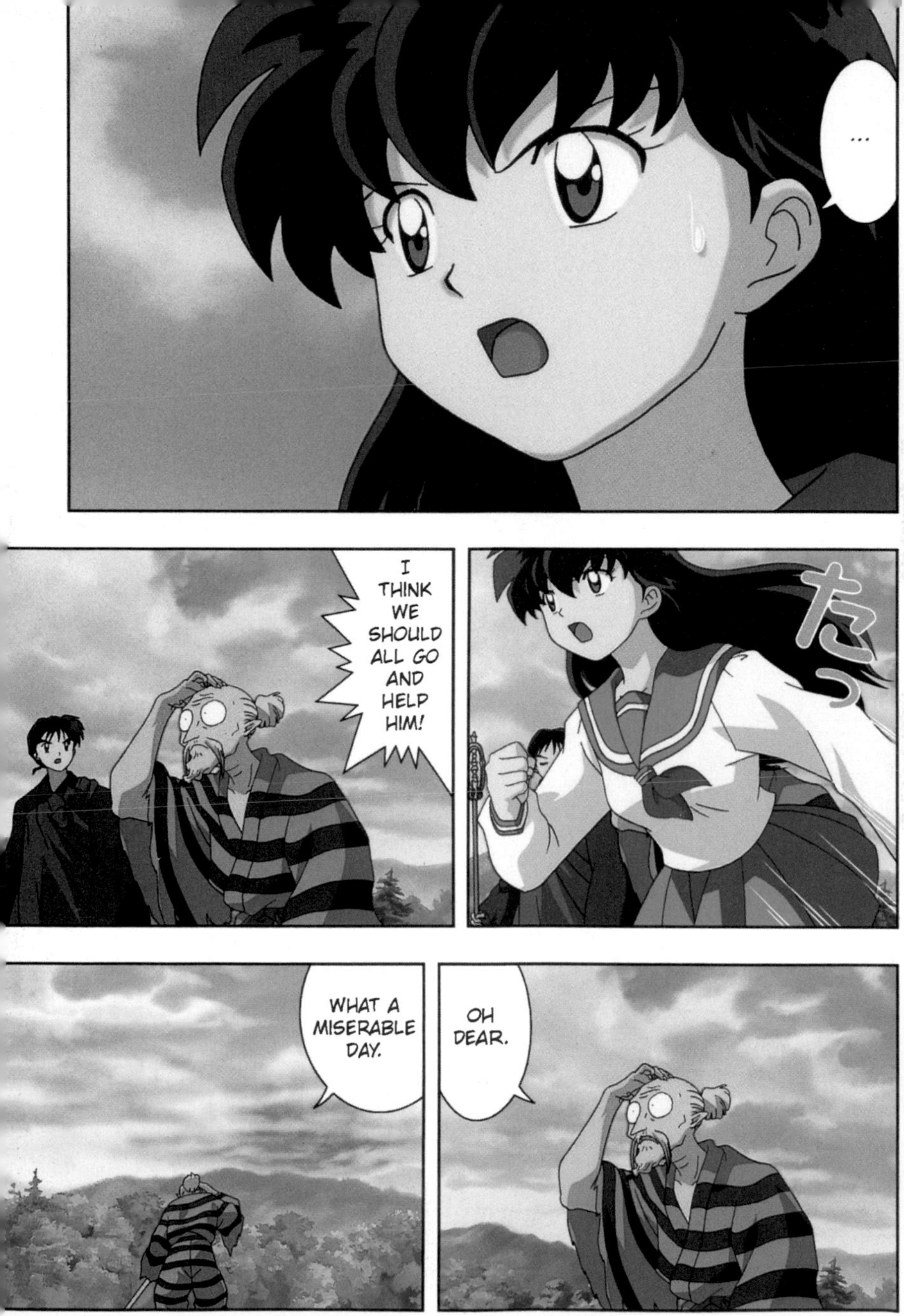
...
たっ
I THINK WE SHOULD ALL GO AND HELP HIM!
OH DEAR.
WHAT A MISERABLE DAY.

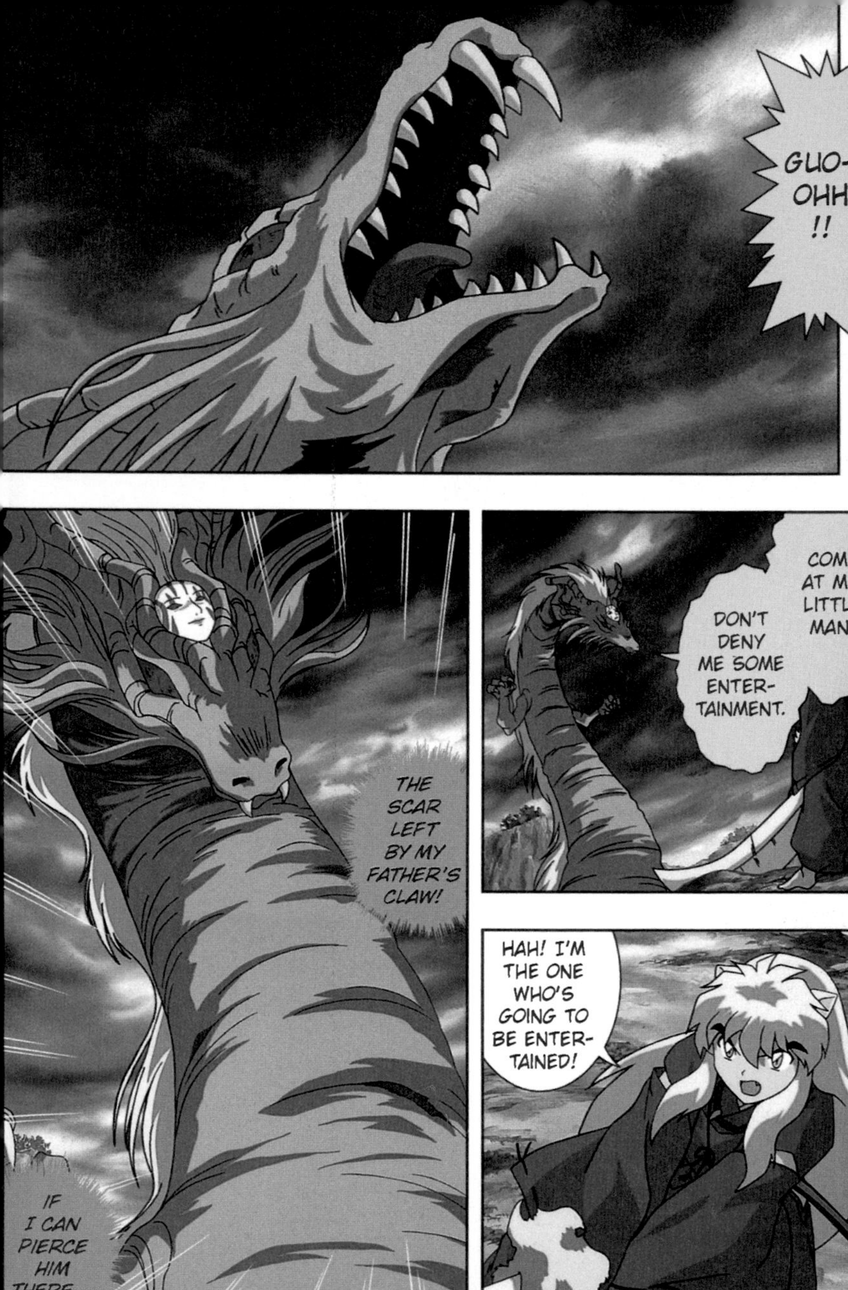
GUO-OHH!!
COME AT ME, LITTLE MAN!
DON'T DENY ME SOME ENTER-TAINMENT.
HAH! I'M THE ONE WHO'S GOING TO BE ENTER-TAINED!
THE SCAR LEFT BY MY FATHER'S CLAW!
IF I CAN PIERCE HIM THERE...

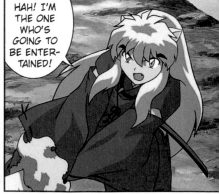

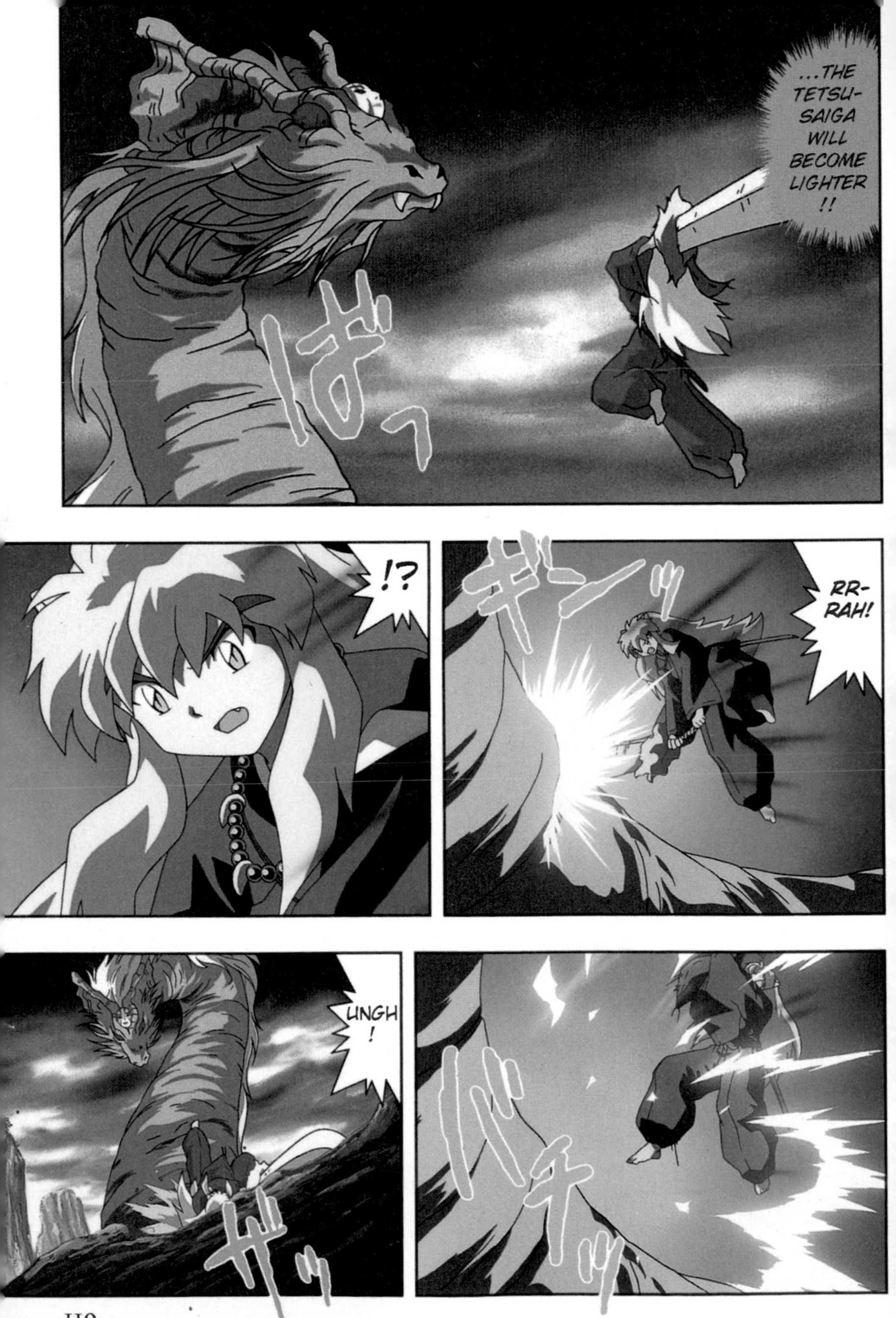
...THE TETSU-SAIGA WILL BECOME LIGHTER !!
ばっ
ギーンッ
RR-RAH!
!?
バチッ
UNGH !
ザッ

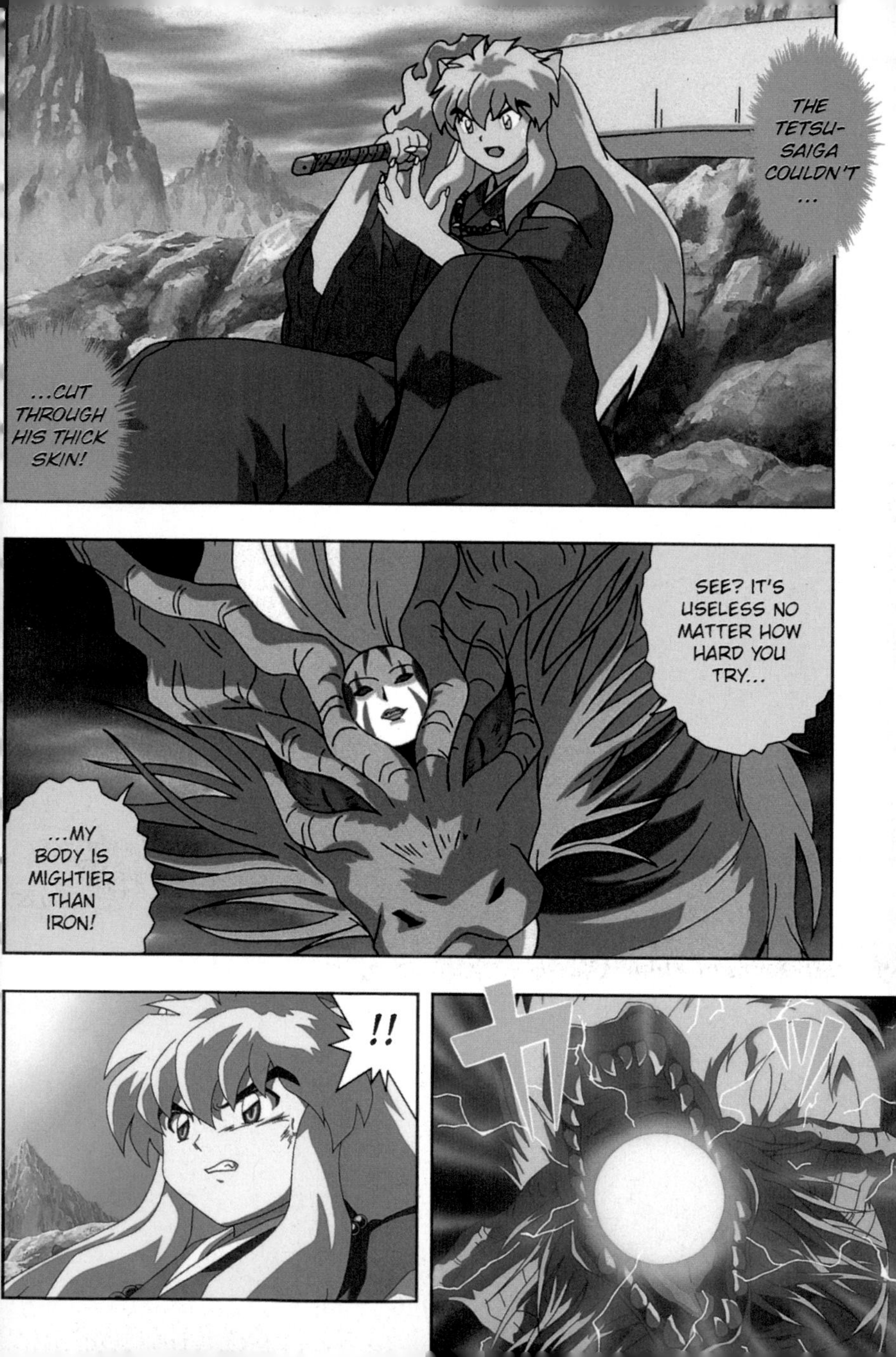
THE TETSU-SAIGA COULDN'T ...
...CUT THROUGH HIS THICK SKIN!
SEE? IT'S USELESS NO MATTER HOW HARD YOU TRY...
...MY BODY IS MIGHTIER THAN IRON!
カッ
!!

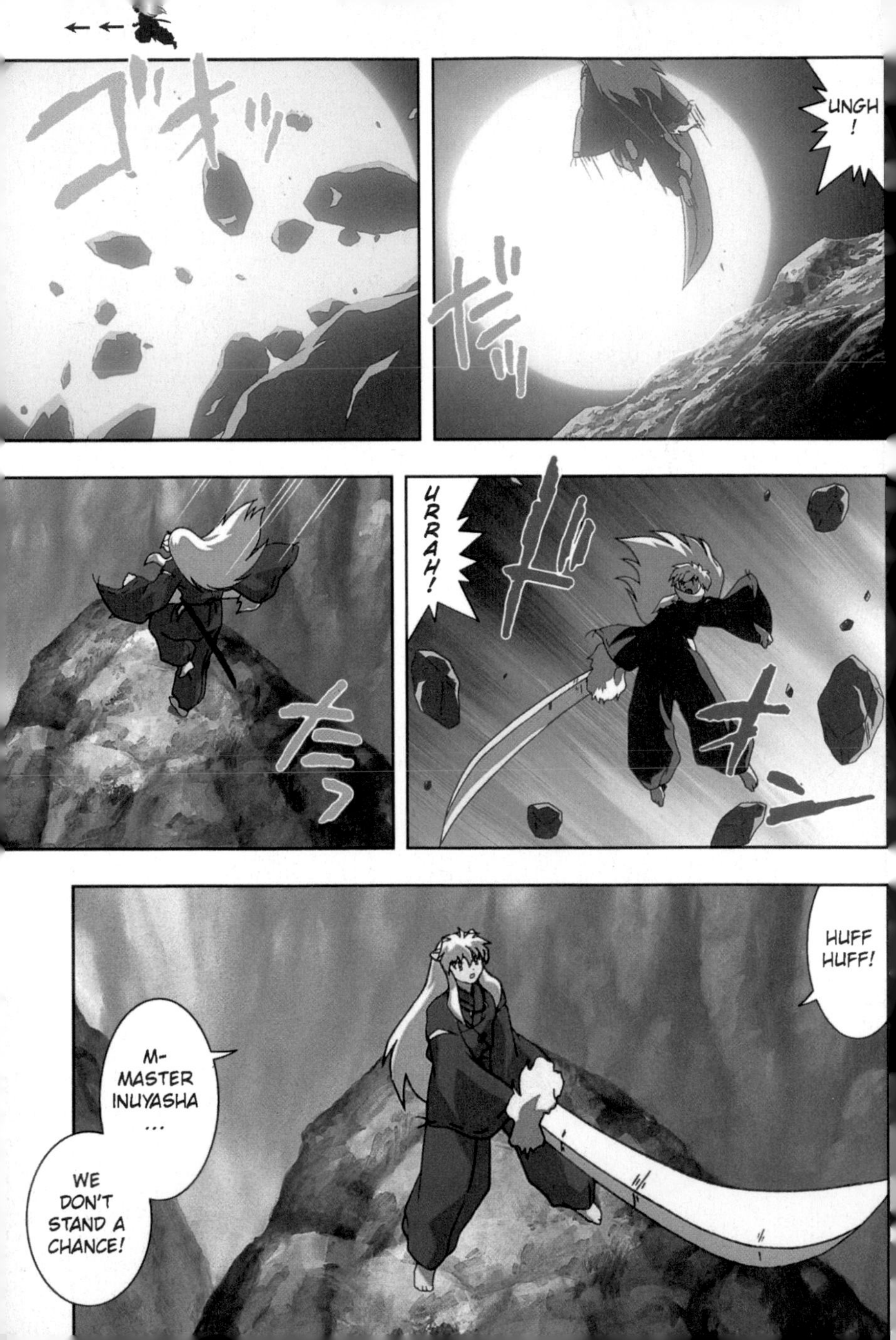
UNGH!
URRAH!
HUFF HUFF!
M-MASTER INUYASHA...
WE DON'T STAND A CHANCE!

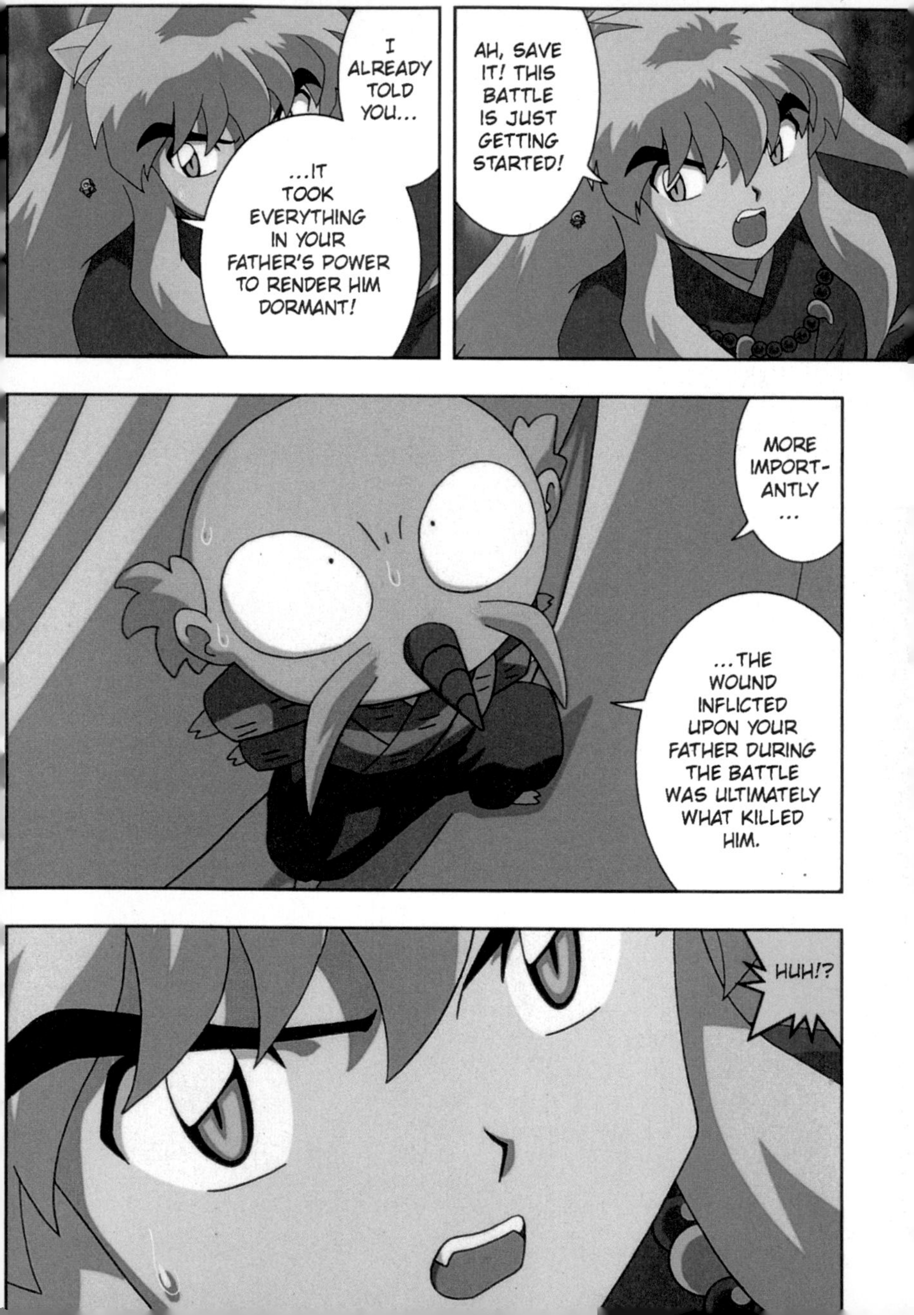
AH, SAVE IT! THIS BATTLE IS JUST GETTING STARTED!
I ALREADY TOLD YOU...
...IT TOOK EVERYTHING IN YOUR FATHER'S POWER TO RENDER HIM DORMANT!
MORE IMPORT-ANTLY...
...THE WOUND INFLICTED UPON YOUR FATHER DURING THE BATTLE WAS ULTIMATELY WHAT KILLED HIM.
HUH!?

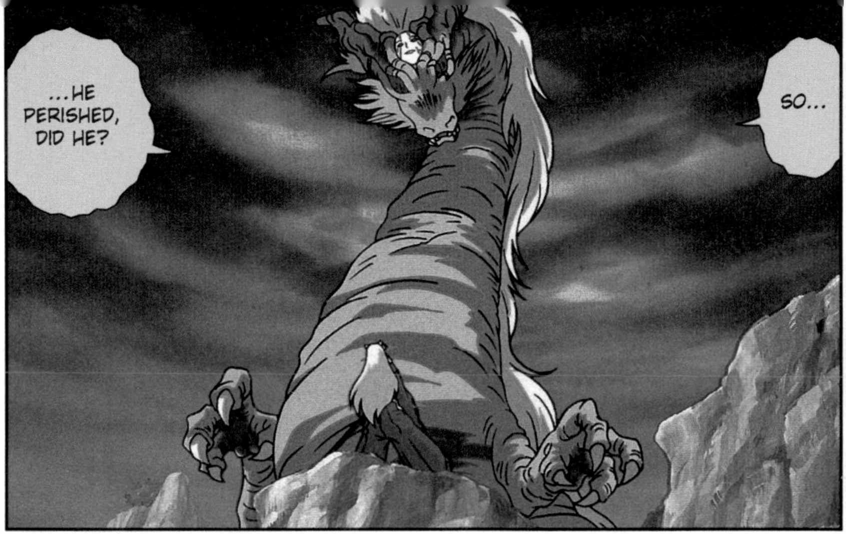
SO...
...HE PERISHED, DID HE?

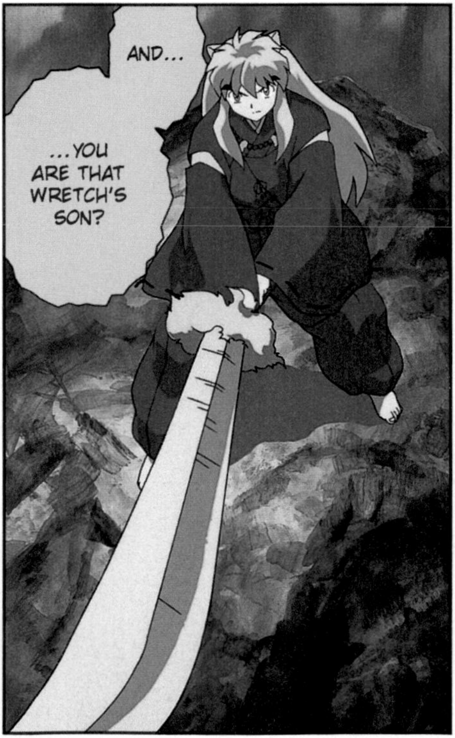
AND...
...YOU ARE THAT WRETCH'S SON?

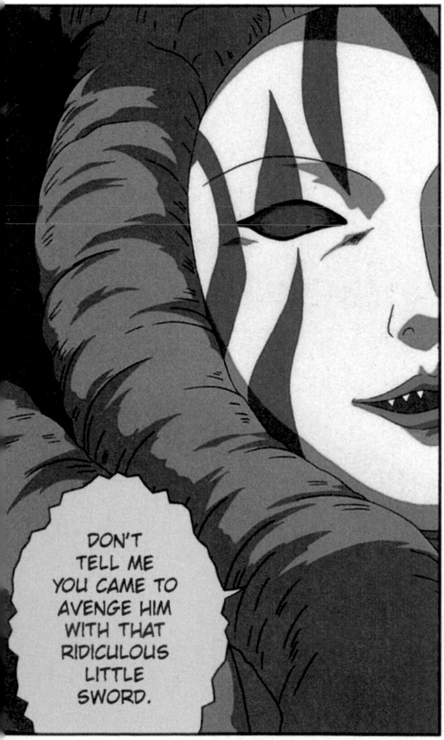
DON'T TELL ME YOU CAME TO AVENGE HIM WITH THAT RIDICULOUS LITTLE SWORD.

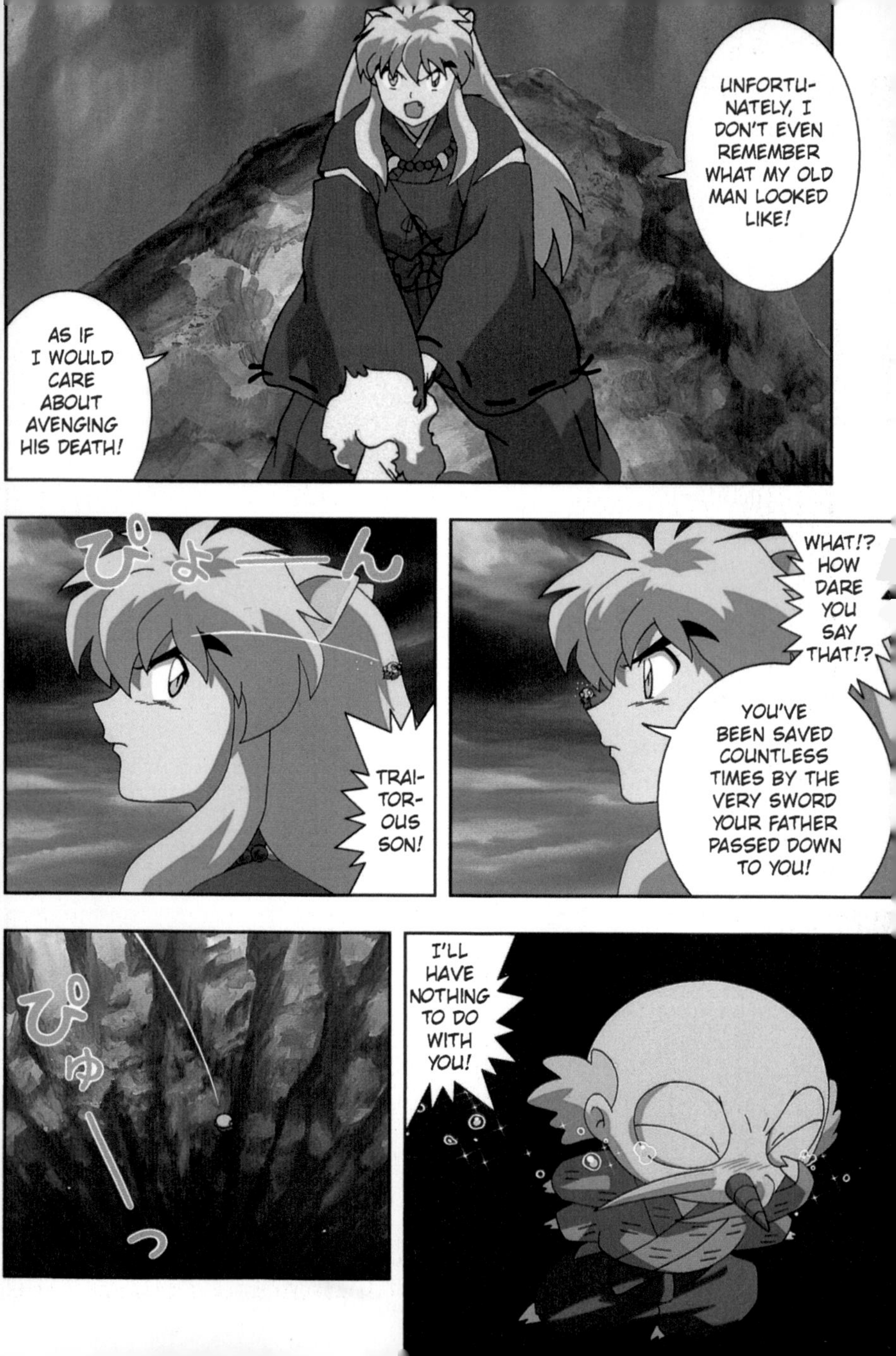
UNFORTU-NATELY, I DON'T EVEN REMEMBER WHAT MY OLD MAN LOOKED LIKE!
AS IF I WOULD CARE ABOUT AVENGING HIS DEATH!
WHAT!? HOW DARE YOU SAY THAT!?
YOU'VE BEEN SAVED COUNTLESS TIMES BY THE VERY SWORD YOUR FATHER PASSED DOWN TO YOU!
ぴょーーん
TRAI-TOR-OUS SON!
I'LL HAVE NOTHING TO DO WITH YOU!
ぴゅーっ

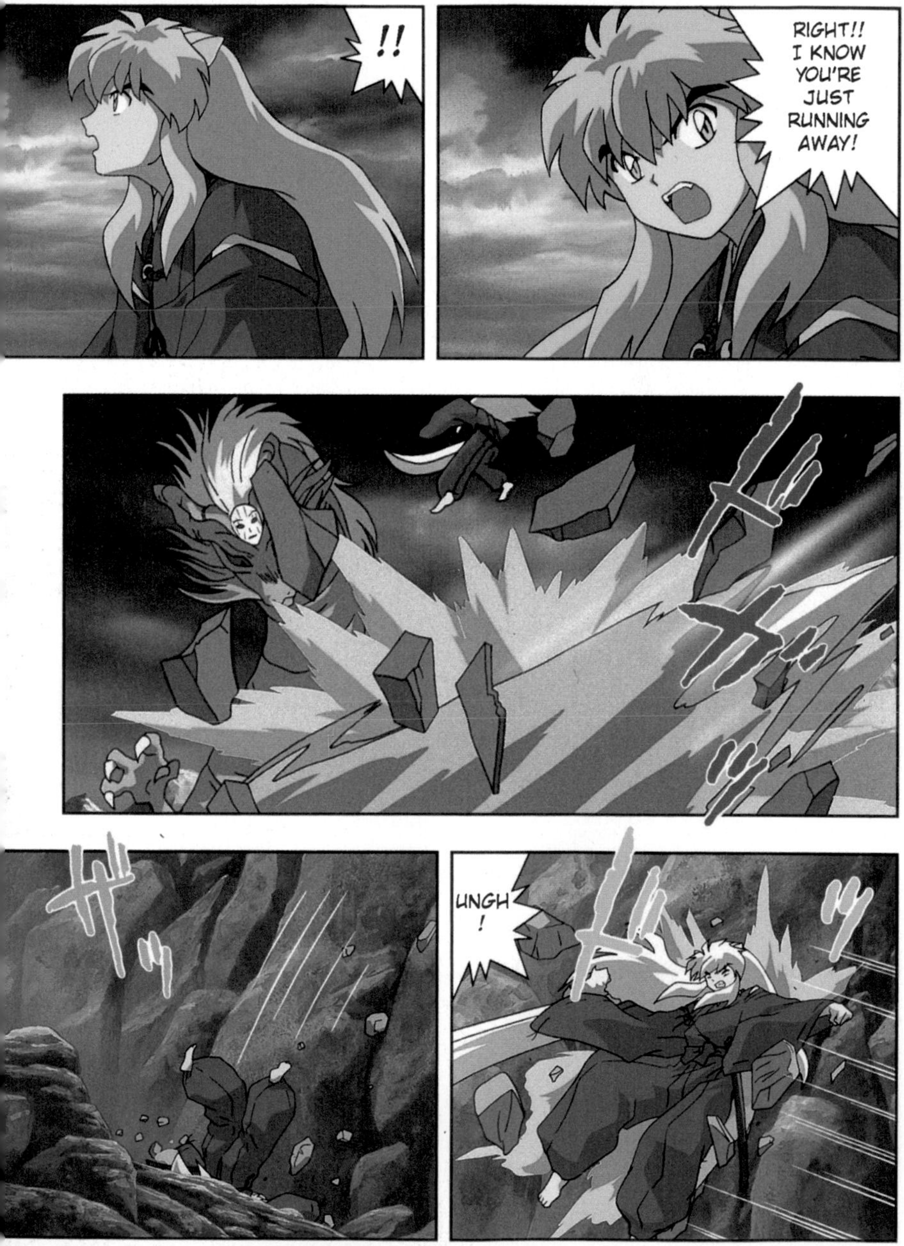
RIGHT!! I KNOW YOU'RE JUST RUNNING AWAY!
!!
UNGH!

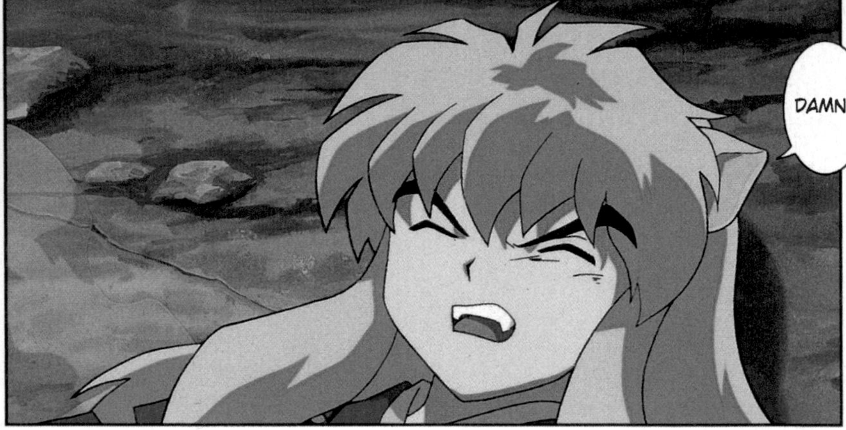
DAMN!
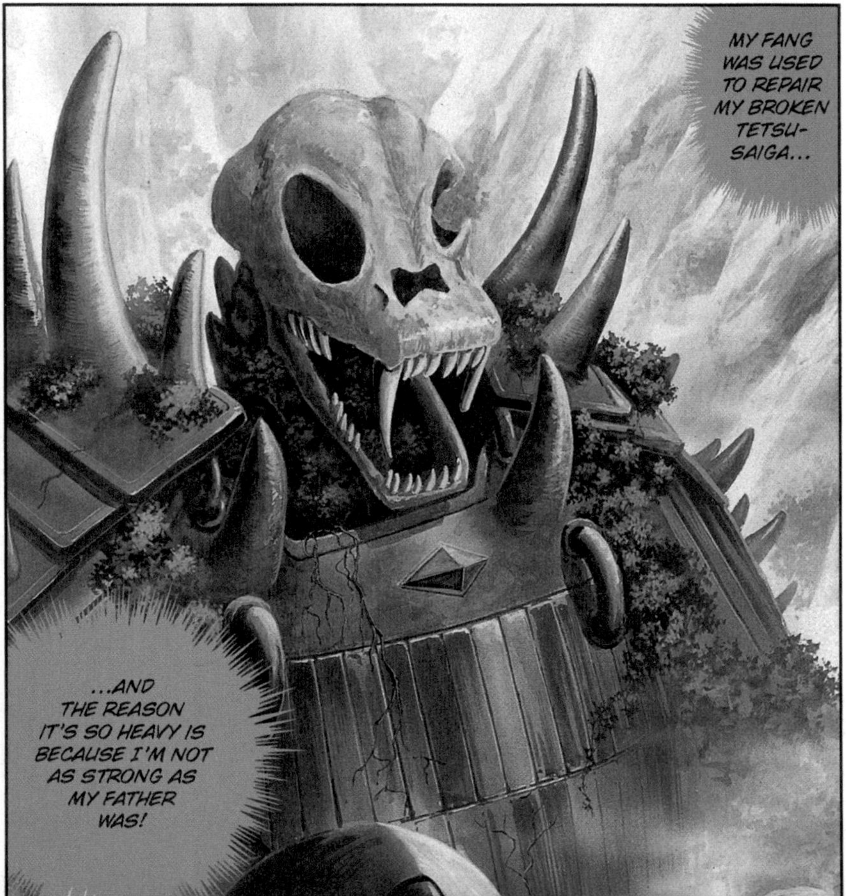
MY FANG WAS USED TO REPAIR MY BROKEN TETSU-SAIGA...
...AND THE REASON IT'S SO HEAVY IS BECAUSE I'M NOT AS STRONG AS MY FATHER WAS!

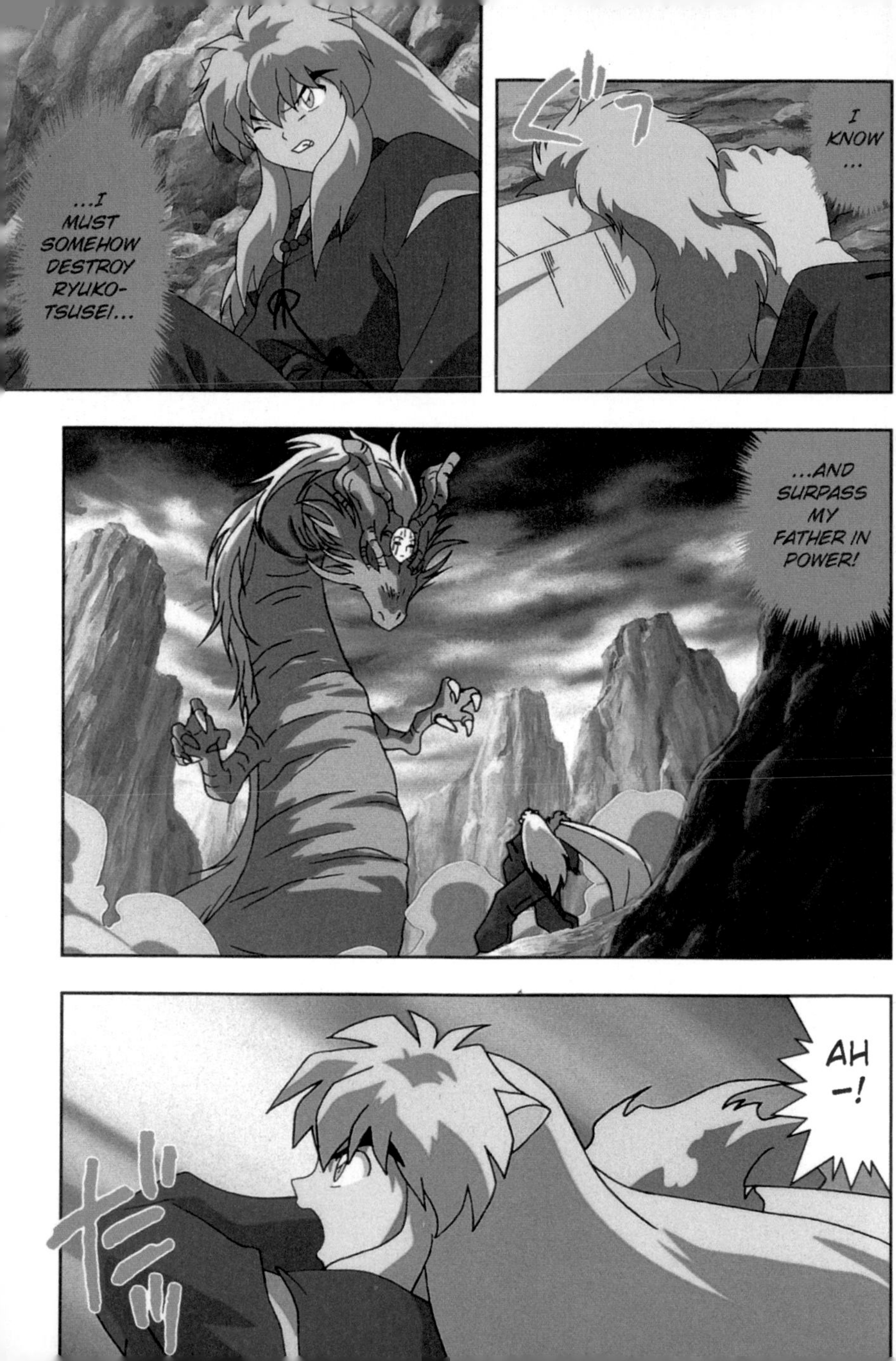
I KNOW ...
...I MUST SOMEHOW DESTROY RYUKO-TSUSEI...
...AND SURPASS MY FATHER IN POWER!
AH —!

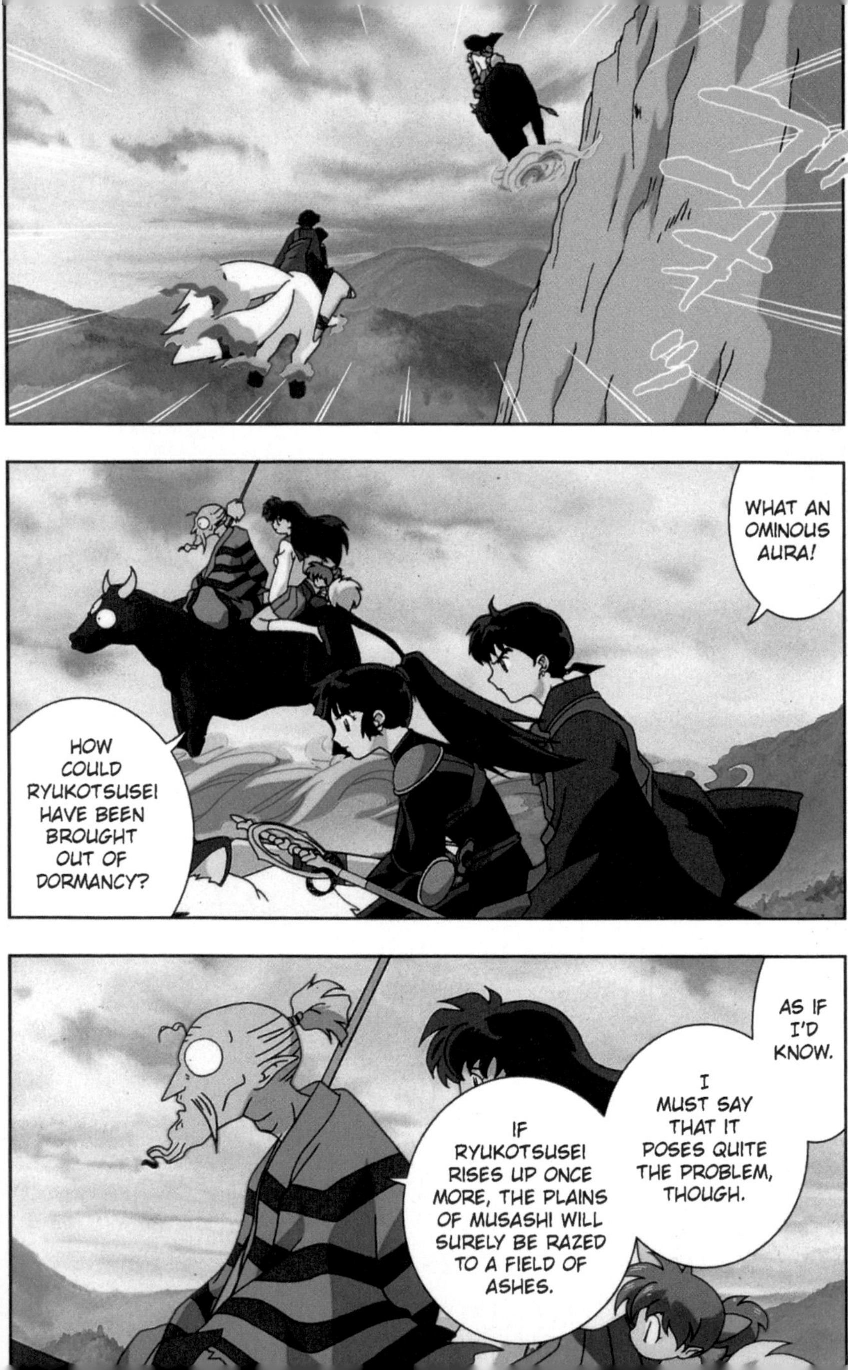
WHAT AN OMINOUS AURA!
HOW COULD RYUKOTSUSEI HAVE BEEN BROUGHT OUT OF DORMANCY?
AS IF I'D KNOW.
I MUST SAY THAT IT POSES QUITE THE PROBLEM, THOUGH.
IF RYUKOTSUSEI RISES UP ONCE MORE, THE PLAINS OF MUSASHI WILL SURELY BE RAZED TO A FIELD OF ASHES.

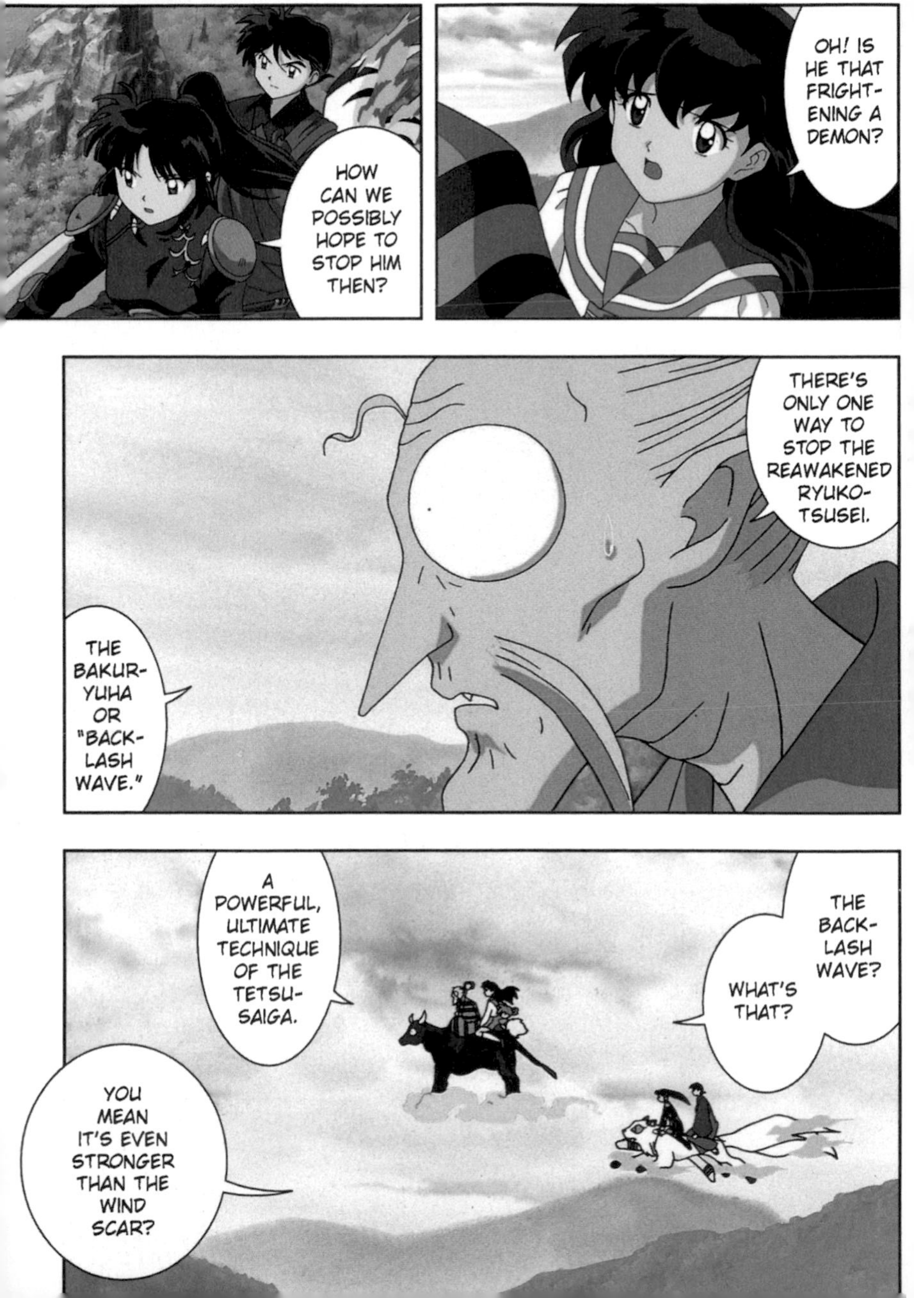
OH! IS HE THAT FRIGHTENING A DEMON?
HOW CAN WE POSSIBLY HOPE TO STOP HIM THEN?
THERE'S ONLY ONE WAY TO STOP THE REAWAKENED RYUKOTSUSEI.
THE BAKURYUHA OR "BACKLASH WAVE."
THE BACKLASH WAVE?
WHAT'S THAT?
A POWERFUL, ULTIMATE TECHNIQUE OF THE TETSUSAIGA.
YOU MEAN IT'S EVEN STRONGER THAN THE WIND SCAR?

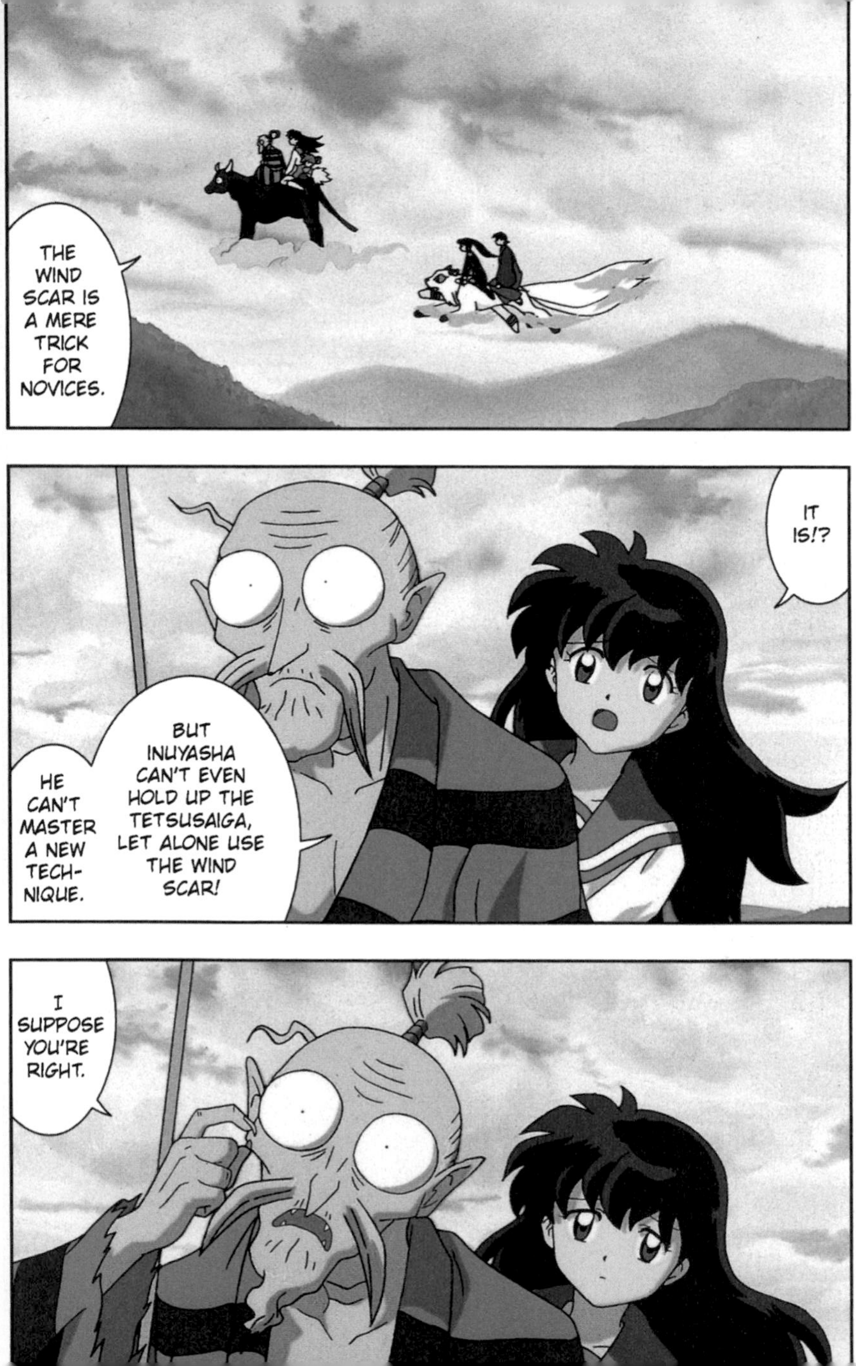
THE WIND SCAR IS A MERE TRICK FOR NOVICES.
IT IS!?
BUT INUYASHA CAN'T EVEN HOLD UP THE TETSUSAIGA, LET ALONE USE THE WIND SCAR!
HE CAN'T MASTER A NEW TECH-NIQUE.
I SUPPOSE YOU'RE RIGHT.

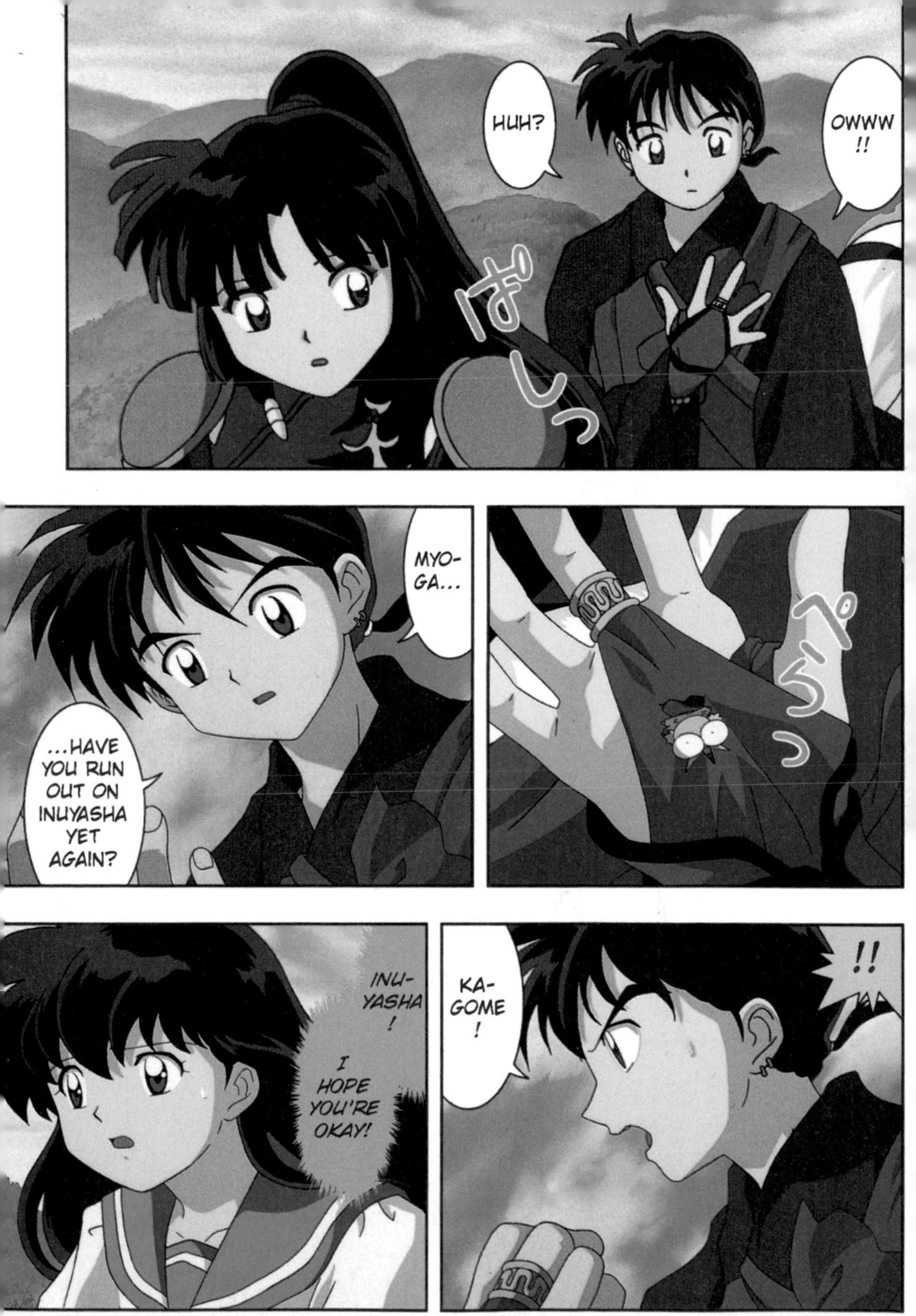
OWWW !!
HUH?
ぱしっ
ぺらっ
MYO-GA...
...HAVE YOU RUN OUT ON INUYASHA YET AGAIN?
!!
KA-GOME!
INU-YASHA!
I HOPE YOU'RE OKAY!

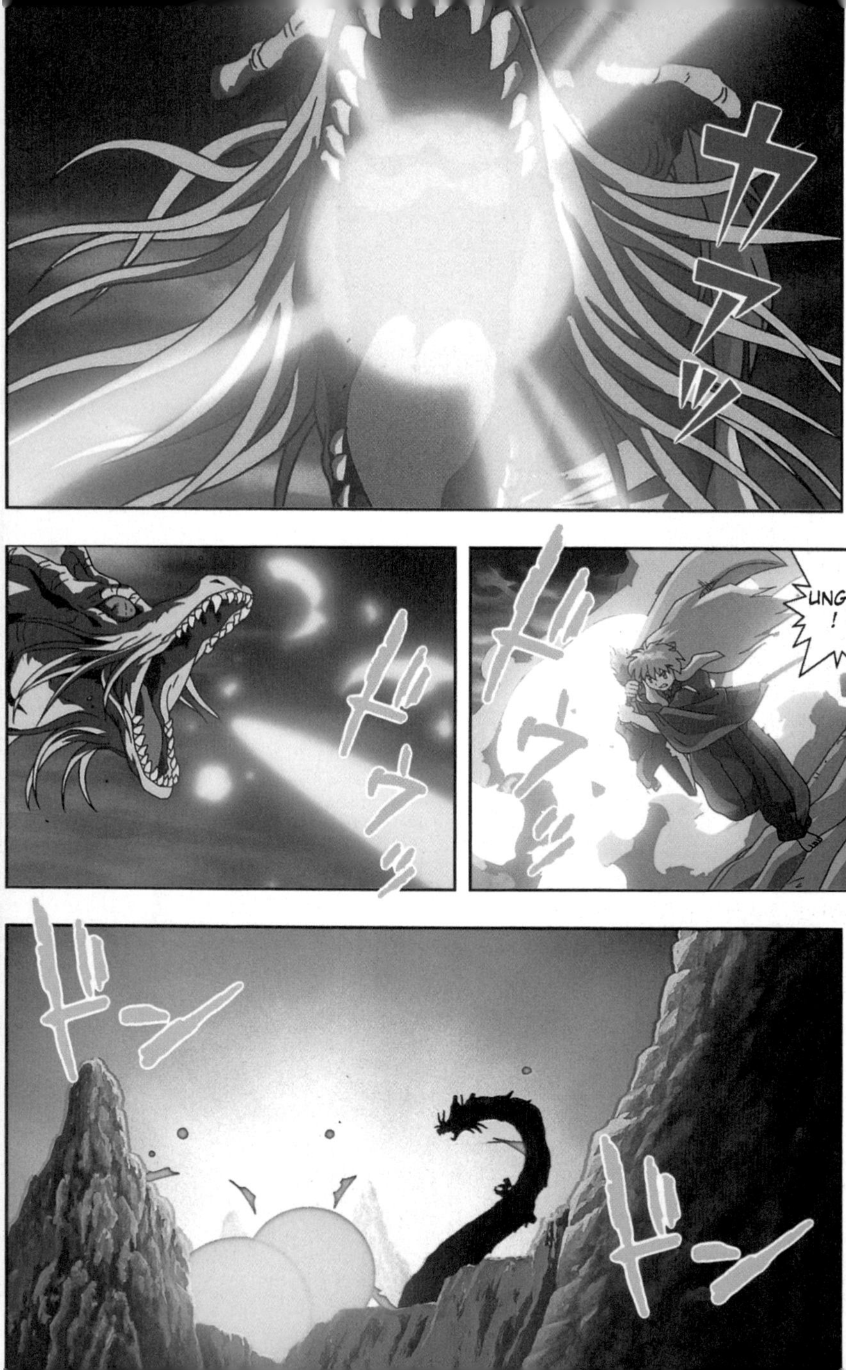
カァッ
ドゥッ
UNGH!
ドゥッ
ドーン
ドーン

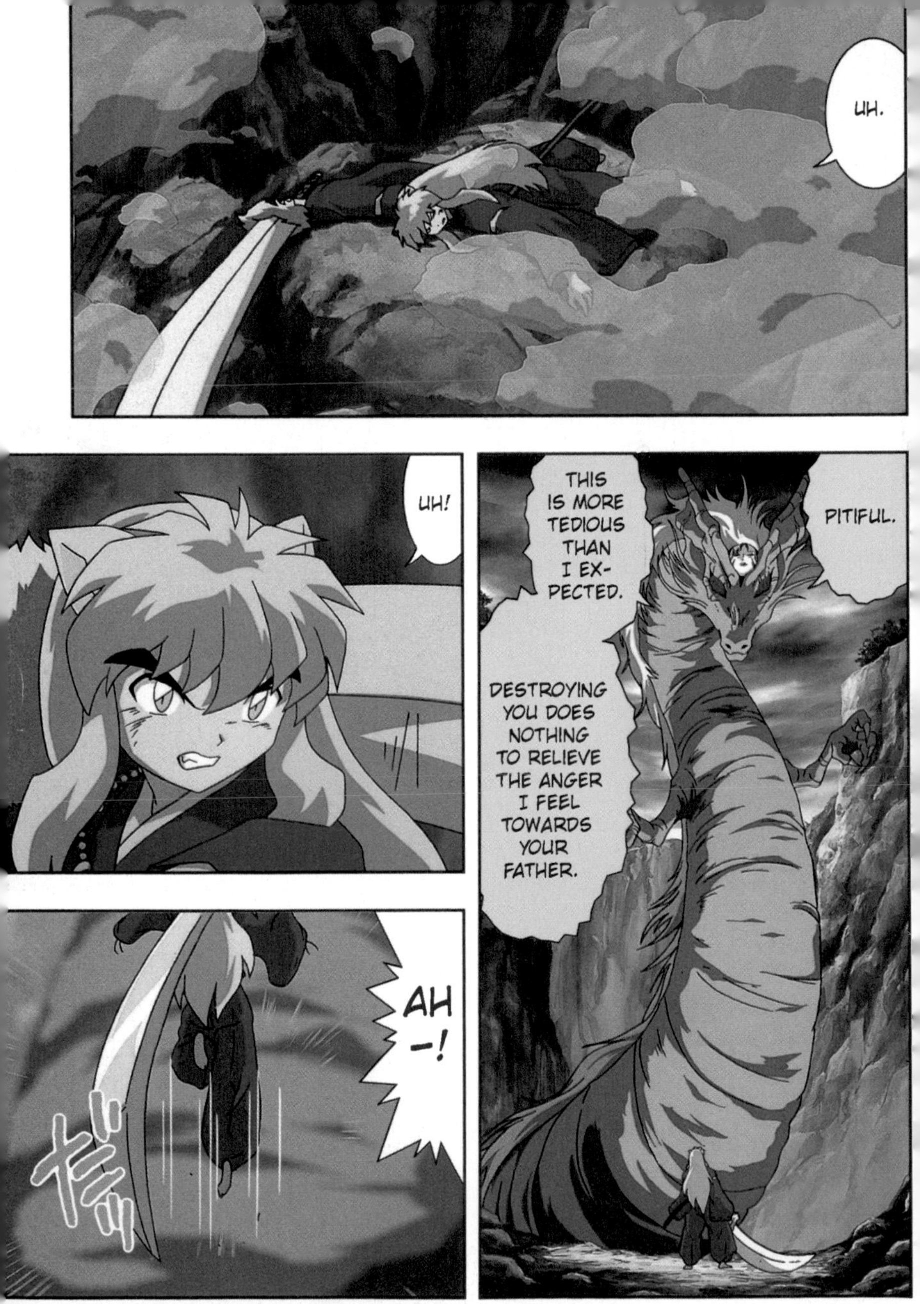
UH.
PITIFUL.
THIS IS MORE TEDIOUS THAN I EX-PECTED.
DESTROYING YOU DOES NOTHING TO RELIEVE THE ANGER I FEEL TOWARDS YOUR FATHER.
UH!
AH-!
ダッ

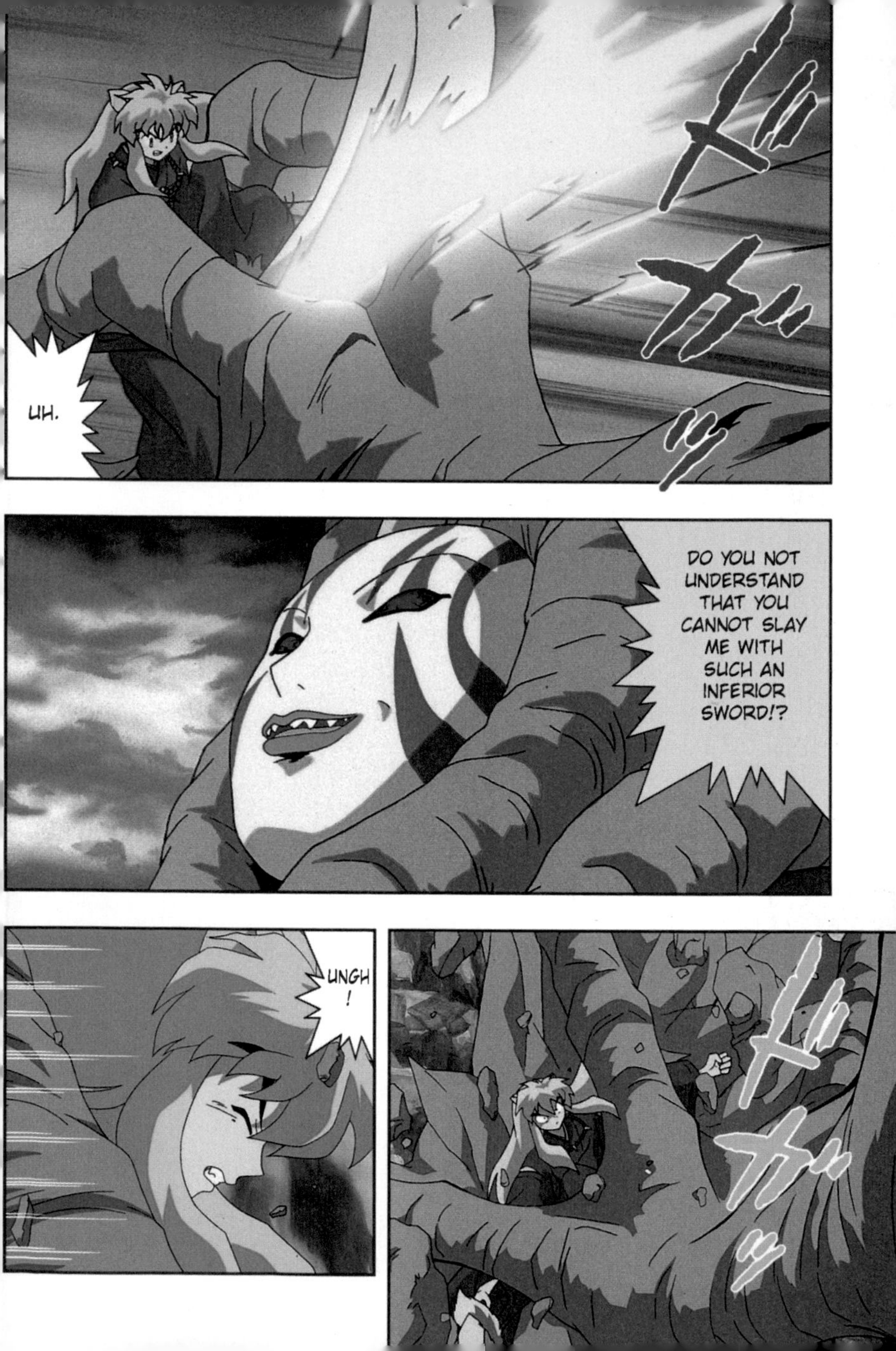
UH.
DO YOU NOT UNDERSTAND THAT YOU CANNOT SLAY ME WITH SUCH AN INFERIOR SWORD!?
UNGH!

ドゴッ
!!
ガラガラ
ポロッ
TETSU-SAIGA!

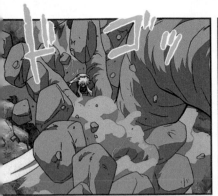

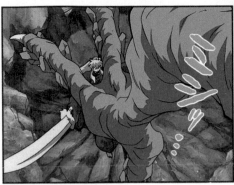

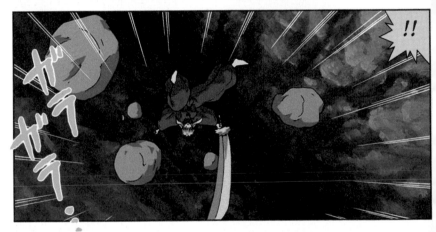

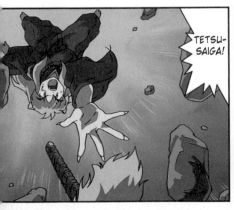

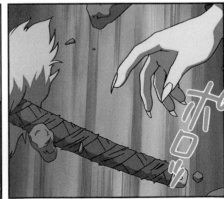

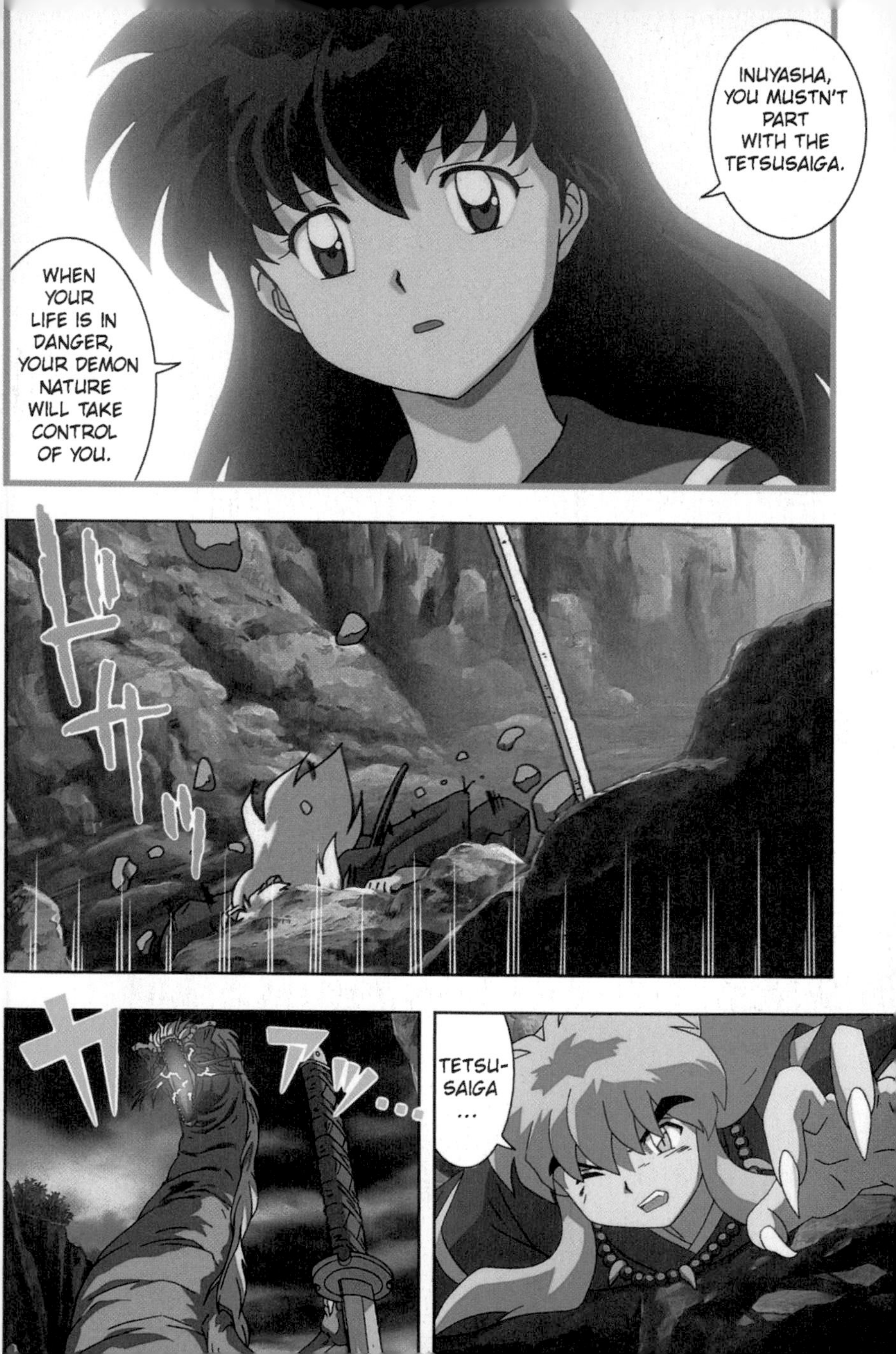
INUYASHA, YOU MUSTN'T PART WITH THE TETSUSAIGA.
WHEN YOUR LIFE IS IN DANGER, YOUR DEMON NATURE WILL TAKE CONTROL OF YOU.
TETSU-SAIGA ...

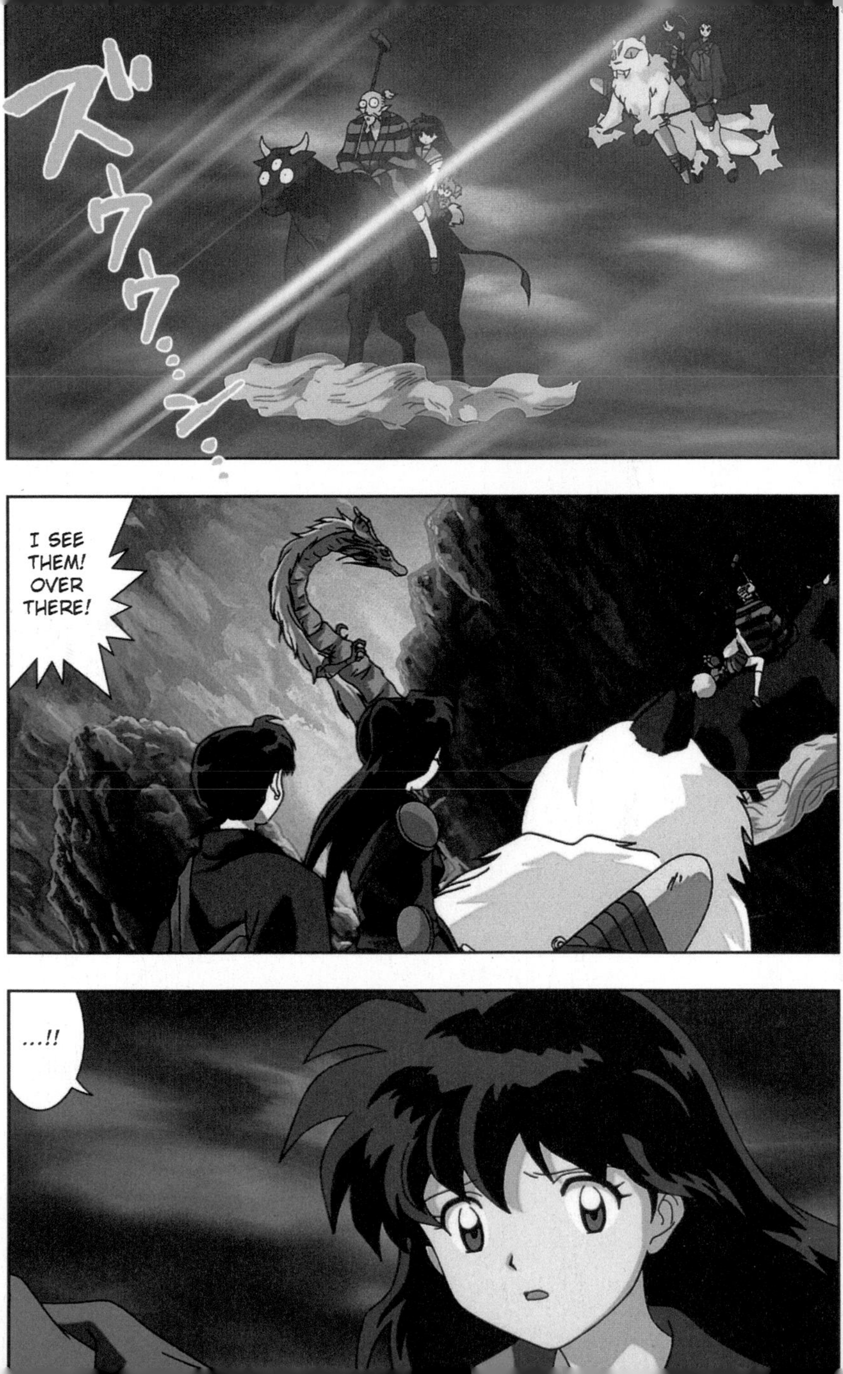
ズウウウ……ン…
I SEE THEM! OVER THERE!
...!!

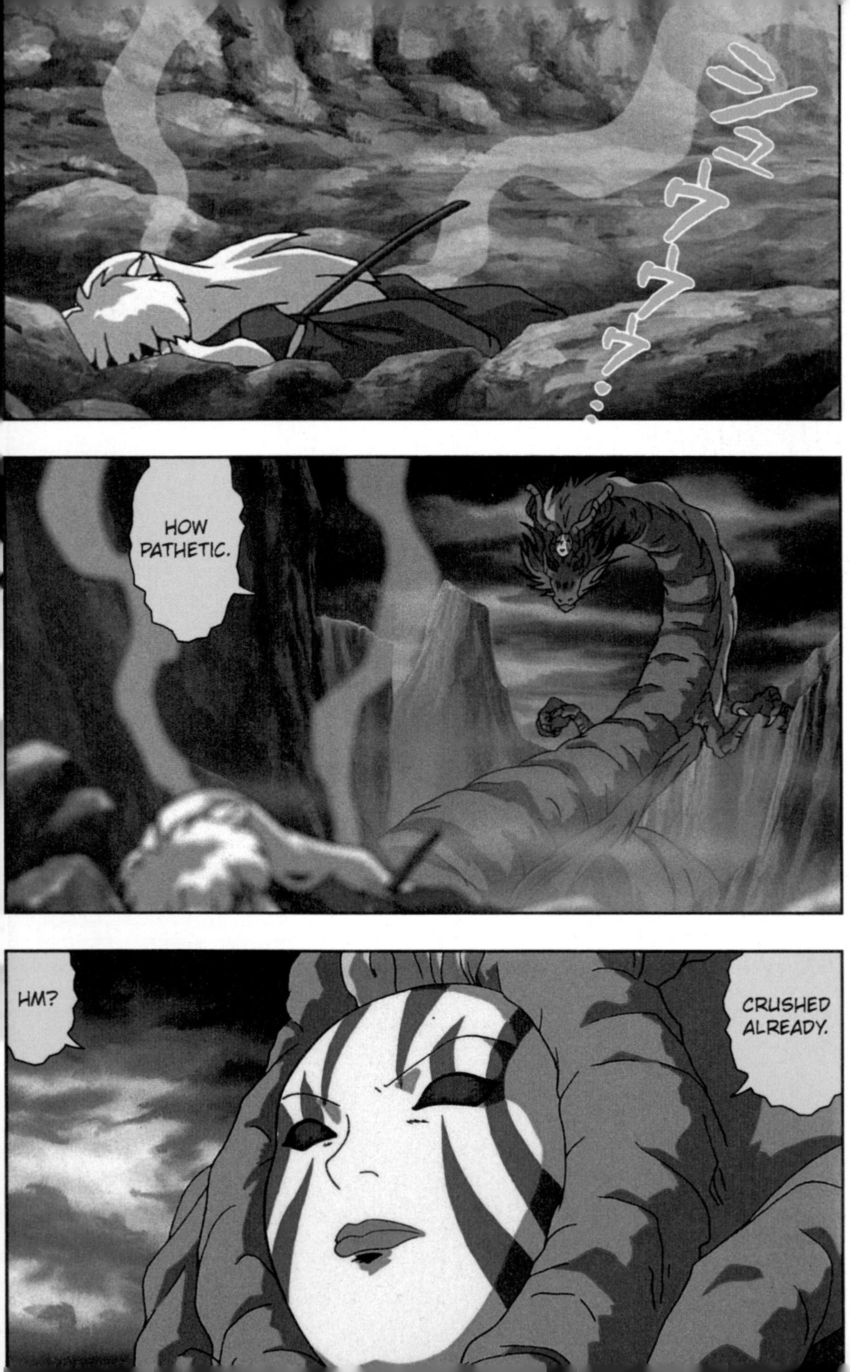
シュゥゥゥ…
HOW PATHETIC.
CRUSHED ALREADY.
HM?

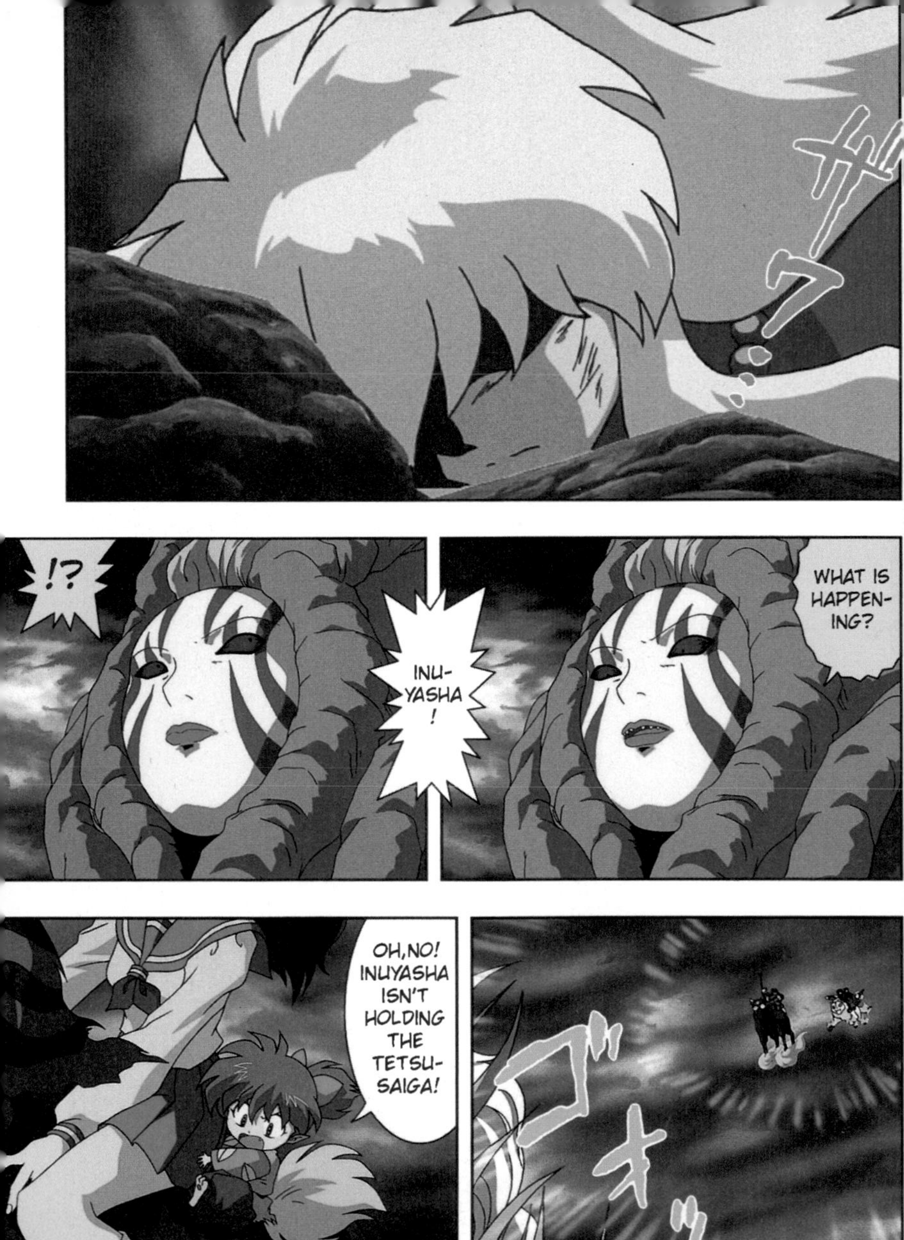

ザク!
WHAT IS HAPPEN-ING?
INU-YASHA!
!?
ゴオッ
OH, NO! INUYASHA ISN'T HOLDING THE TETSU-SAIGA!

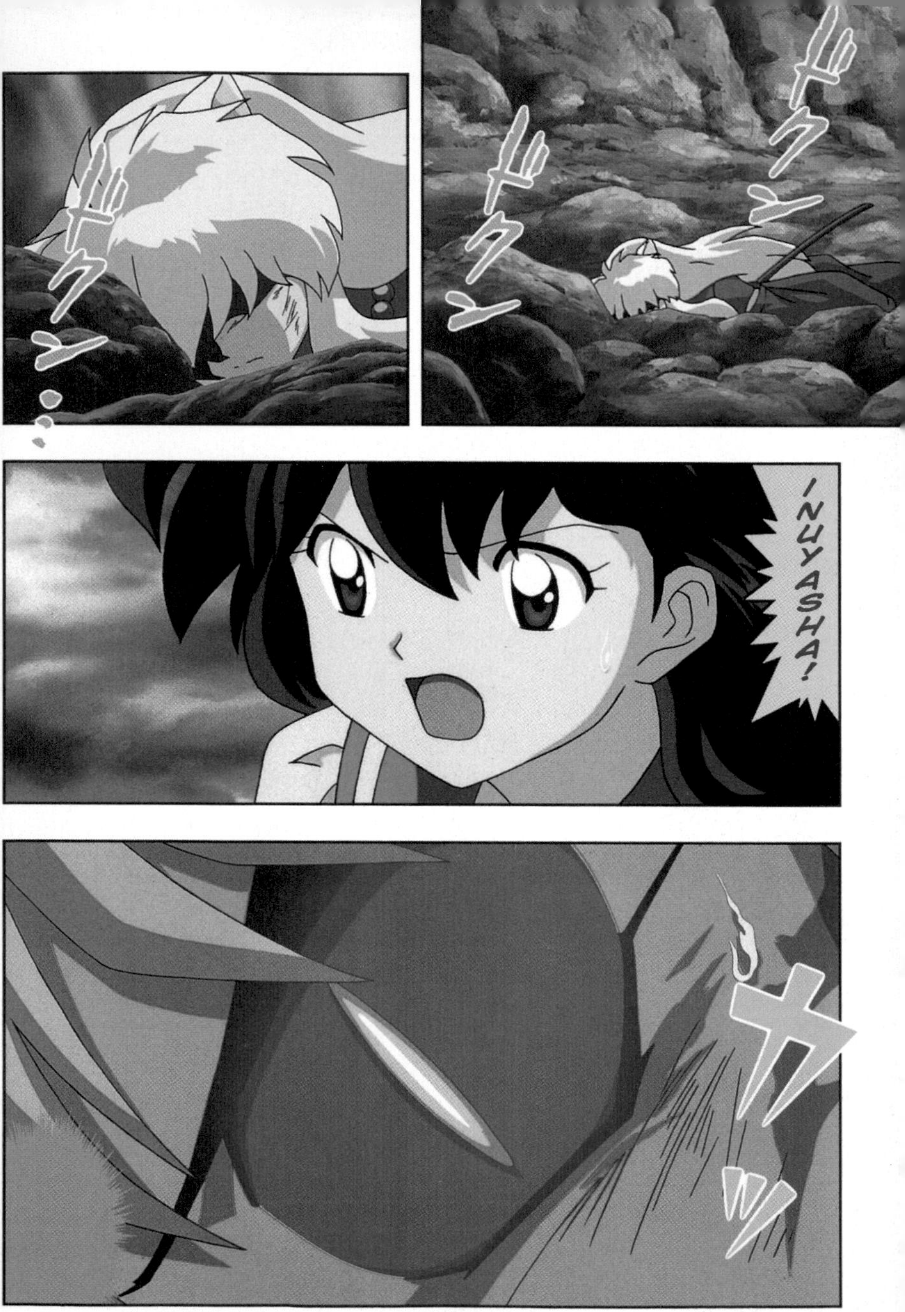
ドクン
ドクン
ドクン…
INUYASHA!
ガッ

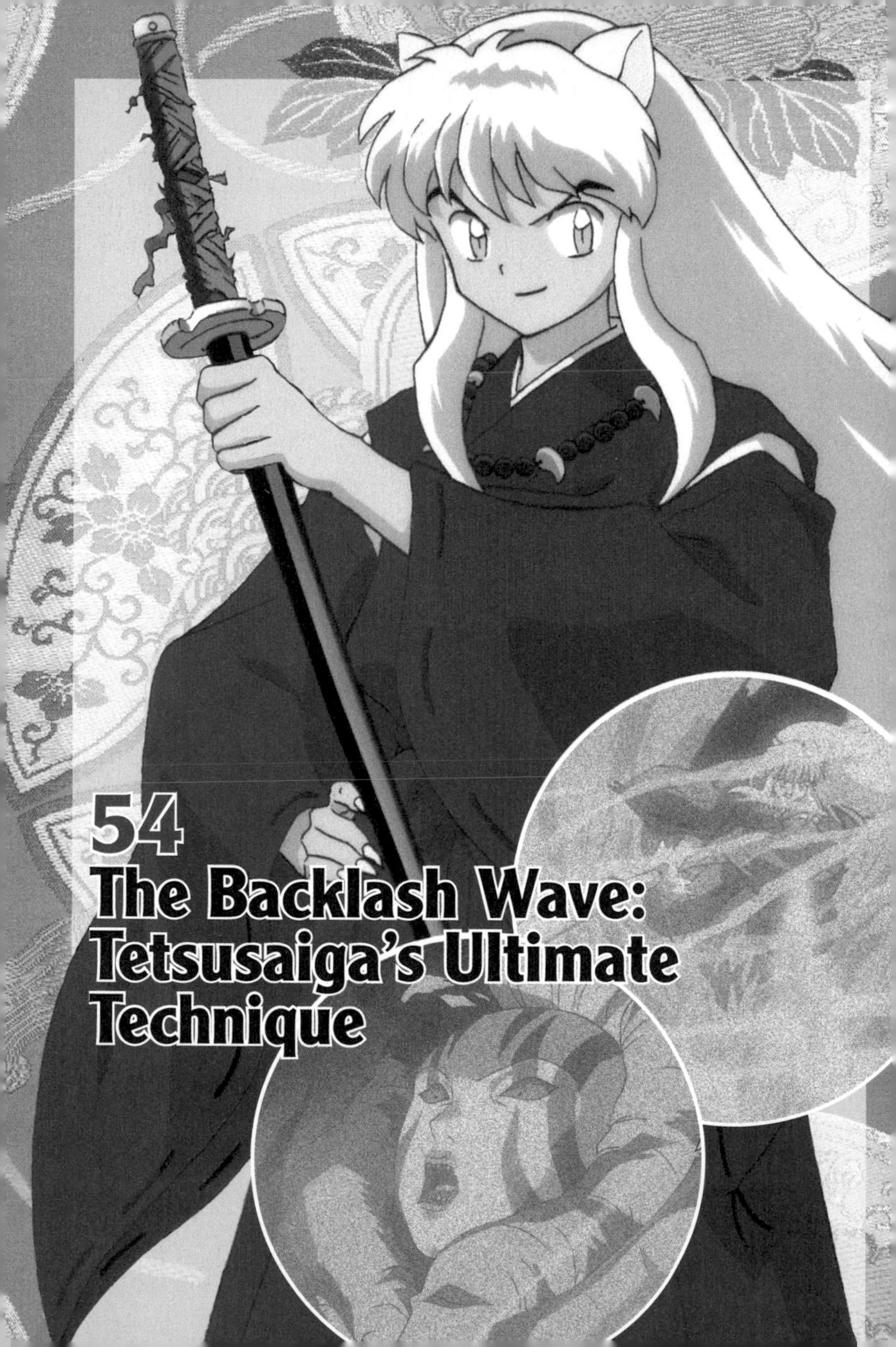

54
The Backlash Wave: Tetsusaiga's Ultimate Technique

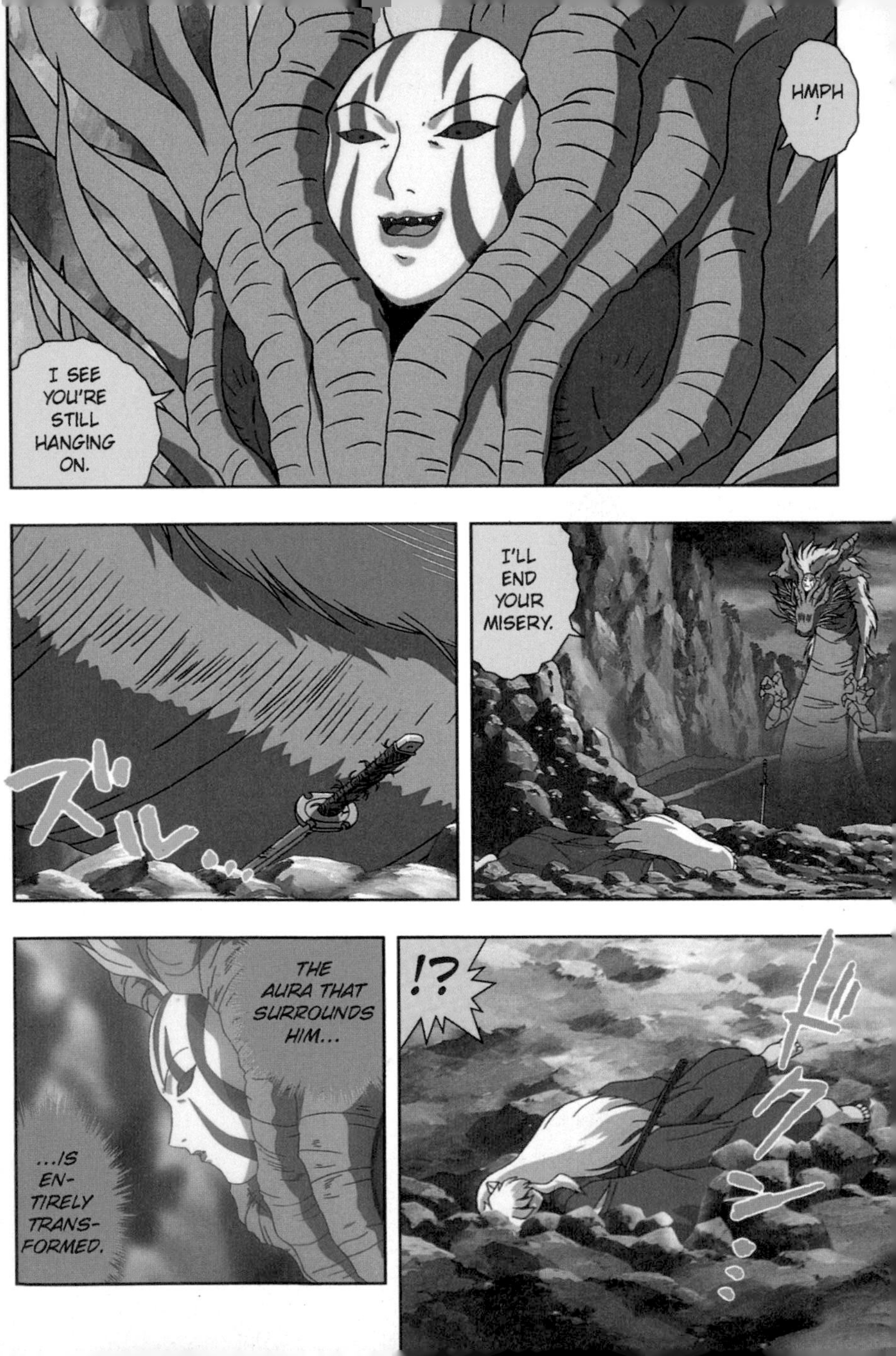
HMPH!
I SEE YOU'RE STILL HANGING ON.
I'LL END YOUR MISERY.
ズル…
!?
ドクン…
THE AURA THAT SURROUNDS HIM...
...IS ENTIRELY TRANSFORMED.

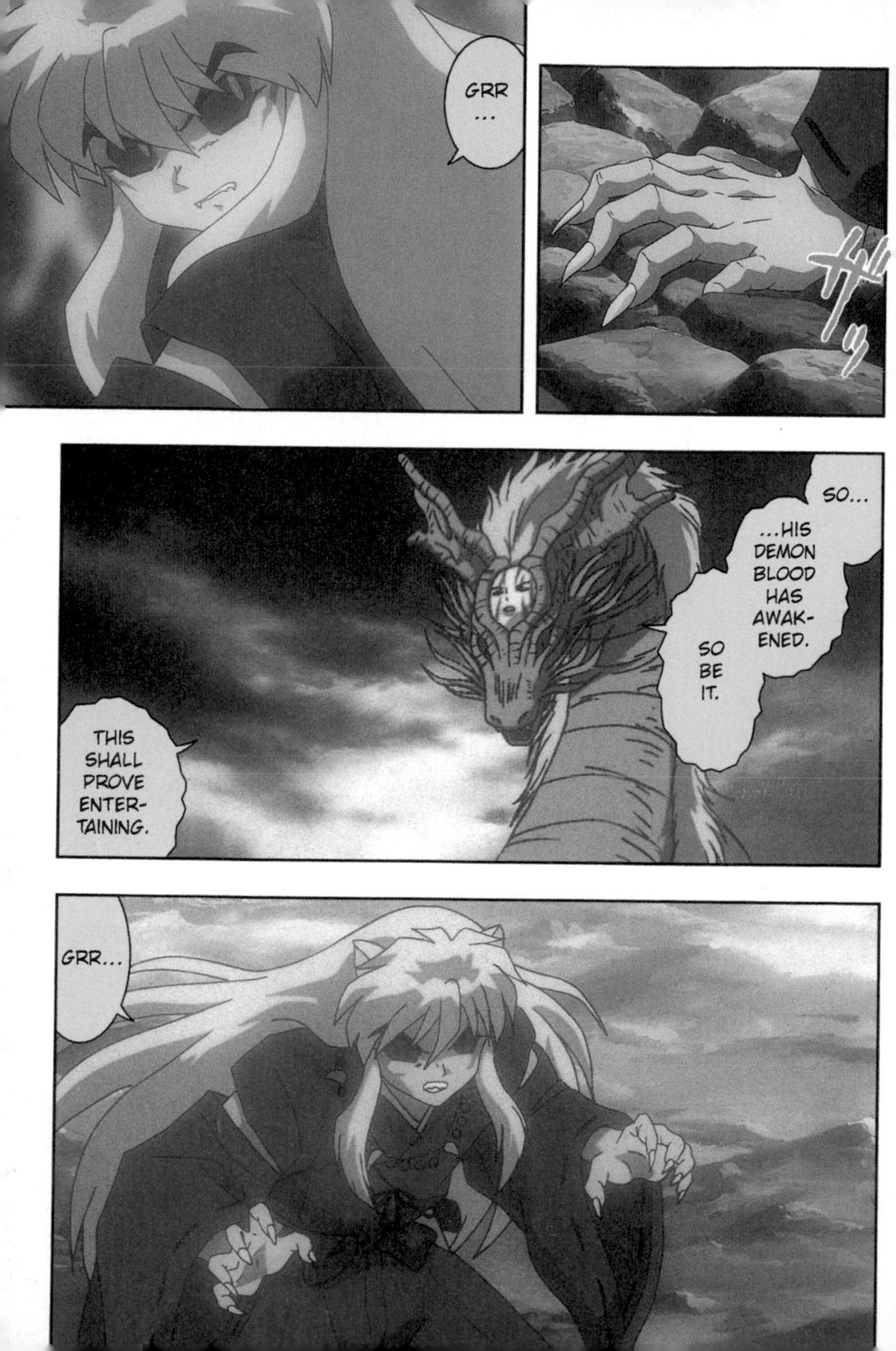
GRR ...
SO...
...HIS DEMON BLOOD HAS AWAKENED.
SO BE IT.
THIS SHALL PROVE ENTERTAINING.
GRR...

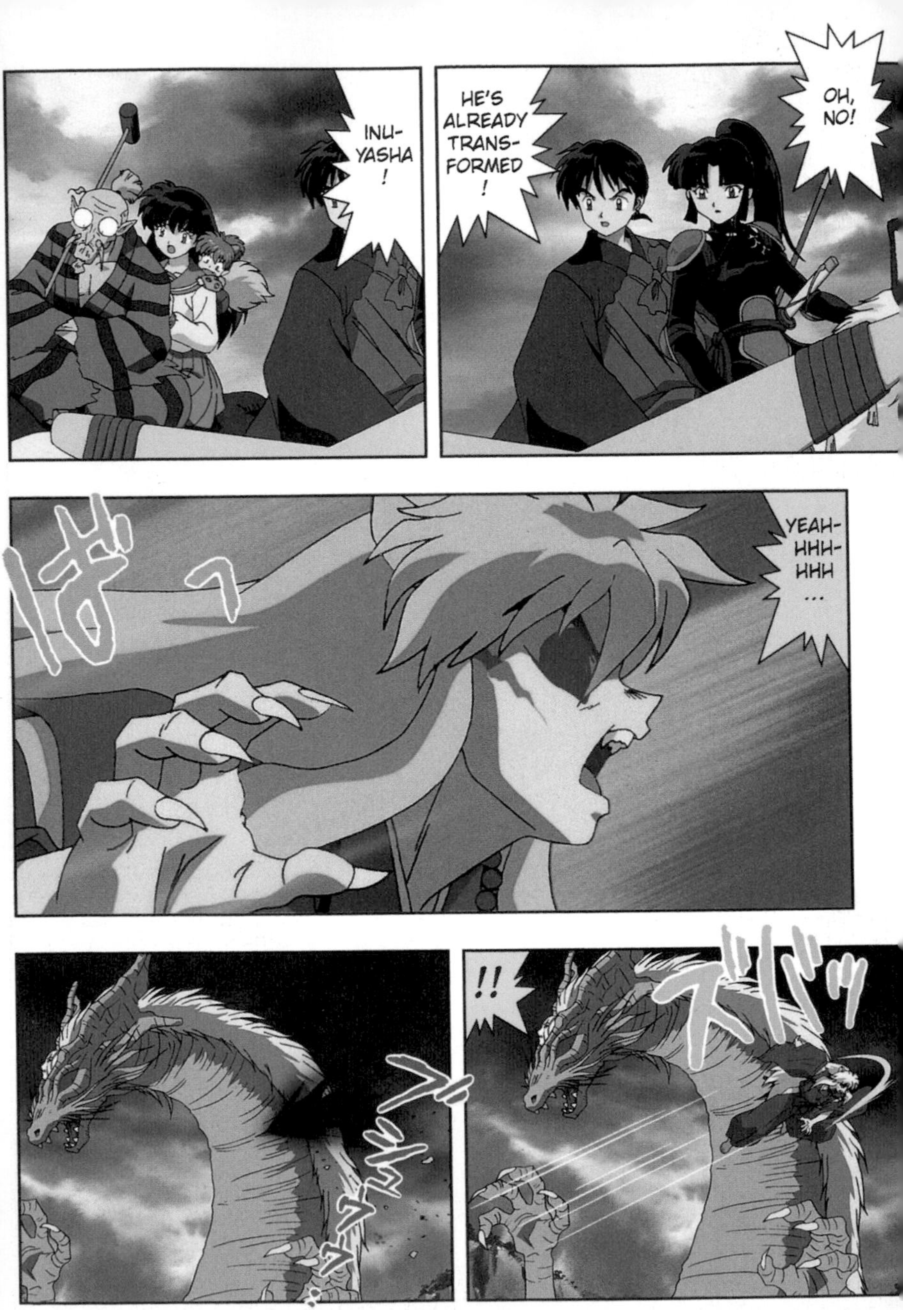
OH, NO!
HE'S ALREADY TRANS-FORMED!
INU-YASHA!
YEAH-HHH-HHH...
ばっ
ズバッ
!!

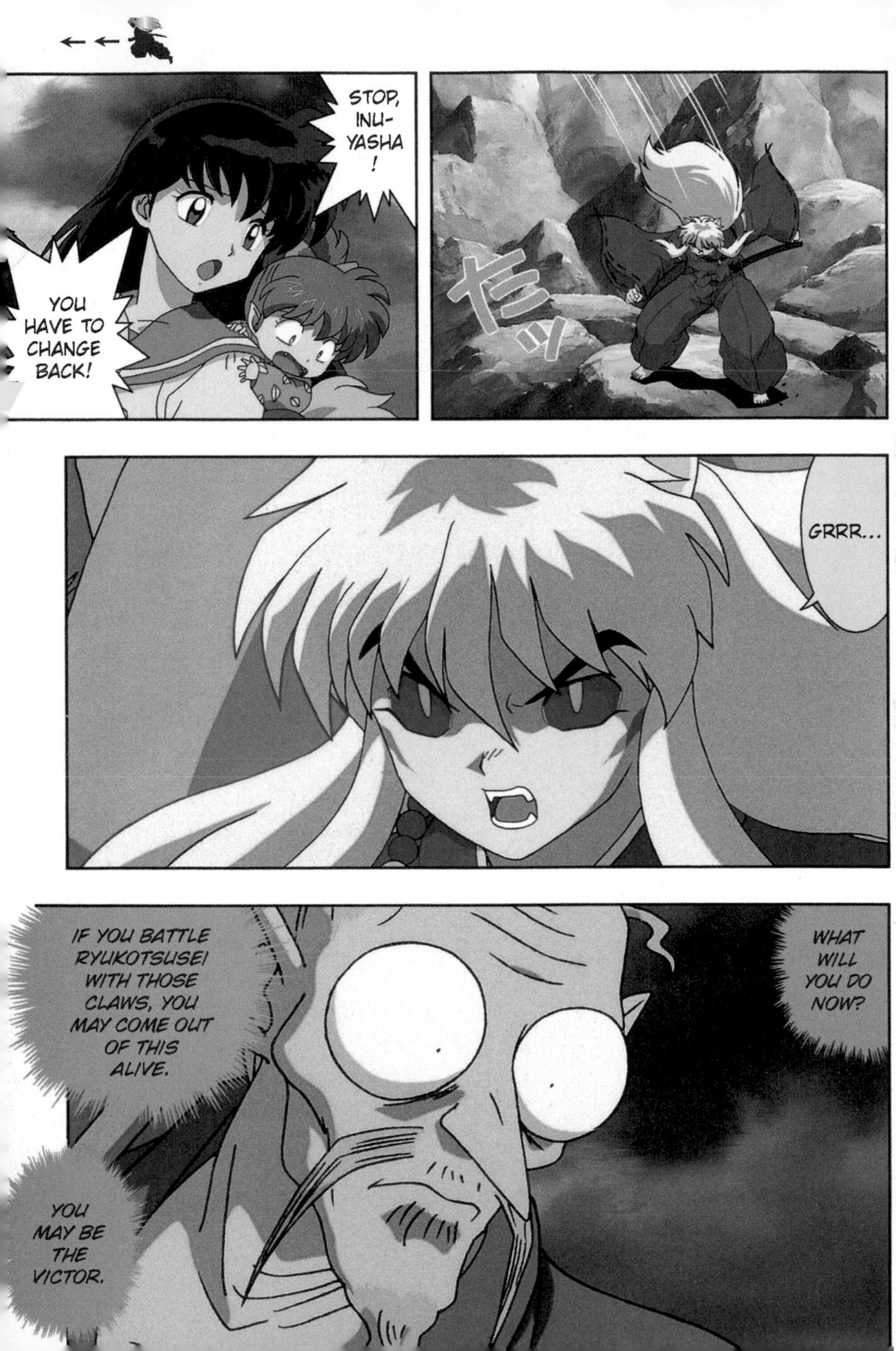
STOP, INU-YASHA!
YOU HAVE TO CHANGE BACK!
GRRR...
WHAT WILL YOU DO NOW?
IF YOU BATTLE RYUKOTSUSEI WITH THOSE CLAWS, YOU MAY COME OUT OF THIS ALIVE.
YOU MAY BE THE VICTOR.

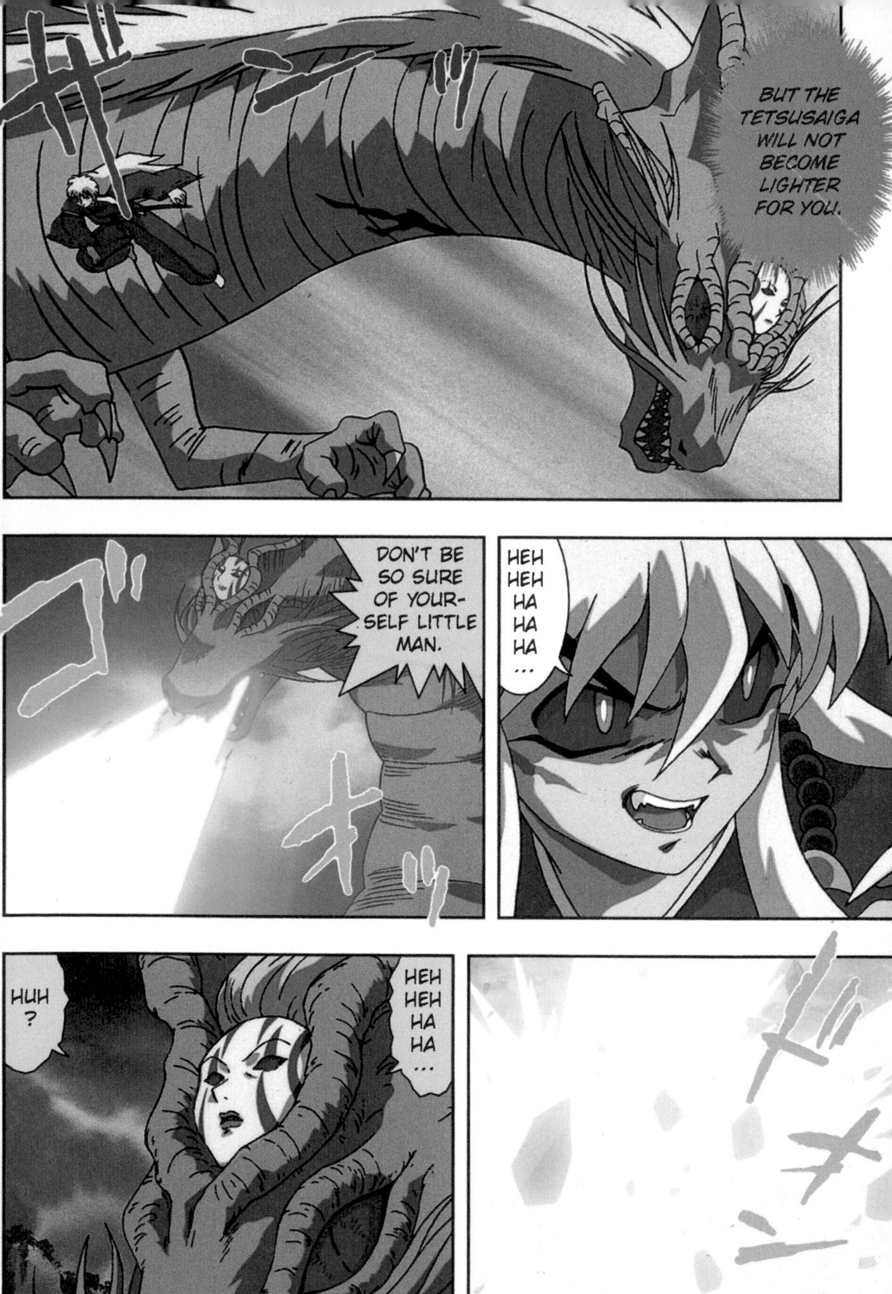
BUT THE TETSUSAIGA WILL NOT BECOME LIGHTER FOR YOU.
HEH HEH HA HA HA ...
DON'T BE SO SURE OF YOUR-SELF LITTLE MAN.
HEH HEH HA HA ...
HUH ?

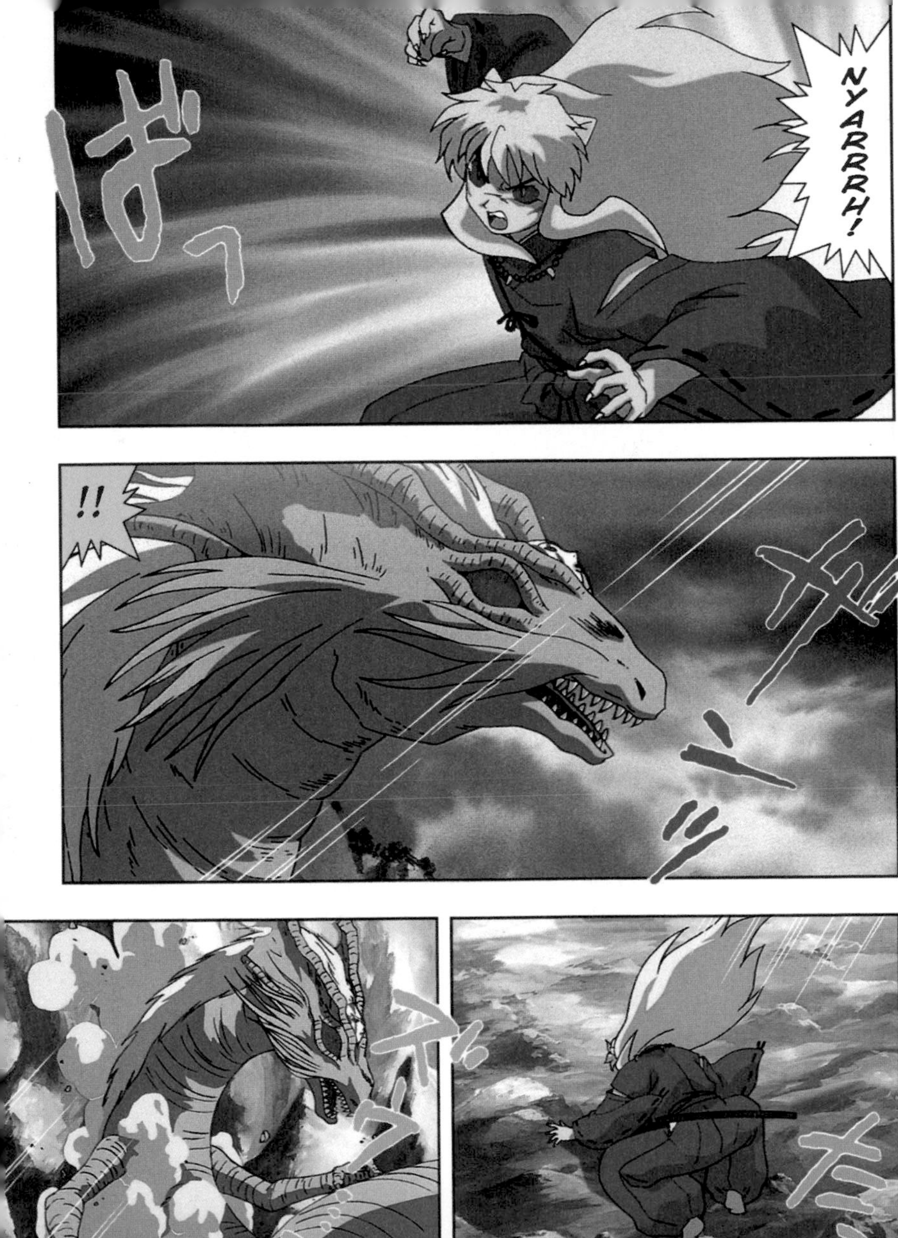
NYARRRH!
ばっ
!!
たっ

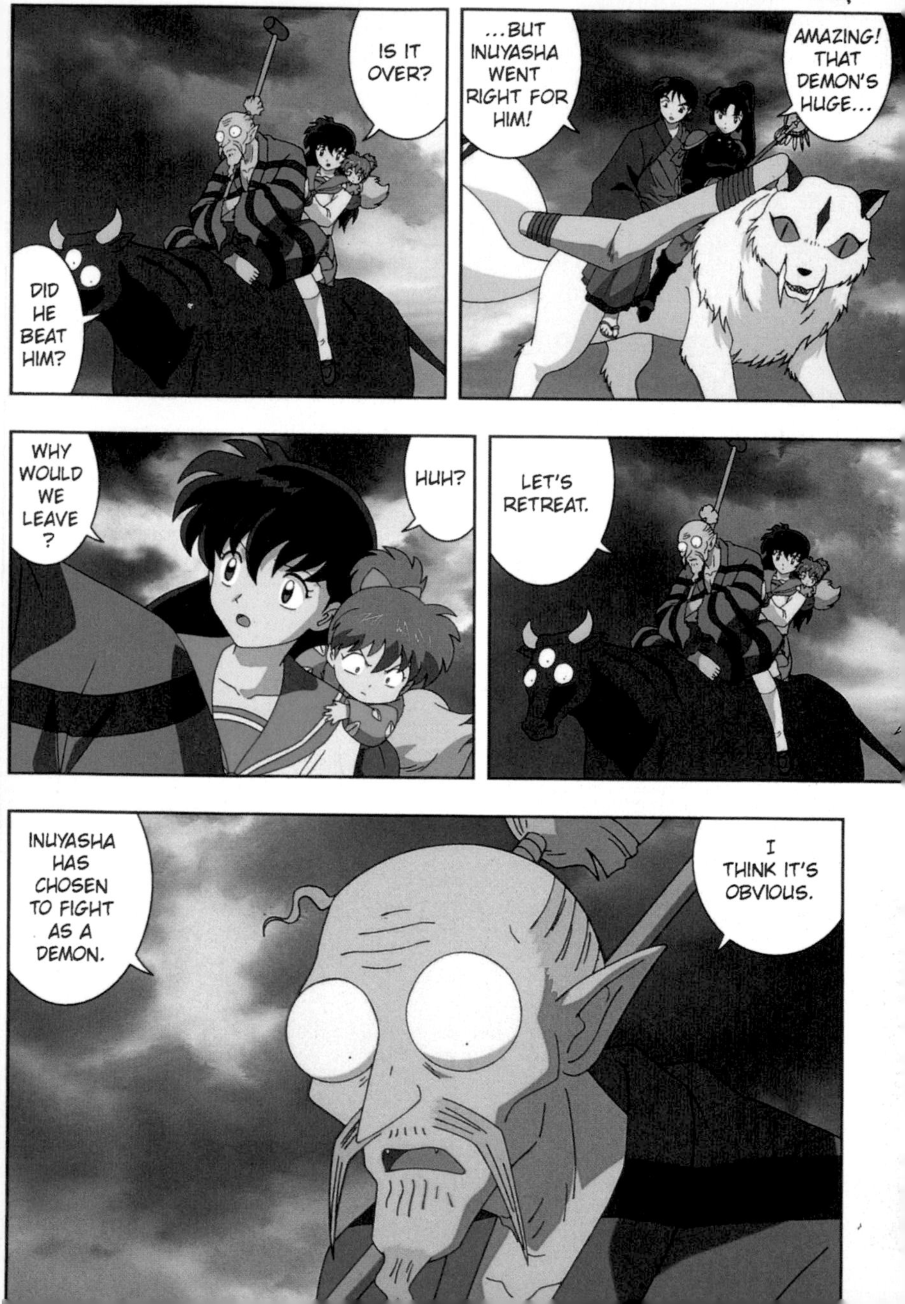
AMAZING! THAT DEMON'S HUGE...
...BUT INUYASHA WENT RIGHT FOR HIM!
IS IT OVER?
DID HE BEAT HIM?
LET'S RETREAT.
HUH?
WHY WOULD WE LEAVE?
I THINK IT'S OBVIOUS.
INUYASHA HAS CHOSEN TO FIGHT AS A DEMON.

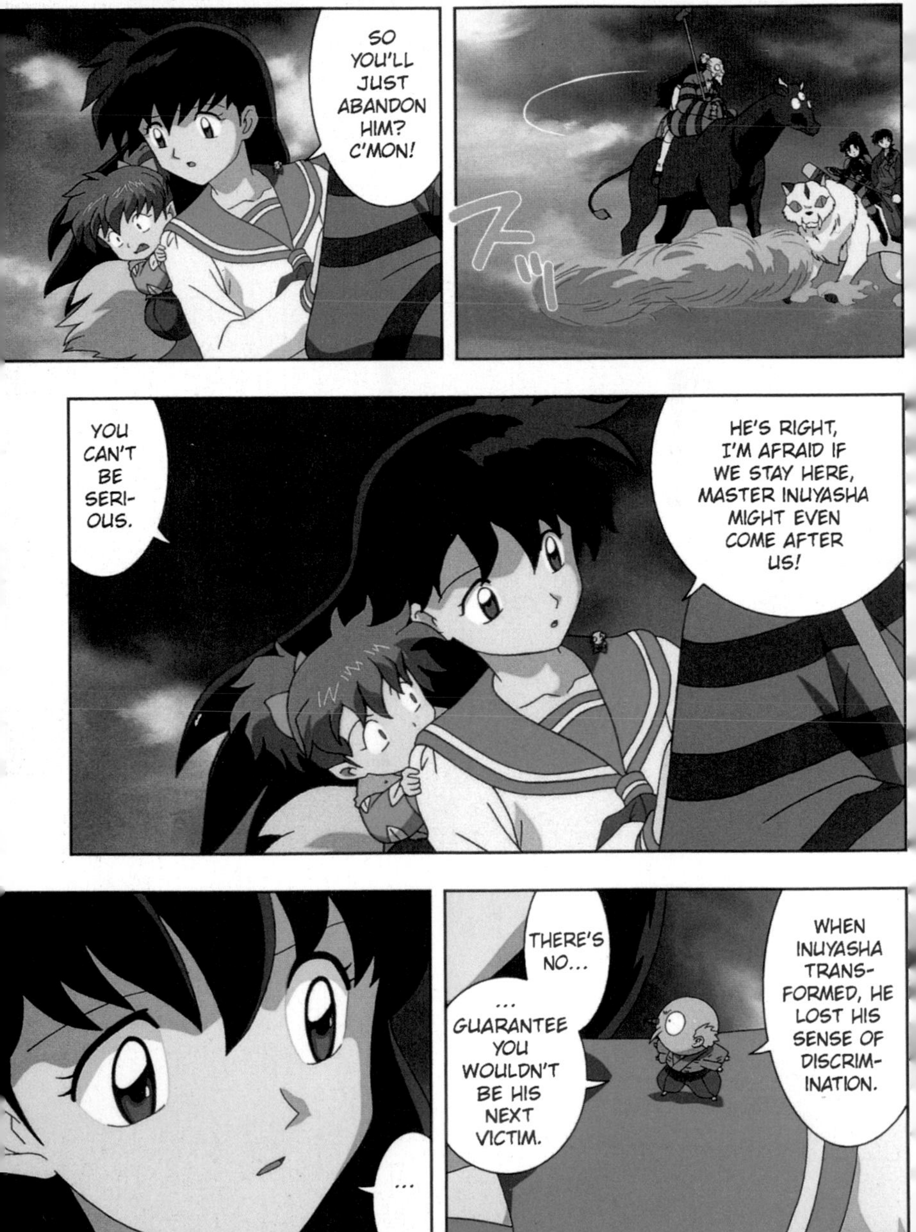
ズッ
SO YOU'LL JUST ABANDON HIM? C'MON!
HE'S RIGHT, I'M AFRAID IF WE STAY HERE, MASTER INUYASHA MIGHT EVEN COME AFTER US!
YOU CAN'T BE SERI-OUS.
WHEN INUYASHA TRANS-FORMED, HE LOST HIS SENSE OF DISCRIM-INATION.
THERE'S NO...
... GUARANTEE YOU WOULDN'T BE HIS NEXT VICTIM.
...

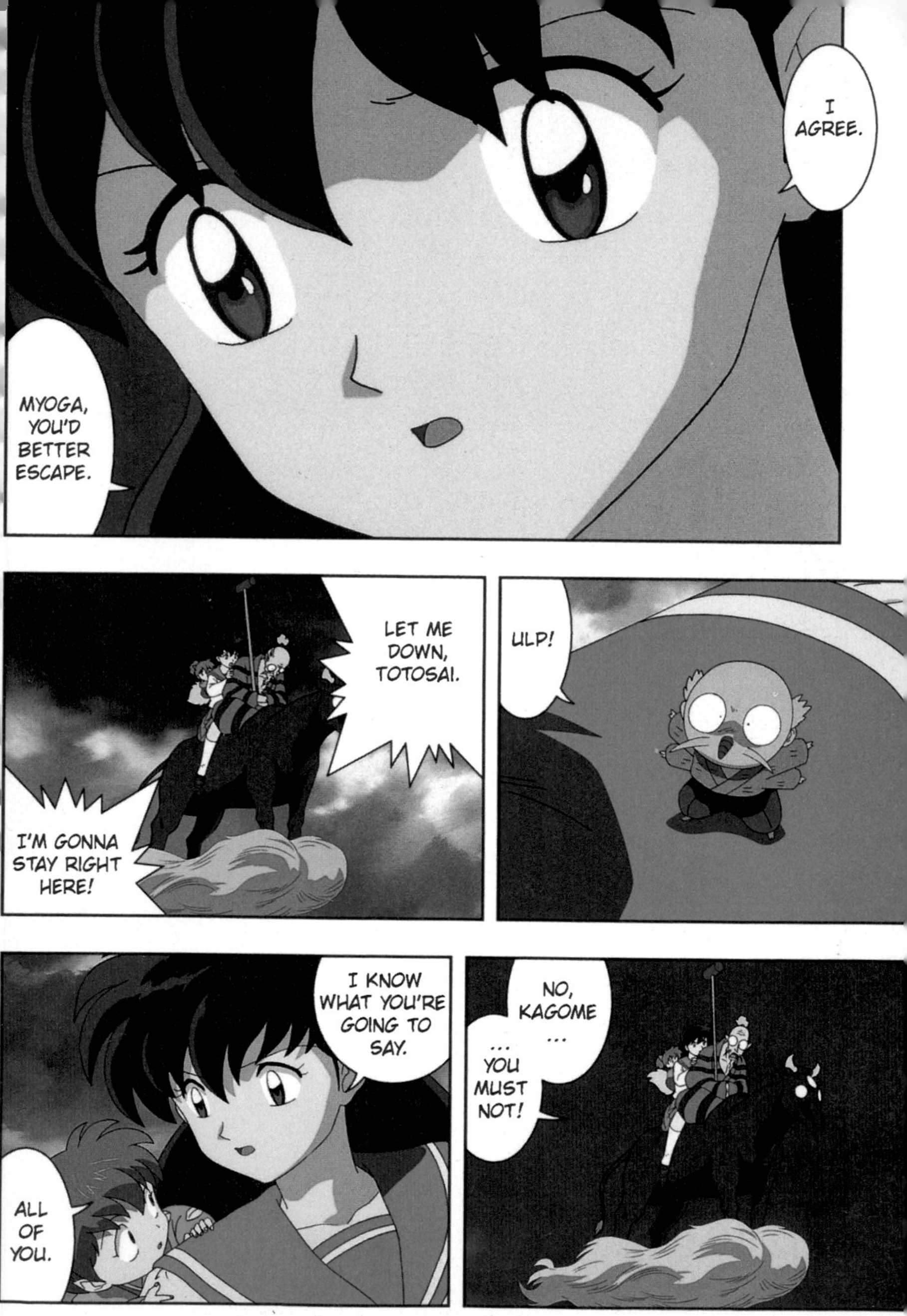
I AGREE.
MYOGA, YOU'D BETTER ESCAPE.
ULP!
LET ME DOWN, TOTOSAI.
I'M GONNA STAY RIGHT HERE!
NO, KAGOME ...
... YOU MUST NOT!
I KNOW WHAT YOU'RE GOING TO SAY.
ALL OF YOU.

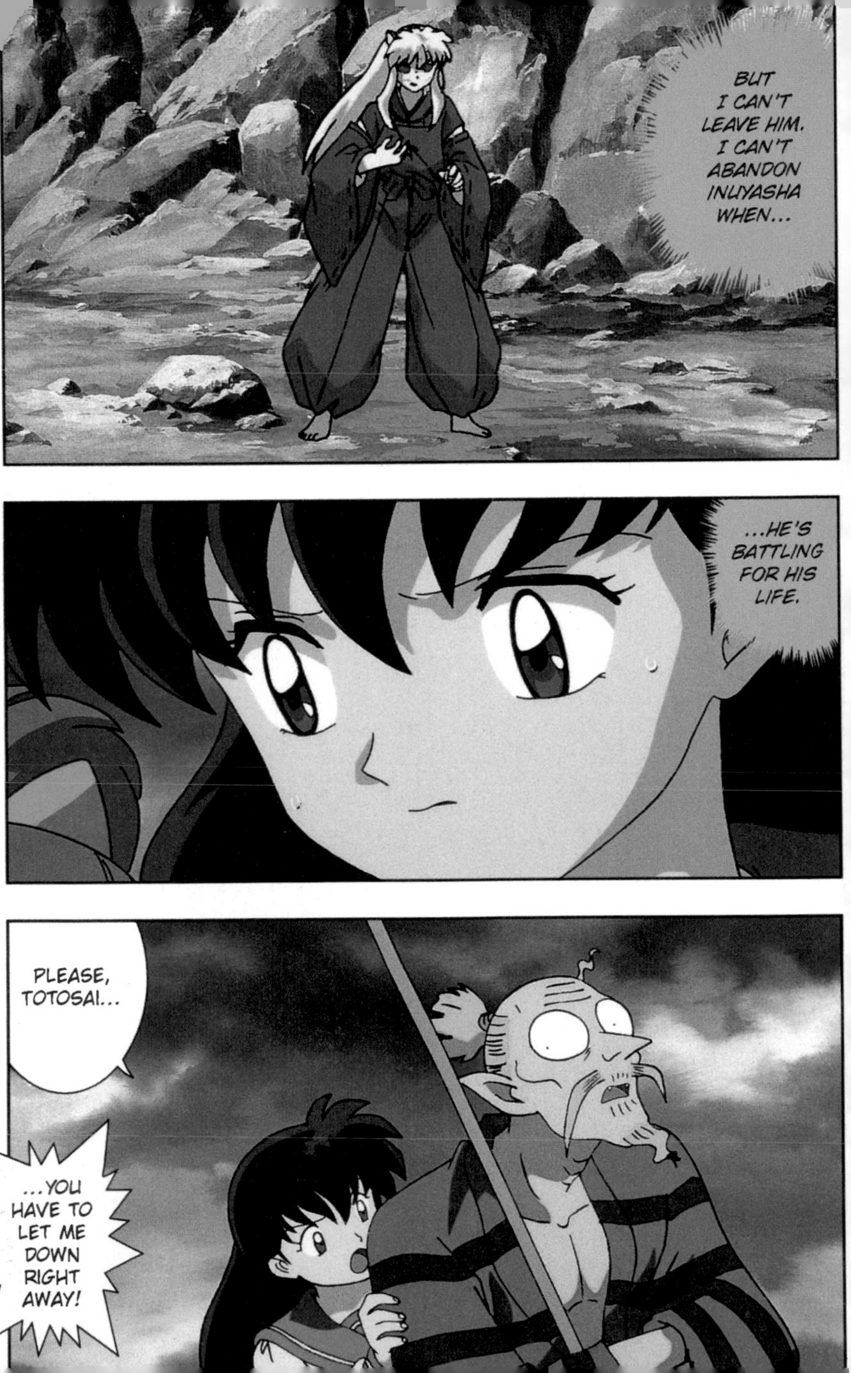
BUT I CAN'T LEAVE HIM. I CAN'T ABANDON INUYASHA WHEN...
...HE'S BATTLING FOR HIS LIFE.
PLEASE, TOTOSAI...
...YOU HAVE TO LET ME DOWN RIGHT AWAY!

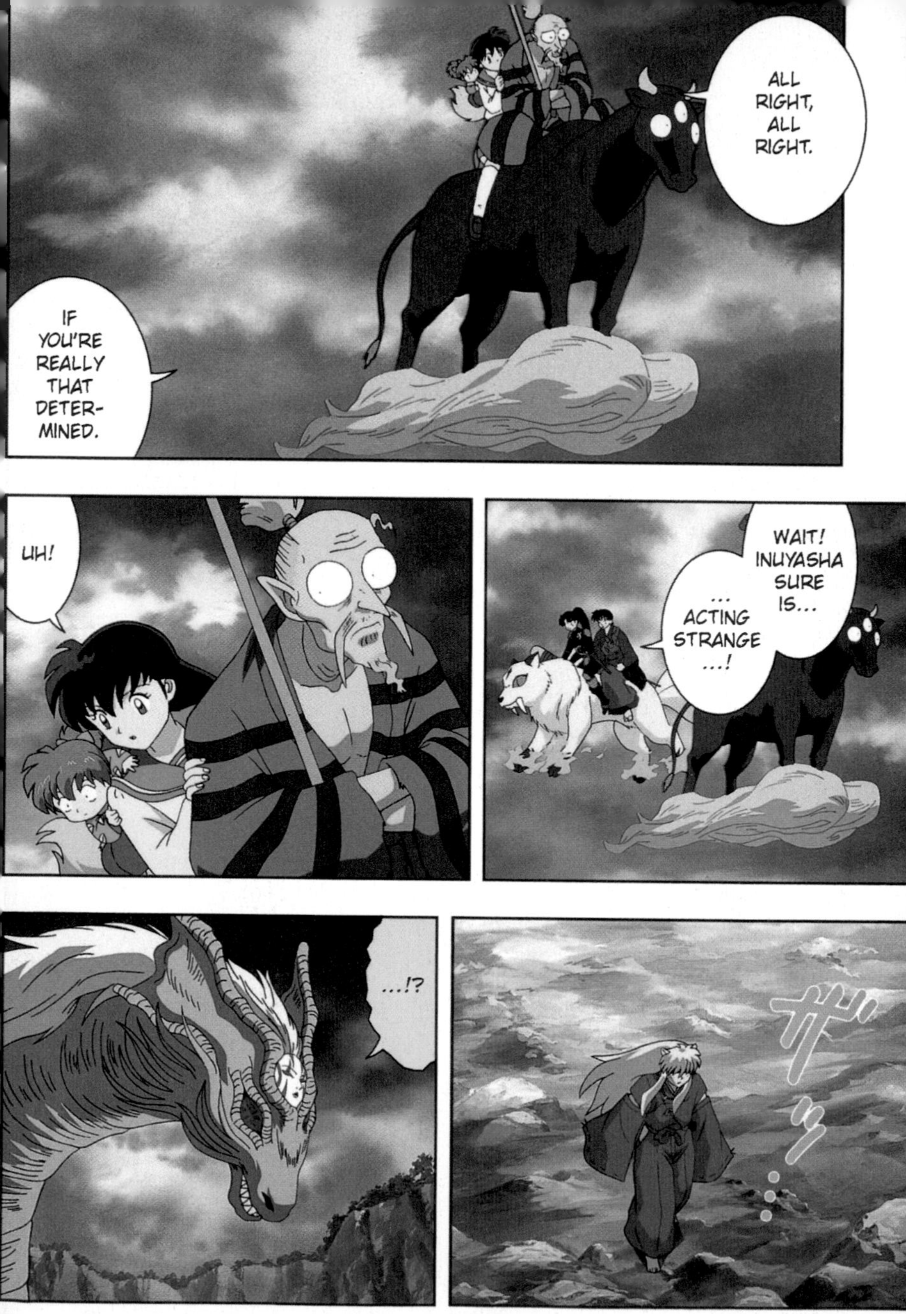
ALL RIGHT, ALL RIGHT.
IF YOU'RE REALLY THAT DETERMINED.
WAIT! INUYASHA SURE IS...
...ACTING STRANGE ...!
UH!
...!?

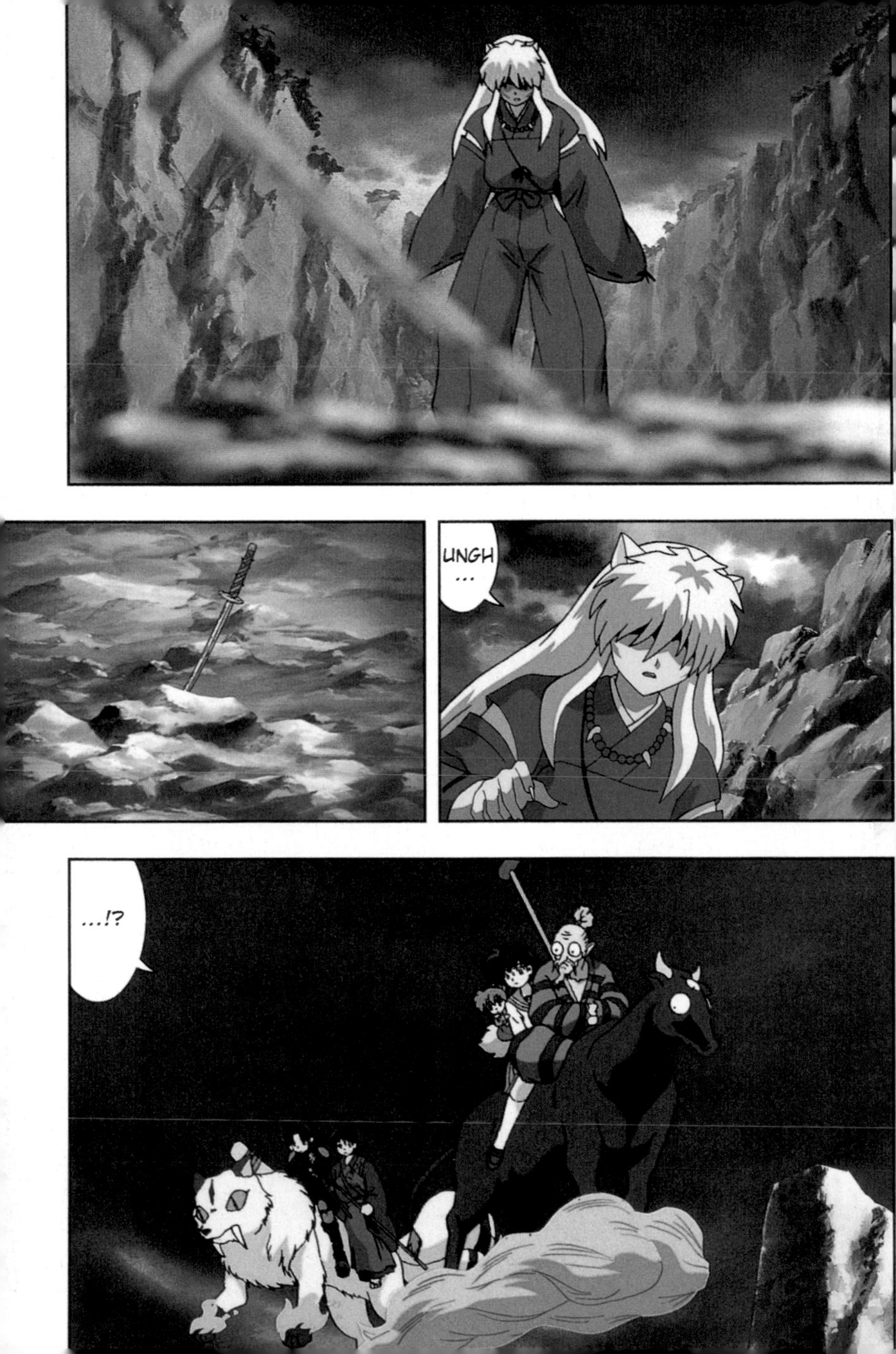
UNGH ...
...!?

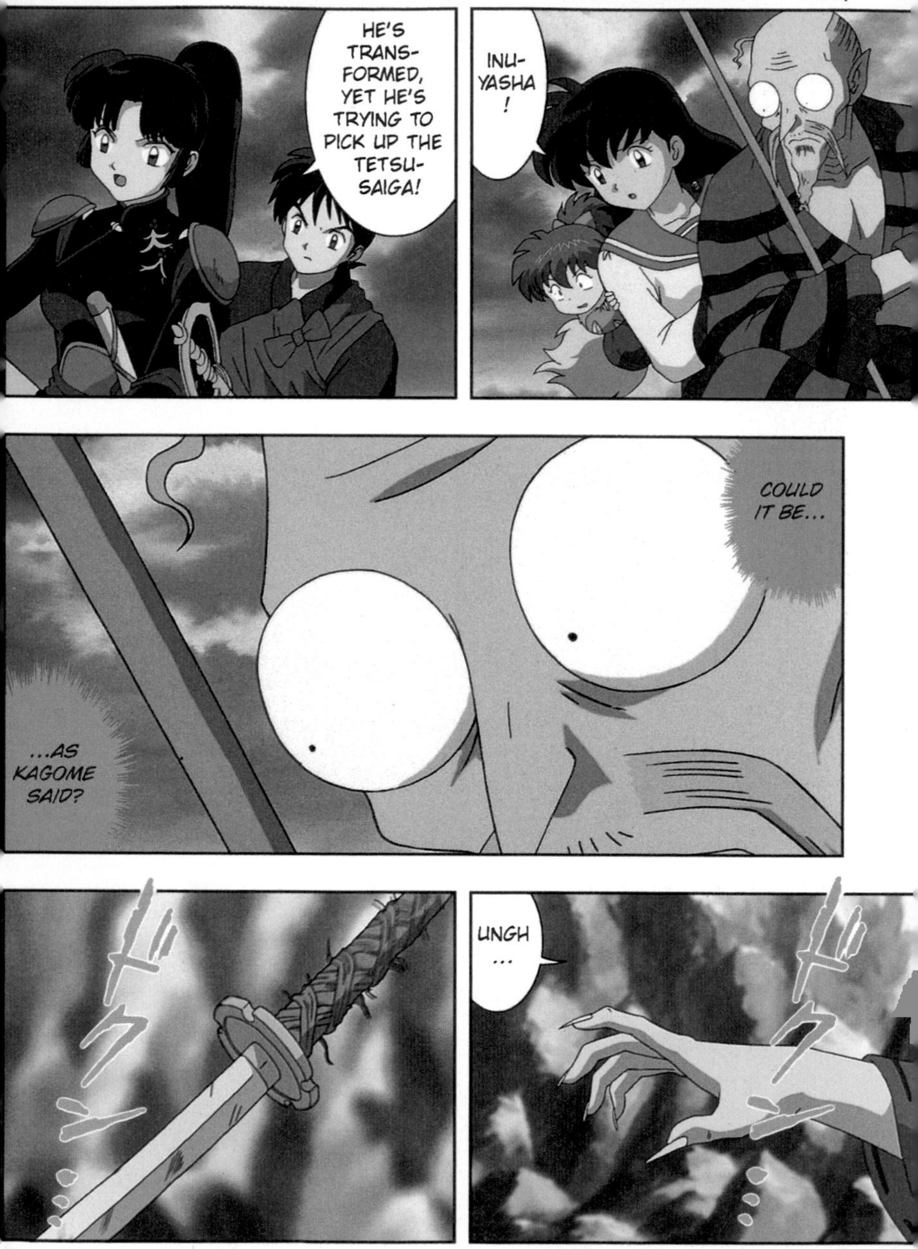
INU-
YASHA
!
HE'S
TRANS-
FORMED,
YET HE'S
TRYING TO
PICK UP THE
TETSU-
SAIGA!
COULD
IT BE...
...AS
KAGOME
SAID?
UNGH
...
ドクン
ドクン

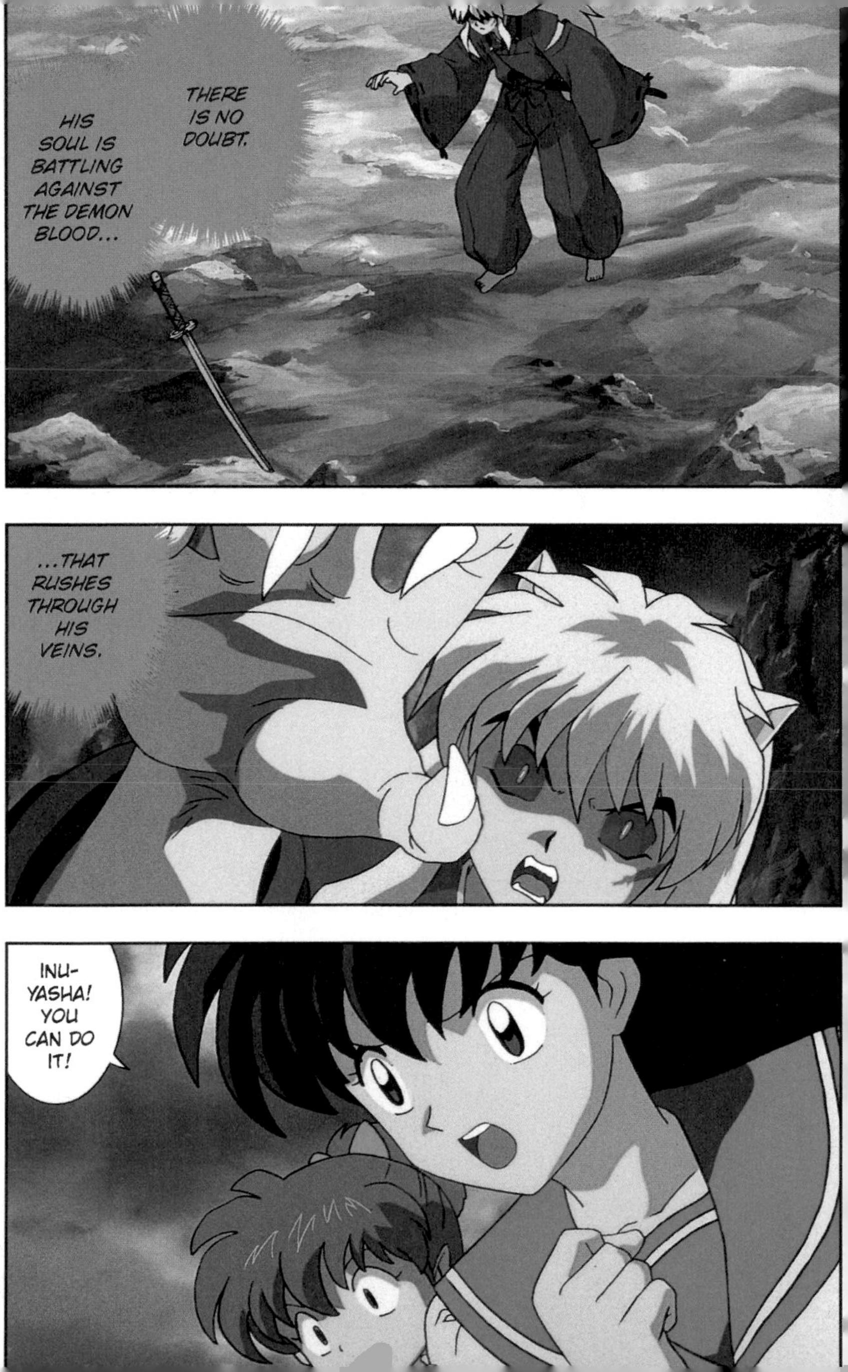
THERE IS NO DOUBT.
HIS SOUL IS BATTLING AGAINST THE DEMON BLOOD...
...THAT RUSHES THROUGH HIS VEINS.
INU-YASHA! YOU CAN DO IT!

HOW DARE HE THINK HE CAN CONQUER ME?

IMPU-DENCE!

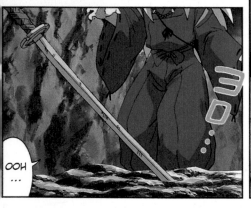

OOH...

PLAYTIME IS OVER!

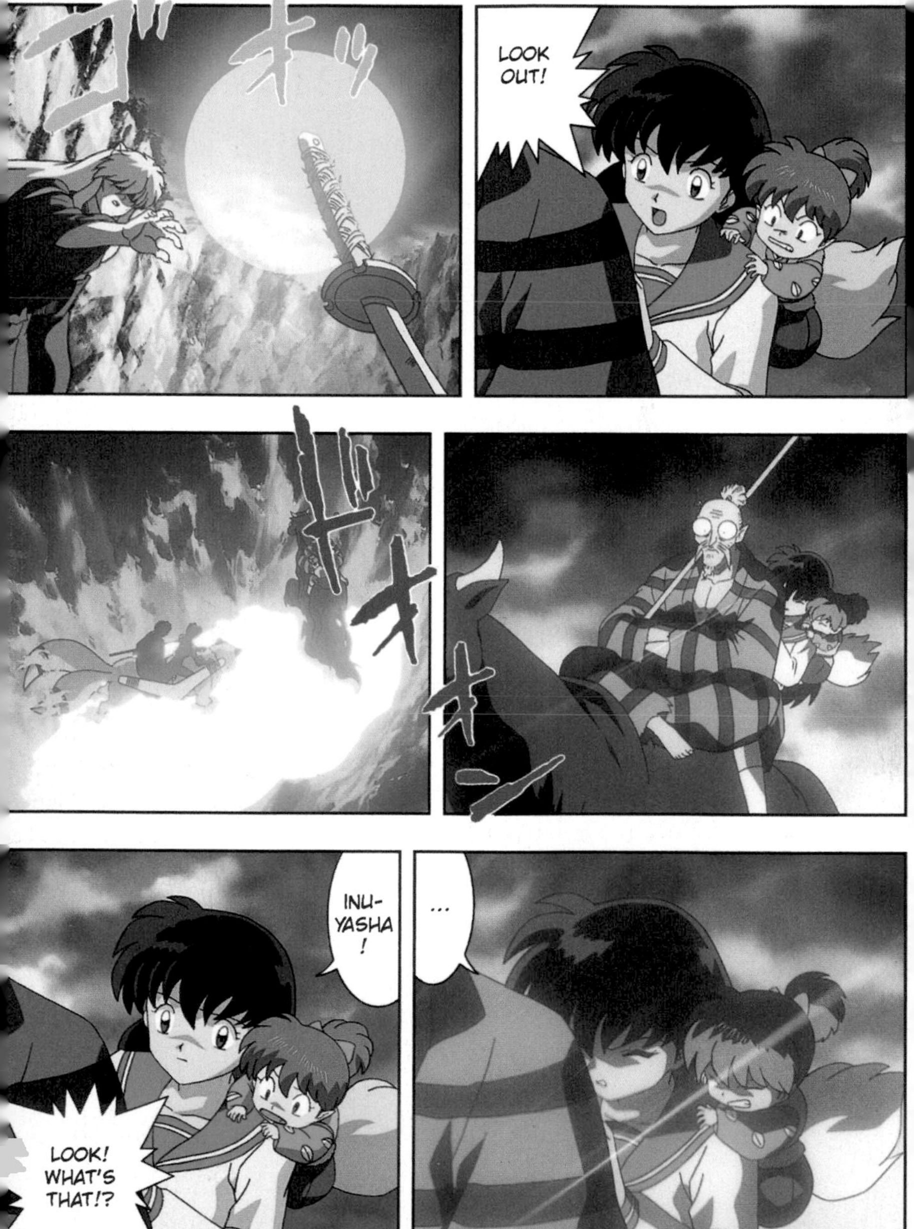
LOOK OUT!
ゴオッ
...
INU-YASHA!
LOOK! WHAT'S THAT!?

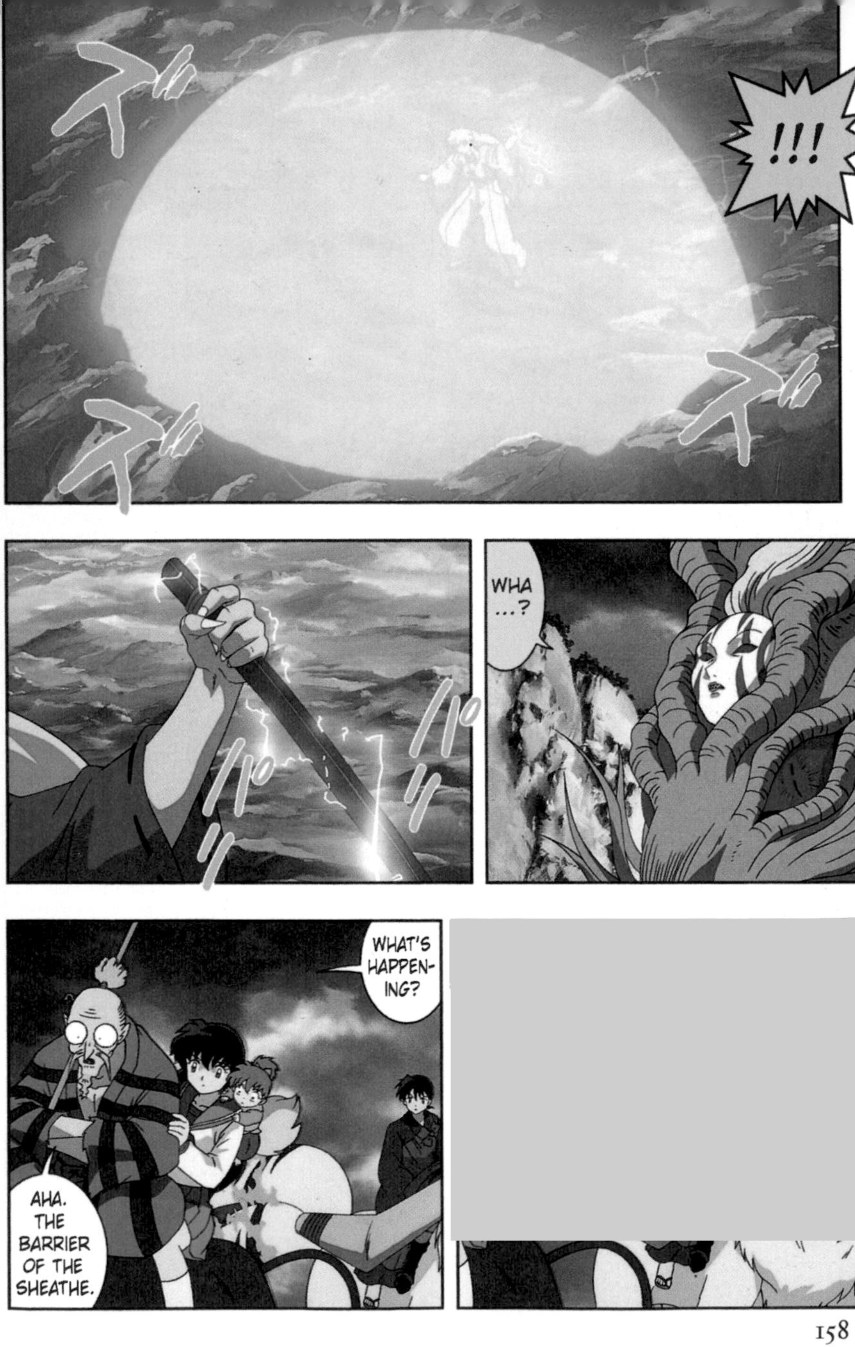
!!!
WHA ...?
WHAT'S HAPPENING?
AHA. THE BARRIER OF THE SHEATHE.

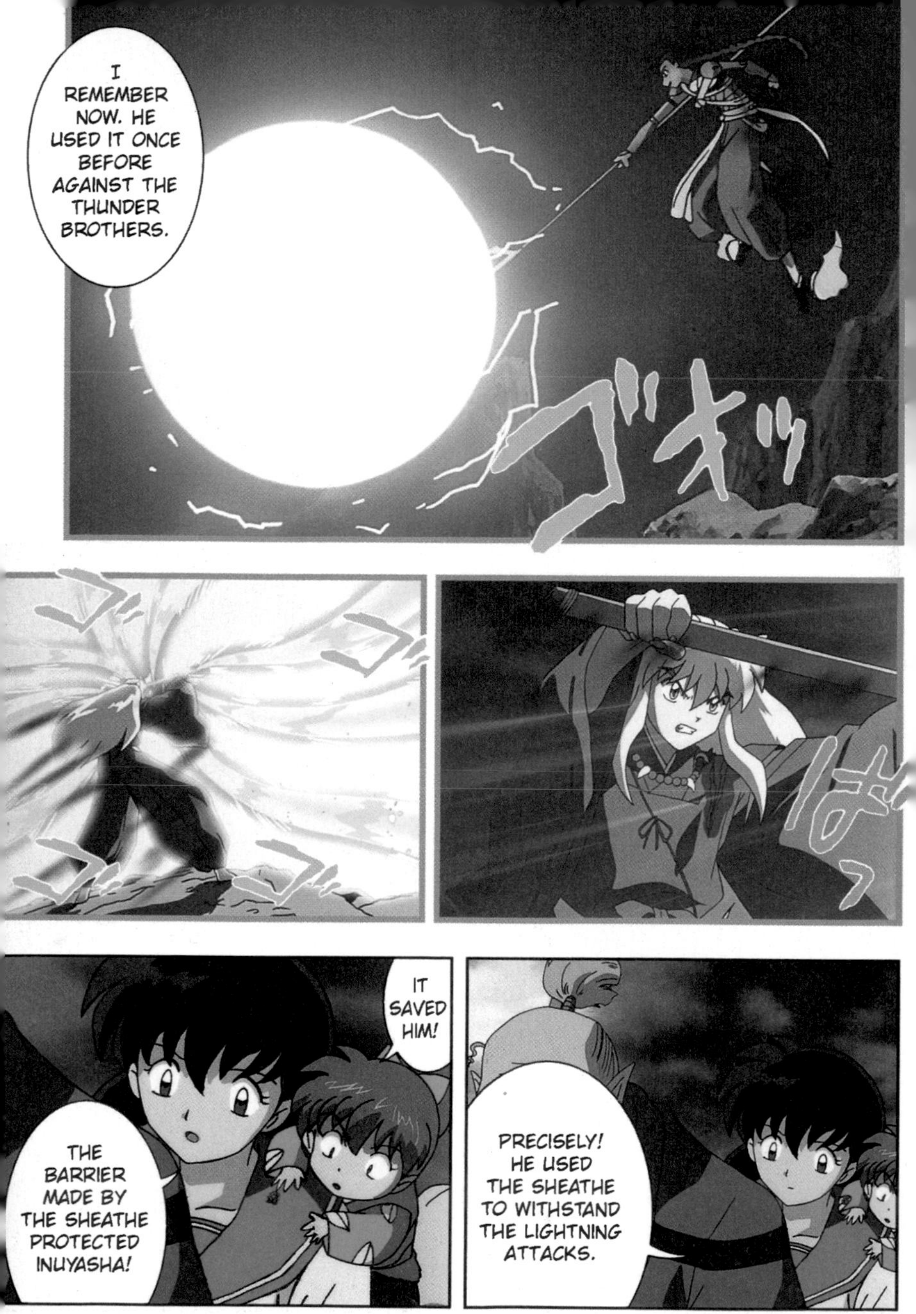
I REMEMBER NOW. HE USED IT ONCE BEFORE AGAINST THE THUNDER BROTHERS.
ゴキッ
はっ
PRECISELY! HE USED THE SHEATHE TO WITHSTAND THE LIGHTNING ATTACKS.
IT SAVED HIM!
THE BARRIER MADE BY THE SHEATHE PROTECTED INUYASHA!

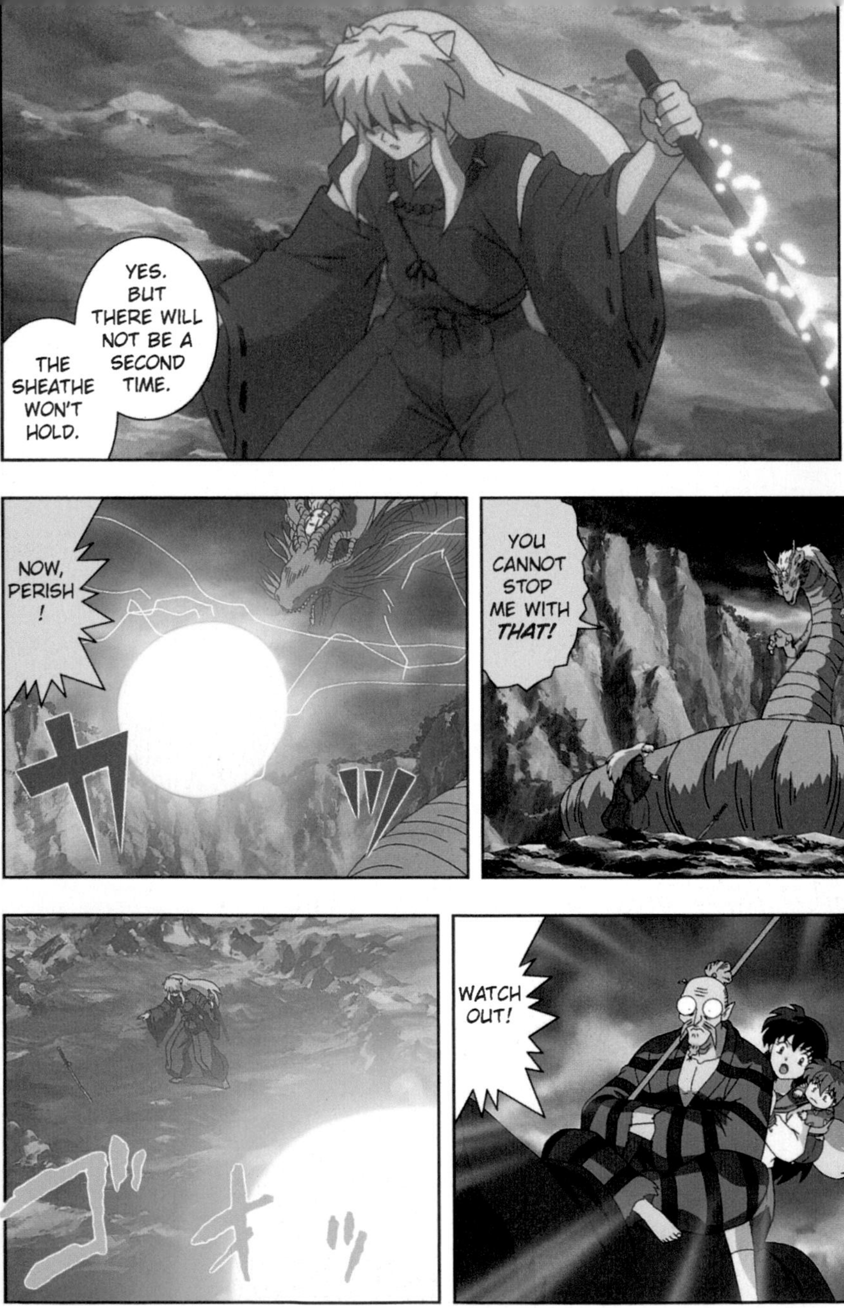
YES. BUT THERE WILL NOT BE A SECOND TIME.
THE SHEATHE WON'T HOLD.
YOU CANNOT STOP ME WITH *THAT!*
NOW, PERISH!
WATCH OUT!

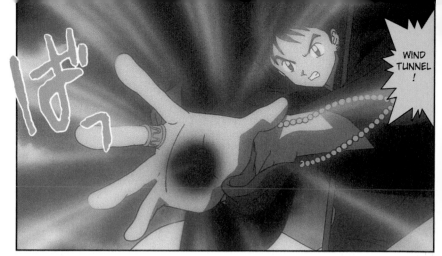

WIND TUNNEL!

ばっ

ゴキォォ…

MIRO-KU!

ゴキォォ…

ゴォォォォォォォォ…

IT'S TOO STRONG!

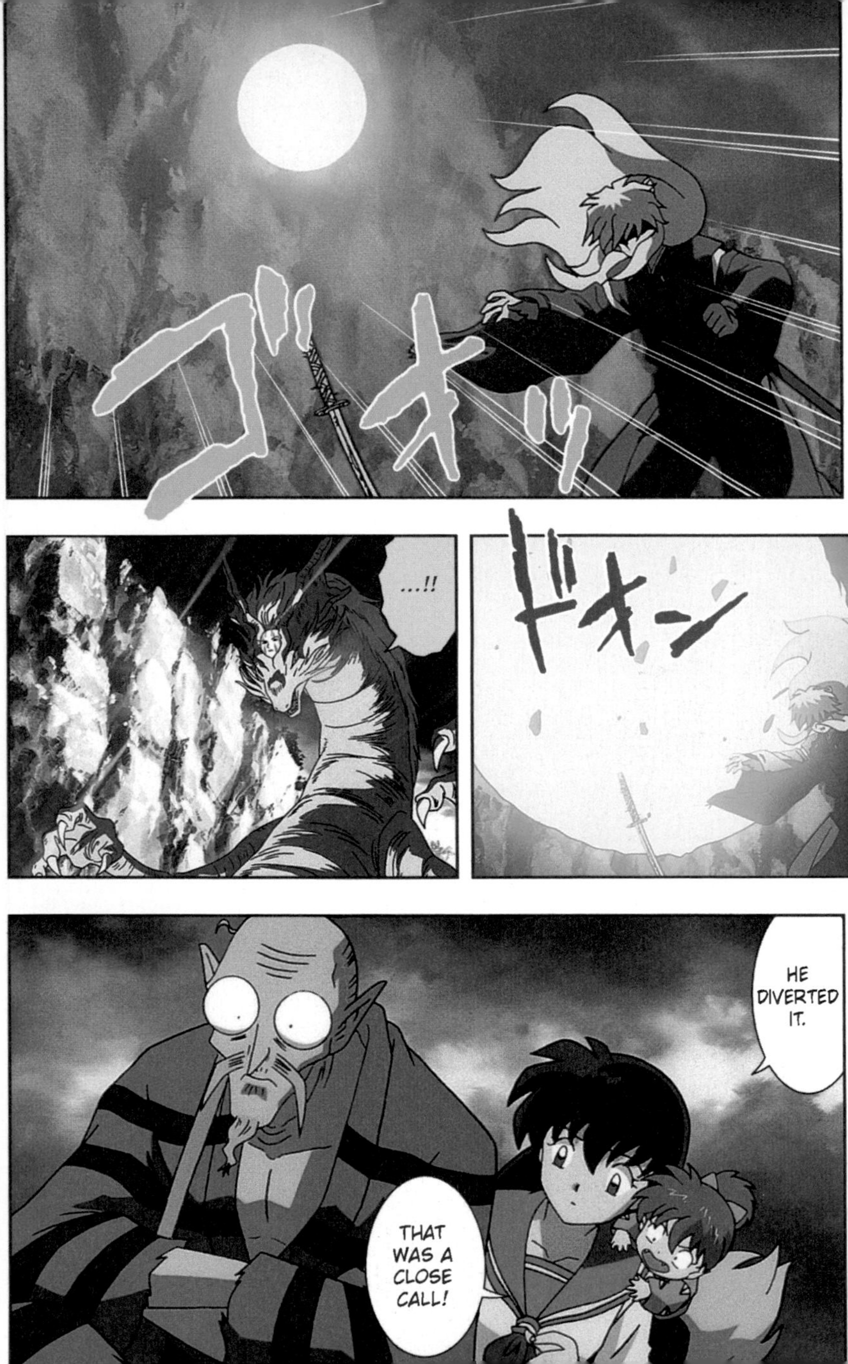
ゴオッ
ドオン
...!!
HE DIVERTED IT.
THAT WAS A CLOSE CALL!

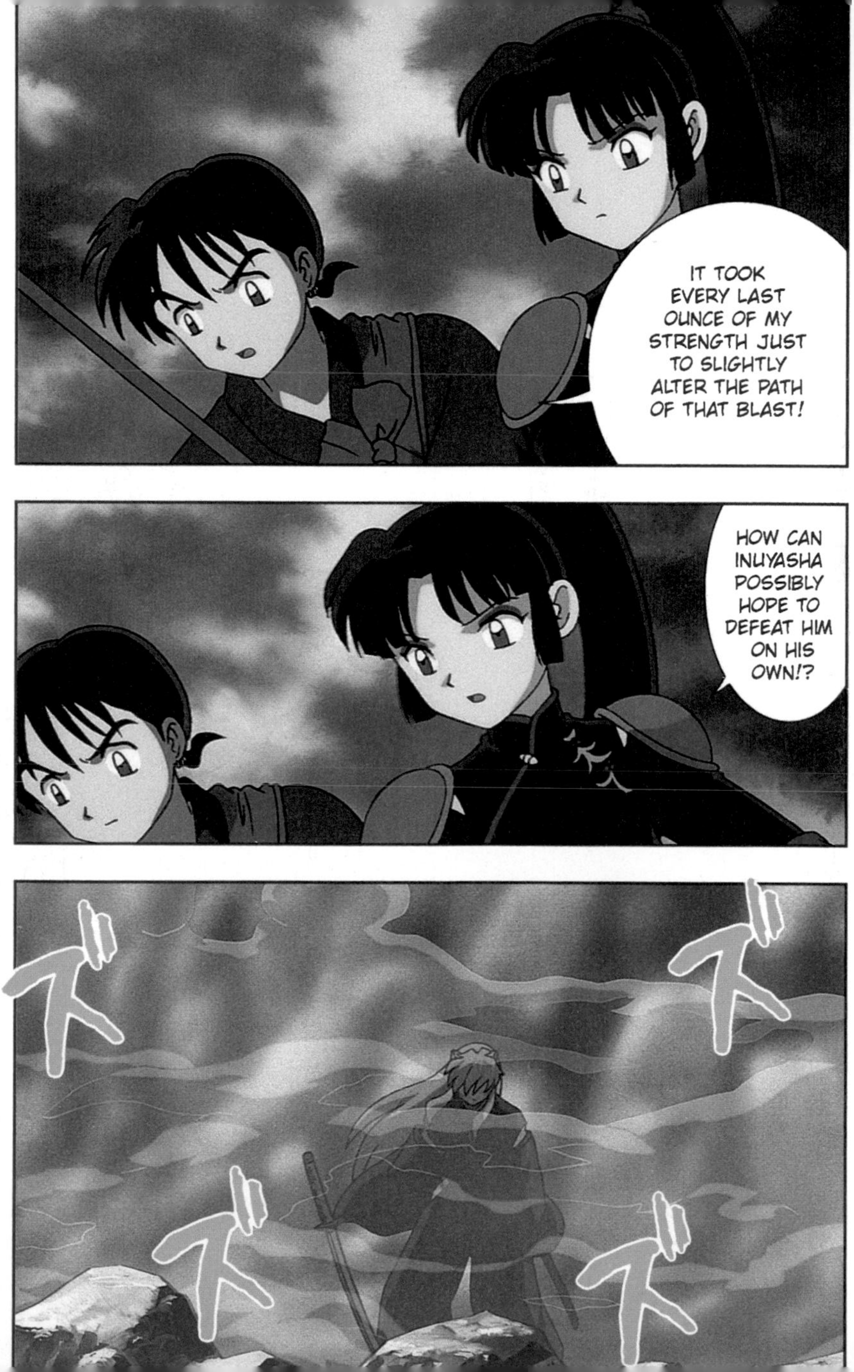
IT TOOK EVERY LAST OUNCE OF MY STRENGTH JUST TO SLIGHTLY ALTER THE PATH OF THAT BLAST!
HOW CAN INUYASHA POSSIBLY HOPE TO DEFEAT HIM ON HIS OWN!?
ズ
ズ
ズ
ズ

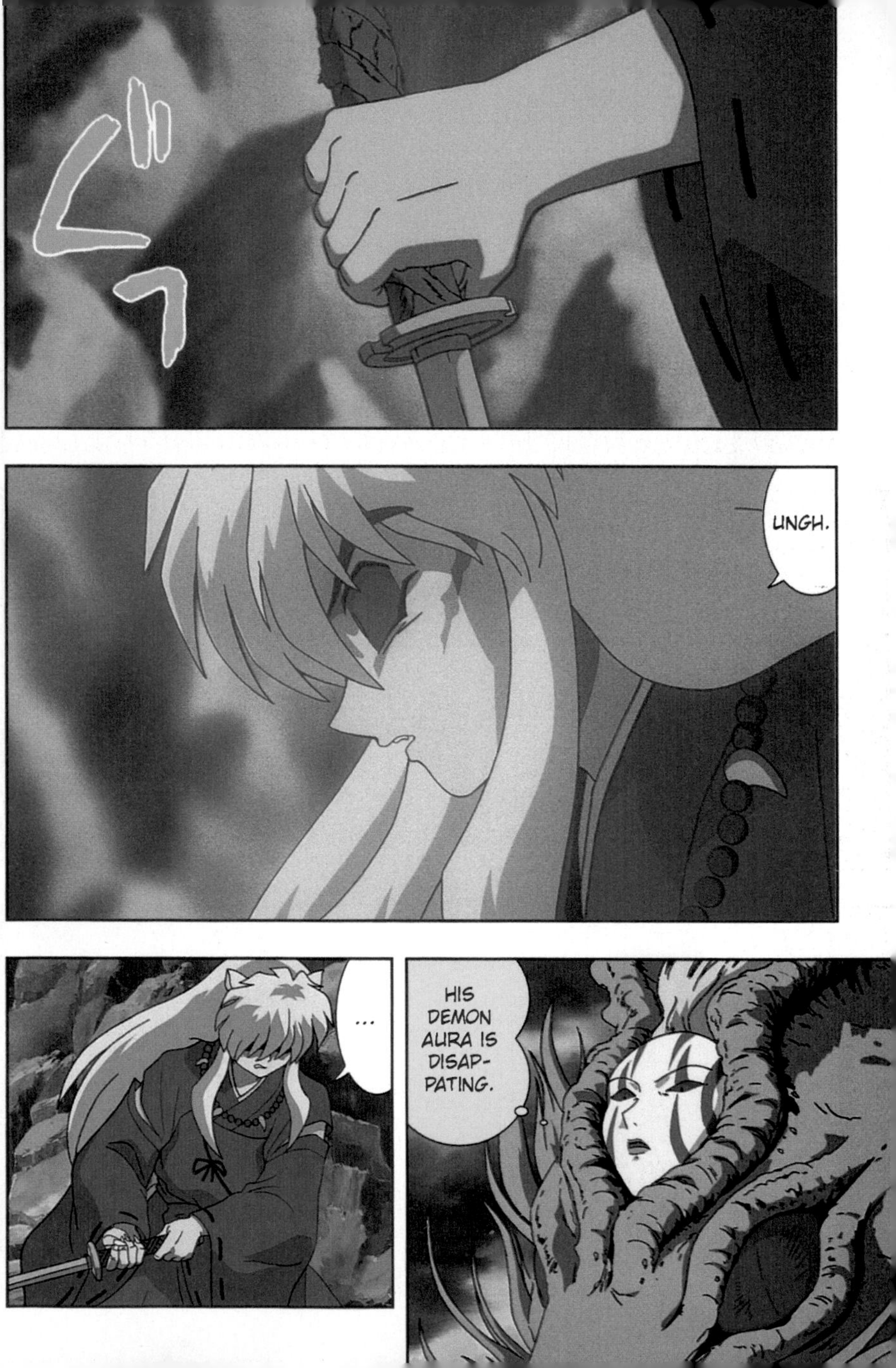
ぐっ
UNGH.
HIS DEMON AURA IS DISAP-PATING.
...

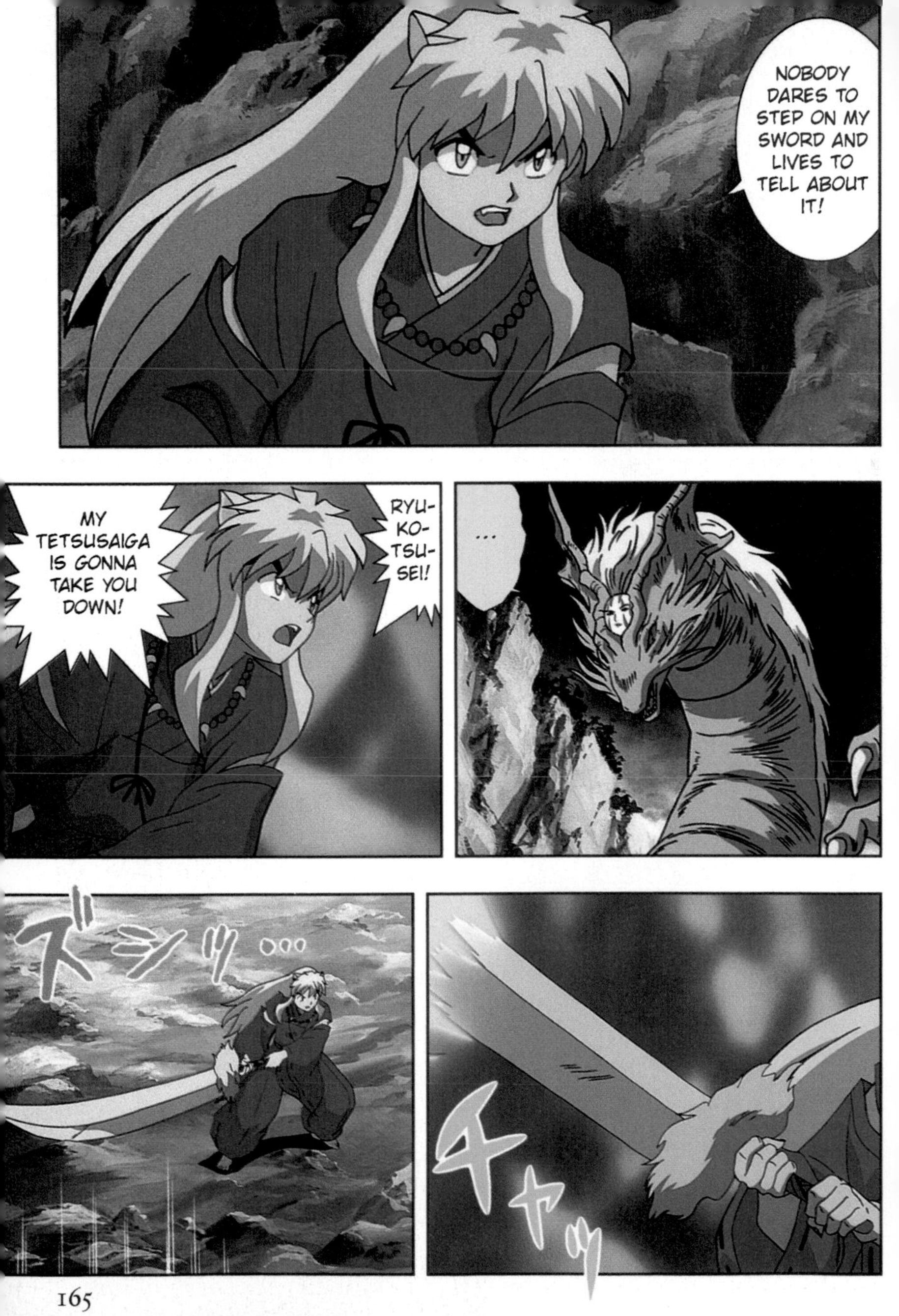
NOBODY DARES TO STEP ON MY SWORD AND LIVES TO TELL ABOUT IT!
...
RYU-KO-TSU-SEI!
MY TETSUSAIGA IS GONNA TAKE YOU DOWN!
チャッ
ズシッ

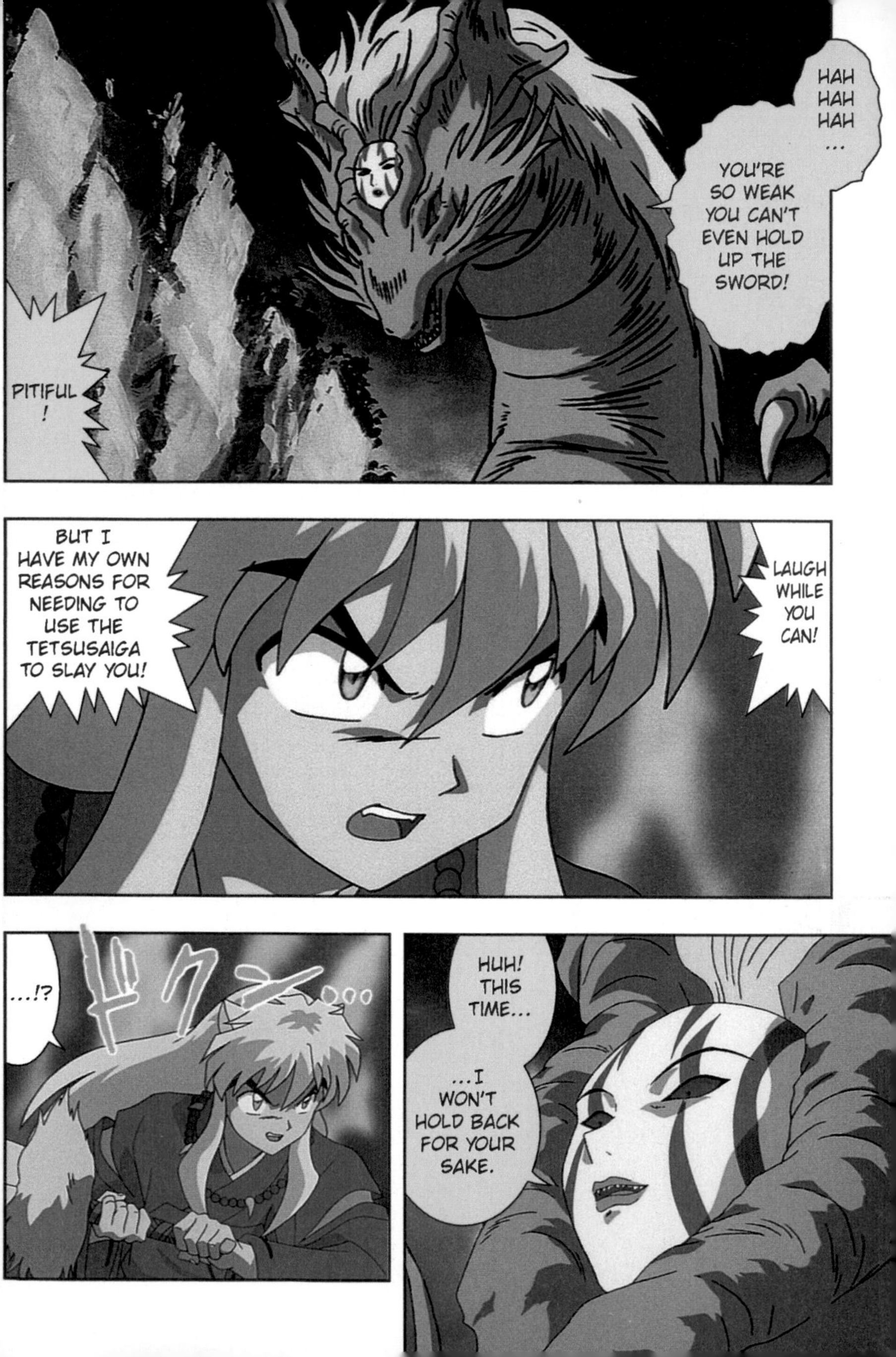
HAH HAH HAH ... YOU'RE SO WEAK YOU CAN'T EVEN HOLD UP THE SWORD!
PITIFUL!
LAUGH WHILE YOU CAN!
BUT I HAVE MY OWN REASONS FOR NEEDING TO USE THE TETSUSAIGA TO SLAY YOU!
HUH! THIS TIME...
...I WON'T HOLD BACK FOR YOUR SAKE.
...!?

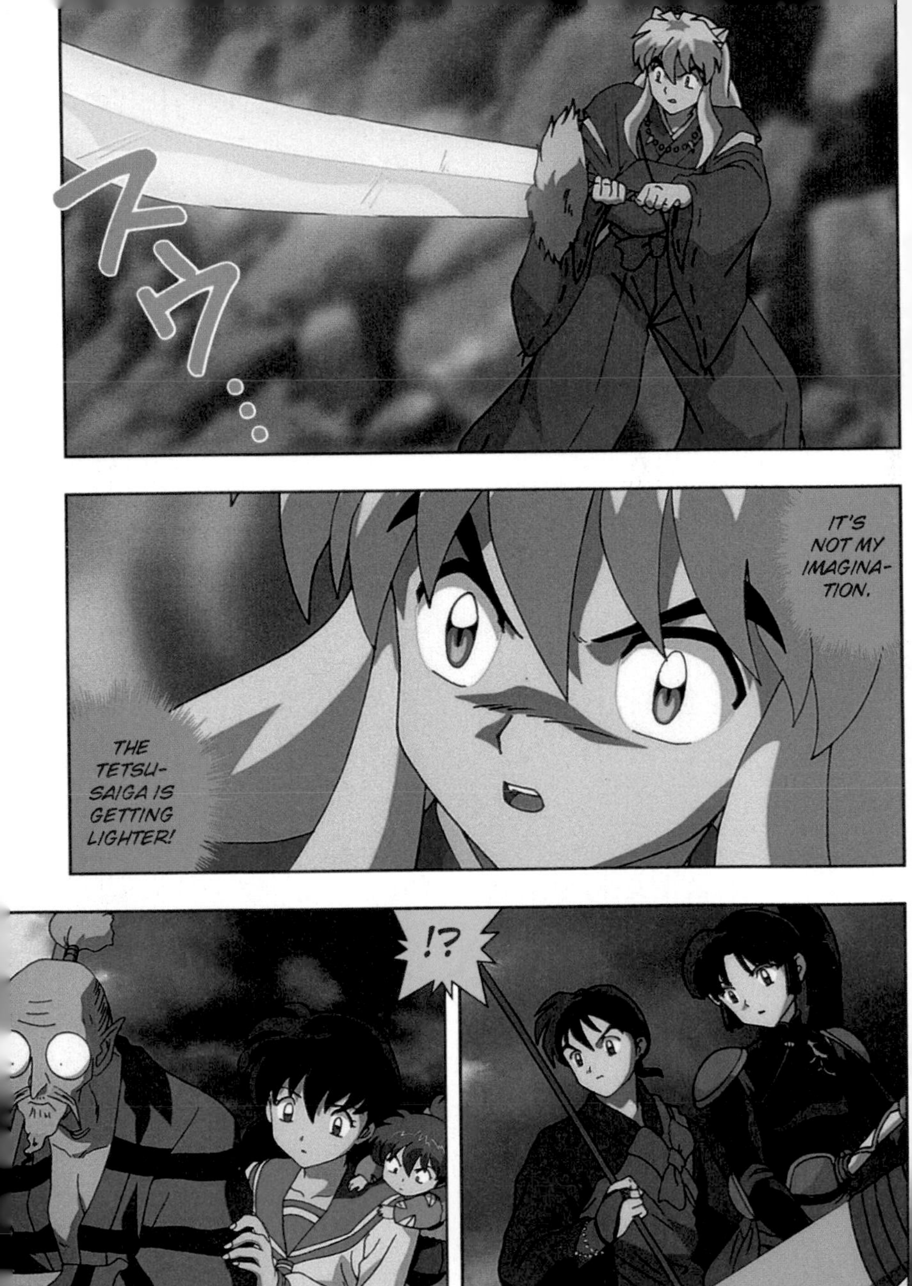
スゥ...
IT'S NOT MY IMAGINATION.
THE TETSU-SAIGA IS GETTING LIGHTER!
!?

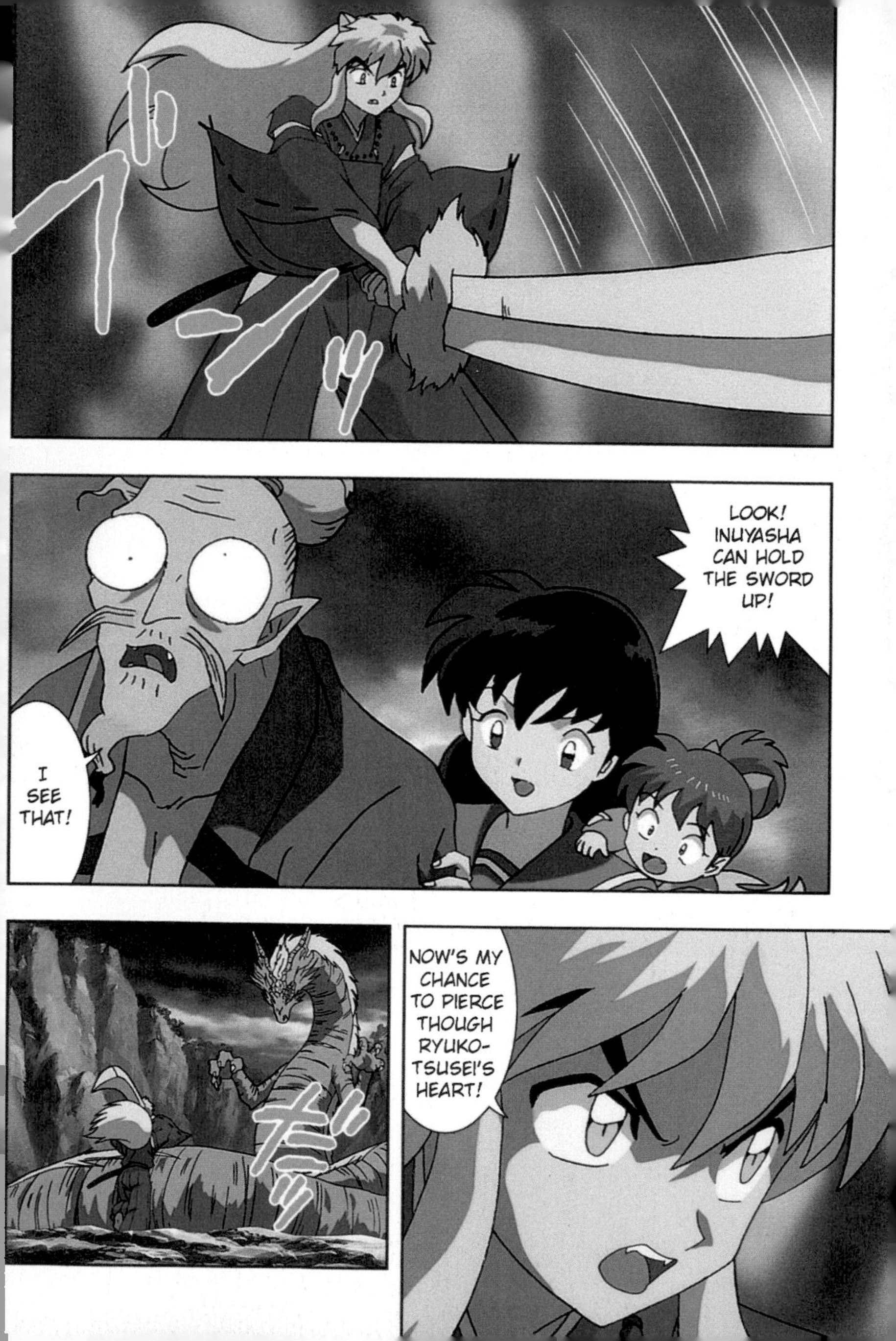
LOOK! INUYASHA CAN HOLD THE SWORD UP!
I SEE THAT!
NOW'S MY CHANCE TO PIERCE THOUGH RYUKO-TSUSEI'S HEART!

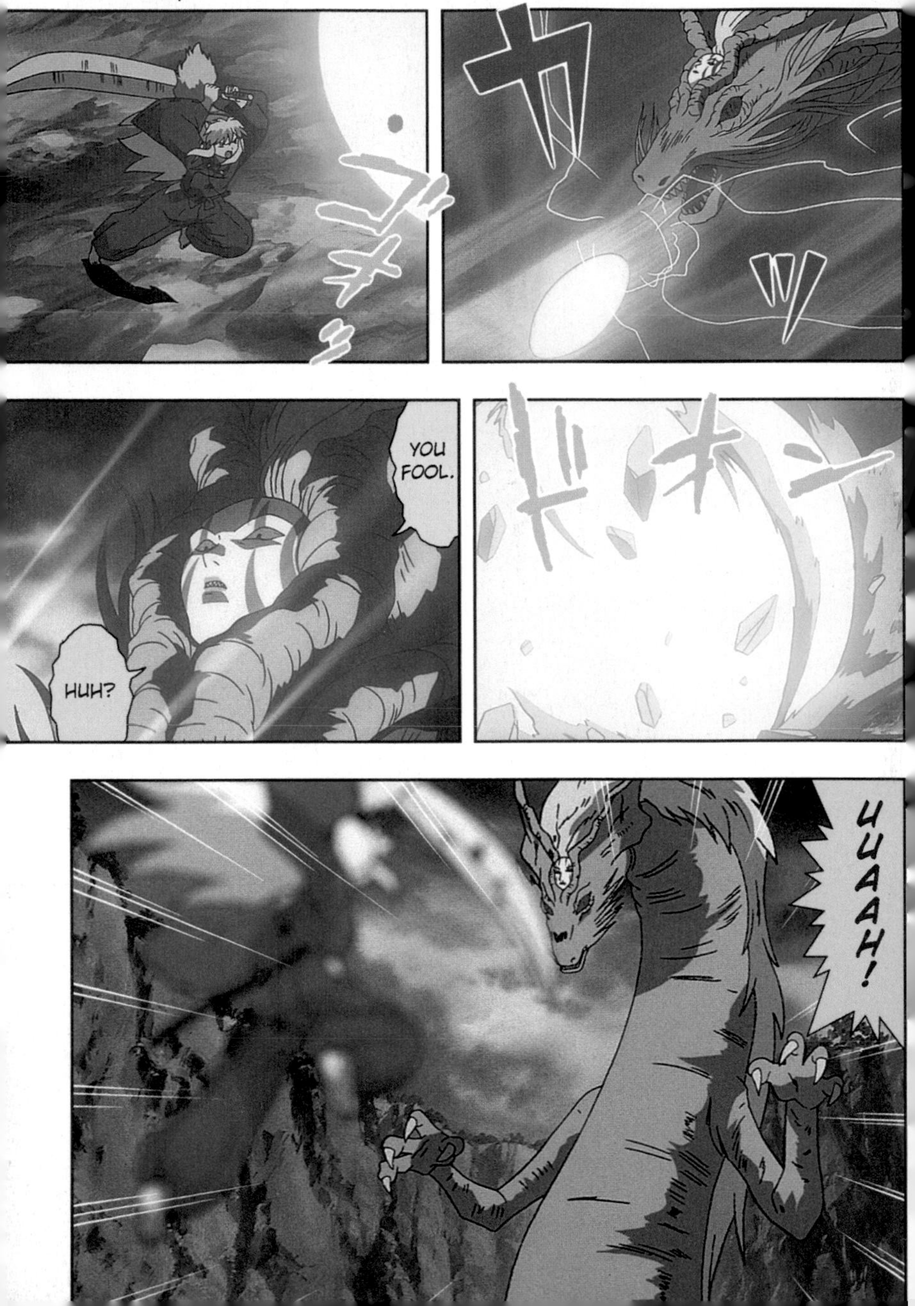
YOU FOOL.
HUH?
UUAAH!

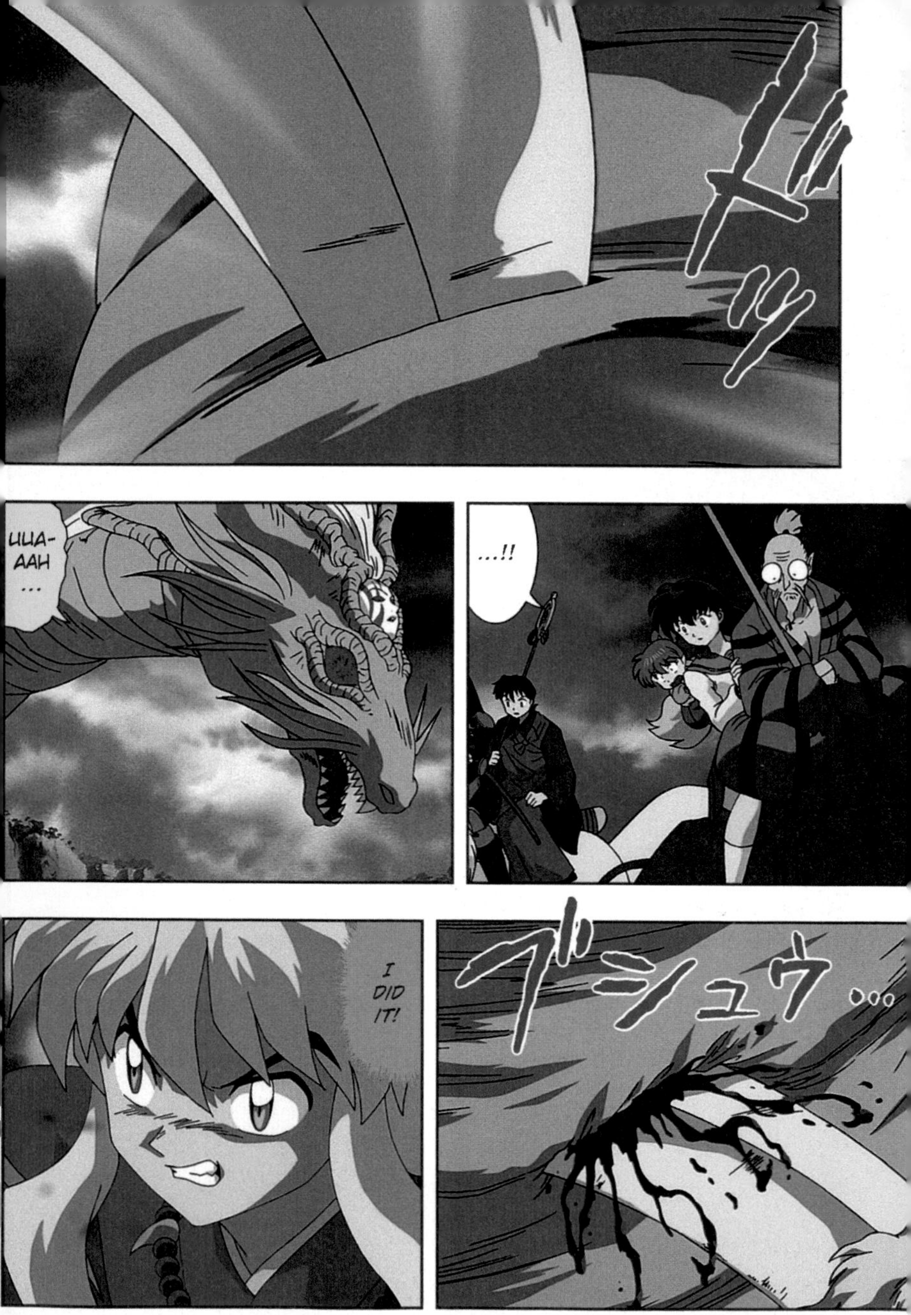
...!!
UUA-AAH ...
ブシュウ...
I DID IT!

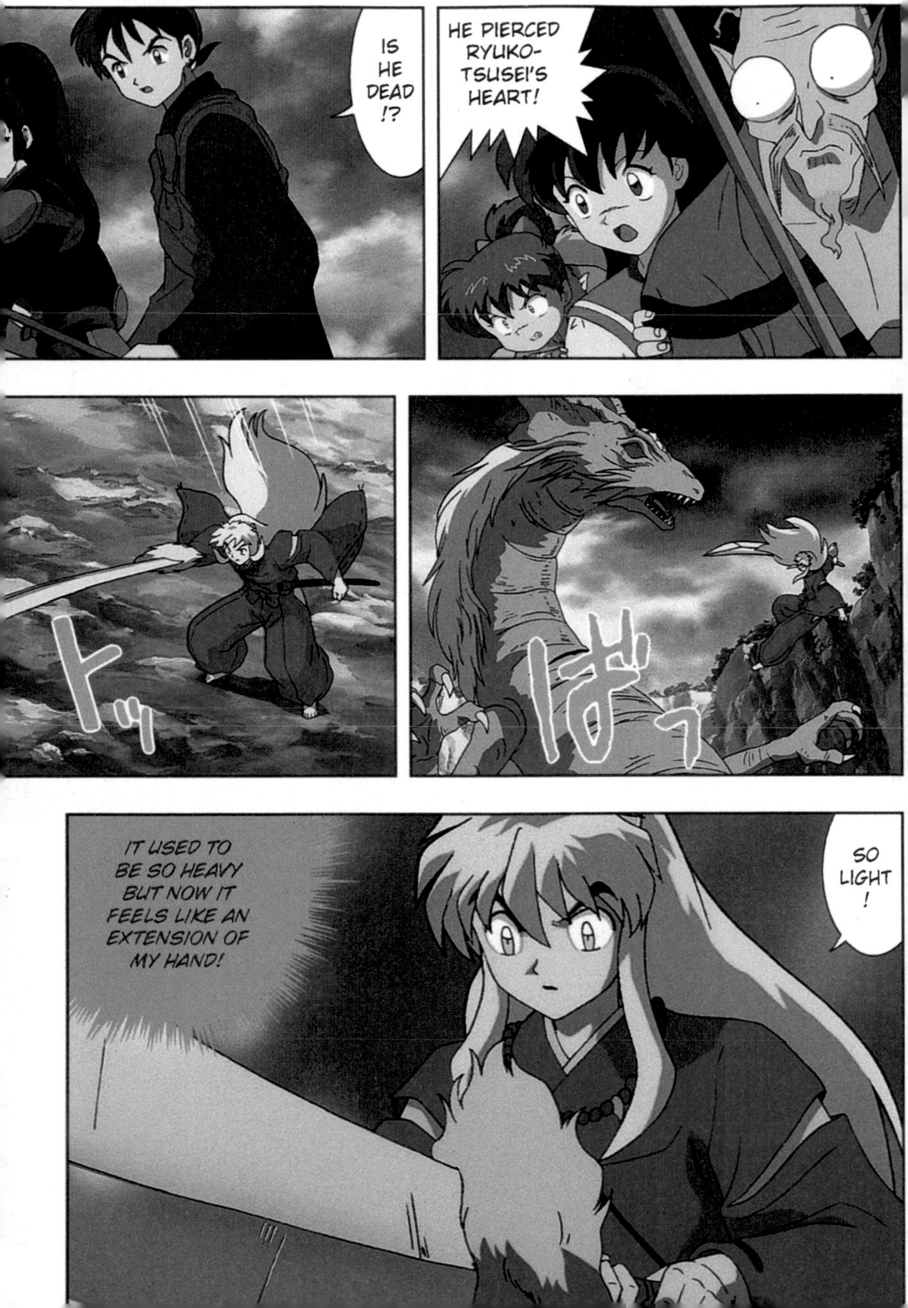
HE PIERCED RYUKO-TSUSEI'S HEART!
IS HE DEAD !?
ぱっ
トッ
SO LIGHT !
IT USED TO BE SO HEAVY BUT NOW IT FEELS LIKE AN EXTENSION OF MY HAND!

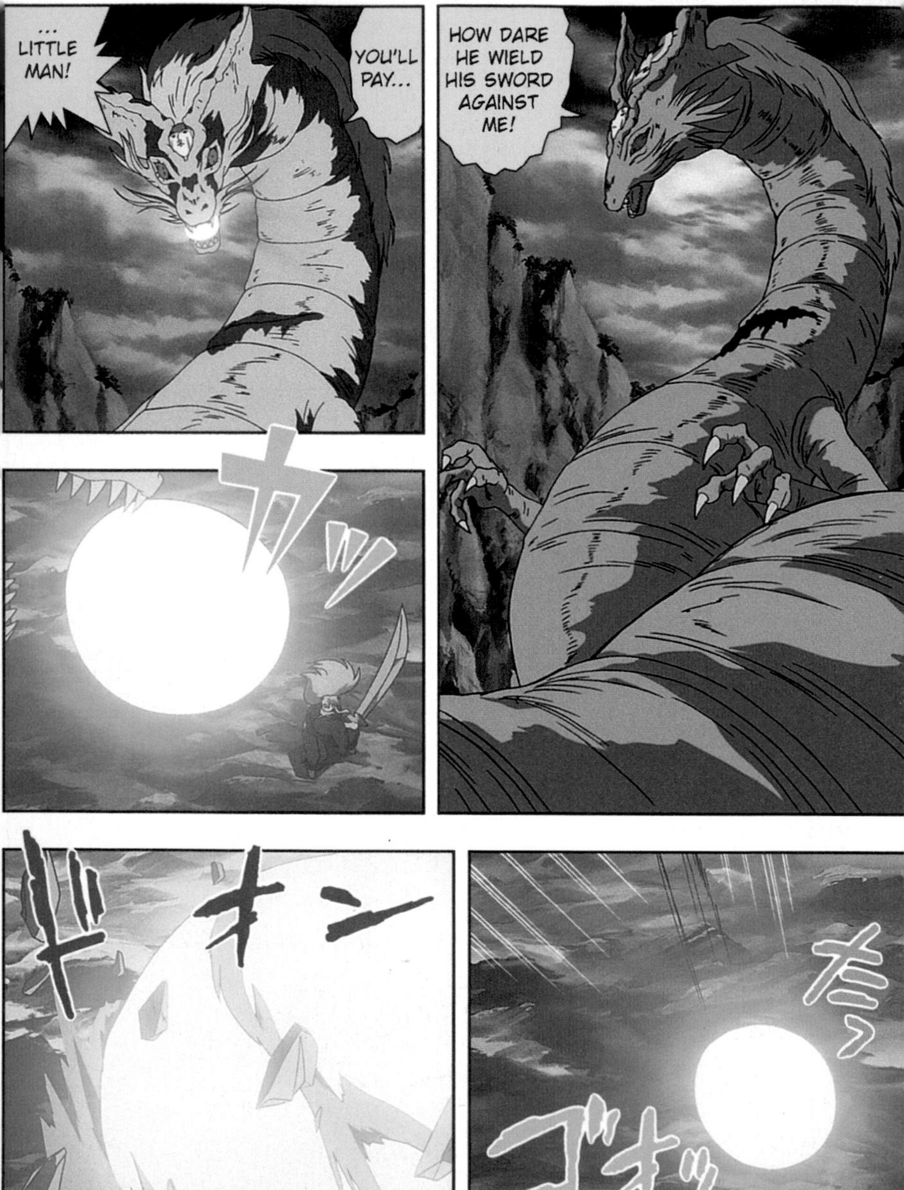
HOW DARE HE WIELD HIS SWORD AGAINST ME!
YOU'LL PAY...
... LITTLE MAN!
カッ
たっ
ゴォッ
ドオン

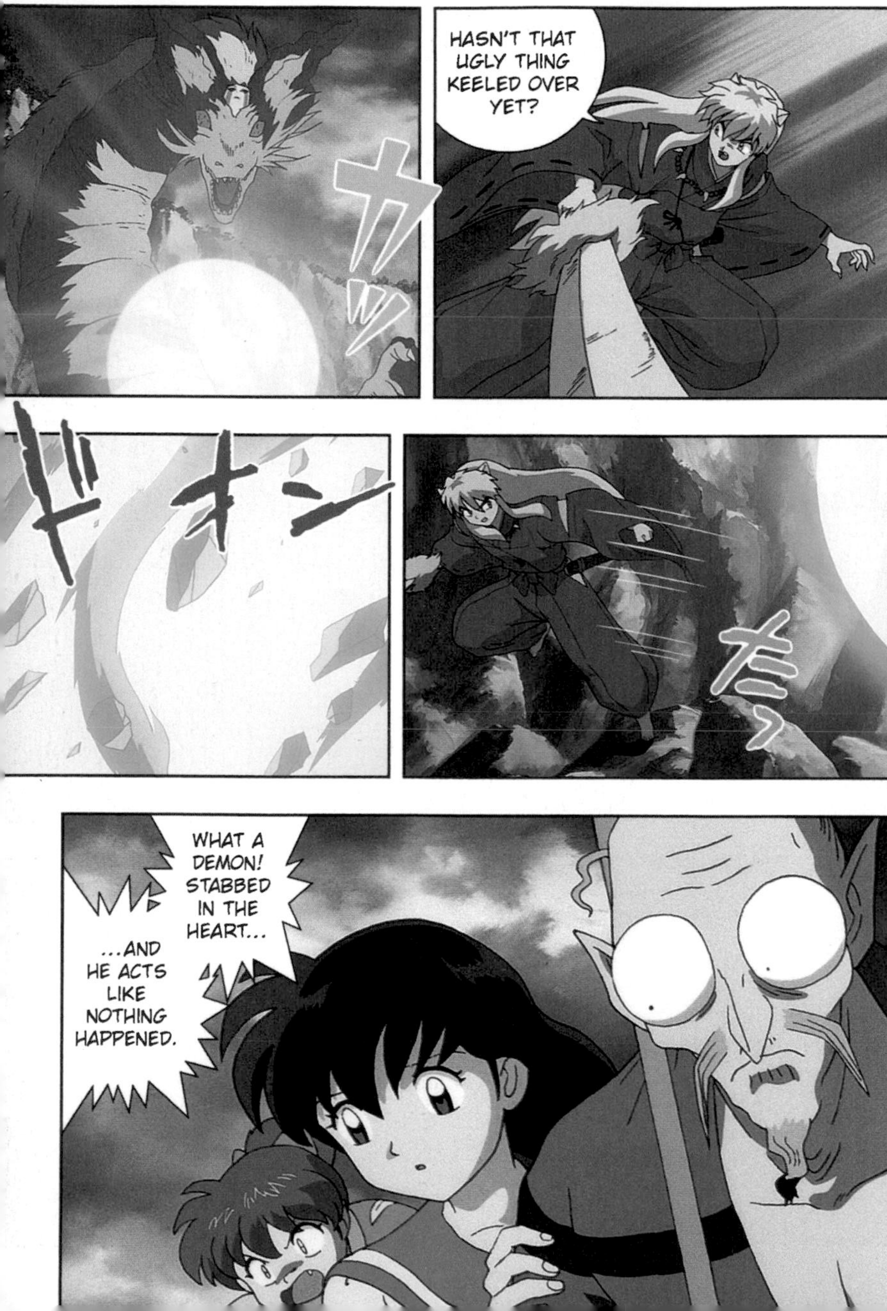
HASN'T THAT UGLY THING KEELED OVER YET?
カッ
たっ
ドオン
WHAT A DEMON! STABBED IN THE HEART...
...AND HE ACTS LIKE NOTHING HAPPENED.

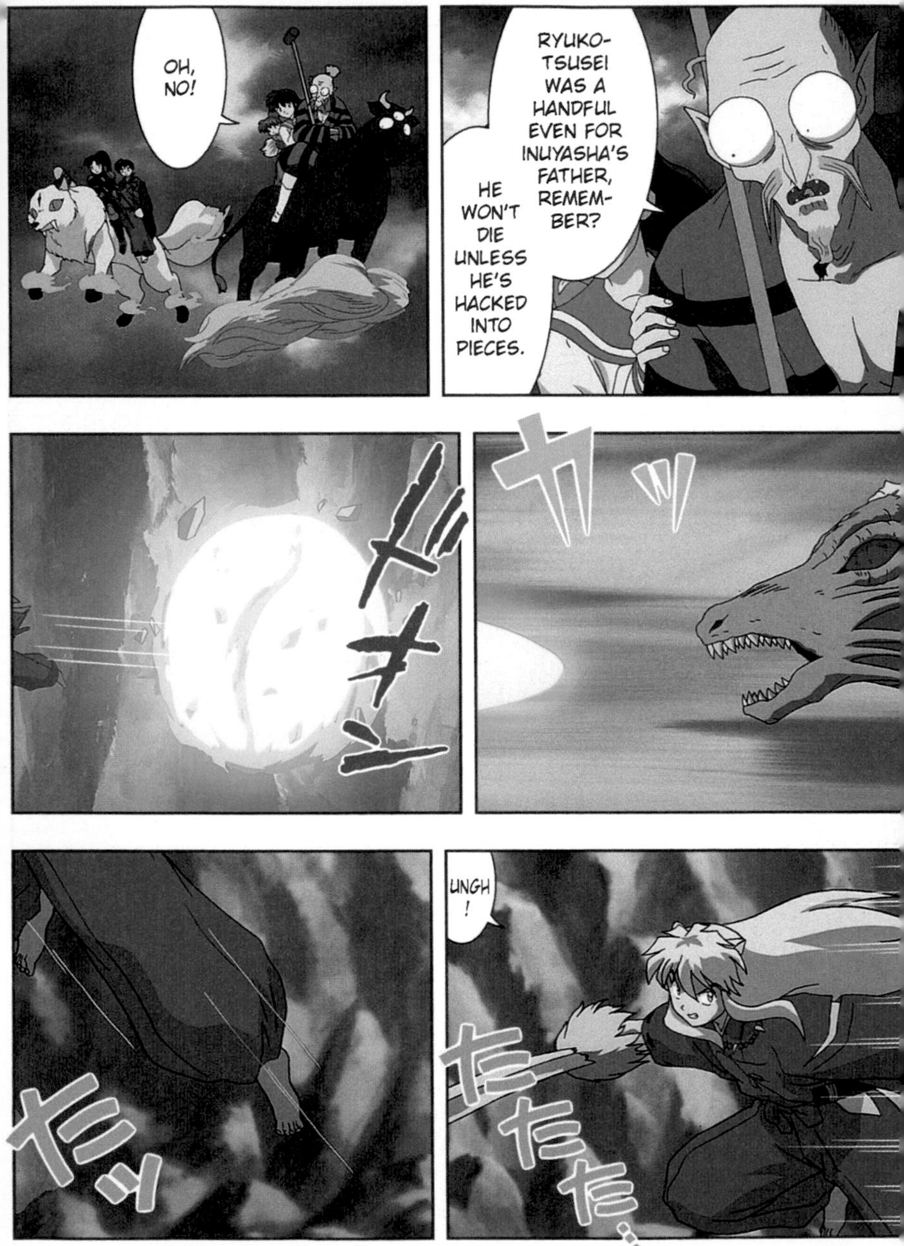
RYUKO-TSUSEI WAS A HANDFUL EVEN FOR INUYASHA'S FATHER, REMEMBER?
HE WON'T DIE UNLESS HE'S HACKED INTO PIECES.
OH, NO!
UNGH!
たたた…

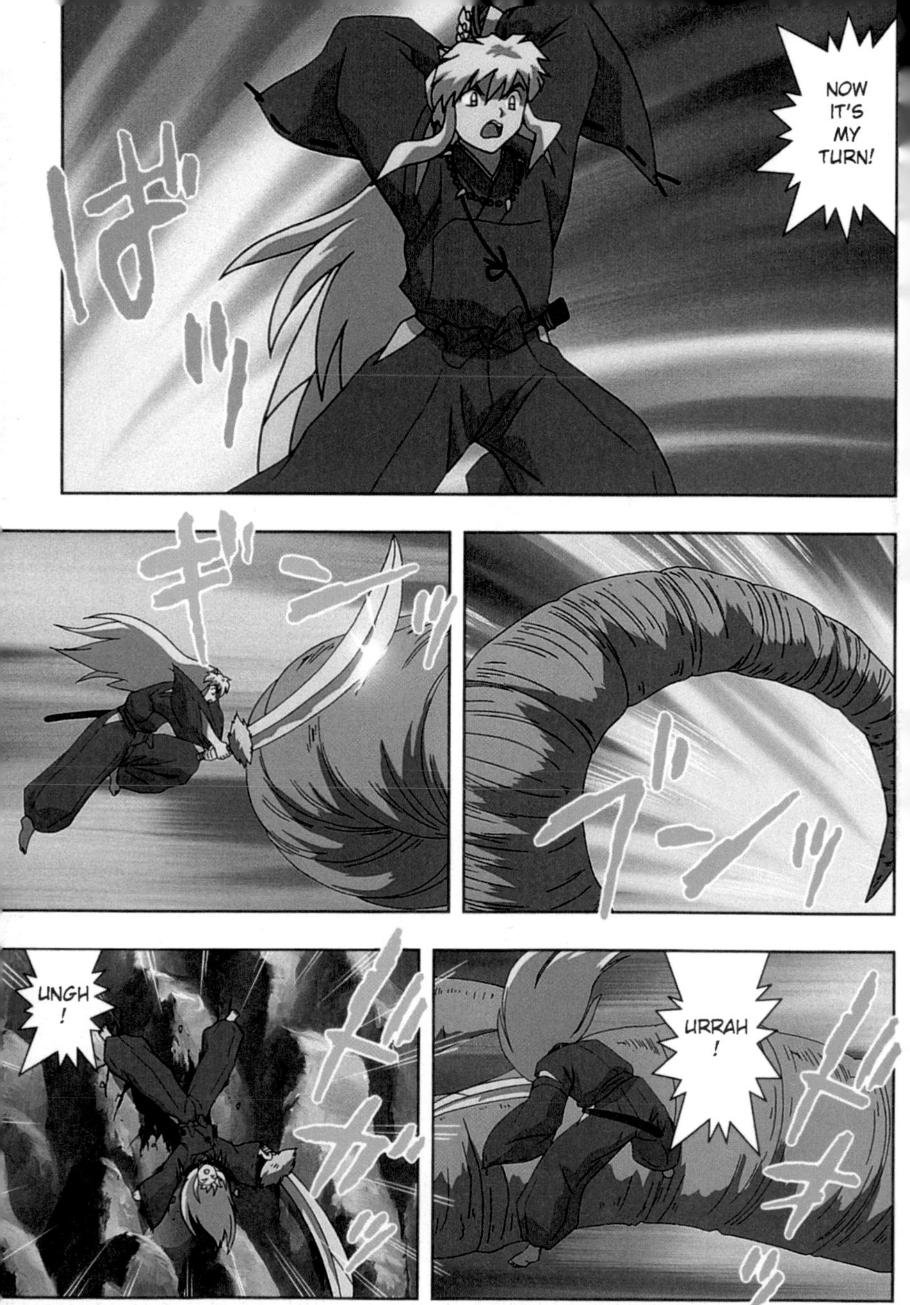
NOW IT'S MY TURN!
ばッ
ブンッ
ギンッ
URRAH!
UNGH!
ドガッ

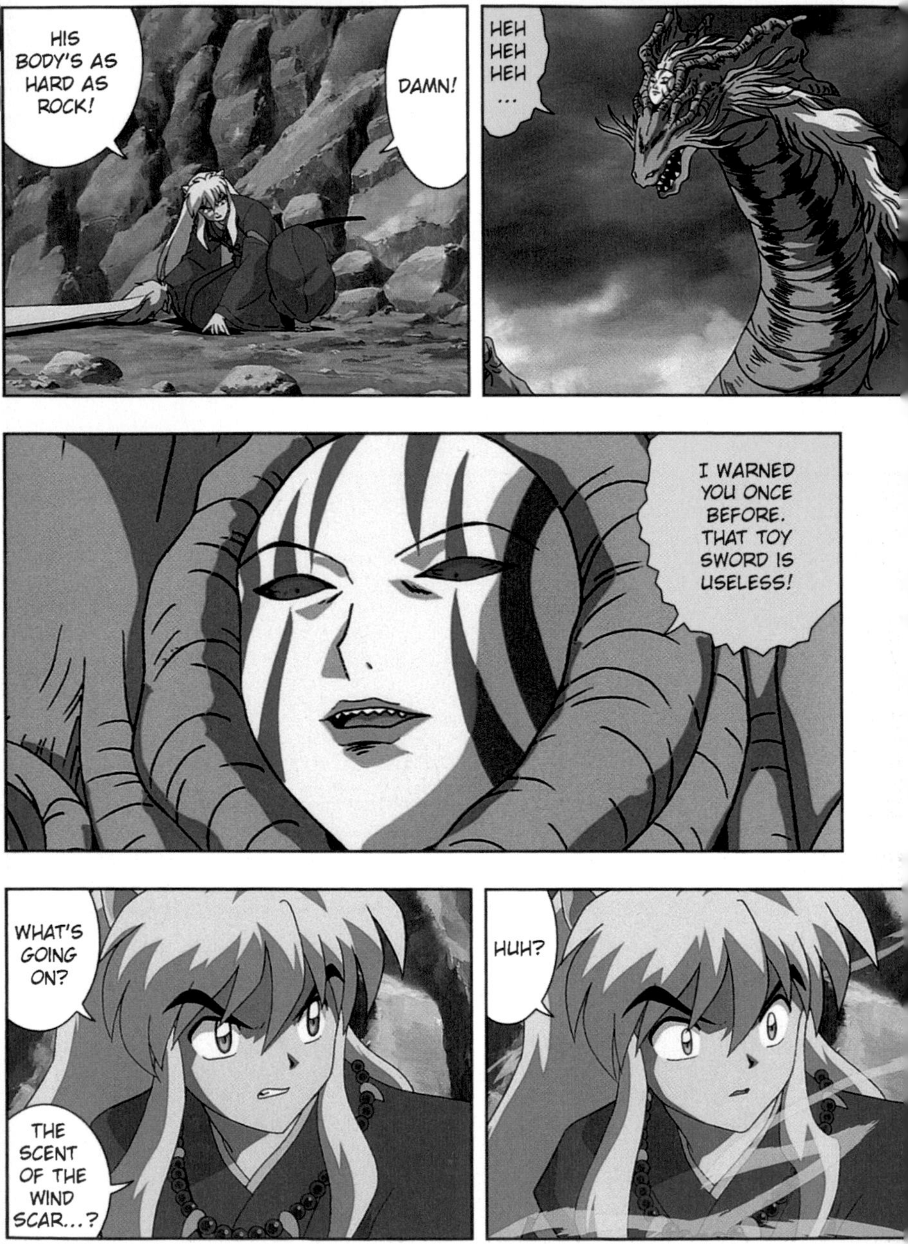
HEH HEH HEH ...
DAMN!
HIS BODY'S AS HARD AS ROCK!
I WARNED YOU ONCE BEFORE. THAT TOY SWORD IS USELESS!
HUH?
WHAT'S GOING ON?
THE SCENT OF THE WIND SCAR...?

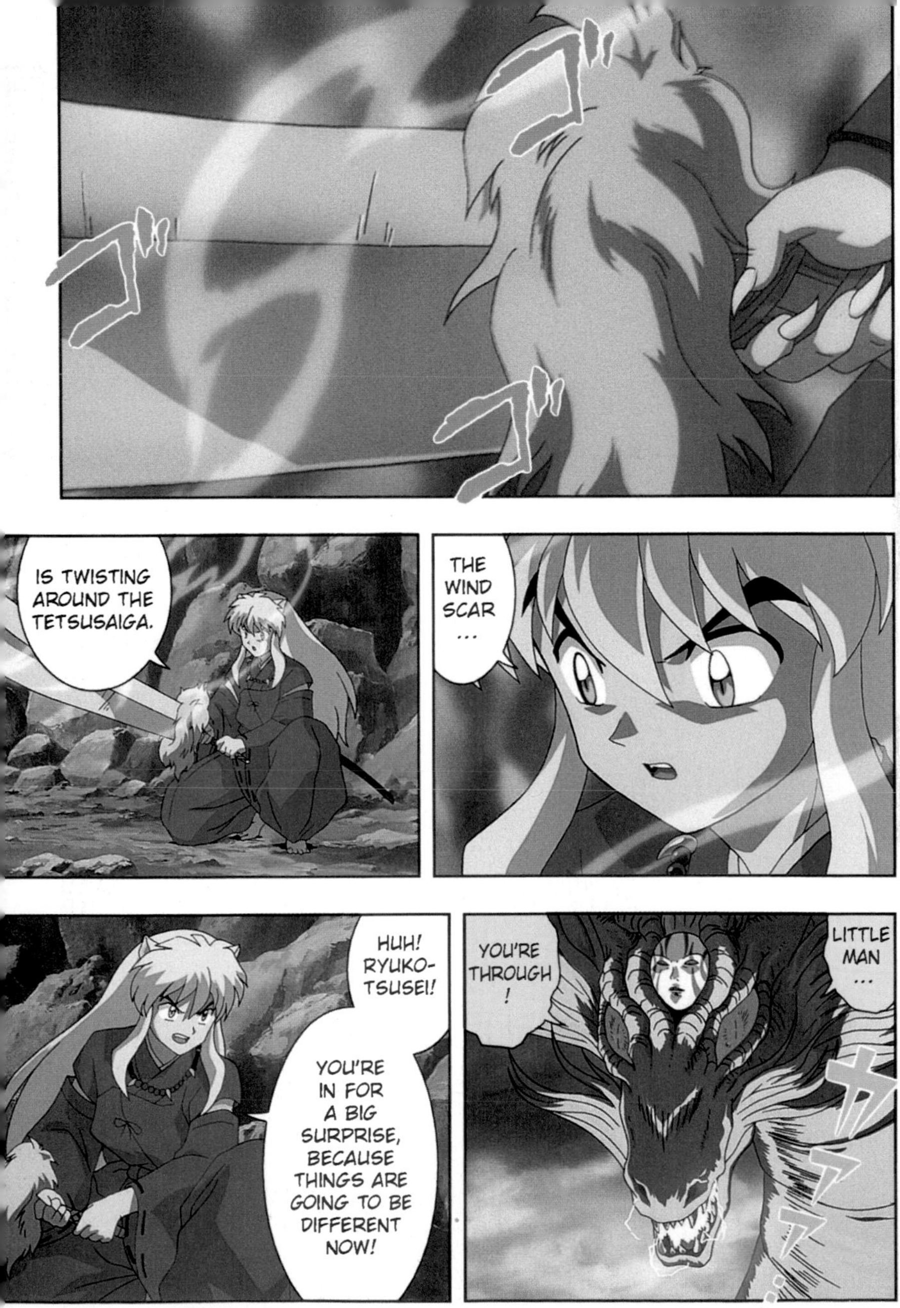
THE WIND SCAR ...
IS TWISTING AROUND THE TETSUSAIGA.
LITTLE MAN ...
YOU'RE THROUGH!
HUH! RYUKO-TSUSEI!
YOU'RE IN FOR A BIG SURPRISE, BECAUSE THINGS ARE GOING TO BE DIFFERENT NOW!

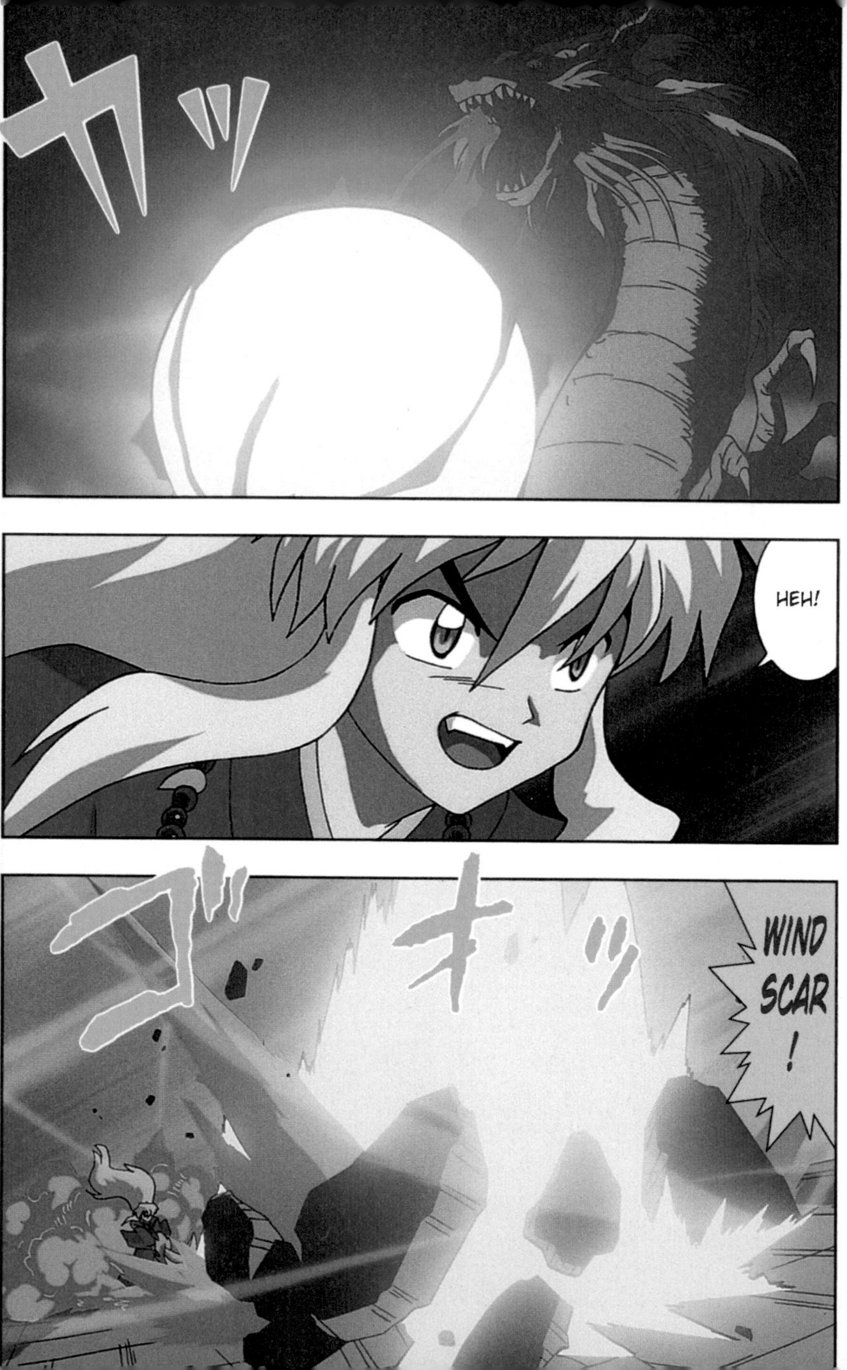
カッ
HEH!
WIND SCAR !
ゴオッ

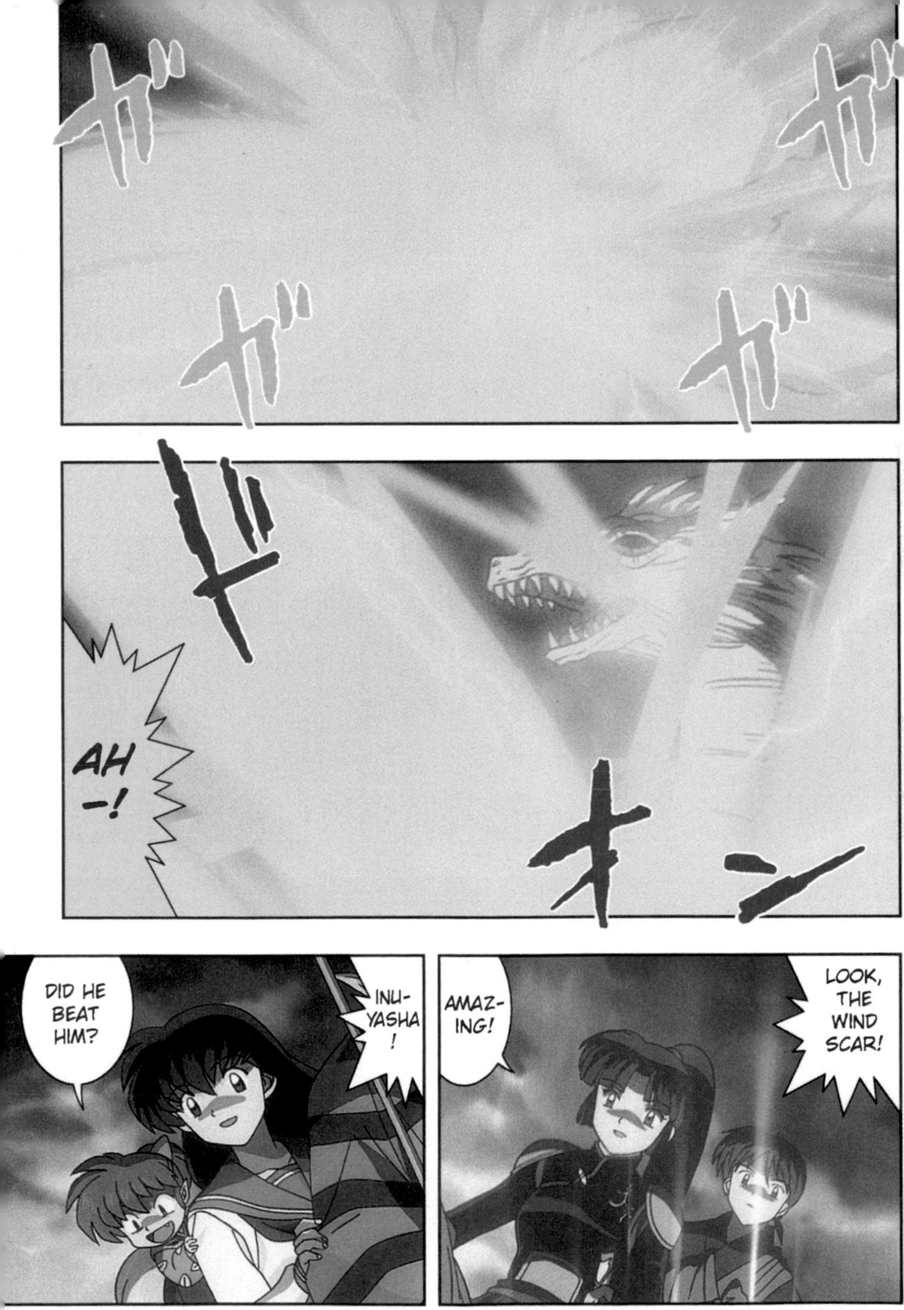
ガ
ガ
ガ
ガ
AH-!
ドオン
LOOK, THE WIND SCAR!
AMAZ-ING!
INU-YASHA!
DID HE BEAT HIM?

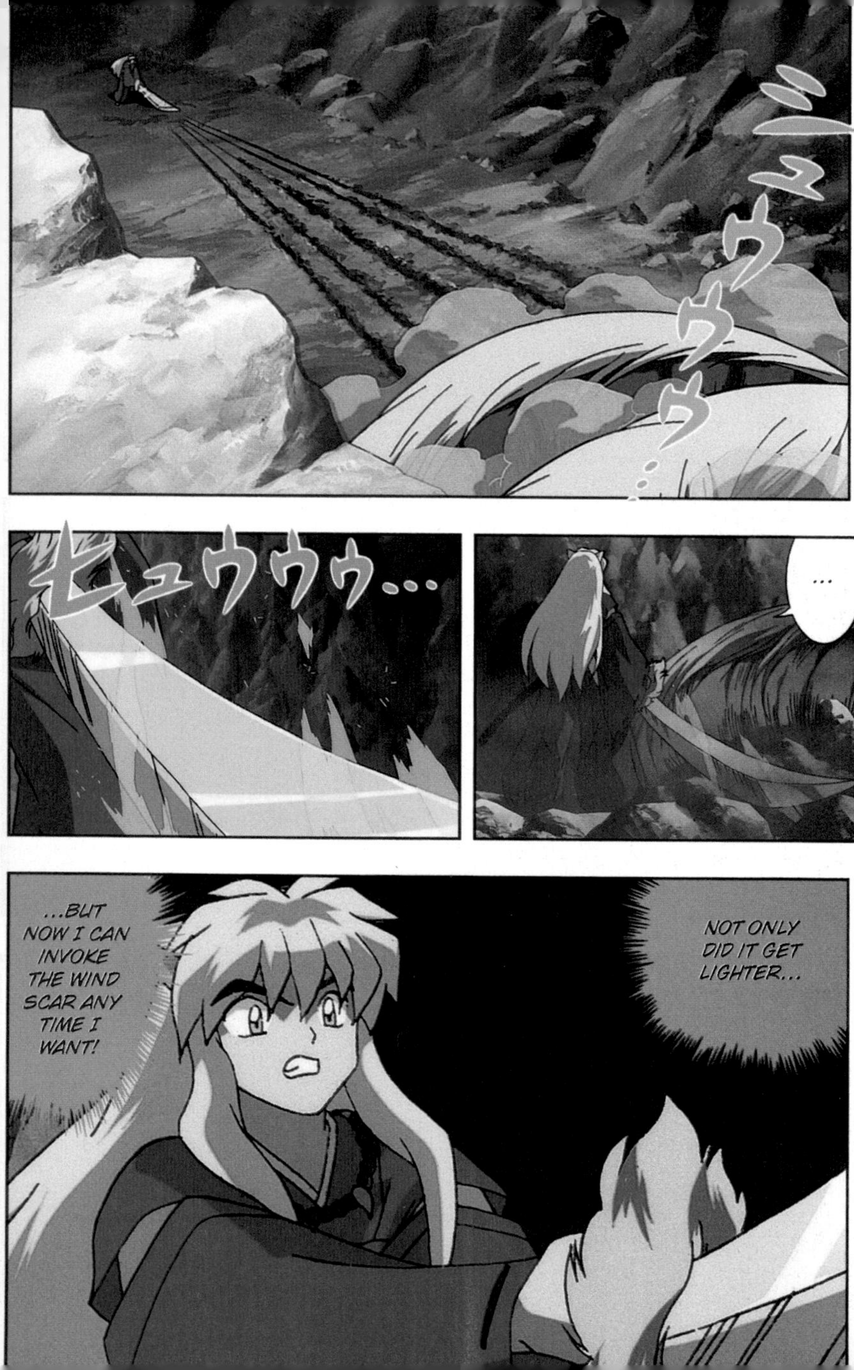
ミュウウウ…
…
ヒュウウウ…
NOT ONLY DID IT GET LIGHTER…
…BUT NOW I CAN INVOKE THE WIND SCAR ANY TIME I WANT!

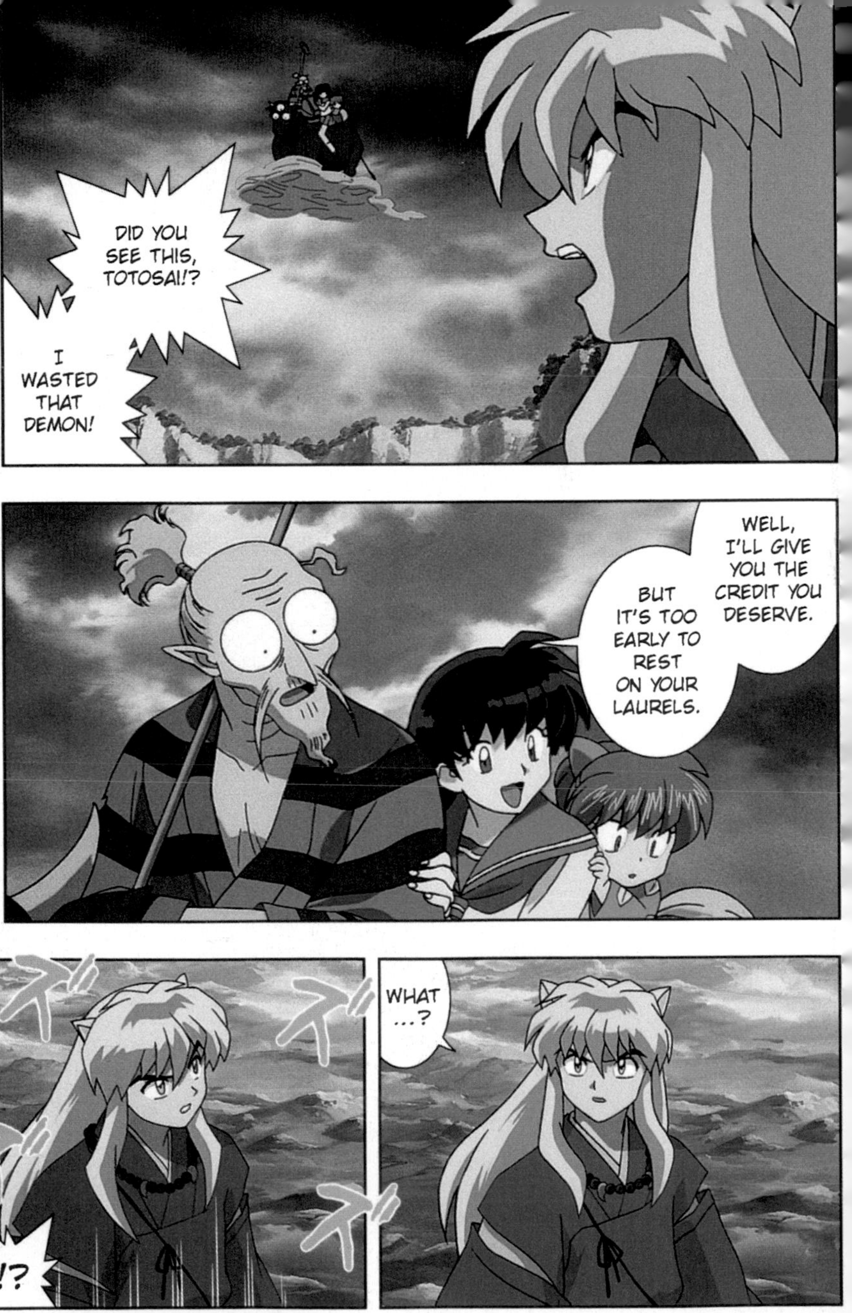
DID YOU SEE THIS, TOTOSAI!?
I WASTED THAT DEMON!
WELL, I'LL GIVE YOU THE CREDIT YOU DESERVE.
BUT IT'S TOO EARLY TO REST ON YOUR LAURELS.
WHAT ...?
ズ
ズ
ズ
ズ
!?

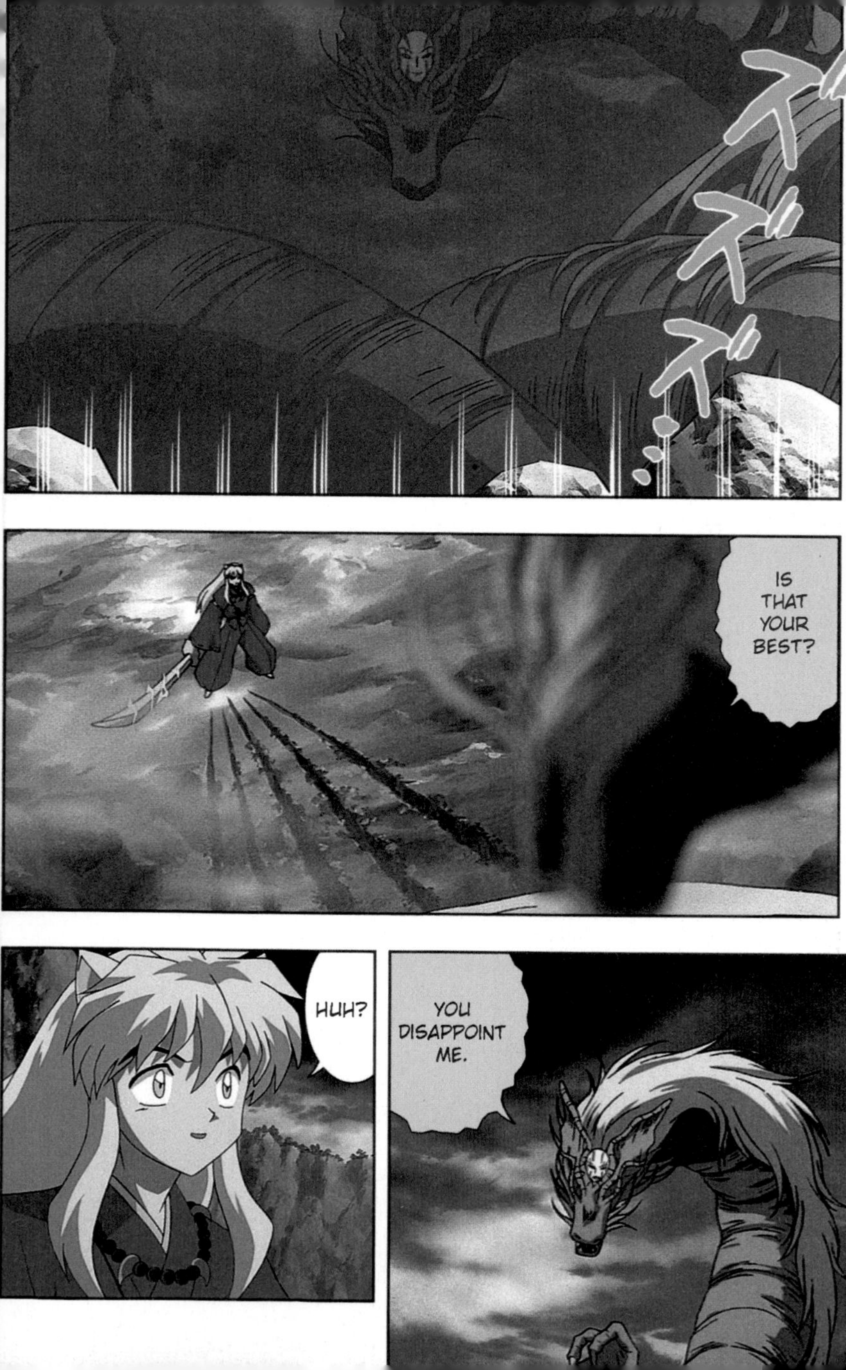
ズズズ…
IS THAT YOUR BEST?
YOU DISAPPOINT ME.
HUH?

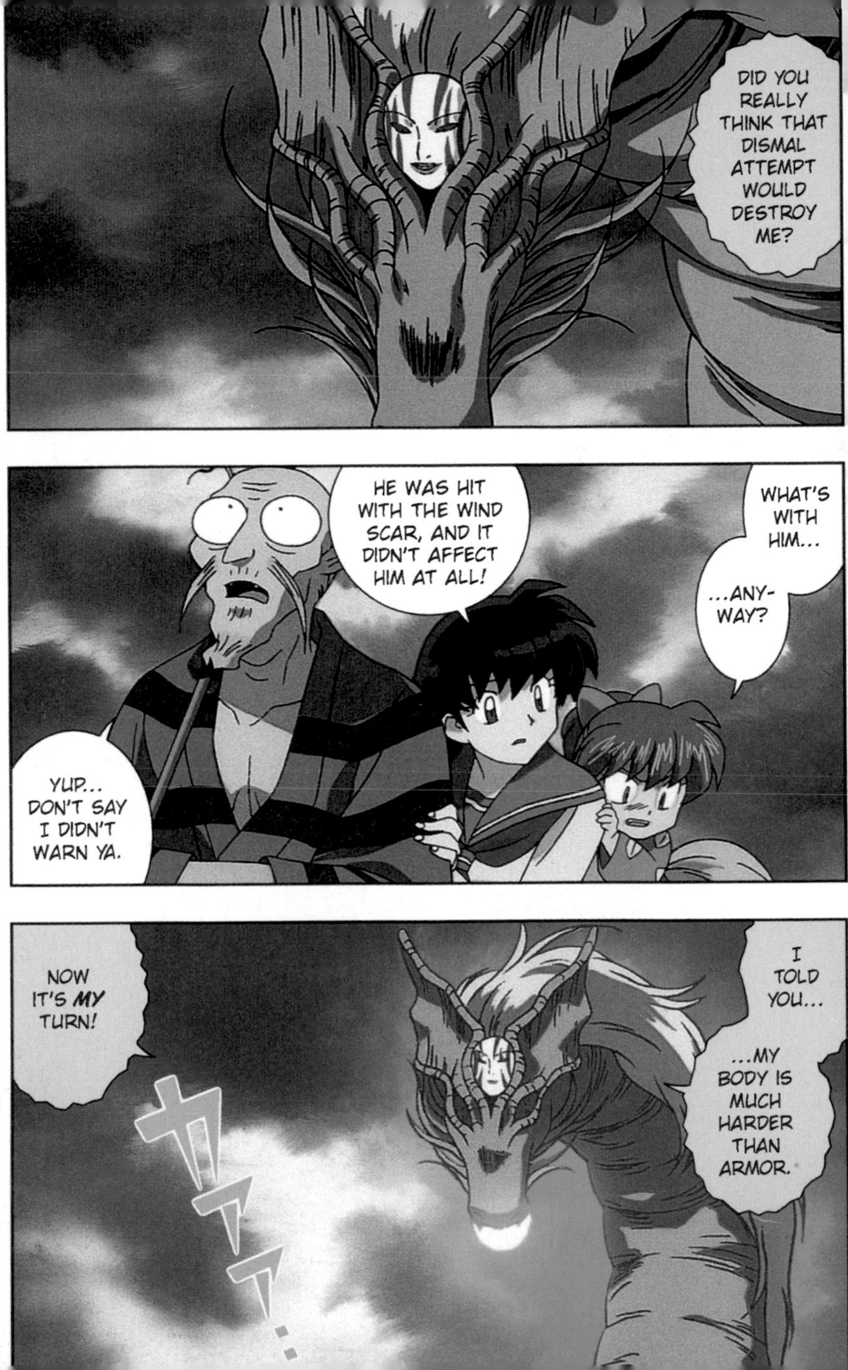
DID YOU REALLY THINK THAT DISMAL ATTEMPT WOULD DESTROY ME?
WHAT'S WITH HIM...
...ANY-WAY?
HE WAS HIT WITH THE WIND SCAR, AND IT DIDN'T AFFECT HIM AT ALL!
YUP... DON'T SAY I DIDN'T WARN YA.
I TOLD YOU...
...MY BODY IS MUCH HARDER THAN ARMOR.
NOW IT'S *MY* TURN!
カァァ..

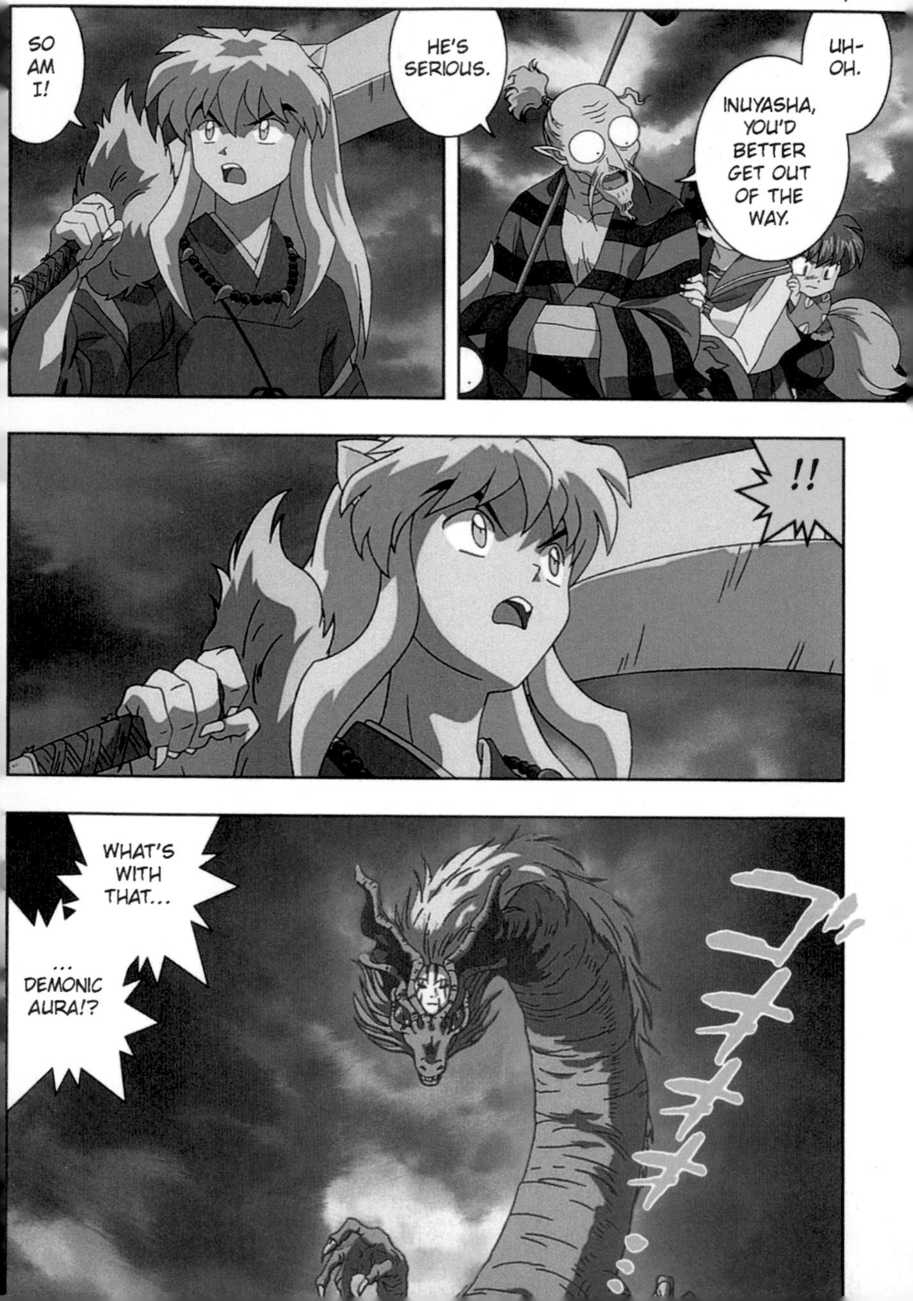
UH-OH.
INUYASHA, YOU'D BETTER GET OUT OF THE WAY.
HE'S SERIOUS.
SO AM I!
!!
WHAT'S WITH THAT...
...DEMONIC AURA!?

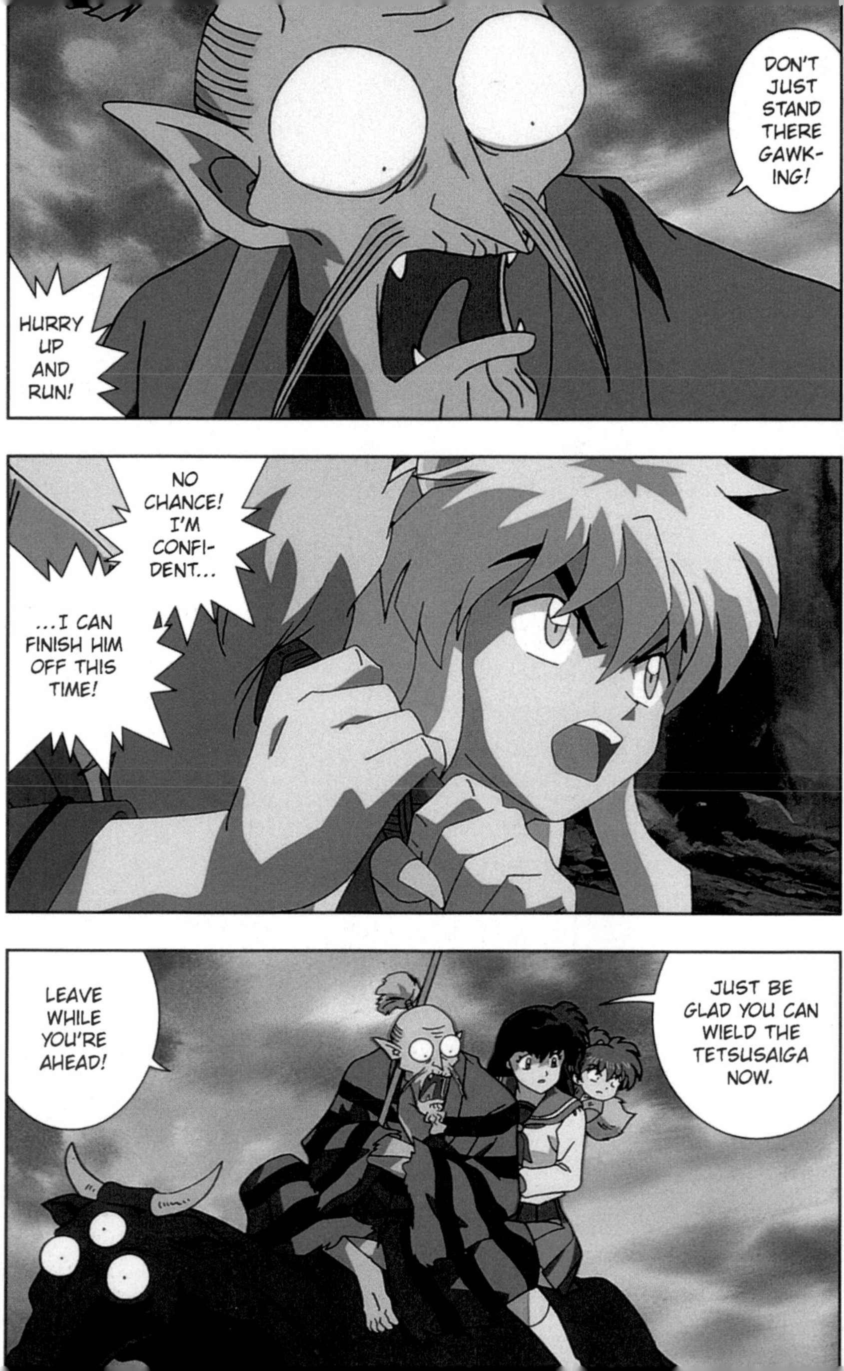
DON'T JUST STAND THERE GAWKING!
HURRY UP AND RUN!
NO CHANCE! I'M CONFIDENT...
...I CAN FINISH HIM OFF THIS TIME!
JUST BE GLAD YOU CAN WIELD THE TETSUSAIGA NOW.
LEAVE WHILE YOU'RE AHEAD!

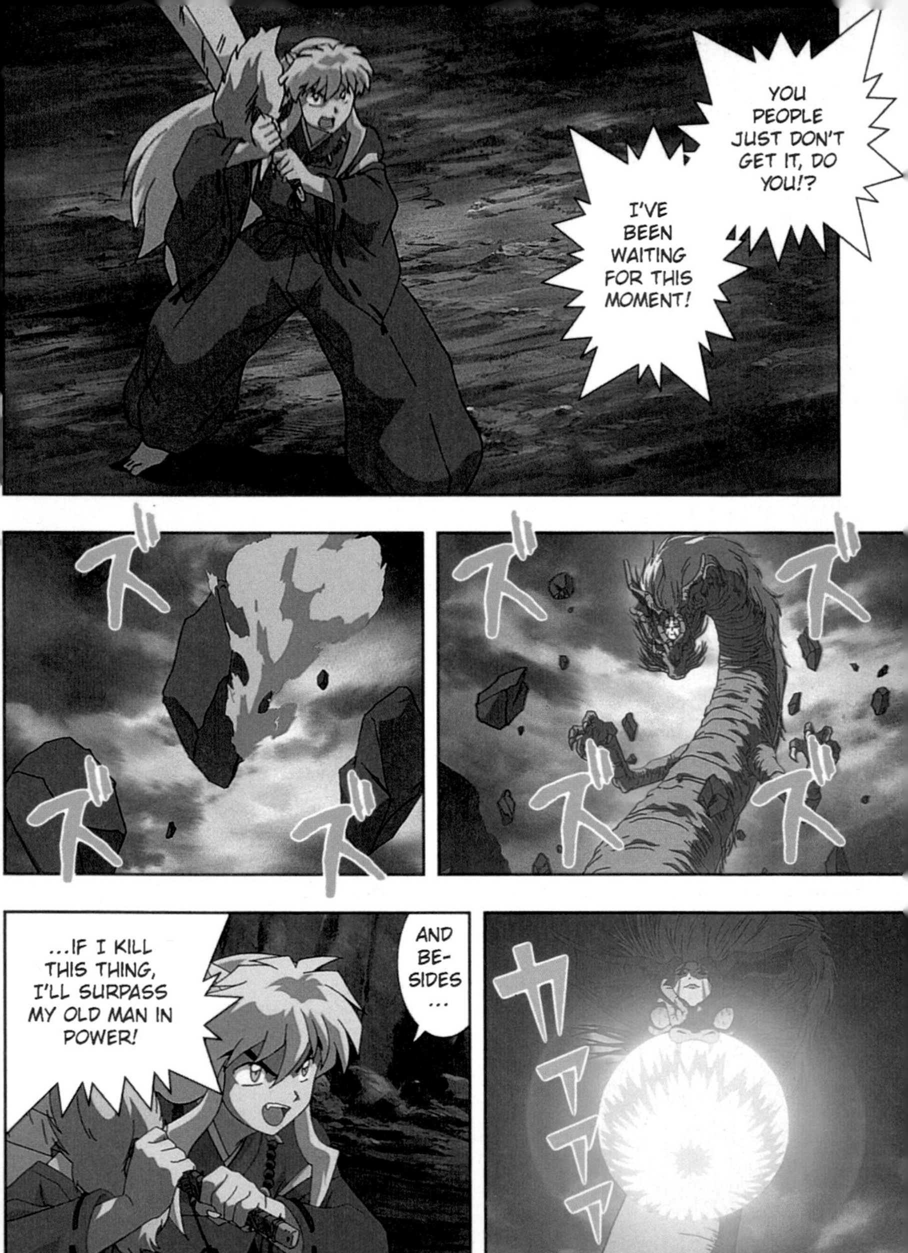
YOU PEOPLE JUST DON'T GET IT, DO YOU!?
I'VE BEEN WAITING FOR THIS MOMENT!
ズ
ズ
ズ
ズ
ズ
ズ
ズ
ヤァァァ…
AND BE-SIDES...
...IF I KILL THIS THING, I'LL SURPASS MY OLD MAN IN POWER!

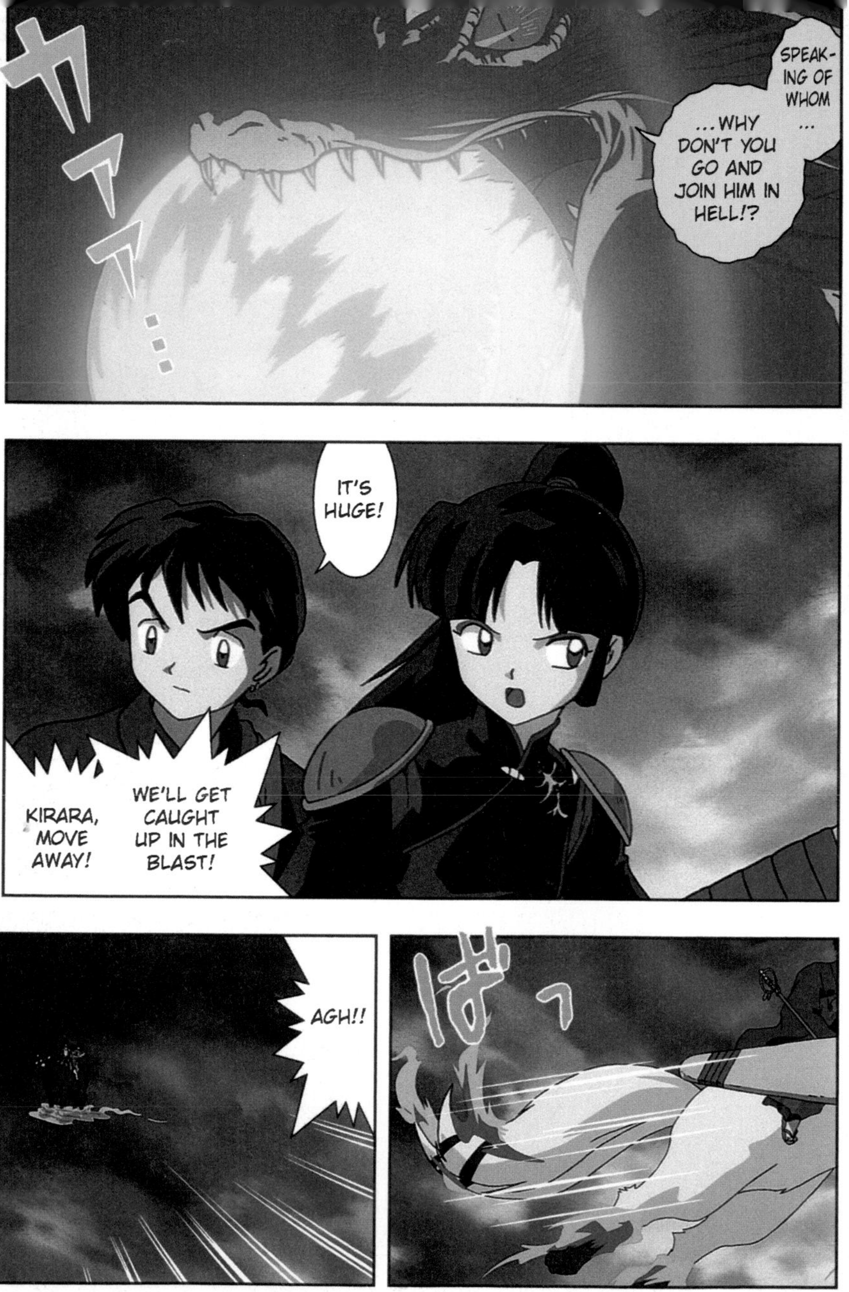

SPEAKING OF WHOM ...
...WHY DON'T YOU GO AND JOIN HIM IN HELL!?
カァァァ…
IT'S HUGE!
WE'LL GET CAUGHT UP IN THE BLAST!
KIRARA, MOVE AWAY!
ばっ
AGH!!

RRAHHH!

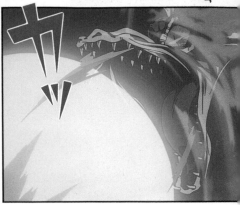

I'VE NEVER SEEN SUCH HUGE BLAST OF DEMONIC ENERGY!

HUH ?

...

GET OUTTA THERE !

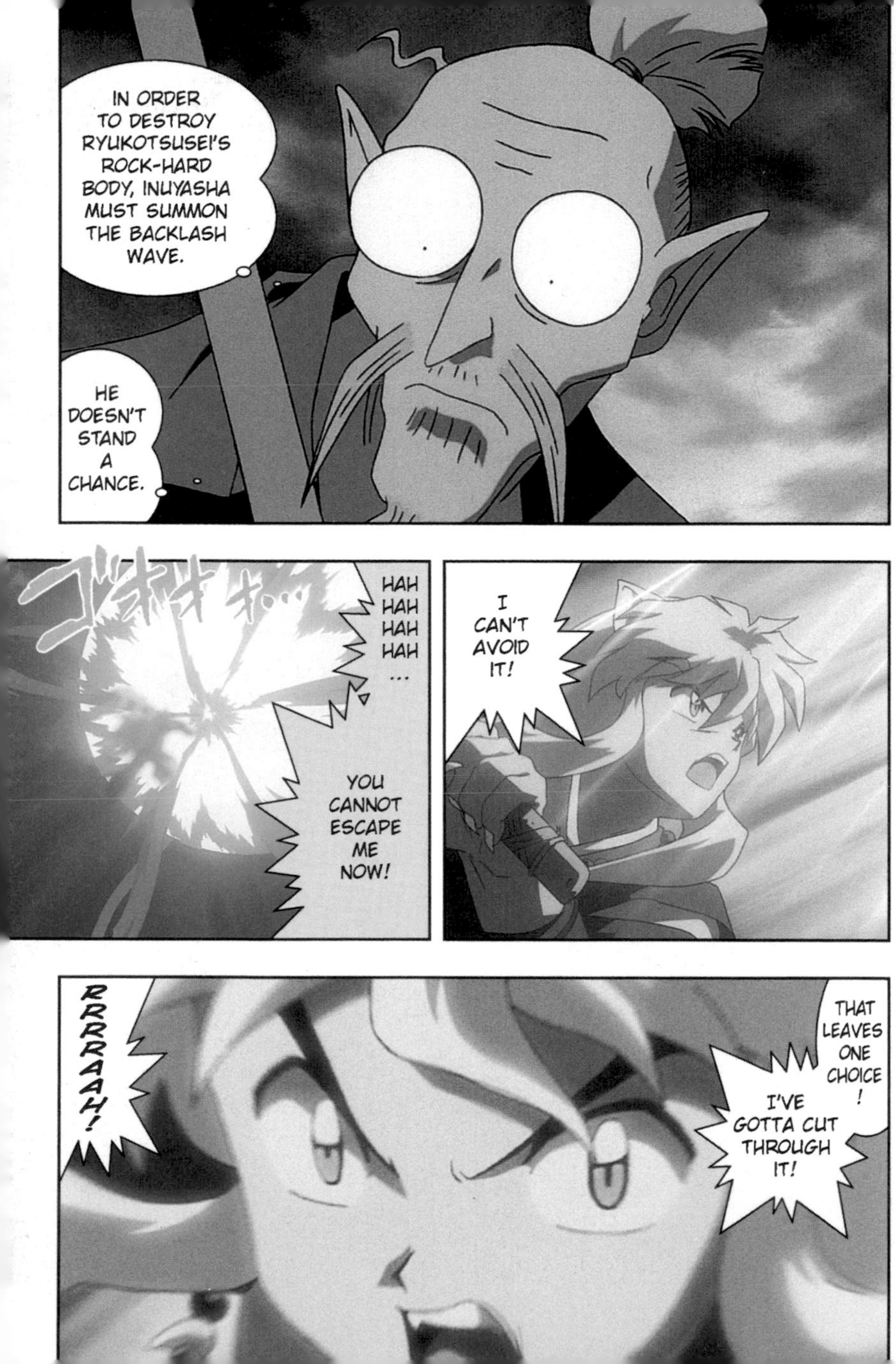
IN ORDER TO DESTROY RYUKOTSUSEI'S ROCK-HARD BODY, INUYASHA MUST SUMMON THE BACKLASH WAVE.
HE DOESN'T STAND A CHANCE.
I CAN'T AVOID IT!
HAH HAH HAH HAH ...
YOU CANNOT ESCAPE ME NOW!
THAT LEAVES ONE CHOICE!
I'VE GOTTA CUT THROUGH IT!
RRRRAAH!

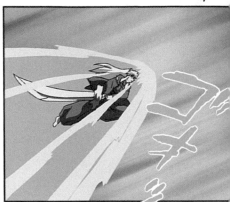

HUH
!?

LOOK!
IT CAN'T
BE!

WHAT
IS
THAT
!?

INCRED-
IBLE!
THAT'S THE
BACKLASH
WAVE.

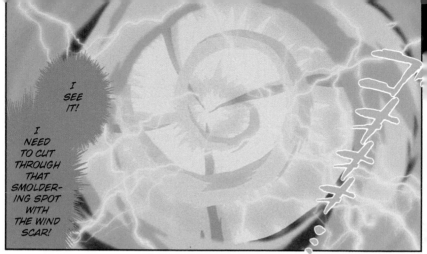

I SEE IT!

I NEED TO CUT THROUGH THAT SMOLDERING SPOT WITH THE WIND SCAR!

RIGHT ABOUT HERE!

シュウウウ···

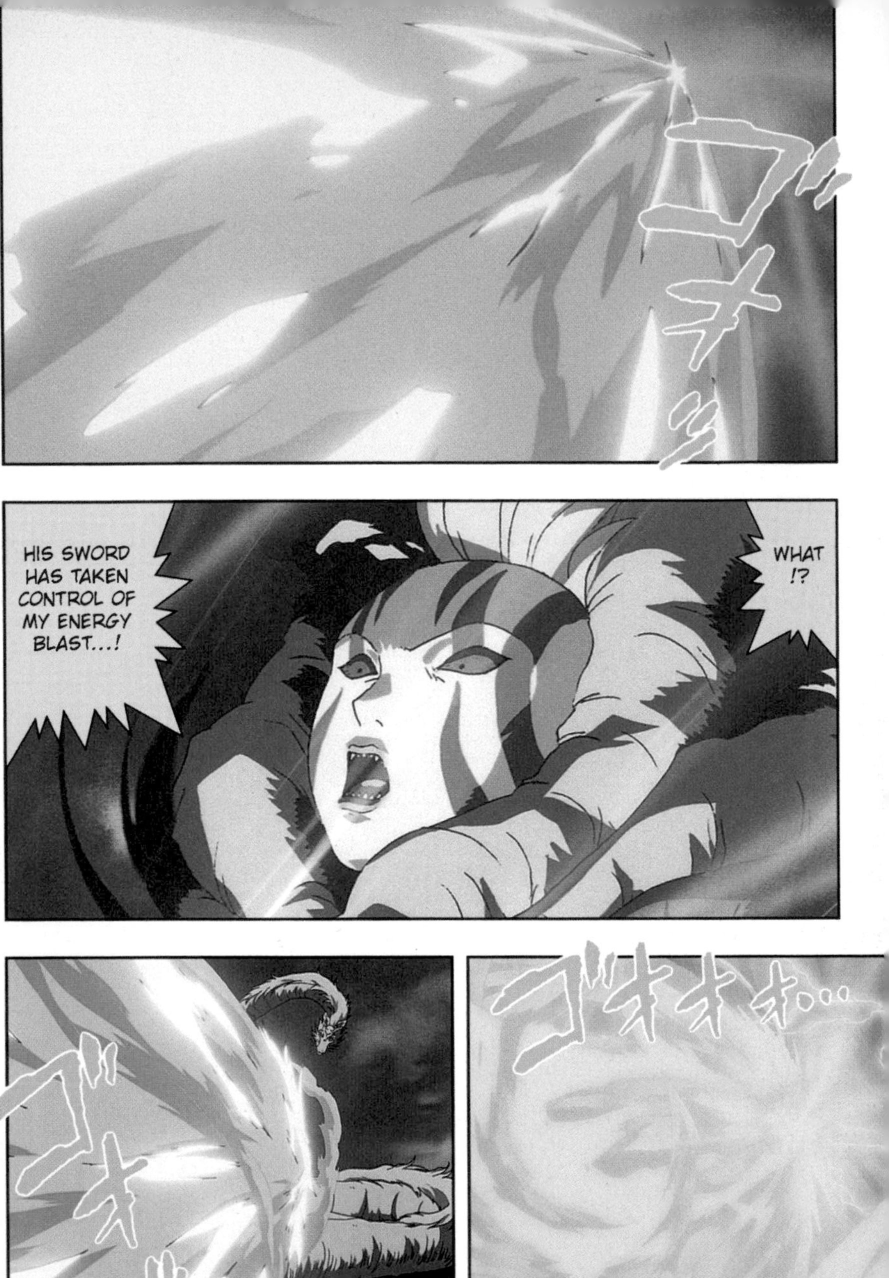
ゴオッ
WHAT !?
HIS SWORD HAS TAKEN CONTROL OF MY ENERGY BLAST...!
ゴオオオ…
ゴオッ

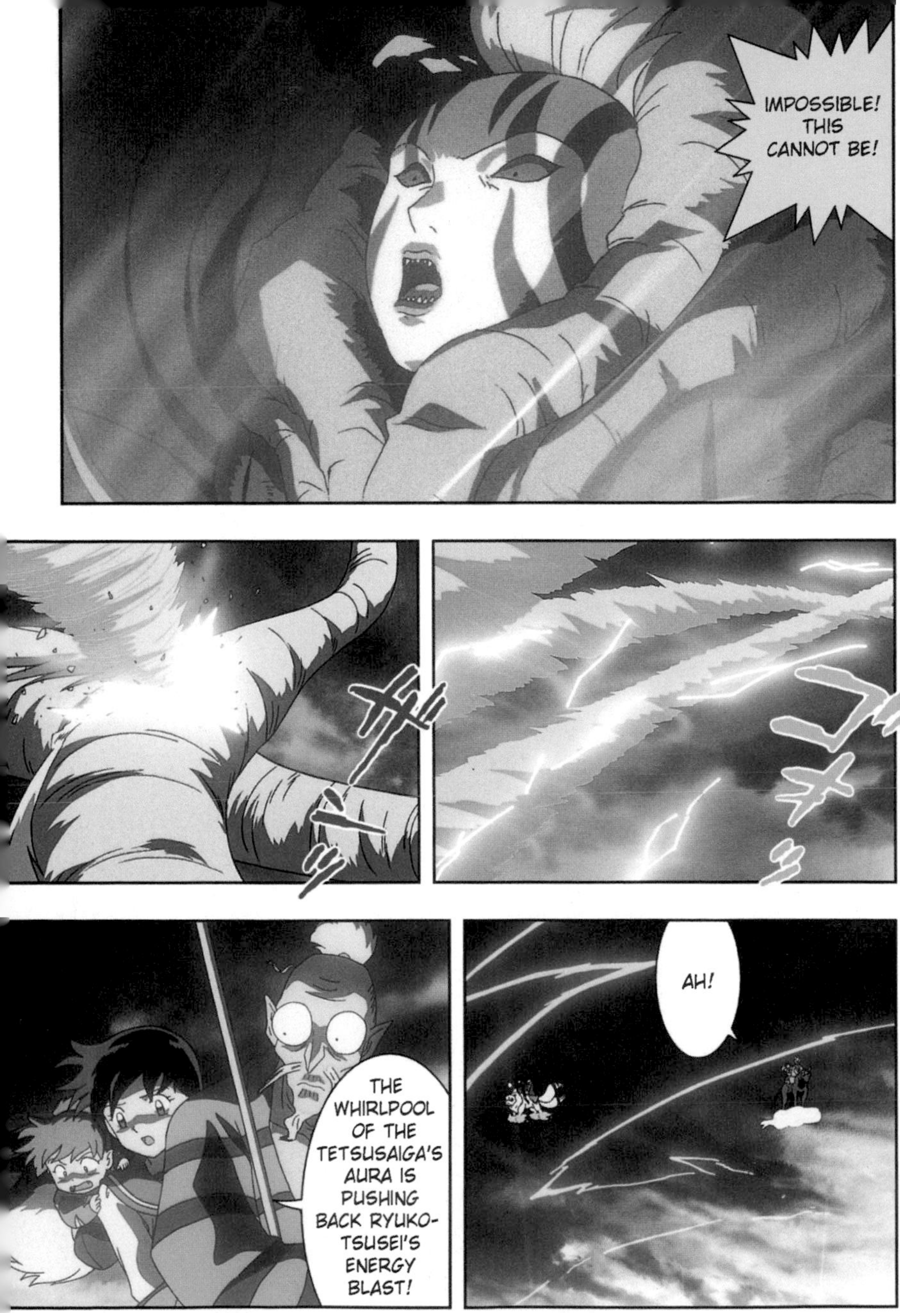
IMPOSSIBLE! THIS CANNOT BE!
AH!
THE WHIRLPOOL OF THE TETSUSAIGA'S AURA IS PUSHING BACK RYUKO-TSUSEI'S ENERGY BLAST!

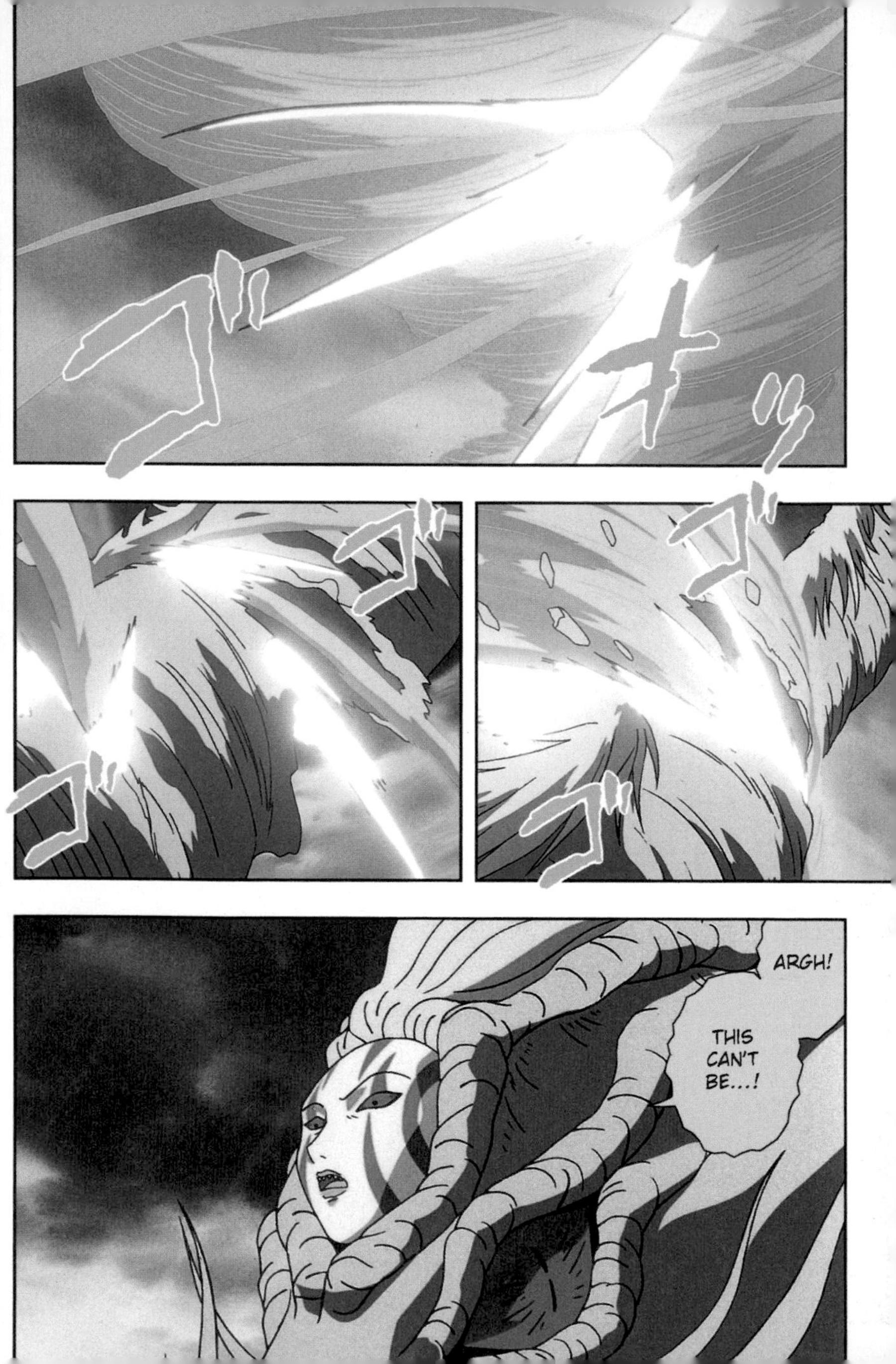
ARGH!
THIS CAN'T BE...!

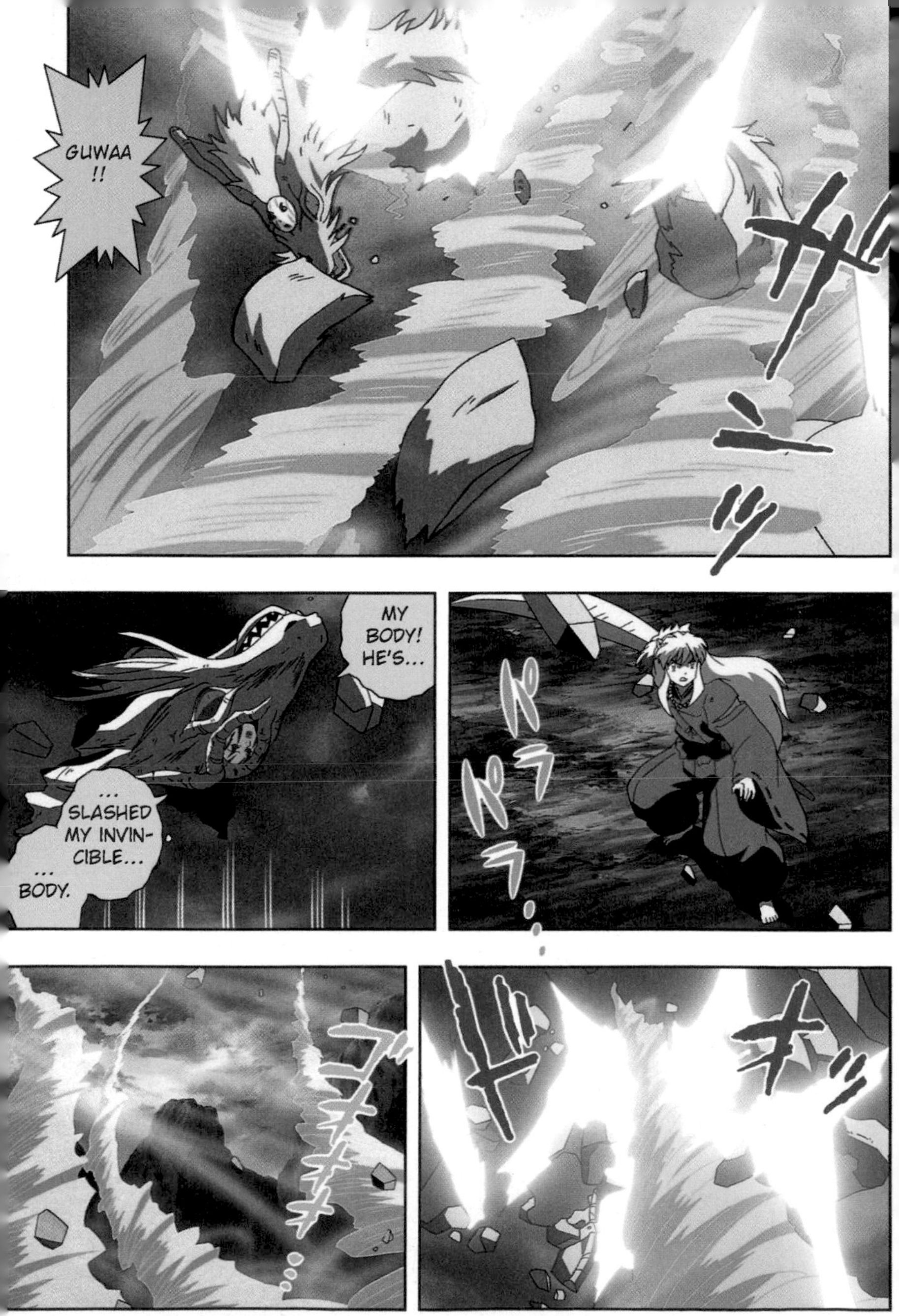
GUWAA!!
パラパラ...
MY BODY! HE'S...
...SLASHED MY INVINCIBLE...
...BODY.

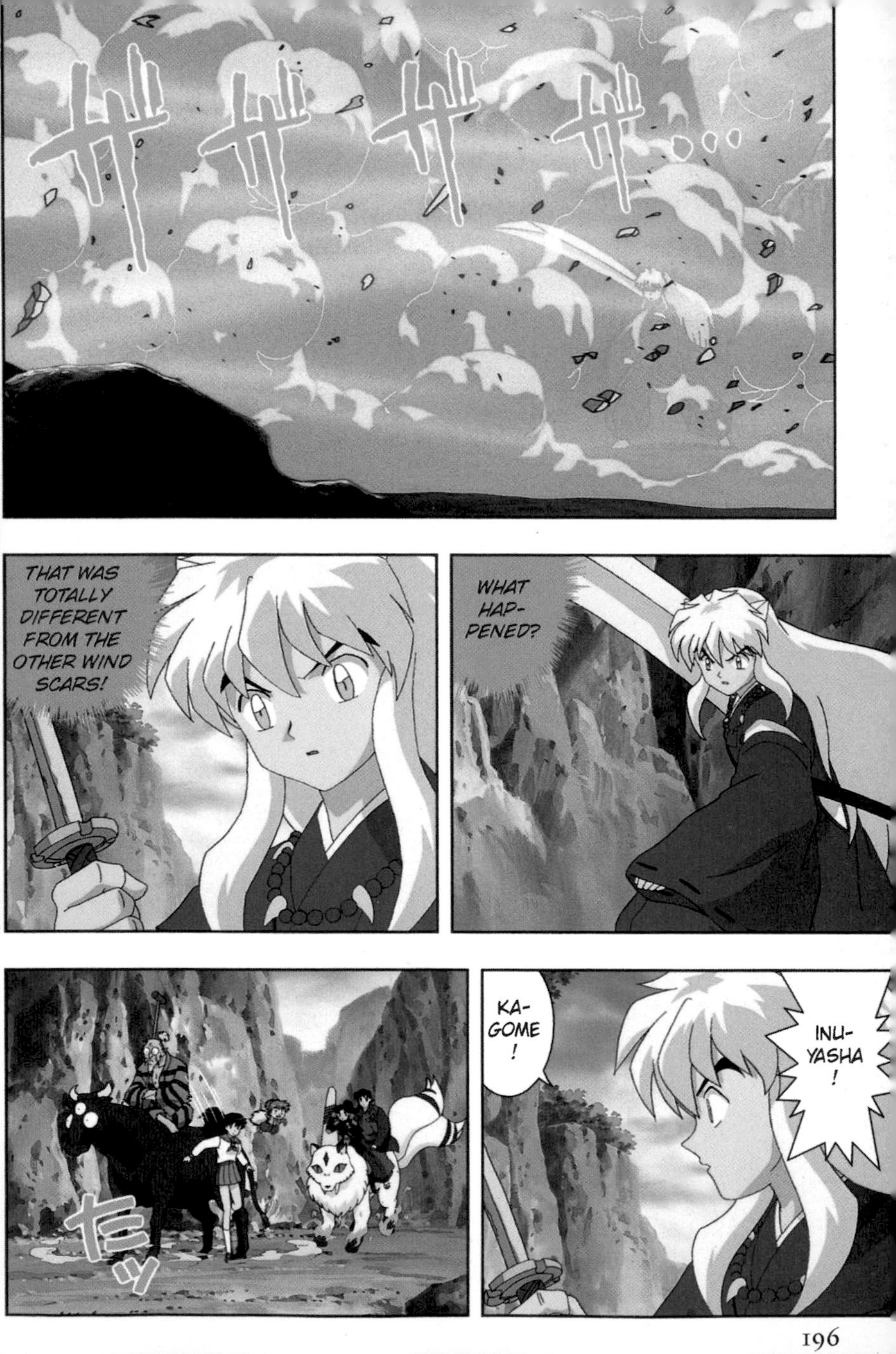
ザザザザ…
WHAT HAP-PENED?
THAT WAS TOTALLY DIFFERENT FROM THE OTHER WIND SCARS!
INU-YASHA!
KA-GOME!
タッ

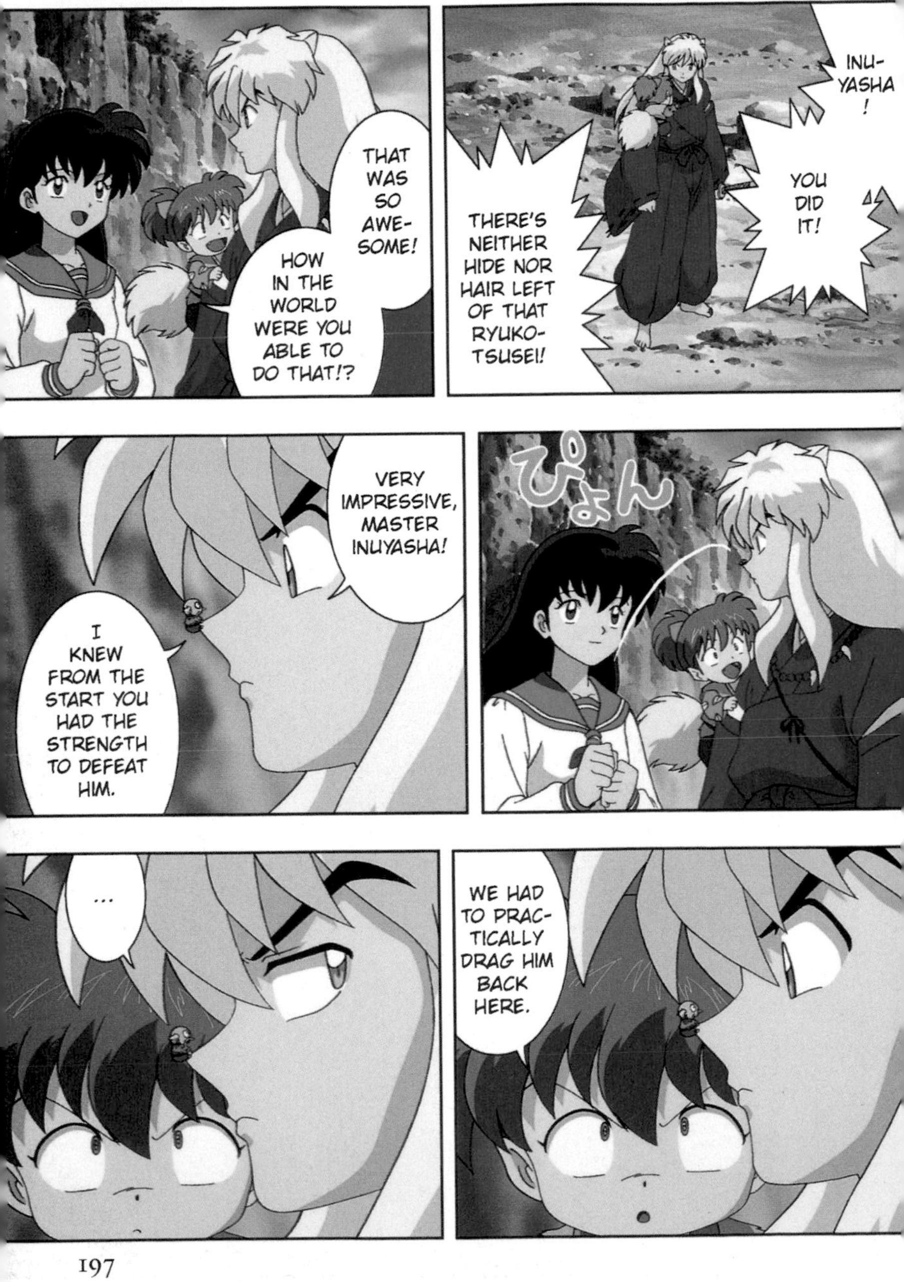
INU-YASHA!
YOU DID IT!
THERE'S NEITHER HIDE NOR HAIR LEFT OF THAT RYUKO-TSUSEI!
THAT WAS SO AWESOME!
HOW IN THE WORLD WERE YOU ABLE TO DO THAT!?
ぴょん
VERY IMPRESSIVE, MASTER INUYASHA!
I KNEW FROM THE START YOU HAD THE STRENGTH TO DEFEAT HIM.
WE HAD TO PRACTICALLY DRAG HIM BACK HERE.
...

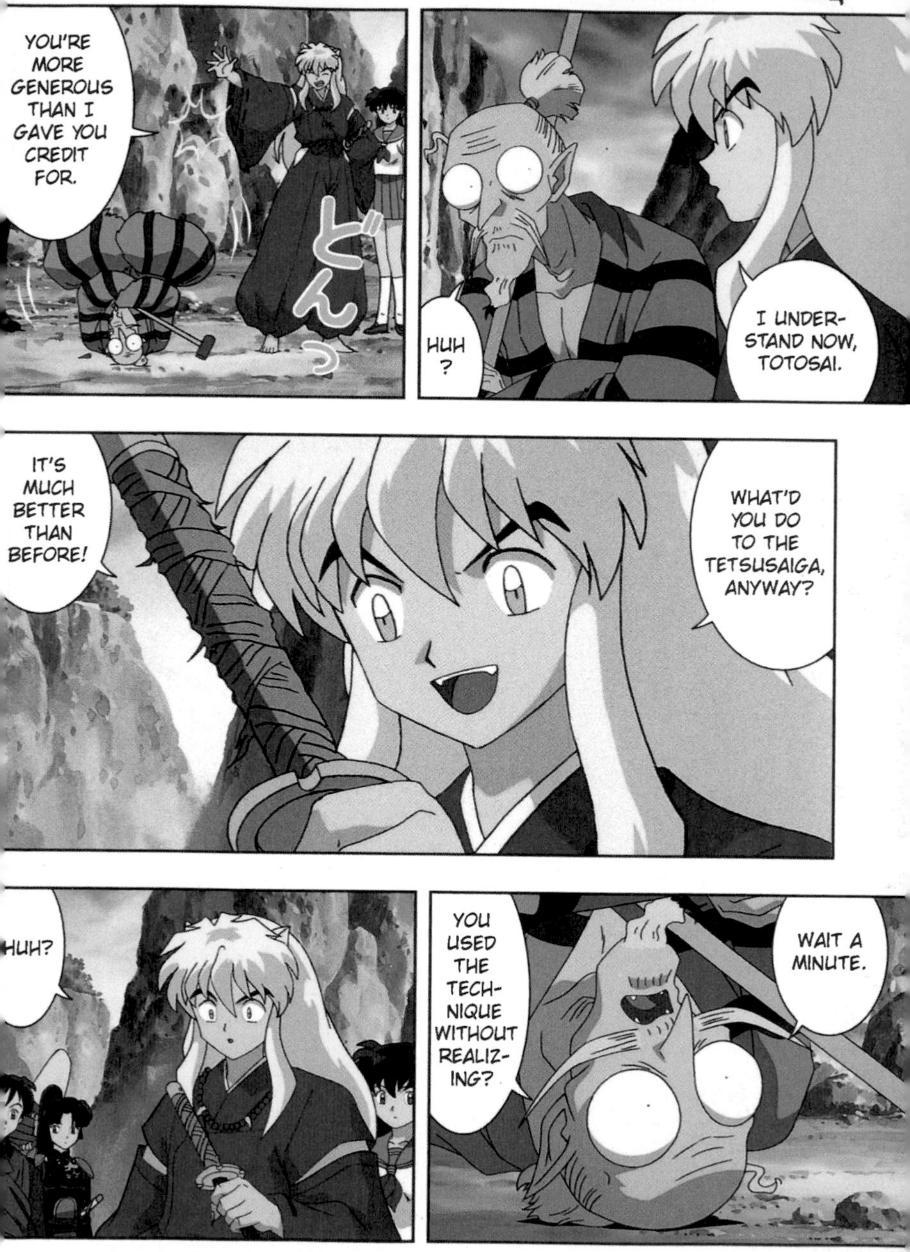
I UNDER-STAND NOW, TOTOSAI.
HUH ?
YOU'RE MORE GENEROUS THAN I GAVE YOU CREDIT FOR.
どんっ
IT'S MUCH BETTER THAN BEFORE!
WHAT'D YOU DO TO THE TETSUSAIGA, ANYWAY?
WAIT A MINUTE.
YOU USED THE TECH-NIQUE WITHOUT REALIZ-ING?
HUH?

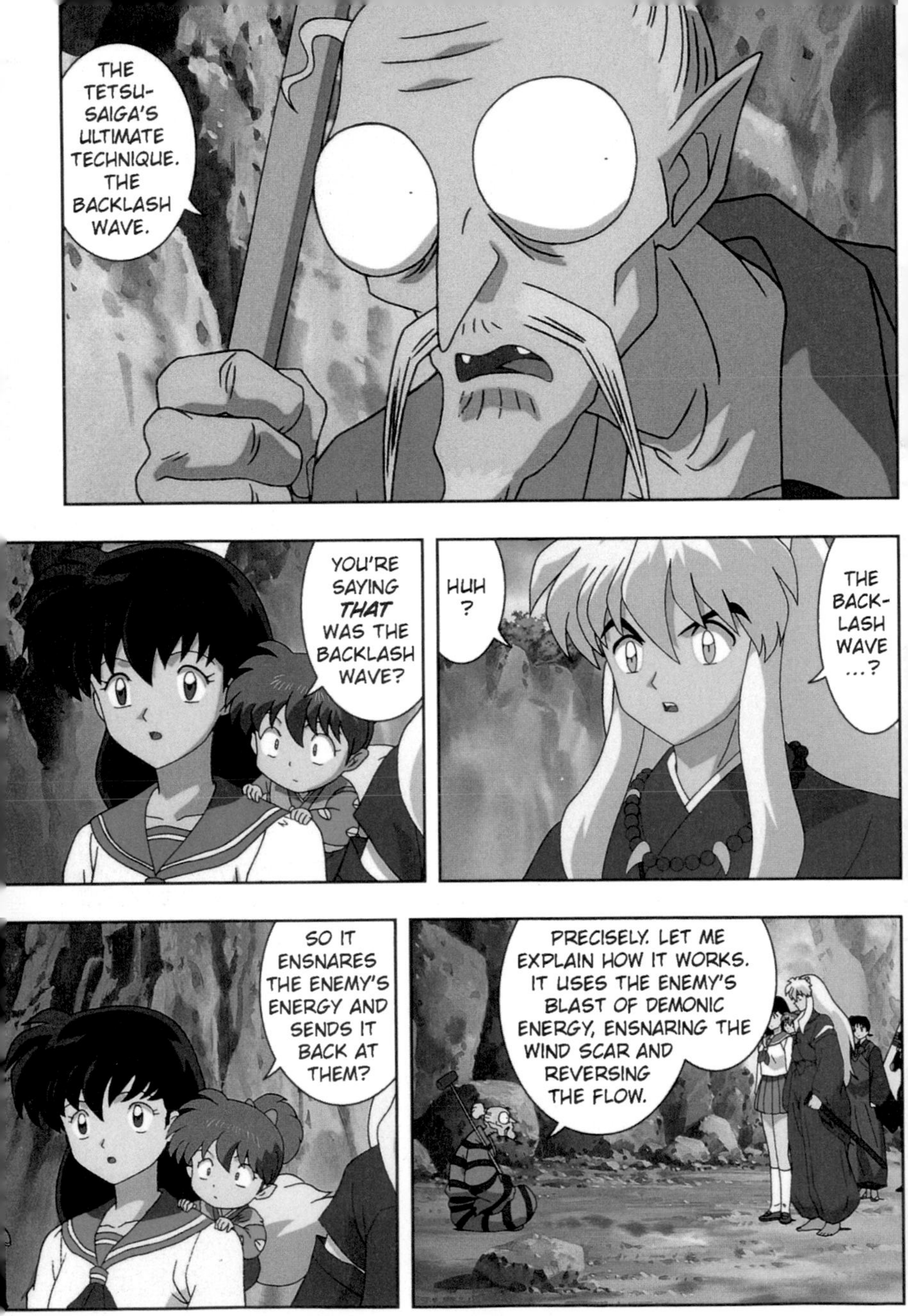
THE TETSU-SAIGA'S ULTIMATE TECHNIQUE. THE BACKLASH WAVE.
YOU'RE SAYING *THAT* WAS THE BACKLASH WAVE?
HUH?
THE BACK-LASH WAVE ...?
SO IT ENSNARES THE ENEMY'S ENERGY AND SENDS IT BACK AT THEM?
PRECISELY. LET ME EXPLAIN HOW IT WORKS. IT USES THE ENEMY'S BLAST OF DEMONIC ENERGY, ENSNARING THE WIND SCAR AND REVERSING THE FLOW.

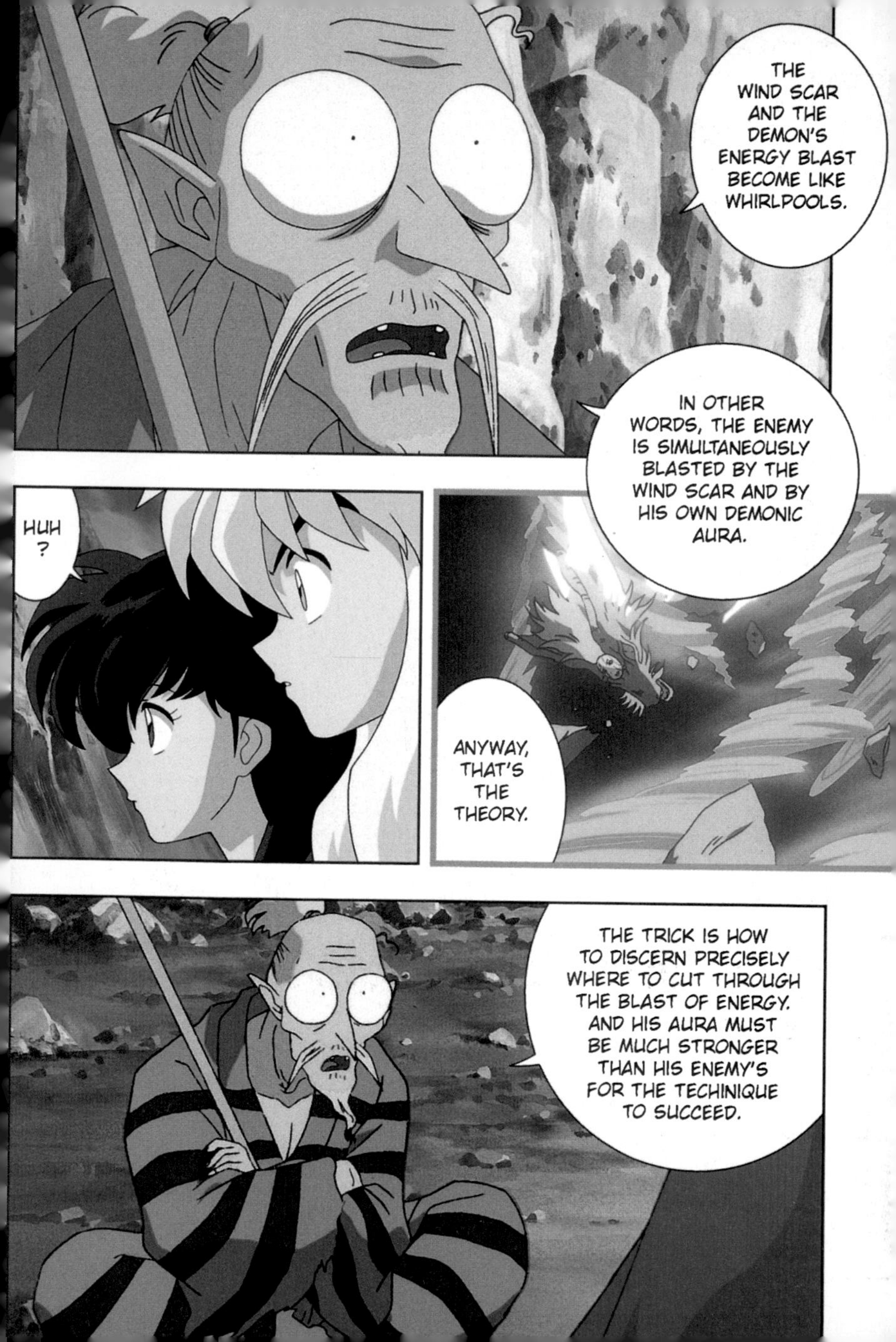
THE WIND SCAR AND THE DEMON'S ENERGY BLAST BECOME LIKE WHIRLPOOLS.
IN OTHER WORDS, THE ENEMY IS SIMULTANEOUSLY BLASTED BY THE WIND SCAR AND BY HIS OWN DEMONIC AURA.
ANYWAY, THAT'S THE THEORY.
HUH ?
THE TRICK IS HOW TO DISCERN PRECISELY WHERE TO CUT THROUGH THE BLAST OF ENERGY. AND HIS AURA MUST BE MUCH STRONGER THAN HIS ENEMY'S FOR THE TECHINIQUE TO SUCCEED.

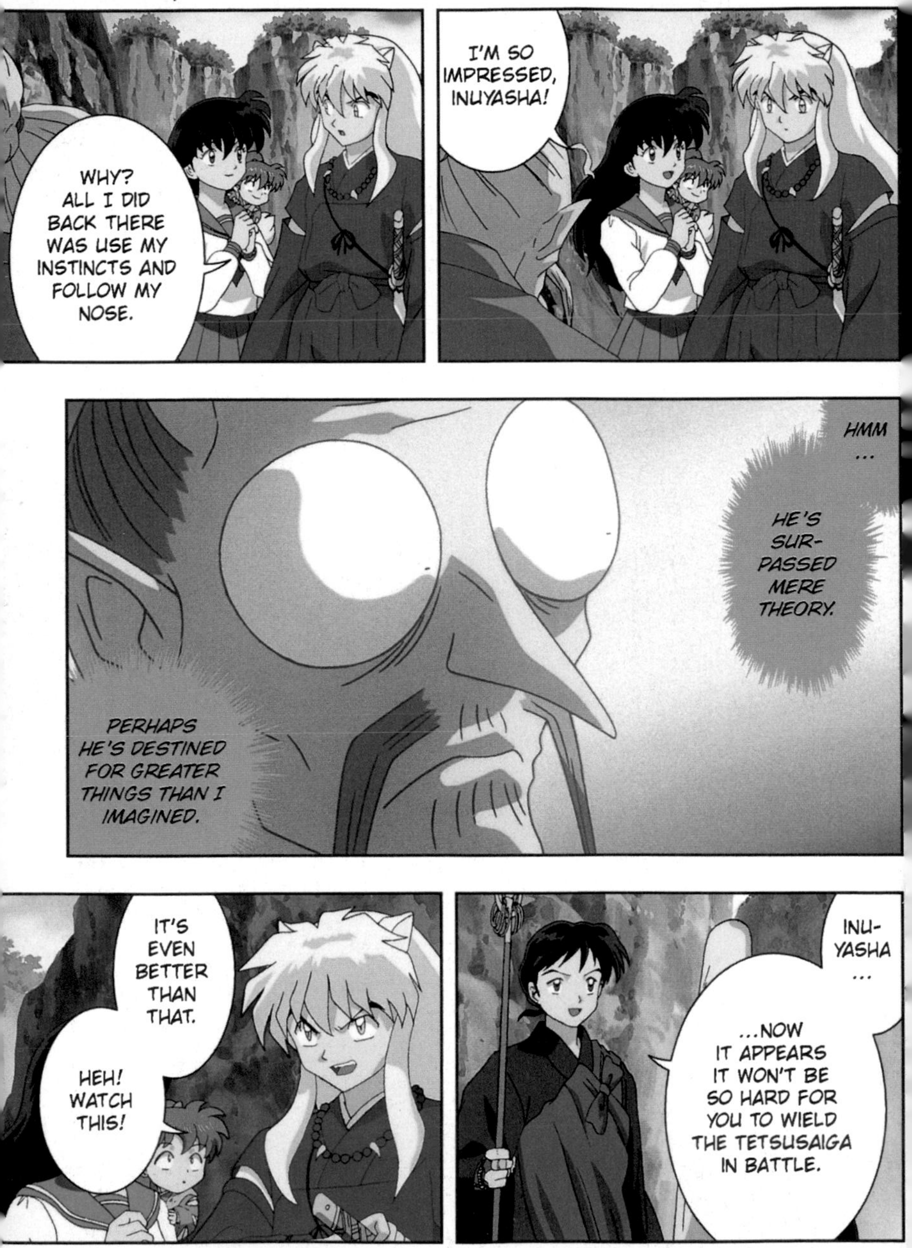
I'M SO IMPRESSED, INUYASHA!
WHY? ALL I DID BACK THERE WAS USE MY INSTINCTS AND FOLLOW MY NOSE.
HMM...
HE'S SUR-PASSED MERE THEORY.
PERHAPS HE'S DESTINED FOR GREATER THINGS THAN I IMAGINED.
INU-YASHA...
...NOW IT APPEARS IT WON'T BE SO HARD FOR YOU TO WIELD THE TETSUSAIGA IN BATTLE.
IT'S EVEN BETTER THAN THAT.
HEH! WATCH THIS!

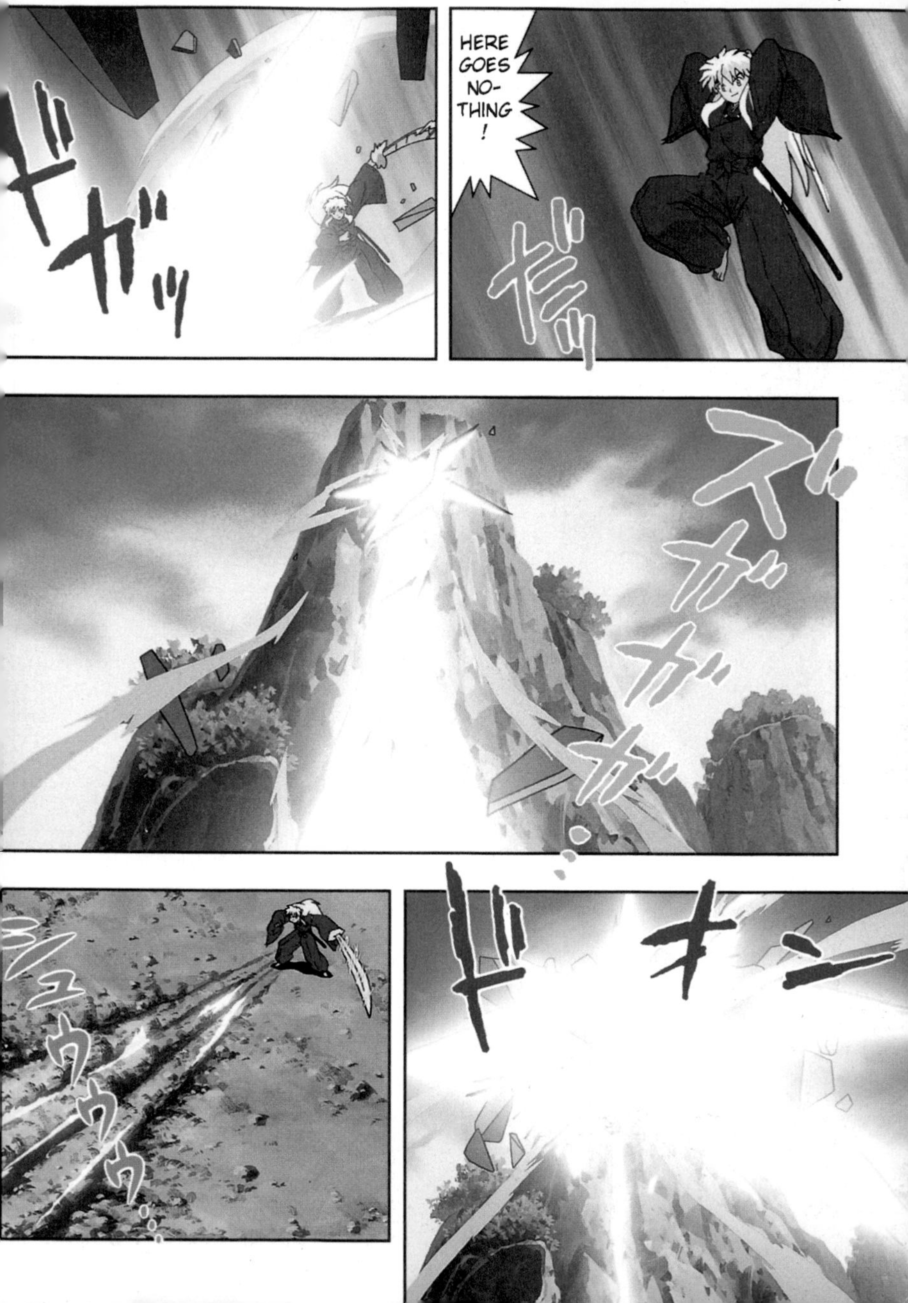
HERE GOES NO-THING!
ダッ
ドガッ
ズガガガ…
ドォン
シュウウウ…

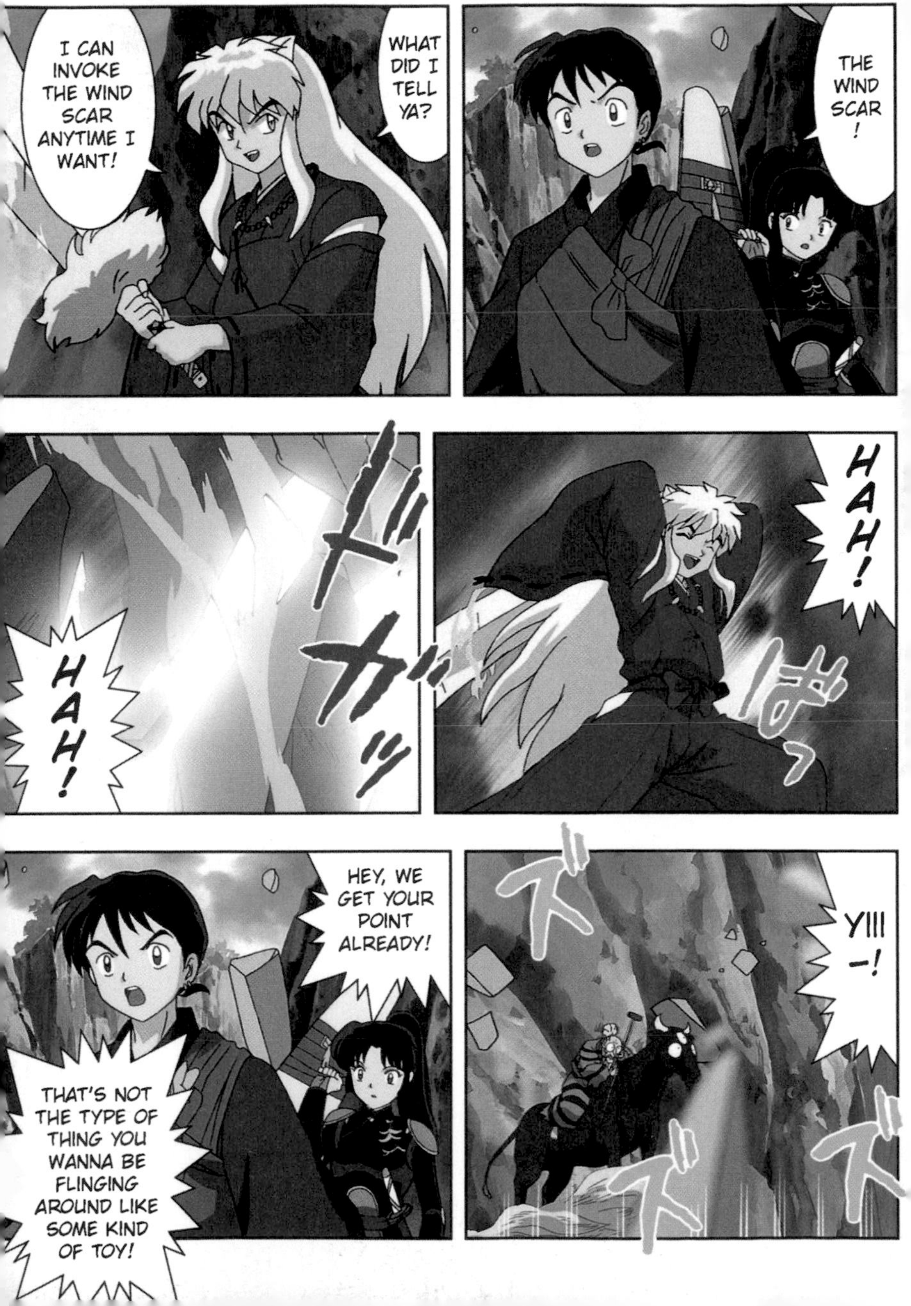
THE WIND SCAR!
WHAT DID I TELL YA?
I CAN INVOKE THE WIND SCAR ANYTIME I WANT!
HAH!
HAH!
YIIII—!
HEY, WE GET YOUR POINT ALREADY!
THAT'S NOT THE TYPE OF THING YOU WANNA BE FLINGING AROUND LIKE SOME KIND OF TOY!

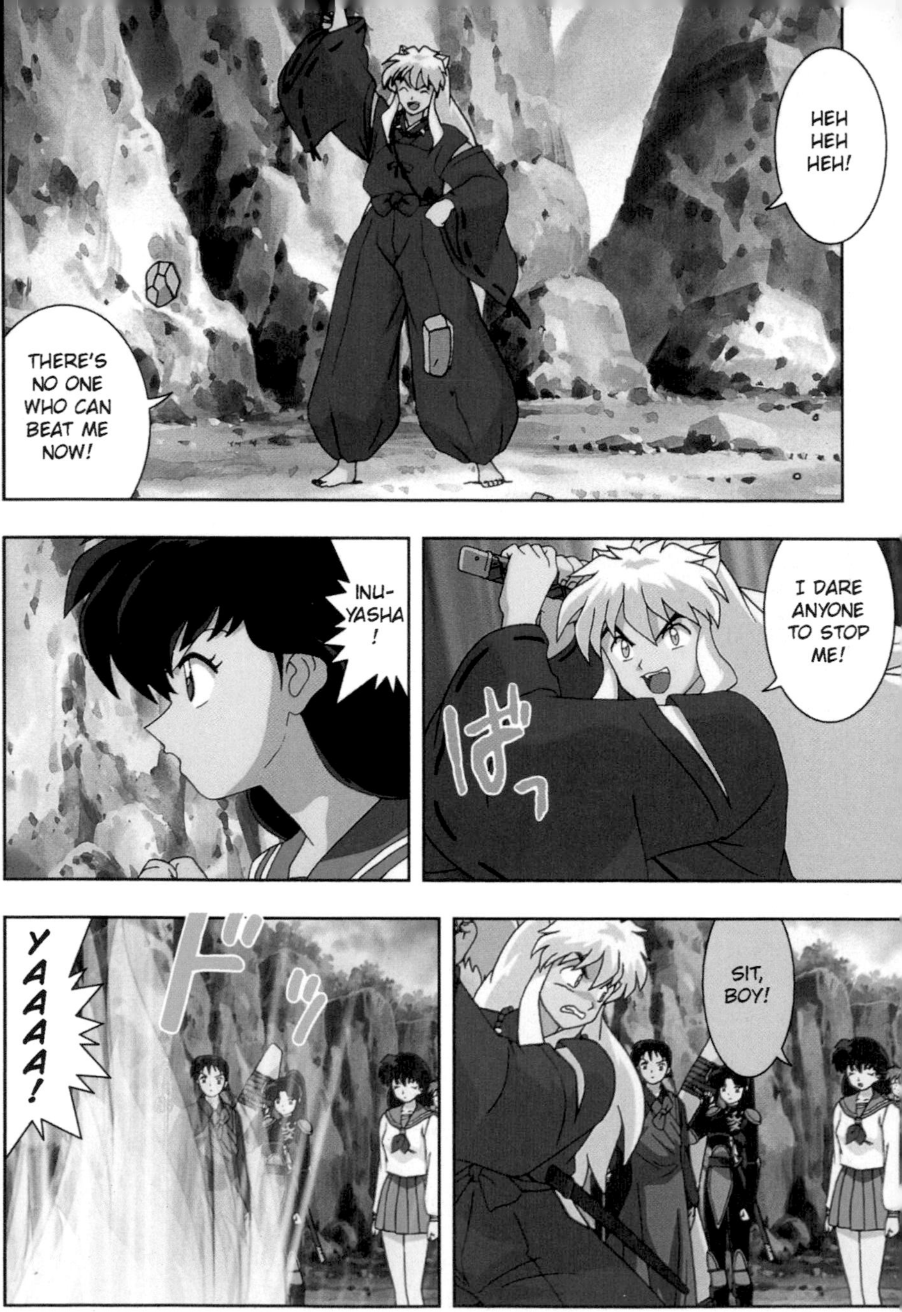
HEH HEH HEH!
THERE'S NO ONE WHO CAN BEAT ME NOW!
I DARE ANYONE TO STOP ME!
ぱっ
INU-YASHA!
SIT, BOY!
ドッ
YAAAAA!

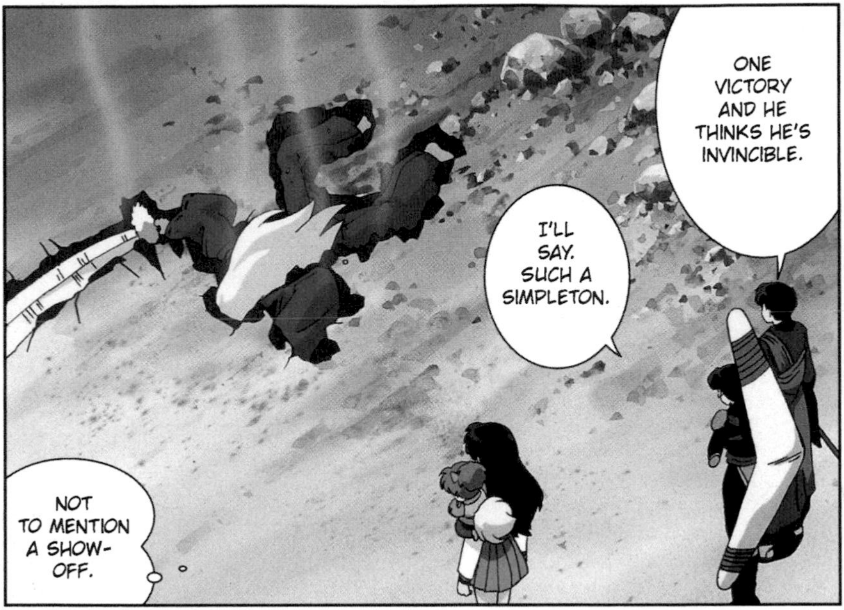
ONE VICTORY AND HE THINKS HE'S INVINCIBLE.
I'LL SAY. SUCH A SIMPLETON.
NOT TO MENTION A SHOW-OFF.
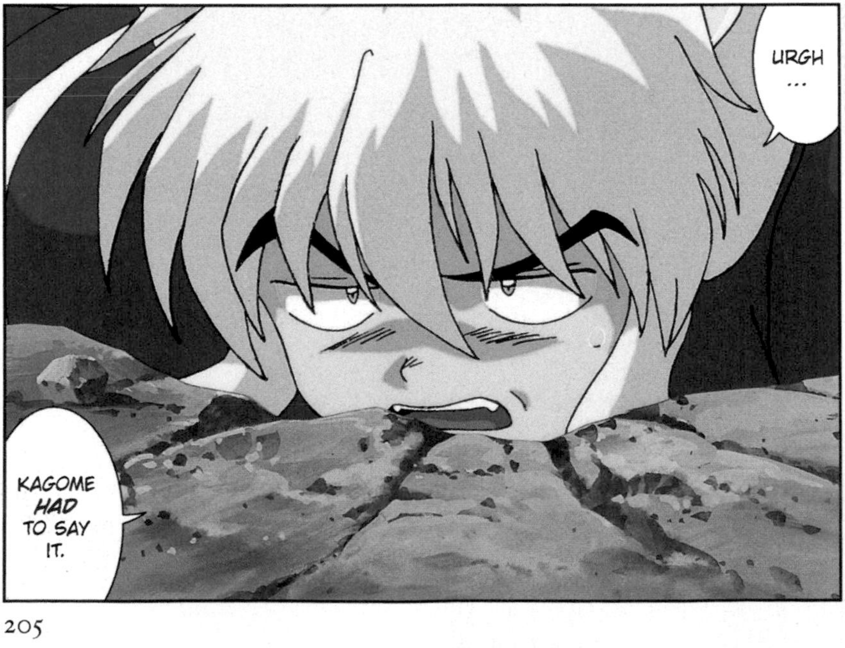
URGH ...
KAGOME ***HAD*** TO SAY IT.

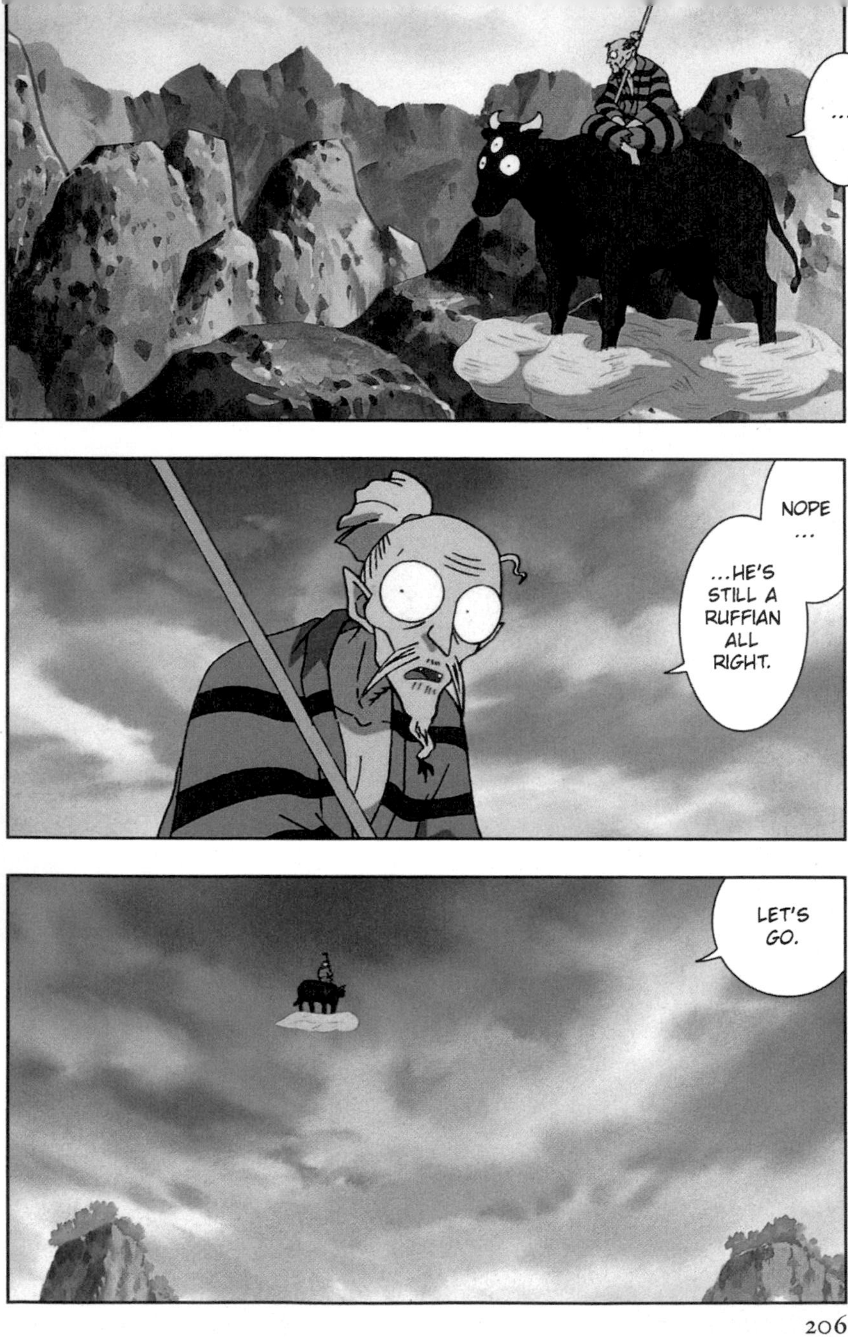
...
NOPE ...
...HE'S STILL A RUFFIAN ALL RIGHT.
LET'S GO.

Glossary of Sound Effects

Each entry includes: the location, indicated by page number and panel number (so 3.1 means page 3, panel number 1); the phonetic romanization of the original Japanese; and our English "translation"—we offer as close an English equivalent as we can.

19.3 FX: Ka (Inuyasha's eyes suddenly glow)

20.1 FX: Gohhhh... (whooshing)
20.2 FX: Doh (Inuyasha suddenly explodes out of poison cocoon)
20.3 FX: Ba (Inuyasha explodes out of cocoon)
20.4 FX: Za (Miroku lands on ground nearby)

21.4 FX: Zuba (a vicious slash)

22.1 FX: Zan (slash)

23.1 FX: Za (Inuyasha lands)

24.2 FX: Ba (Gatenmaru transforms)
24.3 FX: Basa (Gatenmaru's wings unfurl)
24.5 FX: Ban (Gatenmaru's clothing rips from his body)

25.3 FX: Basa (Gatenmaru's wings beat)
25.4 FX: Gohh... (whirlwind forms)
25.5 FX: Gohh... (whirlwind whooshes)

26.2 FX: Da (Inuyasha lunges)
26.3 FX: Ba (Inuyasha bursts through the whirlwind)
26.5 FX: Doh (Gatenmaru falls to Earth)
26.6 FX: Zun... (Gatenmaru collapses)

27.2 FX: Buoh (Gatenmaru spits web stuff)
27.3 FX: Shururuto... (web stuff winds around Inuyasha but does not enclose him)
27.4 FX: Shuuu... (hissing)

28.1 FX: Ba (Inuyasha leaps)
28.2 FX: Zuba (slash)

29.1 FX: Za (slash)
29.2 FX: Da (bandits run off)

31.1 FX: Jita jita (Jaken dances with frustration)

Chapter 52 : A Demon's True Nature

6.5 FX: Kata kata (flask knocks against cup as girl's hands shake)

8.1 FX: Don (push)
8.5 FX: Shuru... (Gatenmaru's tongue snakes out)

9.1 FX: Doh (Gatenmaru's tongue connects)
9.2 FX: Shuuuu... (sucking slurpy sound)

10.2 FX: Dokun... (pounding heartbeat)
10.3 FX: Gaku (Inuyasha collapses forward)

11.3 FX: Jiri... (Grandpa crawling)
11.5 FX: Da (a running step)

12.1 FX: Da (grandpa runs off with the sword)

13.1 FX: Baki (hitting old man with spear)
13.1 FX: Ga ga (stamping on old man)

14.1 FX: Ta (running)

14.3 FX: Ba (whack!)
14.4 FX: Ta (running)
14.5 FX: Doga (kick)
14. 6 FX: Baki (kick)

16.2 FX: Jiri... (men close in)

17.1 FX: Doh doh doh doh (the bandits charge)
17.2 FX: Doga (Sango whacks bandits with the Hiraikotsu)
17.3 FX: Baki (whack!)

18.2 FX: Shuuu... (hissing sound)
18.4 FX: Ju (webs drop on top of Miroku)

19.1 FX: Zawa... (Inuyasha transforms)
19.2 FX: Dokun dokun... (pounding heartbeats)

50.1 FX: Ka (Sesshomaru's blade shines)
50.5 FX: Kiiiii...in... (Sesshomaru holds off a lunging Inuyasha with his sword)
51.3 FX: Doh (Inuyasha flung back)
51.5 FX: Zan (Inuyasha smacks back down to ground)

52.4 FX: Ba (Kagome throws herself on Inuyasha to protect him)

53.3 FX: Da (Sango rushes toward Kagome)

60.1 FX: Da (Jaken runs up to greet Sesshomaru)

65.1 FX: Ba (boy shakes off arm)

68.2 FX: Basha basha (hands splashing in river)

Chapter 53 : Father's Old Enemy: Ryukotsusei

76.2 FX: Gohhh... (whoosh of flame)
76.3 FX: Ka—n ka—n (Totosai forges sword)

78.1 FX: Gohhh... (whoosh as Kirara flies)

83.1 FX: Chiku... (slurp)
83.4 FX: Puchi (squish)
83.5 FX: Harari... (Myoga falls down)

89.3 FX: Bu bu bu... (buzzing)

90.1 FX: Bu bu bu bu (buzzing)

91.3 FX: Buu..n... (buzzing)

93.3 FX: Kaa... (shining)

94.1 FX: Za Za (sound of water)
94.2 FX: Zaaaa... (sound of waterfall)
94.3 FX: Ta (Inuyasha leaps off log bridge)

95.1 FX: Gohhh... (wind blows desolately through mountains)
95.2 FX: Ga (Inuyasha takes a firm hand on rock face)

97.2 FX: Gui (Kagome accidentally pushes Totosai too hard)
97.3 FX: Dosa (Totosai falls on his head)

33.1 FX: Suta suta... (Rin leads A-Un off)

34.1 FX: Doh doh doh (stampeding bandits)
34.3 FX: Da (Inuyasha takes off in pursuit)
34.4 FX: Zuba (slash)
34.5 FX: Za (Inuyasha runs through group of bandits, slashing all the way)

35.1 FX: Doh doh doh... (sound of mass exodus)
35.2 FX: Ba (Inuyasha comes for them)
35.3 FX: Zuba (slash)
35.4 FX: Doka (attack)

36.1 FX: Gu... (Kagome clutches sword)
36.3 FX: Ta (Kagome bolts toward Inuyasha)
36.4 FX: Ta (Sango runs after Kagome)
36.5 FX: Ta ta ta... (Kagome runs)
36.6 FX: Ta ta ta... (running)

37.1 FX: Ta (Inuyasha touches down in front of fleeing bandits)

39.2 FX: Ta (running)
39.4 FX: Ta (Inuyasha leaps away)

42.4 FX: Ba (Inuyasha leaps)
42.5 FX: Cha (Sesshomaru pulls sword from sheath)

43.1 FX: Su... (Sesshomaru brandishes his sword)
43.2 FX: Gohh (Inuyasha whooshes toward Inuyasha)
43.5 FX: Gohh (whooshing)

44.1 FX: Baki (Inuyasha smacks Sesshomaru's blade)
44.5 FX: Bushuu (blood spurts from cuts)

45.2 FX: Da (Inuyasha jumps away)
45.3 FX: Doga (Inuyasha smacks into the dirt)
45.4 FX: Suu... (Sesshomaru's energy attack surrounds Inuyasha)

46.1 FX: Cha (blade noise)
46.2 FX: Doh (energy attack from Sesshomaru's sword)
46.3 FX: Pota pota (blood drips)
46.4 FX: Da (running)

47.4 FX: Ta ta ta... (running)

49.3 FX: Da (Inuyasha lunges)
49.4 FX: Cha (metal sword sound)

98.2/4 FX: Gohhhhhh… (big whooshing of wind between rocks)

104.3 FX: Shuuuu… (hissing as Naraku melts away Inuyasha father's fang)

104.4 FX: Shuuu… (more hissing)
FX: Doro (fang drops off)

105.1 FX: Fu… (Naraku disappears)

105.3 FX: Shuuuu… (hissing)

105.5 FX: Kaaa… (shining)
FX: Dokun (heartbeat)

105.6 FX: Dokun… (heartbeat)

106.1 FX: Dokun… (heartbeat)
FX: Dokun… (heartbeat)

106.2 FX: Piku… (Ryukotsusei's claws move)

106.3 FX: Zawa… (the wicked wind whistles and moans)

106.4 FX: Ka (demon's eye opens)

107.3 FX: Zu zu zu (rocks clatter away as Ryukotsusei breaks free)

107.4 FX: Gara gara… (rocks clattering)

107.5 FX: Zu zu zu (rocks thundering down)

109.1 FX: Cha (Inuyasha pulls Tetsusaiga from scabbard)

110.1 FX: Gao (Rukotsusei rushes at Inuyasha)

110.2 FX: Ta (Inuyasha leaps away from Ryukotsusei's gaping jaws)

110.3 FX: Dogo (Ryukotsusei smacks into rock)

110.4 FX: Suta (Inuyasha alights on Ryukotsusei's back)

110.5 FX: Ta ta ta… (running)

111.1 FX: Ta (Inuyasha leaps)

111.2 FX: Ta ta ta… (running)

111.4 FX: Kaaaaa (glowing as Ryukotsusei conjures up an energy ball)

112.1 FX: Dohh (Ryukotsusei spits energy ball)

112.2 FX: Ta (Inuyasha leaps out of the way of energy ball)

112.3 FX: Dogoh (energy ball blows apart rocks as it strikes)

113.3 FX: Goh (whoosh)

113.5 FX: Goh (whoosh as Ryukotsusei zaps Naraku]

115.4 FX: Cha (Inuyasha brandishes his sword)

117.2 FX: Ta (Kagome takes off running)

119.1 FX: Ba (Inuyasha lunges at Ryukotsusei)

119.2 FX: Gin (clang)

119.4 FX: Bachi (Inuyasha thrown backward)

119.5 FX: Za (Inuyasha falls on ground)

120.3 FX: Ka (glowing energy ball)

121.1 FX: Da (Inuyasha leaps)

121.2 FX: Goh (energy ball whooshes into rocks)

121.3 FX: Dohhn (Inuyasha and rocks displaced by power of energy ball)

121.4 FX: Ta (Inuyasha lands on outcropping)

124.4 FX: Pyo—n (Myoga leaps off Inuyasha)

124.5 FX: Pyu-- (Myoga leaps away)

125.3 FX: Doga (strike)

125.4 FX: doh (Inuyasha lands hard)

125.5 FX: Za (Inuyasha slides down rock face)

127.1 FX: Gu (Inuyasha grabs Tetsusaiga)

127.4 FX: Da (Inuyasha charges)

128.1 FX: Gohh (Sango and Miroku whoosh past)

131.1 FX: Pashi (Miroku unintentionally crunches Myoga)

131.2 FX: Pera (Myoga slips off Miroku's hand)

132.1 FX: Kaa (Ryukotsusei forms another shining energy ball)

132.2 FX: Dohh (energy ball strikes behind Inuyasha)

132.3 FX: Dohh (Ryukotsusei spits another energy ball)

132.4 FX: Dohn dohn (energy balls strike one after another in the distance)

133.4 FX: Da (Inuyasha leaps)

134.1 FX: Doga (strike)

134.3 FX: Doga (Ryukotsusei pins Inuyasha to cliff face)

135.1 FX: Mishi… (squishing sound)

135.2 FX: Dogo (impact)

135.3 FX: Gara gara… (rocks fall)

135.4 FX: Poro (Inuyasha drops sword)

136.2 FX: Dosa (Inuyasha lands in a heap)

136.4 FX: Kaa (shining)

137.1 FX: Suuuu…n… (the rest of the gang thunders toward our hero)

138.1 FX: Shuuuu… (hissing of smoke/dust rising from ground)

139.1 FX: Zawa… (rustling as Inuyasha transforms, eyes open)
139.5 FX: Gohh (Miroku and Sango whoosh down)

140.1 FX: Dokun dokun (Inuyasha's heartbeats)
140.2 FX: Dokun (another heartbeat)
140.4 FX: Ka (Inuyasha's eyes snap open, glowing)

Chapter 54 : The Backlash Wave: Tetsusaiga's Ultimate Technique

142.3 FX: Zuru… (Ryukotsusei steps on the Tetsusaiga)
142.4 FX: Dokun (heartbeat)

143.1 FX: Za (scrape of Inuyasha's hand on ground)

144.3 FX: Ba (Inuyasha prepares to slash with claws)
144.4 FX: Zuba (slash)
144.5 FX: Bushuuu… (hissing of blood escaping)

145.1 FX: Ta (Inuyasha touches down)

146.1 FX: Zan (slash)
146.3 FX: Goh (Ryukotsusei spits energy blast)
146.4 FX: Dohn (impact of energy blast)

147.1 FX: Ba (Inuyasha prepares to attack)
147.2 FX: Zan (Inuyasha slashes as he rushes past Ryukotsusei)
147.3 FX: Ta (Inuyasha lands)
147.4 FX: Zu… (Ryukotsusei crashes into cliff face)

149.1 FX: Su (Totosai does an about face)

152.4 FX: Za… (Inuyasha walking with his feet dragging)

154.4 FX: Dokun… (Tetsusaiga pulses)
154.5 FX: Dokun… (Tetsusaiga pulses)

156.3 FX: Yoro… (Inuyasha being unsteady on his feet)
156.4 FX: Ka (shining of energy ball)

157. 2 FX: Gohh (whooshing)

157.3/4 FX: Dohhn (impact of energy ball)

158.1 FX: Zu zu zu (glow grows mysteriously bigger)
158.3 FX: Pari pari (crackling)

159.1 FX: Goh (whooshing)
159.2 FX: Ba (Inuyasha brandishes the sheathe)
159.3 FX: Go go go go (whooshing of power around Tetsusaiga's sheathe)

160.3 FX: Ka (shining)
160.5 FX: Gohh (energy ball whooshes toward Inuyasha)

161.1 FX: Ba (Miroku thrusts out his hand as he opens the Wind Tunnel)
161.2 FX: Gohhh… (energy ball dragged slightly toward Miroku's Wind Tunnel)
161.3 FX: Gohh… (whooshing)
161.4/5 FX: Gohhhhhhh… (whoooooosh)

162.1 FX: Gohh (whooshing)
162.2 FX: Dohn (energy ball explodes)
162.3 FX: Zu zu zu zu (dust clears)

164.1 FX: Gu (Inuyasha grips sword)

165.4 FX: Cha (Tetsusaiga transforms)
165.5 FX: Zushi… (Tetsusaiga thunks to the ground)

166.4 FX: Dokun… (Tetsusaiga's pulse)

167.1 FX: Suu… (Inuyasha lifts up Tetsusaiga)

168.1 FX: Bun (Inuyasha moves sword)
168.4 FX: Da (Inuyasha charges Ryukotsusei)

169.1 FX: Ka (glowing)
169.2 FX: Gohh (whooshing)
169.3 FX: Dohn (energy ball explodes)

170.1 FX: Doh (Tetsusaiga pierces Ryukotsusei's thick hide)
170.4 FX: Bushuu… (sound of blood spurting out of Ryukotsusei)

171.3 FX: Ba (Inuyasha leaps backwards off Ryukotsusei)
171.4 FX: Toh (Inuyasha touches down)

172.3 FX: Ka (shining)
172.4 FX: Gohh (whooshing of energy ball)

172.4 FX: Ta (Inuyasha dodges)
172.5 FX: Dohn (energy ball explodes)

173.2 FX: Ka (shining of energy ball)
173.3 FX: Ta (Inuyasha dodges)
173.4 FX: Dohn (energy ball strikes where Inuyasha just was)

174.3 FX: Ka (shining of energy ball)
174.4 FX: Dohn (energy ball hits)
174.5 FX: Ta ta ta… (running)
174.6 FX: Ta (Inuyasha leaps)

175.1 FX: Ba (Inuyasha gets ready to hit)
175.2 FX: Bun (Inuyasha swings the Tetsusaiga)
175.3 FX: Gin (clang)
175.4 FX: Dohh (Inuyasha thrown by blade deflecting off thick skin)
175.5 FX: Doga (Inuyasha falls to ground)

177.1 FX: Go go go (mist whooshes about the Tetsusaiga)
177.4 FX: Kaaa… (shining)

178.1 FX: Ka (shining of energy ball)
178.3 FX: Goh (whoosh)

179.1 FX: Ga ga ga ga (Wind Scar energy deflects energy ball)
179.2 FX: Dohn (energy flung back at Ryukotsusei)

180.1 FX: Shuuuu… (Inuyasha skids back)
180.3 FX: Hyuuuu… (hissing)

181.4 FX: Zu zu zu zu (rumbling as dragon stirs, but we're no supposed to know that until after the page turn)

182.1 FX: Zu zu zu… (Ryukotsusei gets up)

183.3 FX: Kaaa… (shining)

184.4 FX: Gohhhh… (whooshing)

186. 2 FX: Zu zu zu zu (rocks vaporize)
186.3 FX: Zu zu zu (more rocks vaporize)
186.4 FX: Kaaaa… (shining)

187.1 FX: Kaa (shining of energy ball)
187.3 FX: Ba (Kirara moves away)

188.1 FX: Ka (shining)

188.3 FX: Gohh (whooshing)

189.3 FX: Gohhhh… (whooshing of energy ball)

190.1 FX: Gohh (whooshing)
190.2 FX: Gohhh… (more whooshing)

191.1 FX: Gohhhh… (whooshing)
191.2 FX: Shuuuu… (smoldering hiss)
191.4 FX: Zuba (slash)

192.1 FX: Goh (whoosh)
192.3 FX: Gohhh… (whooshing)
192.4 FX: Goh (whooshing)

193.2 FX: Goh (whooshing)
193.3 FX: Zan (whirlwind strikes Ryukotsusei)

194.1 FX: Goh (whoosh)
194.2 FX: Go go (energy whooshes about and severs stuff)
194.3 FX: Go go (more severing)

195.1 FX: Zan (Rukotsusei's head is severed)
195.2 FX: Para para (falling pebbles)
195.4 FX: Doh (Ryukotsusei's head explodes)
195.5 FX: Gohhh… (whooshing)

196.1 FX: Za za za za (Ryukotsusei crumbles to dust, blows away)
196.5 FX: Ta (Kagome alights, runs toward Inuyasha)

197.3 FX: Pyon (sproing as Myoga hopping onto Inuyasha's nose)

198.2 FX: Don (Inuyasha enthusiastically pushes Totosai, knocking him over)

202.1 FX: Da (Inuyasha leaps)
202.2 FX: Doga (big slash)
202.3 FX: Zugagaga (Wind Scar travels up mountain)
202.4 FX: Dohn (and explodes out of the top of it)
202.5 FX: Shuuuu… (aftermath of Wind Scar; stuff burning and rubble falling)

203.3 FX: Ba (Inuyasha lifts sword to strike)
203.4 FX: Doga (strike)
203.5 FX: Zu zu zu (falling rubble)

204.2 FX: Ba (Inuyasha gets ready to slash)
204.5 FX: Ba (Inuyasha gets ready to slash)

GERHART HAUPTMANN

was born November 15, 1862, in the
Silesian village of Obersalzbrunn.
After studying, successively, agriculture,
art, and sculpture, in 1885 Hauptmann
became interested in politics and in the
theater. He began to write plays for
Otto Brahm's Free Stage in Berlin. His
work provoked excitement and comment
because of its naturalism, and in 1892
Hauptmann won world fame with *The
Weavers*. This play with its collective hero—a
village of starving workmen—became a
rallying point for socialists and labor. As a
social dramatist, Hauptmann received the
Nobel Prize for Literature in 1912.

A BANTAM CLASSIC